Natural Resource Management and Policy

Volume 42

There is a growing awareness to the role that natural resources, such as water, land, forests and environmental amenities, play in our lives. There are many competing uses for natural resources, and society is challenged to manage them for improving social well-being. Furthermore, there may be dire consequences to natural resources mismanagement. Renewable resources, such as water, land and the environment are linked, and decisions made with regard to one may affect the others. Policy and management of natural resources now require interdisciplinary approaches including natural and social sciences to correctly address our society preferences.

This series provides a collection of works containing most recent findings on economics, management and policy of renewable biological resources, such as water, land, crop protection, sustainable agriculture, technology, and environmental health. It incorporates modern thinking and techniques of economics and management. Books in this series will incorporate knowledge and models of natural phenomena with economics and managerial decision frameworks to assess alternative options for managing natural resources and environment.

More information about this series at http://www.springer.com/series/6360

Paolo Verme · Abdelkrim Araar
Editors

The Quest for Subsidy Reforms in the Middle East and North Africa Region

A Microsimulation Approach to Policy Making

Springer

Editors
Paolo Verme
The World Bank
Washington, DC
USA

Abdelkrim Araar
University of Laval
Quebec, QC
Canada

Natural Resource Management and Policy
ISBN 978-3-319-52925-7   ISBN 978-3-319-52926-4 (eBook)
DOI 10.1007/978-3-319-52926-4

Library of Congress Control Number: 2017930138

Printed on acid-free paper

This Springer imprint is published by Springer Nature
The registered company is Springer International Publishing AG
The registered company address is: Gewerbestrasse 11, 6330 Cham, Switzerland

Acknowledgements

This book is the product of a team of nineteen authors including World Bank staff and external consultants. The team was led by Paolo Verme (World Bank) and Abdelkrim Araar (University of Laval), who also edited all chapters. This book was prepared for the chief economist office of the Middle East and North Africa (MENA) Region under the guidance of Chief Economist Shanta Devarajan and practice manager Benu Bidani. Finance was provided by the MENA Chief Economist Office and the Poverty and Social Impact Analysis (PSIA) Multi-donor Trust Fund. The authors thank the World Bank Country Director Ferid Belhaj, and acting Country Directors Joelle Businger and Poonam Gupta, who at various stages provided comments and cleared the country chapters. Numerous colleagues provided guidance and comments. We wish to thank Jean-Pierre Chauffour, Charles Cormier, Shanta Devarajan, Ferhat Esen, Stafania Fabrizio, Vivien Foster, Gabriela Inchauste, Philippe Leite, Esther Loening, Masami Kojima, Lili Mottaghi, Mustapha Nabli, Lucian Pop, Guido Rurangwa, and Maria Vagliasindi. A special thanks to our copyeditor Carolyn Goldinger.

Contents

About the Editors

Paolo Verme is a senior economist at the World Bank. A Ph.D. graduate of the London School of Economics, he was a visiting professor at Bocconi University in Milan (2004–09) and at the University of Turin (2003–10) before joining the World Bank in 2010. For almost two decades, he has served as adviser and project manager for multilateral organizations, private companies, and governments on labor market, welfare, and social protection policies. His research is widely published in international journals, books, and reports, and he has worked extensively on subsidies in the MENA Region and elsewhere. He is the coauthor of the subsidies simulation model SUBSIM (www.subsim.org).

Abdelkrim Araar received his Ph.D. in economics from Laval University in 1998. He is a World Bank consultant and a resource member at the Partnership for Economic Policy (PEP) network. Abdelkrim has been involved in designing and conducting training activities, developing training material, and conducting fundamental research. He has provided theoretical and technical supports to many researchers, especially those in developing countries. He is the coauthor, with Paolo Verme, of the Stata SUBSIM package. Also he is the coauthor, with Jean-Yves Duclos, of the book *Poverty and Equity: Measurement, Policy and Estimation with DAD*, the DASP Stata package, and DAD software.

Abbreviations

AIDS	Almost Ideal Demand System
CGE	Computable general equilibrium
CIF	Cost, insurance, and freight
CNG	Compressed natural gas
CPU	Consumer price index
DP	Market price
FAO	Food and Agriculture Organization
FDI	Foreign direct investment (FDI)
GDP	Gross domestic product
HBS	Household Budget Survey
HEIS	Household Expenditures and Income Survey
HFO	Heavy fuel oil
HH	Households
IBT	Increasing block tariffs
IMF	International Monetary Fund
IP	International reference price
kWh	Kilowatt hours
LPG	Liquefied petroleum gas
mbd	Million barrels per day
MENA	Middle East and North Africa
NP	Nonsubsidized price
OECD	Organisation for Economic Co-operation and Development
OPEC	Organization of the Petroleum Exporting Countries
PG	Price gap
PGI	Poverty gap index
PMT	Proxy means test
ppm	Parts per million
PPP	Purchasing power parity
PSIA	Poverty and Social Impact Analysis
QAIDS	Quadratic Almost Ideal Demand System

SBA	Standby arrangement
SMEs	Small- and medium-size enterprises
SR	Subsidy rate
SUBSIM	SUBsidy SIMulation
VAT	Value-added tax
VDT	Volume-differentiated tariffs
WHO	World Health Organization

Djibouti

DF	Djibouti franc
DISED	Department of Statistics and Demographic Studies
EBC	Enquête de Budget et Consommation (Budget and Consumption Survey)
EDAM	Enquête Djiboutienne auprès des ménages
Eq. Ad.	Equivalence adult scale
ESMAP	Energy Sector Management Assistance Program
SDVK	La Société de Distribution et de Vente de Kérosène
SESN	National Solidarity
TIC	Domestic consumption tax

Egypt, Arab Republic of

CAPMAS	Central Agency for Public Mobilization and Statistics
GoE	Government of Egypt
LE	Egyptian pound
MB	Muslim Brotherhood
PT/kWh	Piastre per kilowatt hour
SAM	Social accounting matrix

Iran, Islamic Republic of

Rl	Iranian rial
SCI	Statistical Center of Iran

Jordan

DOS	Department of Statistics
EDCO	Electricity Distribution Company
EMRC	Energy and Minerals Regulatory Commission
IDECO	Irbid District Electricity Company
JD	Jordanian dinar
JD/kWh	Jordanian dinar per kilowatt hour
JEPCO	Jordan Electric Power Company

SPEAKS	Social Protection Evaluations of Attitudes, Knowledge and Support Survey
NAF	National Aid Fund
NEPCO	National Electricity Power Company
NUR	National Unified Registry

Libya

LD	Libyan dinar

Morocco

BARS	Bureau d'Approvisionnement des Régions Sahariennes
CDC	Caisse de Compensation
DH	Moroccan dirham
DH/L	Moroccan dirham per liter
HCP	High Commission for the Plan
LSS	Living Standards Survey
ONEE	National Electricity Company
ONICL	Office National Interprofessionnel des Cereales et des Legumineuses
RAM	Royal Air Maroc
SAMIR	Societé Anonyme Marocaine de l'Industrie du Raffinage

Tunisia

BAD	Banque Africaine de Développement
ENBCV	Enquête Nationale sur le Budget, la Consommation et les Conditions de Vie des Ménages
INS	Institut National de la Statistique
PNAFN	Programme National d'Aide aux Familles Nécessiteuses
TD	Tunisian dinars

Yemen

PDRY	People's Democratic Republic of Yemen
PEC	Public Electricity Corporation
SWF	Social Welfare Fund
YAR	Arab Republic of Yemen
YRl	Yemini rial

List of Figures

List of Tables

List of Boxes

Overview

Background and Motivation for the Book

The past decade saw extraordinary changes in the Middle East and North Africa (MENA) Region and consumers' subsidies have been at the core of these changes. Oil prices rose to unprecedented levels during the decade that spanned from 2005 to 2014 and this contributed to generate a global rise in food and commodities prices that severely affected poor and middle-income countries. The widespread practice of regulating prices of essential energy and food consumer products in the MENA Region amplified these global shocks in a region already affected by increasing social tensions and in 2011 social tensions erupted into revolutions, regime changes, and political reforms that made subsidy reforms very difficult to implement for the new political establishments. Meanwhile, the economic decline resulting from revolutions and political changes made the budget crisis worse, increasing the urgency for subsidy reforms. On the one hand, the budget pressure for reforms was mounting. On the other hand, the political and social instability rendered these reforms a political hazard.

Faced with this dilemma, some governments in the MENA Region decided to push subsidy reforms through while others opted to avoid reforms altogether. These decisions were suffered and came after prolonged periods of discussions and negotiations that saw the World Bank playing an active role. Between 2010 and 2014, several governments in the MENA Region repeatedly called on the World Bank to assist them with the analysis of subsidies and the design of subsidy reforms, and by 2014, the World Bank was working in seven countries[1] in collaboration with local ministerial teams. This, in turn, offered to the World Bank a unique opportunity to work intensively and continuously on consumers' subsidies for a prolonged stretch of time and learn firsthand the nuts and bolts of subsidies

[1]Djibouti, the Arab Republic of Egypt, Jordan, Libya, Morocco, Tunisia, and the Republic of Yemen.

reforms. It was also an opportunity to develop specific modeling devices that could be deployed quickly and homogenously across countries.

The objective of this book is to capitalize on the work undertaken by the World Bank in the MENA Region between 2010 and 2014 using a particular model specifically designed for the distributional analysis of subsidies and the simulation of subsidies reforms. The model is called "SUBSIM" and has been used uniformly in all the seven countries where the World Bank operated. This allowed us to collect the results of the country works into one volume and compare results cross-country in a way that was not possible before.

The focus of this book is the distribution of subsidies and the simulation of subsidy reforms in a partial equilibrium framework. The distributional analysis of subsidies provides information on who benefits from existing subsidies, and the simulations of subsidy reforms provide information on the outcomes of the reforms in terms of government budget, household welfare, poverty, inequality, and the trade-offs between these outcomes. It is a partial equilibrium approach in that we focus on the final consumption market only.

The countries covered are Djibouti, the Arab Republic of Egypt, the Islamic Republic of Iran,[2] Jordan, Libya, Morocco, Tunisia, and the Republic of Yemen. Thus, we have four countries from North Africa and four from the Middle East. We also cover net oil exporters as well as net oil importers and low-income countries and as middle-income countries. This choice provides a certain heterogeneity of experiences that helped us to derive some general lessons for policy.

This book covers energy and food subsidies. The coverage of energy subsidies is rather complete, meaning that we cover almost all subsidized products in all countries considered. The coverage of food subsidies is limited to few countries and few products. The reason is that it was difficult to identify with precision the subsidized products in household surveys and in macroeconomic input–output tables. Moreover, information on the unit subsidies of these products was scarce because none of the countries considered undertook subsidies reforms of food items.

Where possible, we estimated direct and indirect effects of subsidy reforms. By direct effects, we mean first-round effects or short-term effects of changes in subsidized products on final household consumption via the consumption of subsidized products. By indirect effects, we mean second- and higher-order long-term effects of subsidy reforms on subsidized products and on nonsubsidized products that are affected by price changes in subsidized products. SUBSIM can estimate direct and indirect effects, but the data necessary for estimating indirect effects were available only for a few countries.

This book does not cover some other important aspects of subsidies and subsidies reforms. We do not estimate general equilibrium effects or the effects of subsidy reforms in all markets, such as the financial market or the labor market.

[2]The World Bank did not work in Iran during the period, but it commissioned a chapter on Iran to academics specialists in the field who agreed to use SUBSIM for the analysis.

We do not estimate the effects on production incentives or consider direct subsidies to enterprises, only final subsidies to consumers. With one exception, we are not making use of qualitative surveys and surveys designed to capture people's views of subsidies and we do not analyze the role of public information campaigns during subsidies reforms. We also do not attempt to estimate environmental effects, changes in gas emissions, or other social costs and benefits induced by subsidies or subsidy reforms.

Further, for the case of energy consumption such as electricity or natural gas, this book does not cover nonresidential consumers. This is relevant because in some countries nonresidential customers account for a substantial share of energy consumption and removal of subsidies for these types of consumers poses its own challenges. Also, in the case of electricity, a large share of the subsidies burden is explained by the high cost of production. This book does not discuss issues of production costs or efficiency, which for several countries like Jordan are the answer to the subsidies crisis. In these cases, reforming subsidies is strictly related to medium- and long-term energy policies that aim at reducing production and environmental costs.

Data on energy consumption from residential customers, which are captured in household surveys, have their own limits. For example, in some countries we found evidence of households owing multiple meters for the same property in an effort to exploit the benefits of lower tariffs at low consumption levels. In other cases, we found anecdotal evidence of households illegally attached to other households' meters and in some other cases small businesses confound voluntarily or involuntarily household and business meters. These phenomena exist and distort the information reported by households on expenditure. The countries observed in this book are mostly middle-income countries with electricity coverage that are close to universal coverage in many countries. Therefore, the phenomena described are less acute than in poor countries. These phenomena can also work in opposite directions, inflating or deflating reported expenditure. As a result, we have not made any attempt to artificially correct this information and for this reason some of the results may be moderately over or under estimated.

Finally, electricity or natural gas bills may include payments for previous periods (arrears) or they may relate to different tariffs depending on the type of consumer. For example, some countries apply different tariffs to households who own meters of different power (say 3 kW as opposed to 6 kW) while other countries may use regional tariffs. These two factors evidently complicate the accurate estimation of expenditure and consumption for the period or tariff block considered. This book does not attempt to correct for issues related to arrears because proper information was not available. We made an effort instead to use the appropriate tariffs depending on types of consumers and location although this was not always possible.

Clearly, this book is narrow in its scope, but it is precisely this focus and the use of the same model in all countries considered that allowed us to be more accurate in our comparisons across countries.

Structure of the Book

This book is organized in 2 parts and 10 chapters. Part I, Cross-Country Analyses, covers the comparative analyses across countries. Chapter 1 provides a synthesis of what we learned about subsidies reforms from a political economy perspective. Chapter 2 provides a comparative analysis of subsidies and subsidies reforms across countries in US dollars at purchasing power parity (PPP) values. Using the same data used by the country studies, this chapter shows the relative importance of subsidies across countries and income groups and the main winners and losers of subsidy reforms. Part II, Country Case Studies, includes the country-specific analyses. All of the chapters in this part were developed along a similar structure with an introduction, followed by a brief history of subsidies, and then the distributional analysis of subsidies, simulations of subsidies reforms, the political economy of reforms, and a conclusion. All chapters are based on primary microdata and macrodata, and each chapter provides two simulations of reforms. The first simulation was chosen based on what was deemed more relevant for the policy dialogue at the time of preparing the chapters. The second simulation is standard across all chapters and includes the full elimination of subsidies. This book includes as an appendix the User Manual for SUBSIM that illustrates the use of the model and provides all formulas used for the estimations throughout the book.

Products Considered

The number of products that remained subsidized at the beginning of the reform process in 2010 is not large. The principal subsidized energy products are gasoline, diesel, liquefied petroleum gas (LPG), kerosene, electricity, and natural gas. Among food products, only bread (or flour) and sugar remained subsidized in several countries, and only one country (Libya) maintained a wide array of subsidies on food products. Egypt and Tunisia also subsidized several food products, but these products could not be analyzed for lack of data.

Table 1 reports all the products considered in the country chapters for the distributional analysis and for the simulation of subsidies reforms. We can see, for example, that all case studies consider gasoline and LPG, most case studies consider electricity and diesel, and selected case studies consider kerosene and natural gas. Given our data limitations, only three chapters consider bread and sugar, and two consider flour, vegetable oil, and milk for children. When possible, we have also attempted to provide indirect effects of subsidies reforms in addition to direct effects. Table 1 shows that we were able to estimate indirect effects in four of the eight countries considered (Morocco, Tunisia, Jordan, and the Islamic Republic of Iran) for all subsidized products considered in these countries.

Table 1 Summary of products considered by country (direct and indirect effects)

	North Africa								Middle East							
	Morocco		Tunisia		Libya		Egypt, Arab Rep.		Jordan		Yemen, Rep.		Djibouti		Iran, Islamic Rep.	
	Dir.	Ind.	Dir.	Ind.	Dir.	Ind.	Dir.	Ind.	Dir.	Ind.	Dir.	Ind.	Dir.	Ind.	Dir.	Ind.
Energy																
Gasoline	X	X	X	X	X	–	X	–	X	X	X	–	X	–	X	X
Diesel	X	X	X	X	X	–	–	–	X	X	X	–	X	–	X	X
LPG	X	–	X	X	X	–	X	–	X		X	–	–	–	X	X
Kerosene	X	–	–	–	X	–	–	–	X			–	X	–	X	X
Electricity	X	X	X	X	X	–	X	–	X	X	X	–	–	–	X	X
Natural gas	–	–	–	–	–	–	X	–	–	–	–	–	–	–	X	X
Food																
Flour	–	–	–	–	X	–	–	–	–	–	–	–	X	–		
Flour-bread	X				X	–	–	–	–	–	–	–	–	–	X	X
Semolina	–	–	–	–	X	–	–	–	–	–	–	–	–	–	–	–
Rice	–	–	–	–	X	–	–	–	–	–	–	–	–	–	–	–
Sugar	X				X	–	–	–	–	–	–	–	X	–	–	–
Tea	–	–	–	–	X	–	–	–	–	–	–	–	–	–	–	–
Macaroni	–	–	–	–	X	–	–	–	–	–	–	–	–	–	–	–
Vegetable oil	–	–	–	–	X	–	–	–	–	–	–	–	X	–	–	–
Paste tomatoes	–	–	–	–	X	–	–	–	–	–	–	–	–	–	–	–
Milk for children	–	–	–	–	X	–	–	–	–	–	–	–	X	–	–	–
Milk (concentrated)	–	–	–	–	X	–	–	–	–	–	–	–	–	–	–	–

Data Overview

For all countries considered in this book, we were able to obtain and use the latest available household budget survey (HBS) containing information on household expenditure by product, including subsidized products. Because some of these household surveys are not recent, we used the gross domestic product (GDP), the consumer price index (CPI), and population statistics to update monetary and population data to 2014, the baseline year considered in this book. Table 2 provides the basic statistics from each survey after the update. We can see that some surveys, such as those for Egypt and the Islamic Republic of Iran, were quite recent, while others such as the one for Morocco and the Republic of Yemen were quite old.

For all countries, we followed the same approach to update the household survey to the most recent year (2014). Updates were made using published IMF macroindicators for inflation and gross domestic product (GDP) per capita as well as population statistics. These data were taken from the IMF *World Economic Outlook* database (April 2015) and can be consulted in Table 2.11. Data used to update the household budget surveys to 2014 are provided in Table 2.12. Tables 2.11 and 2.12 contain the specific information used for the comparative analysis of Chap. 2. The country chapters followed the same approach although some of the primary data may derive from national statistical institutes' sources.

No particular assumptions were made on elasticities between GDP growth and household expenditure growth. We simply applied the same growth rates of GDP to household expenditure. In the short run, this assumption may not hold for all countries, but in the long run, the two growth rates are expected to converge. We did not make any assumption on asymmetric growth rates across the distribution of incomes. The GDP growth rate was applied equally to the expenditure of all households so that the distribution of incomes of the last available survey remained unaltered.

In total, we worked with 121,615 household observations with an average size of 4.6 people and representing a population of almost 250 million people, approximately 62% of the total population of the MENA Region.

Table 2 Data summary

Country	HBS year	Obs.	Population (m)	HH size	I/O tables
Djibouti	2012	5,880	0.94	5.6	No
Egypt, Arab Rep.	2013	15,057	85.83	5.2	No
Iran, Islamic Rep.	2013	38,316	77.97	3.6	Yes
Jordan	2010	11,223	6.69	5.4	Yes
Libya	2008	19,660	6.21	6.3	No
Morocco	2007	7,062	33.18	4.7	Yes
Tunisia	2010	11,281	11.06	4.3	Yes
Yemen, Rep.	2005	13,136	27.46	7.5	No
Total	–	121,615	249.35	4.60	–

Note HH household; *HSB* household budget survey; *I/O* input–output tables; *Obs.* observations

Summary of Simulations

Each of the eight country chapters provides two alternative simulations of subsidies reforms. One simulation was selected on the basis of its relevance for the current debate on subsidies. For Egypt, Morocco, and the Republic of Yemen, we simulated ex-post the impact of recent reforms, which amounts to an evaluation of these reforms. In Libya and the Islamic Republic of Iran, we considered the partial elimination of subsidies, and in Tunisia and Jordan, we considered the total elimination of subsidies with compensation. The other set of simulations we did for all countries was the total elimination of subsidies with no compensation. Table 3 summarizes the reforms scenario considered with the order of simulations followed in each country (note that the total elimination of subsidies can be the first or second simulation depending on the country).

The comparative chapter (Chap. 2), where we harmonized data in US$-PPP values across countries, provides a cross-country comparative distributional analysis and an analysis of a 30% reduction of subsidies in each country and across all products. Given that the amounts of subsidies and the distribution of expenditure are different across countries and products, results are evidently different. These results are also not directly comparable with the results in the country chapters because of the US$-PPP conversions and other choices made to harmonize variables across countries. However, Chap. 2 uses the same price data used in the country chapters. All choices regarding data and conversion factors are reported in annex to Chap. 2.

Table 3 Summary of simulations by country

Country	Simulation 1	Simulation 2
Morocco	October 2014 reforms: increases in gasoline, diesel, and electricity prices; changes in electricity tariffs' blocks	Full elimination of subsidies
Tunisia	Full elimination of subsidies	Full elimination of subsidies with cash compensation
Libya	30% cut in subsidies on all products	Full elimination of subsidies
Egypt, Arab Rep.	25% increase in prices of all energy products	July 2014 reforms: price increases for gasoline, diesel, natural gas, and fuel oil
Jordan	Full elimination of subsidies	Full elimination of subsidies with cash compensation
Yemen, Rep.	August 2014 reforms: Increase in gasoline (50%), diesel (20%), and kerosene (100%) prices	Full elimination of subsidies
Djibouti	Removal of tax benefits on gasoline and diesel	Introduction of consumer tax on powdered milk, flour, cooking oil, and sugar
Iran, Islamic Rep.	10% price increase for all products	Full elimination of subsidies

Simulations of subsidies reforms make also use of own price elasticities. These elasticities vary across products and countries. This question was left to the country teams to decide and is discussed in each chapter. Our recommendation to the teams was to follow the recommendations provided by the SUBSIM manual available in this book. The manual explains that for subsidized prices that are very far from free market prices (unit subsidies are very high) a good approach is to use very low own price local elasticities following a suggested formula provided by the guide. For products with low subsidies, the recommendation was to use known free market price elasticities such as those observed in similar countries. As a result, own price elasticities can vary between 0.1 and 0.5 across products and countries. The exception is the comparative analysis of Chap. 2 where we used the same elasticities for the same products to render results comparable across countries.

SUBSIM as an Analytical Tool

This book uses a single tool for analysis in Chap. 2 and across all the eight countries considered. This tool is a subsidy microsimulation model developed by the World Bank called SUBSIM. As already discussed, it was specifically developed to provide rapid distributional analyses of subsidies and simulation of subsidies reforms to respond to the numerous and increasing requests for assistance that the World Bank received starting in 2010.

The World Bank has a long tradition in subsidies analyses and has developed over the years several analytical tools that can be used for subsidies analysis, including general equilibrium models, partial equilibrium models, or microsimulation models of various kinds. Before undertaking the project of designing a new model, we reviewed 13 different models that were in use at the World Bank. We concluded that we did not have a dedicated model for subsidies analysis that could provide simple results quickly and accurately, which severely constrained our ability to respond in a timely manner to government requests. As a consequence, we decided to undertake the project of constructing a new model in 2010.

Since its first version in 2011, SUBSIM has been used in eight countries in the MENA Region and other countries in other regions, and this experience has contributed to the improvement of the model, which is now in its third version. The model is accompanied by a user manual included in this book and is available free of charge for downloading from our Web site (www.subsim.org). The Web site also includes reports and publications based on SUBSIM work and additional useful information for users.

SUBSIM is programmed in Stata, is automatically added to the Stata menu when installed, and has an easy-to-use Windows interface. The model estimates the impact of subsidies reforms on household welfare, poverty, and inequality, and on the government budget with or without compensatory cash transfers. It can estimate direct and indirect effects using household budget survey data and input–output matrixes, can be applied to energy and food subsidies, and accommodates linear and nonlinear pricing. It produces 22 tables and 10 graphs of standard output in English or French and allows the user to save input data for future reference.

The model comes in two flavors, one that estimates direct effects only and a second that estimates direct and indirect effects. The direct effects module requires at least one household budget survey that contains information on household expenditure on subsidized products. It relies on standard microeconomic theory and uses as measure of welfare the Laspeyres variation formula by default, which is the standard welfare measure used by organizations such as the World Bank or the IMF for policy simulations. However, as explained in the user manual in more detail, the Laspeyres formula becomes inadequate for large price variations and SUBSIM offers users the option to use a Cobb–Douglas utility function to model a standard demand function and provide results accordingly. This is the option used in this book for simulations of large price variations. The direct effects module also provides the option of introducing own price elasticities, a choice left to users.

The direct–indirect effects module of SUBSIM requires input–output tables in addition to at least one household budget survey. Users need to prepare the two sources of data in advance in a way that SUBSIM can recognize the same economic sectors and products from the two data sources and match them. Direct and indirect effects are obtained by shocking sectors in the input–output tables and measuring the first-order and higher-order effects on final prices. These price effects are then applied to household data to measure total effects. Thanks to a specially designed matrix formula for the input–output tables, this last module allows users to present direct and indirect effects separately, an option usually unavailable in other models. Users have also the option of measuring first-order or higher-order effects for short- or long-term estimations.

The SUBSIM team was embedded in the governments' policy reforms teams that designed and implemented reforms in seven of the eight countries we consider in this book. This collaboration gave us privileged access to information that was later used to provide assistance across countries and revise the SUBSIM model to suit subsidy situations in diverse contexts. Our country teams changed over the four years of work, and the authors of the eight country chapters are those who worked on these countries last, but many more people contributed to the SUBSIM effort over the years and we are grateful to them for all inputs received.

The use of the same model in all of the case studies provided a unique opportunity to standardize data and results and compare products and reforms across countries. The standard tables and graphs produced by SUBSIM are directly comparable across countries and chapters, and we also developed a separate version of SUBSIM that can compare the same products across countries in US dollars and purchasing power parity. This version of the model was used to prepare the cross-country analysis of Chap. 2.

Part I
Cross-Country Analyses

Chapter 1
Subsidy Reforms in the Middle East and North Africa Region: A Review

Paolo Verme

Introduction

Between 2010 and 2014 MENA, the Middle East and North Africa Region, experienced an extraordinary wave of energy and food subsidies reforms. These reforms did not achieve the objective of removing subsidies completely—far from it, but they were extraordinary in two important respects. They were unprecedented because no other period in the history of the Region had seen such a wave of subsidies reforms and because they occurred during an extremely complex period from a social and political perspective—a period of war, revolutions, and social upheavals.

What triggered the reforms? Who reformed, when, how, and why? What are the pros and cons of reforms? These are the questions we discuss in this chapter. Using the information contained in the comparative analysis of Chap. 2 and eight country case studies, this chapter summarizes events and reflects on some of the choices made by policymakers and emerging (although still unfolding) lessons. A brief history of subsidies will show how their evolution followed a similar pattern across the countries of the Region, a pattern mainly guided by oil prices and shifts in the dominant political views of the time. We then ask what triggered the reforms and try to pinpoint the key factors that eventually forced governments to take action on reforms. Next is a summary of the essential elements of the subsidy reforms in those countries that implemented reforms between 2010 and 2014. Last is a discussion of reforms and the challenges that remain in completing the reforms.

P. Verme (✉)
The World Bank, Washington, USA
e-mail: pverme@worldbank.org

P. Verme and A. Araar (eds.), *The Quest for Subsidy Reforms in the Middle East and North Africa Region*, Natural Resource Management and Policy 42,
DOI 10.1007/978-3-319-52926-4_1

A Brief History of Subsidies

Consumer subsidies are part of the history of the MENA Region. In some countries, subsidies were already present during the colonial period and were part of the colonial heritage when countries became independent. Each case study in this book briefly reviews the origin and evolution of subsidies during the postindependence period, and this section reviews some of the salient features of this history.

Consumer subsidies have evolved to serve different purposes depending on the country considered and the historical period. Most of the consumer subsidies systems as we know them today were introduced in the MENA Region between the 1940s and 1970s. **Price stabilization** was the initial motivation for these subsidies. As countries emerged first from World War II and then from the colonial struggles, one of their main concerns was price instability and rising prices on basic consumer goods. This situation encouraged several governments to experiment with price stabilization mechanisms whereby price increases and decreases would be mitigated via a price adjustment mechanism designed to keep price variations contained within established margins. The initial idea was not to subsidize products, but to contain price fluctuations. In the francophone countries of the Maghreb these mechanisms became known as *caisses de compensation* (compensation fund) precisely to underline their stabilization role as opposed to a subsidy role.

Some of these *caisses de compensation,* such as the one established in Morocco during World War II, maintained financial stability for fairly long times, while other similar experiments incurred financial constraints early on. All these stabilization mechanisms eventually turned into subsidies systems. The reasons are multiple, but three factors are sufficient to explain the incapacity of these stabilization mechanisms to maintain financial rigor. The first is that nominal prices tend to increase in the long term, so that periods when the stabilization mechanism earned an income were few. The second is that it is politically convenient for a government to keep prices fixed when international prices rise but much harder politically to keep domestic prices high when international prices decrease. There is a behavioral asymmetry here explained by politics and subsidies progressively became a political instrument to buy political consensus. The third factor is related to the businesses and the interest groups that are generated by the very existence of subsidies and that become with time an obstacle to reforms.

As price stabilization mechanisms turned into subsidies systems, the rationale for these subsidies also started to change into a system of **social protection**. This change coincided with the turning of the MENA Region toward socialism and the revolutions that put dictators into power between the 1950s and the 1970s. As the political and economic systems became more centralized, subsidies became instrumental in supporting the regimes. After Muammar Gaddafi's revolution, Libya quickly introduced in 1971 a national institution to oversee the prices of basic commodities, which contributed to the expansion of subsidies across food and energy items and which became one of the main instruments of the regime to quell discontent. But subsidies fitted well with all other types of regimes in the Region, whether they were monarchies, democracies, pseudodemocracies, or dictatorships. During this period, the state takes a paternalistic role with a mix of socialist and Islamic ideology that sees subsidies as a form of social protection. Populations start to see subsidies as a human right or natural entitlements; governments are happy to use subsidies as a tool to gain consensus and are unprepared to take the risks associated with removing them. Countries that attempted major reforms in the 1970s and 1980s had to backtrack these reforms such as Tunisia in the aftermath of the 1983 reform.

The prolonged use of subsidies and the benefits that they provided to some enterprises generated a new rhetoric for their use as **enterprise support mechanisms**. Import substituting, infant industry protection, or export-oriented growth are some of the terms used to justify subsidies in this context. These terms were used to defend a system of production born and raised with subsidies. Enterprises found themselves in the middle of the subsidy system in two different but connected ways. On the one hand, consumer subsidies covered domestically produced products so that consumer subsidies had first to pass through producers. For example, bread subsidies were and are still administered by subsidizing flour for bakeries. This kind of subsidy evidently creates distortions on the production side and incentives for the creation of shadow markets. Subsidies on liquefied petroleum gas (LPG) are administered by financing the distributors of LPG bottles, which creates an entire distribution system around this product alone. Moreover, some consumer products such as diesel or sugar are widely used as production inputs by enterprises, artificially reducing costs. On the other hand, producer subsidies accompanied consumer subsidies throughout the period. This combination of producer and consumer subsidies generated a much distorted apparatus of production highly dependent on subsidies. Not surprisingly, general equilibrium models often find that when subsidies are removed, the gross domestic product (GDP) declines in the medium term. The reason is that many businesses are expected to survive and export only in the presence of subsidies and they become noncompetitive and go out of business when subsidies are removed.

The 1990s were characterized by a structural transformation of the economies, but became somehow a **lost decade** in terms of subsidies reforms. The socialist period in the MENA Region came to an end during the 1990s when enlightened dictators, presidents, and monarchs started to implement structural reforms, including privatization, liberalization and financial stabilization in the aftermath of the fall of the Berlin Wall. Subsidies were seen as a possible area of reform, but little was accomplished in terms of removing existing subsidies for two good reasons. One is that oil prices were extremely low (around US$20 per barrel) and the second is that countries started to grow thanks to the initial reforms. These two factors resulted in subsidies being a relatively small share of GDP decreasing the pressure for reforms. It is, however, a lost decade for subsidies reforms in that low oil prices would have allowed governments to remove price regulation mechanisms and subsidies with a small impact on household welfare as compared to the decade that followed.

The 2000s brought about the first urge for reforms but no reforms; rather, it was a period that could characterize subsidies as **one of the last instruments for fragile governments to maintain power**. The change in attitudes toward subsidies was generated by two concomitant factors. The first follows from the previous period. As countries start to reform their economies, it becomes increasingly clear among international observers that subsidies are an obstacle to further reforms, and this idea starts to generate a debate on subsidies reforms also within countries. The second and most important factor is oil prices. Starting from the beginning of the decade the price of oil rises with a relentless growth process, which drastically changes the weight of subsidies on the economy. Subsidies, for the first time, become an unsustainable burden for the budget. Increasing oil prices have a double cost: they not only increase subsidies but also contribute to higher prices of non-subsidized products, including food. This general increase in prices, in turn, generates resentments on the part of the population and a wall of adversity toward subsidy reforms. Moreover, through the 2000s none of the countries in the Region goes through political reforms, and rulers continue to use subsidies as a tool to contain discontent. In Libya, for example, Gaddafi implemented a drastic reform of food subsidies in 2008 only to roll it back completely on the eve of the Libyan revolution as one of his last attempts to contain discontent. Hence, subsidies become increasingly a burden for state budgets, but they remain a political hazard for fragile rulers.

The incapacity of governments to remove subsidies during a period of hard budget constraints relates to oil prices and government instability but also finds its roots in a combination of factors that, taken individually, may seem reasonable to many observers. Table 1.1 shows ten factors that justify removing subsidies as well as ten factors that would seem to justify subsidies. Subsidies are costly to the government and tax payers; they distort investments, production, and consumption; and they can support nondemocratic institutions. Yet, subsidies are easily portrayed as good policies. Politicians are rightly concerned about the risk of political uprising, various stakeholders benefit indirectly from subsidies thanks to established monopolies or oligopolies. Export-oriented firms benefit from lower input costs and can better compete on international markets. Consumers benefit from reduced prices and reduced volatility on prices, and this applies to all consumers. Subsidies also worked as a social protection mechanism, compensating for the general increase in prices of the late 2000s, and in many countries of the MENA Region, subsidies are perceived as an acquired right.

All these reasons for keeping subsidies appear to be legitimate but each of these reasons is linked to a particular interest group and result in a net cost for the economy at large. For example, the risk of social uprising is real, but delaying reforms does not address the problem. Export-oriented firms benefited from increased export competitiveness but only in the short term and at the expense of reduced growth in production and productivity in the medium and long term. Subsidies worked as social protection mechanisms but in a much less efficient way than cash transfers targeted to the poor. In other words, although removing subsidies may result in a positive social outcome overall and in a better allocation of

Table 1.1 Pros and cons of subsidy reforms

Ten reasons to remove subsidies	Ten reasons to keep subsidies
Economic	*Economic*
Distort consumption	Reduce production costs and increase export competitiveness
Distort production	Reduce price volatility, financial risks, and uncertainty for households
Distort investments	*Political*
Delay important strategic decisions on energy	Risk of social uprising
Encourage informality and illegality	Buy political consensus
Political	Benefit established monopolies/oligopolies related to politicians
Support undemocratic regimes and populists governments	*Social*
Nontransparent to the population	Work as social protection mechanism
Social	Compensate for general increases in prices
Costly for the tax payers	Benefit the poor, the middle class, and the rich
Inequitable and prorich	Perceived as a basic human right
Costly for the environment	Increased demand for subsidies due to economic decline in the MENA Region

resources in the long run, the potential loss of short-term gains from particular interest groups are a powerful constraint to reforms. This was why it was so difficult to remove subsidies. The voices of the different interest groups were louder than the overall economic rationale of the social planner, a voice that few governments were willing to heed. It is natural to ask next, therefore, what broke this equilibrium and made governments move on with reforms.

What Triggered Reforms?

The recent wave of subsidies reforms really starts with the 2010 reforms in Iran and progressively expands to other countries of the MENA region in the midst of political turmoil. A combination of factors explains this wave of reform, each of which cannot explain the reforms alone. One possible factor is the extent of the political changes that took the Region by storm. Regime changes in the Arab Republic of Egypt, Libya, Tunisia, and the Republic of Yemen altered the political settings in these countries and had a demonstrative effect on countries that did not experience revolutions first hand. The popular revolutions affected the politics of other countries of the MENA Region, and in some countries political changes occurred without a revolution. The new class of politicians was less averse to subsidies reforms than the previous regimes, perhaps because they were typically less connected than the old regimes to the benefits derived from subsidies. The spirit of change created a new social contract with the populations, who became less averse to reforms although subsidies remained in great demand.

But the main factors that explain reforms are economic and relate to the price of oil, regulated prices and the economic decline generated by the political changes. The period considered thus far was exceptional for world energy and food prices. Figure 1.1 shows average monthly oil prices (U.S. and European FOB prices in US $ per barrel, left axis) and the price of gasoline (U.S. FOB price in US$ per gallon, right axis) between May 1987 and April 2016.[1] Four distinct periods emerge. The first period, between 1987 and 2003, is characterized by oil prices below US$40 per barrel. During this period, U.S. and European prices overlap, and the price of gasoline follows closely the oil price. A second period is characterized by a steep surge in oil prices between 2003 and 2008 when price volatility increases and the price of gasoline follows less closely the oil price. The third period starting in 2009 follows the global financial crisis and is characterized by high and volatile oil prices where the U.S. and European prices and the price of gasoline increasingly diverge. The fourth period shows the most recent decline in oil and gasoline prices and also continued price volatility. The period considered by this book (2010–2014) is unique in terms of both the level and volatility of oil prices.

The picture is similar if we consider the commodities indexes for fuel and food (Fig. 1.2). The fuel energy index, which combines fuel products, shows that its trend overlaps with the oil trend up until the 2008 global financial crisis when we start to see more volatility and a certain divergence between the two trends. The food price index is naturally less associated with changes in the oil price but nevertheless is correlated with it. In particular, during the period that we consider more closely (2010–14) both the food and energy indexes show high levels and high volatility. In their reforms efforts, governments faced increasing fiscal pressure and increasing uncertainty. This aspect is crucial to understanding the political economy of reforms and why most governments in the Region have put subsidies reforms at the top of their agenda in recent years.

The next issue to consider is the regulated prices that MENA countries were confronted with when they were forced to introduce reforms. Table 1.2 shows the average regional prices for four energy products—gasoline, diesel, kerosene, and LPG—comparing the main regions of the world. It is striking how the MENA Region distinguishes itself from the others by having, by far, the lowest average regional prices. For example, the price of gasoline, on average, was US$0.67, about half the price of other regions. The price of LPG was US$0.4, which is less than a third of the average price in South Asia and about a third of the price in East Asia and the Pacific. Similarly, for diesel and kerosene, the prices in the MENA Region were a fraction of the prices in other regions. Hence, the worldwide push for

[1]Note that the difference between the Cushing OK WTI Spot price and the Europe Brent price may be due to infrastructure constraints in the United States (the location of oil pipelines relative to that of major refineries exporting refined products, for example) combined with the ban on crude oil exports. The three series are plotted to show that the trends are the same despite differences in absolute values.

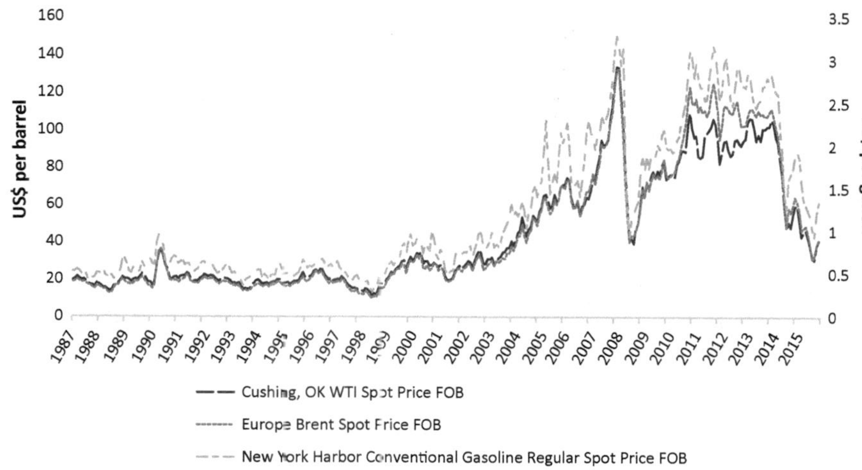

Fig. 1.1 U.S. and European oil prices, May 1987–April 2016. *Source* Elaborated from data available at EIA (2015)

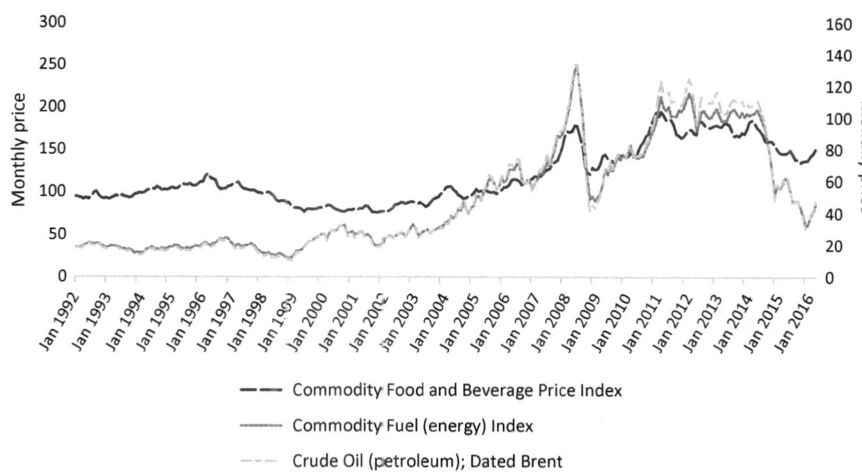

Fig. 1.2 Commodities and oil prices, January 1992–May 2016. *Sources* Elaborated from http://www.indexmundi.com/ and World Bank Commodities Prices database

subsidies reforms that took place in virtually all regions of the world since 2010–11 was particularly acute in the MENA Region when growth took a negative turn due to political instability. These two factors together with the economic decline generated by the political changes were the driving factors of subsidies reforms that eventually overruled the other logics for maintaining subsidies.

Table 1.2 Average regional prices of petroleum products, in US$ (January 2013)

	Gasoline	Diesel	Kerosene	LPG
East Asia and Pacific	1.25	1.03	1.11	1.20
Europe and Central Asia	1.16	1.23	n.a.	n.a.
Latin America and the Caribbean	1.24	1.14	1.18	1.01
Middle East and North Africa	0.67	0.44	0.41	0.40
South Asia	1.25	0.91	0.86	1.44
Sub-Saharan Africa	1.24	1.22	0.96	0.97

Source Elaborated from Kojima 2013
Note The table is based on a sample of 63 countries. Data on Europe and Central Asia (ECA) countries may not be representative due to the small sample size

Who Reformed, When, How, and Why?

An overview of reforms undertaken during this period shows that of the eight countries considered in this book, six implemented substantial reforms. In chronological order of reforms, these countries are the Islamic Republic of Iran, Yemen, Jordan, Morocco, Egypt, and Tunisia. The other two countries of Djibouti and Libya did not implement any reforms and will not be covered in this section. In what follows, we focus on the key reforms undertaken between 2010 and 2014, summarizing the background, contents, and outcomes of the reforms.

Islamic Republic of Iran: December 18, 2010

On January 5, 2010, the government of the Islamic Republic of Iran introduced the Targeted Subsidy Reform Act, a major subsidy reform designed to eliminate most subsidies and compensate the population with a cash transfer. Due to political and organizational constraints, the implementation of the act was delayed for almost a year and the reform was finally launched on December 18, 2010. The reform was originally planned to be implemented over a period of five years to coincide with the fifth five-year economic, social, and cultural development plan. The act estimated the expected net gain at 200 trillion rials but did not indicate the price increase to be applied to subsidized products. The reform was preceded by an extensive public relations campaign to educate the population on the costs and benefits of the reform (Guillaume et al. 2011). The government also made clear that protests would not be well received. Budget savings deriving from the reforms were expected to be partly redistributed in the form of transfers to the population (50%), partly used by the government for administration (20%), and for improving the efficiency of the energy, transport, and industry sectors (30%).

The actual reforms that unfolded in the weeks following December 18, 2010 included major prices increases for all fuel products, electricity, water, transport, and bread. The price of gasoline increased fourfold from the equivalent of US$0.10 per liter to US$0.40 per liter for quotas[2] and from US$0.60 per liter to US$0.70 per liter for nonquotas. The price of diesel increased tenfold from US$0.06 per gallon to US$0.6, and the price of natural gas for domestic consumption increased at least fivefold from 1–1.3 to 7 cents per cubic meter. Prices for electricity and water also increased by around 300% on average, and the reform did not spare public transport or bread, with prices increasing by more than 200%.[3]

The price reform was accompanied by a compensatory cash transfer of 445,000 rials per person per month, an amount equivalent to 28% of the median household income and 50% of the income of a minimum wage worker with a family of four (see Chap. 10). This transfer was quasi-universal. About 80% of households were made eligible on the eve of the reform, and more households were added later. The cash transfer was administered via bank accounts. The first transfer was deposited in accounts in advance of the price increases in an effort to minimize protest and distrust for reforms.

The reform had a clear impact on prices, which increased during the first half of 2011 across main consumption items, with average increases around 30% and peak increases around 100%. Consumption of fuel products such as gasoline and liquefied gas decreased by about 10%. In January 2012 the government estimated that total savings from the reform amounted to an equivalent of US$15 billion. The simulations provided in Chap. 10 show that the compensatory cash transfers provided were excessive to compensate for the reforms and that a large part of the transfers accrued to the nonpoor. Perhaps because of these large effects, the government partly rolled back reforms in March 2012 when the parliament amended the Targeted Subsidies Reform Act

The main trigger for reforms was the size of subsidies, which by 2010 were estimated at the equivalent of US$100 billion, an amount larger than the total oil revenues and over 20% of GDP. The scope and size of the reform was unprecedented not only for Iran but also for any other economy that embarked on subsidy reforms. Indeed, the outcomes of this reform have produced large changes in consumption patterns, inflation, and government revenues and expenditure. However, despite the large increases in prices, the reform did not remove price controls and four years later Iran found itself again with very large subsidies, the second largest provider of subsidies in the MENA Region after Libya, as shown in Chap. 2. Therefore, although the reform partly succeeded in readjusting consumption and prices, it failed in its attempt of removing subsidies.

Subsidy reforms in Iran have also been carried out in a complex economic environment characterized by international sanctions and large social programs, such as the Maskan Mehr low-cost housing program, which contributed to a prolonged period of stagnation and inflation. The outcomes of these other factors merged with the outcomes of the subsidy reforms and eventually created public

[2]Since June 2007 gasoline has been subject to a quota system administered with electronic cards.
[3]See also https://en.wikipedia.org/wiki/Iranian_subsidy_reform_plan.

resentments against the reforms (see Chap. 10). The continuation of reforms during the five-year period that was initially envisioned did not happen as expected, and further subsidy reforms remain as problematic as ever.

Yemen: 2010–2014

Recent subsidies reforms in Yemen initiated around 2005 with World Bank and IMF support. Initial reforms included several rounds of price increases that more than doubled prices between 2005 and 2010. In 2010, the government introduced further price increases for fuel products of about 30% and for LPG of about 100%. This was followed in 2011 and 2012 by further increases of prices of gasoline by 66% and diesel and kerosene by about 100%. These large price increases were not accompanied by significant public protests. In July 2014, the government decided to remove subsidies and initially increased prices by 60–90% depending on the product, but this move lacked a proper public information campaign and resulted in violent protests that forced the government to partially reverse reforms in September of the same year. As a result, gasoline and diesel experienced a net increase of 50 and 20% respectively. This last round of reforms also foresaw compensatory measures in terms of an expansion of funding and coverage for the social welfare fund. However, these compensatory measures were not clearly explained to the public and they took some time to be enforced, which partly explains why they were not effective in preventing public protests. It is also important to note that these reforms occurred in the midst of high political instability that eventually turned into civil war. If we consider the political climate, the government took bold and risky reforms during the period that could have further compromised the political environment.

Jordan: November 13, 2012

The government of Jordan introduced a major subsidies reform on November 13, 2012. This move occurred unexpectedly, despite a prolonged period of public discussion about subsidies reforms. The reform reintroduced the automatic pricing adjustment mechanism on petroleum products and thereby discontinued the practice of discretionary adjustments. The liberalization of prices caused immediate increases in the prices of 90 octane gasoline and kerosene (+14.3%, from 700 to 800 fils per liter for both products), diesel (+33% from 515 to 684 fils per liter), and LPG (+53.8%, from JD 6.5 to JD 10 per cylinder of 12.5 kg). This rise followed an initial price increase of the other petroleum products, including 95 octane gasoline, introduced during the second quarter of 2012. The reform was accompanied by the precautionary measure of freezing the price of bread, but the Ministry of Transport was instructed to adjust public transport tariffs according to the new fuel prices.

The Jordanian reform also included a compensation of JD 70 per person per year with a maximum ceiling per household of JD 420 per year, an amount excluded from any form of taxation or deductions. The only eligibility criteria were Jordanian residency and an annual household income below JD 10,000. An estimated 70% of the population were expected to be eligible for the program, and the administrators used several public databases to exclude noneligible households, including the rosters of public sector employees and retirees, military personnel and retirees, and social security subscribers. Beneficiaries of the National Aid Fund (NAF) would receive the compensation without application, but all other eligible citizens (private sector employees, the unemployed, and the inactive) had to apply by filling out a specific form. The start of the compensation was set for November 18, 2012, and payments were scheduled to be made every four months. Payments were also anchored to the average international price of oil with an automatic discontinuation of benefits if the price of oil per barrel fell below US$100 in the four months preceding any payment. The generous cash transfer that accompanied the reform probably contributed to quell protest, as the reform did not result in any social backlash.

Arab Republic of Egypt: July 5, 2014

The Arab Republic of Egypt undertook substantial reforms of fuel prices on July 5, 2014. The government announced increases in prices for all fuels with the sole exception of LPG. Gasoline prices rose from LE 0.9 to LE 1.6 for 80 octane, from LE 1.85 to LE 2.6 for 92 octane, and from LE 5.75 to LE 6.25 for 95 octane; natural gas for cars rose from LE 0.45 to LE 1.1; and diesel from LE 1.1 to LE 1.8. Prices for natural gas and fuel for commercial uses were also increased significantly. Electricity prices for all residential customers rose by about 50% on average; smaller increases were applied to commercial customers for whom the initial price had been much higher. These were all major price increases in percentage terms but still insufficient to eliminate subsidies as the starting prices were very low. The government also announced a complete phase out of subsidies over a five-year period, estimated savings of about LE 51 billion and planned to allocate part of these savings to social expenditure—about LE 27 billion on health, education, and social protection programs.

The July 2014 reform aimed at addressing the major budget liability stemming from the prolonged growth of subsidies. For example, fuel subsidies had increased at a compound annual growth rate of 26% between 2002 and 2013. Their share of the government budget increased from 9% in 2002 to 22% in 2013, and their share in Egypt's GDP increased from 3 to 7% in the same period (see Chap. 6). The weight on the budget was already very high in 2011, but the Egyptian revolution stalled any possible reforms. The new government of Mohamed Morsi preferred to delay major reforms and focus instead on administrative adjustments such as the much needed corrections to the LPG distribution system. It is only with the arrival of the government of Abdel Fattah el-Sisi that the political commitment and capacity to implement reforms became stronger. The popularity that this government enjoyed during the first few months in office and the inherited budget deficit contributed to create the conditions for reforms.

Morocco: September 16, 2013–October 1, 2014

Major reforms to the subsidy system in Morocco began on September 16, 2013, with the decision to reactivate the price indexation mechanism for liquid petroleum products, including gasoline, diesel, and fuel oil. The new system imposed a cap on the unit subsidies with the remaining price differential to be passed through to domestic prices. This first measure helped the government to reduce subsidies by an estimated 1.3 percentage points of GDP.

On February 1, 2014, the government stopped supporting prices of gasoline and industrial fuel oil. The price of gasoline in January 2014 was not very far from the nonsubsidized price. As a result, the price increase that occurred in February 2014 was relatively small, from DH 12.02 to DH 12.8. As fuel oil was used for the generation of electricity, the government introduced a lump-sum transfer to the national electricity company to be phased out over a period of three years during which electricity tariffs were to progressively increase starting from August 2014. The August reforms of electricity included an increase of the number of blocks from four to six. Tariffs were adjusted, and starting from the third block, the tariff system changed from increasing block tariffs (IBT) to volume differentiated tariffs (VDT).[4] Diesel unit subsidies were also subjected to a gradual dismantling with a progressive phase out from DH 2.15 per liter in January 2014 to DH 0.80 per liter in October. Subsequently, the government removed diesel from its list of subsidized products.

As of January 2015 the only remaining subsidized products in Morocco were LPG, flour, and sugar. However, the government decided to continue administering prices of liquid petroleum products through the implementation of the indexation mechanism until November 2015, when prices of all liquid petroleum products would be fully liberalized. Prices of these products would thereafter be subject to competition among the distributors (see Chap. 3).

The political economy of subsidy reforms in Morocco has been driven largely by the global prices of strategic commodities and by the increasing cost of subsidies to the state's budget. Subsidy reforms were complemented by other fiscal consolidation measures, including a freeze on wages and limits to hiring civil servants to stop the rise of the public wage bill, and improvements to the tax collection system

[4]Increasing block tariffs (IBT) apply when the tariff corresponding to a particular block applies only to the latest block of consumption, and tariffs for the previous blocks of consumption apply to the previous blocks. Volume differentiated tariffs (VDT) apply is when the tariffs corresponding to a particular block is applied to all quantities consumed up to that block.

through the extension of the tax base, harmonization of tax rates, and an effort to stop tax evasion.

The evaluation of the 2013–14 reforms in Chap. 3 shows that the reforms are unlikely to have had any impact on poverty and inequality and they did protect the most vulnerable parts of the population while contributing significantly to reducing the budget deficit. The evaluation of the 2014 subsidy reforms has shown that the government has made a set of proper choices from a distributional and budget perspective. Subsidies have been eliminated on those products, such as gasoline, that were more prorich and affected poverty the least, while the reform of products that would hurt the poor the most, such as LPG, has been delayed. Electricity tariffs have been increased in a sensible way by increasing the number of blocks (and thereby reducing the consumer surplus) and by raising tariffs only on the upper blocks, protecting in this way the poor and the middle class. The 2014 reforms had important indirect effects, particularly for diesel, and these had an impact on poverty but still modest overall. All reforms were implemented without compensatory cash transfers, and the reforms did not provoke any significant social backlash.

Tunisia: 2012–14

As with the other reformist countries, Tunisia was forced to embark into subsidy reforms because of budget constraints. Between 2005 and 2013, the combined spending on energy, food, and transportation more than tripled, rising from 2% of GDP in 2005 to 7% in 2013. Energy subsidies, in particular, increased fourfold, reaching 4.7% of GDP in 2013. Due to the 2011 revolution and the economic decline and political instability that followed the revolution, reforming subsidies proved difficult between 2011 and 2012.

In 2012 the government of Tunisia began implementing a gradual strategy of subsidy reduction and improvement in public spending targeting. As reported by the IMF (2014), the prices of gasoline, diesel, and electricity increased by 7% in September 2012, followed by similar increases in March 2013. Energy subsidies to cement companies were halved in January 2014 and fully removed in June of the same year. Electricity tariffs on low and medium voltage consumers were increased in a two-step process, by 10% in January 2014 and another 10% in May 2014. The government introduced a lifeline electricity tariff for households consuming less than 100 kilowatt hours (kWh) per month in 2014. Also in January 2014 the government established a new automatic price formula for gasoline to align domestic prices to international prices over time, but without a clear calendar (see Chap. 4).

The government also introduced other social reforms with the potential to mitigate the impact of subsidy reforms, although not designed specifically for that purpose. It launched a new social housing program (which was never really implemented), increased income tax deductions for the poorest households, and committed to creating a unified registry of beneficiaries of social programs and to improving social spending targeting (to be finished in 2015). In addition, the government continued to expand the cash transfer program (PNAFN) while attempting to reduce its exclusion error.

Policy Options

In what follows we discuss the pros and cons of these different approaches to reforms and other important questions and choices that policy makers are called to address when reforming subsidies such as introducing compensatory measures or not, prepare the public with public information campaigns or be silent, follow a product by product approach as opposed to uniform reforms across products, target the poor, the middle class or both, start from energy subsides as opposed to food subsidies or vice versa, consider direct as opposed to indirect effects, and the choice of the political timing of reforms. Rather than providing recommendations, the following sections review and compare the choices made by the sample of countries we consider in this book.

Radical Versus Gradualist Approach

Looking at the contents, duration, and outcomes of the reforms, we can classify the countries observed into four categories. The first category is made of those countries that followed a *radical approach* to reforms. This category includes Iran and Jordan, the countries that introduced a substantial set of reforms at one particular point in time. The second category is made of those countries that carried out a significant amount of reforms over a period of time using a *gradualist approach*. This category includes Morocco and Tunisia, but the extent of the reforms and their impact have been quite different, with Morocco implementing much deeper reforms than Tunisia. The third category includes Egypt and Yemen, two countries that stepped up reforms in 2014 after a period of gradual reforms. The fourth category of countries is represented by the *nonreformers*, which includes Djibouti and Libya. Djibouti had relatively little subsidy in place to start with and distributed it only in the form of tax exemptions. Libya did not reform because of political instability and civil conflict.

Were Iran and Jordan more successful than Morocco and Tunisia? The answer is not univocal, but there is something to learn by comparing these two sets of countries. Iran did implement profound reforms in terms of price increases, and these reforms did provide some extra revenues for the government, real benefits to the poor, and reduced energy consumption. However, they also brought about inflation, were costly in terms of compensation, and were carried out in the midst of other important economic changes such as international sanctions and housing reforms. Moreover, these reforms failed to liberalize prices of subsidized items. The result is that four years later subsidies had returned to very large levels, and the population remains confused as to the benefits of the reforms. The job is not done, and pushing further reforms will be more difficult than before. The scale of the reforms in Jordan was much lower, but Jordan managed to liberalize prices of gasoline and diesel in one stroke and to buy support with substantial cash transfers. Jordan solved one problem but has yet to tackle the remaining LPG and electricity subsidies. Electricity subsidies in particular represent the main budget problem in Jordan today and the reforms did not address this problem.

Morocco prepared reforms carefully, implemented them in an orderly fashion following an open dialogue with the population, discontinued subsidies altogether for gasoline and diesel, started to implement a clear plan for the removal of electricity subsidies, and designed a plan for discontinuing subsidies on LPG. This country has now eliminated most subsidies and is expected to eliminate all of them within three years. This country started from a relatively low level of subsidies as compared to other countries in the region partly because it was more rigorous in applying the price transfer mechanisms in place and also removed subsidies on other consumers' products such as edible oil early on in the years 2000s. Tunisia implemented simpler reforms with gradual increases of prices and tariffs every quarter. This approach went well with the population, but the country has failed to remove subsidies altogether for any energy product and, at the end of 2014, still maintained subsidies on several food products.

Those countries that did not reform was either because they had low subsidies (Djibouti) or they faced insurmountable political challenges due to internal civil conflict (Libya). Otherwise, these countries too might have gone through reforms during the exceptional convergence of factors of the 2010–14 period. Overall, considering the sample of eight countries and the 2010–2014 period covered by the book, the gradualist approach has been the dominant approach to reforms.

Compensation Versus Noncompensation

The more radical approach followed by the Islamic Republic of Iran and Jordan was accompanied by large cash compensations. In both countries these compensations were seen as indispensable to assist the poor and the middle class and discourage any form of social protest. In this sense, compensations were effective. In contrast to the countries that followed a radical approach, neither Morocco nor Tunisia resorted to comprehensive cash compensation although Tunisia expanded the cash transfer program during the period of subsidy reforms; instead, they paired reforms with other mitigating fiscal reforms. These countries not only avoided any form of social unrest but also gained relatively more from reforms than countries that resorted to compensation. The lack of compensation did not result in an overall reduction in poverty, as in the Islamic Republic of Iran and Jordan, but the overall impact on poverty was very low, also because of the initial low level of subsidies.

In essence, the two dominant approaches to reforms have been the radical approach with compensation and the gradualist approach without compensation. However, several other factors can come into play that may affect the decision about compensation such as the political climate, the overall initial level of subsidies or the existence or introduction of other social protection measures in concomitance with subsidies reforms. Depending on these factors, governments may also consider compensation in the course of gradualist reforms.

It is important for the social planner to have a good knowledge of the distribution of income and expenditure prior to reforms and simulate the impact on household welfare of alternative compensation strategies. The optimal mix between price increases and cash compensation depends largely on the distribution of household incomes, and the effect of price increases on different households depends on household expenditure on subsidized products. In absolute terms, the cost of price increases for richer households tends to be higher than the cost for poorer households because richer households consume more. But in relative terms (relative to total household expenditure) subsidized products tend to be more important for the poor with the exception of a few products. Chapter 2 and the country chapters have shown how SUBSIM can be used to simulate and evaluate these trade-offs.

Other forms of mitigating measures are also possible. Iran, Morocco, and Tunisia accompanied their reforms with fiscal policies that could mitigate the impact of reforms, even if these reforms were not always explicitly linked to the subsidy reforms. Iran launched a major housing scheme (in addition to cash compensation); Tunisia passed a housing program and tax deductions, and Morocco acted on the macro side with macro stabilization and fiscal policies. These reforms and their relation with subsidies reforms are effectively difficult to evaluate and they cut short of addressing the most challenging task of compensation measures, which is targeting the poor properly.

More promising are reforms that aim at improving the targeting capacity of the social protection systems in place. The cost of compensation can be much reduced by passing from quasi-universal systems, such as those implemented by Iran and Jordan, to systems targeting the poor only. Poverty-focused compensations proved difficult to introduce for all countries that moved on with subsidies reforms for the simple reason that these countries did not have proper social protection systems in place. In essence, cash compensation for the poor is the most obvious social policy that would address the poverty question, reduce budget costs and be easy to evaluate in cost-benefit terms. However, this policy remains constrained because the social protection systems in the MENA Region are still underdeveloped and do not guarantee proper targeting of the poor. This contributes to explain why countries that opted for compensation did so using quasi-universal coverage rather than targeting the poor only.

Public Information Versus No Information

This is not an aspect that the book has focused on but it is useful to note the contrast between the different approaches followed by the countries considered. Iran is perhaps the only country that implemented a specific public information campaign before launching the reforms. But Jordan and Morocco kept the discussion on subsidies reforms in the news for a long time before implementing reforms and Morocco was rather specific in explaining reforms when it started the process. Egypt introduced reforms in July 2014 quickly, without a proper information campaign by simply explciting the popularity of the incoming government whereas in Yemen poor communication with the public resulted in social unrest. In essence, the degree of information provided by governments prior to reforms or in the course of reforms varied significantly across countries and it was not necessarily related to the scale or pace of reforms or to social unrest. The only common denominator across countries is that nowhere reforms passed without an interest on the part of the press and some degree of public debate witnessing, once more, the importance of the topic for the region.

Piecemeal Versus Wholesale Reforms

We define "piecemeal" reforms as those carried out product by product, tailoring price increases and product restructuring to each individual product subject to reforms. We define "wholesale" reforms as those carried out uniformly across products: for example, a 20% increase in the price of a set of products. All countries considered made an effort to follow a piecemeal approach. However, Tunisia has used in a couple of occasions homogeneous price increases for different products and those countries that followed a radical approach to reforms did so by treating several products at the same time. Gasoline and diesel were the first products to be reformed in all countries, then electricity, and LPG always came later. Reforms were almost never uniform across products with the exception of price increases in Tunisia at one point in time and for only two products.

Products are different in their production and distribution processes, they target different types of consumers in different ways, the price structure may be different, and reforms may affect different stakeholders and touch upon different interest groups. Comprehensive wholesale reforms are often tempting because they appear simple in their design and their effect can be better measured in terms of budget outcome. The reality on the ground, however, is much more complex. As shown by the simulations in Chap. 2 and the country chapters, uniform price increases across products result in very different outcomes in terms of budget, welfare effects and effects on the various stakeholders managing subsidized products. This may explain why all governments with few exceptions opted for a piecemeal approach to reforms.

Poor Versus Middle Class

Who is really hurt by the reforms and who is most likely to complain? In absolute terms, the answer to both questions is the middle class. The middle class receives more subsidies in dollar amounts than the poor, and the urban middle class has generally more voice when it comes to protests. Political leaders are understandably aware and worried about this fact when it comes to subsidy reforms. The very generous compensation packages designed by Iran and Jordan extended well beyond the middle class, and although the rhetoric may have been around protecting the poor, the real target of quasi-universal cash transfers is the middle class. Egypt, Morocco, and Tunisia, however, did not formally compensate either the poor or the middle class. As already discussed, countries that opted to provide compensation did so with quasi-universal coverage. This is one area where a lot more can be done. If governments opt for compensation and in preparation for the reforms, it is important to simulate reforms and measure the budget cost of compensation under different coverage scenarios as we show throughout the book, and it is equally important to improve the targeting capacity of the social protection systems so as to be able to reach the intended population.

Energy Versus Food Subsidies Reforms

In addition to their investigation of energy products, some of the researchers who contributed to this book were able to consider a limited set of food products in selected countries. The list of food products and countries that administer food subsidies is, however, not complete. For example, Egypt and Tunisia are two countries that administer food subsidies, but the case studies dedicated to these countries focused on energy subsidies only. Still, the evidence of asymmetry in reforms between energy and food items is clear. The subsidies reforms we observed have been largely on energy products, and virtually all governments had a clear preference for postponing or avoiding food subsidies reforms. This choice is partly explained by the fact that energy subsidies weigh more on the government budget than food subsidies (but not true for Libya), and the resistance to this type of reform often comes from fear of hurting the poor and the middle class and causing social unrest. Also, food subsidies are thought to work better than energy subsidies as social protection mechanisms because they tend to be allocated to primary food products largely consumed by the poor and there is also a nutrition angle to consider that may be important for the poorest countries. For example, Libya in 2010 and Egypt in 2014 opted to increase food subsidies while trying to reduce energy subsidies.

But in other cases countries have successfully removed food subsidies (edible oil in Morocco in the early 2000s and edible oil, tomato paste, tea, and dry yeasts in Libya in the mid-2000s) with marginal impact on welfare, no compensation, and no social implications. Therefore, countries in the MENA region showed a clear preference for reforming energy subsidies as opposed to food subsidies but history shows that it is possible to reform food subsidies with moderate social consequences.

Direct Versus Indirect Effects

In the country chapters of this book, indirect effects for food products have been estimated only for two products (bread and sugar) in only one country (Morocco) and results show that these effects are negligible. Indirect effects related to energy products have been estimated in four of the eight countries considered (Morocco, Tunisia, Jordan and Iran) and, in the case of Iran, indirect effects are only available for all products aggregated. Therefore, tentative conclusions on the role of indirect effects for energy products can be made comparing three countries (Morocco, Tunisia, Jordan) and three products (electricity, gasoline and diesel). Moreover, in the case of Morocco, gasoline and diesel effects have been estimated jointly and cannot be separated. Comparing available countries and products, we can nevertheless derive three tentative conclusions on the role of indirect effects (see Table 1.3): (1) For electricity, the share of indirect effects on total effects seems quite consistent across countries and estimated around 40%; (2) The share of indirect effects of petroleum products is greater than the share of non-petroleum products; and (3) The share of indirect effects of diesel is around 80% and generally higher than the share of gasoline. The last two points are expected given the role of petroleum products and diesel in particular in the production processes. Results on electricity are perhaps more interesting and point to a regularity that would call for further research. See also Coady et al. (2015) on indirect subsidies.

Political Timing of Reforms

It is also instructive to reflect on the timing of reforms in relation to the political context in which they occurred. This chapter has argued that reforms were implemented during an extraordinary period of political and social changes for the Region and that this extraordinary period has been partly responsible for the

Table 1.3 Shares of indirect effects over total effects (%)

	Morocco	Tunisia	Jordan
Gasoline	87.8	51	14
Diesel	87.8	89.1	77
Liquefied petroleum gas (LPG)	n.a.	14.4	n.a.
Kerosene	n.a.	n.a.	n.a.
Electricity	36.6	40.7	41

reforms. But it is also true that not all countries experienced the same political changes and not all countries reformed equally. For example, it is clear that Morocco and Jordan had a comparative advantage in relation to Tunisia, Libya or Yemen in that these countries introduced political changes in a piecemeal manner and managed to avoid a revolution and its economic costs.

Political stability evidently provided the government of Morocco with more time and resources to prepare and carry out reforms in an orderly fashion while allowed Jordan to be rather bold with radical reforms. Egypt implemented the first radical reform when El-Sisi came to power and had the political and administrative force to bring about the reforms that had proved difficult to implement under previous political settings. In Libya, Gaddafi brought about radical reforms of food subsidies in the mid-2000s, when he enjoyed political stability and a certain international support, only to backtrack on all reforms when he needed to buy support during the period that preceded the 2011 revolution. Libya has not carried out any reform between 2011 and 2014 despite the size of subsidies in this country because internal civil conflict and political instability made reforms very risky. Although the budget crisis has provided the main impetus for reforming subsidies, the political setting has determined how and when reforms were actually implemented.

Unfinished Business

Chapter 2 offers a comparative analysis of subsidies and simulations of further subsidy reforms. The eight case studies (Chaps. 3 through 10) also simulate the impact of the total removal of subsidies on welfare, poverty, inequality, and the government budget. The results of these investigations show that subsidy reforms in 2014 were far from complete, not only in the countries that have still to embark on reforms but also in countries that went through deep reforms such as Iran and Jordan. The complete elimination of subsidies is hard to accomplish and requires strong political will as well as a convergence of other elements that facilitate reforms such as favorable international oil prices, a stable social situation and a well-structured reform package.

Progress on subsidy reforms also depends on the product considered. By the end of 2014, and with the notable exceptions of Iran and Libya, subsidies on gasoline and diesel were reduced to small amounts. Further reforms on these products will imply ending price regulations or adopt automatic indexation mechanisms that result in zero subsidies. Independently of the cost and benefits of this move, this is an epochal change for governments that have controlled prices of these commodities for decades and will require a strong political will.

Different is the question of LPG. None of the countries studied carried out comprehensive reforms of this product in a consistent manner. A couple of countries increased the price of LPG, but most did not touch this price, and all now face enormous challenges. Before the fall in oil prices, the elimination of subsidies on LPG entailed price increases from 44% (Yemen) to 947% (Libya). With the exception of Morocco, none of the countries studied had a clear strategy to eliminate LPG subsidies in 2015 or in the years to come. LPG is a product used by households for cooking and is largely used by the poor, which makes governments reluctant to touch the price of this product. The production and distribution of LPG is mostly in the hands of few entities that may block reforms.

Reforming LPG subsidies is, however, possible. Egypt and Tunisia have explored the possibility of combining the expansion of the natural gas network with the reduction in the use of LPG bottles. Natural gas networks are expanding in these countries, and their governments could facilitate the expansion of the network in poorer urban neighborhoods by subsidizing connections to the network. The cost of natural gas for household use is competitive with LPG, and even poor households may be willing to switch to the new system, which was the experience in Europe during the 1960s and 1970s. To encourage this process while reducing subsidies, governments could proceed with small but regular increases in the price of the LPG bottle and use the revenue to expand the natural gas network further or compensate communities that cannot be reached. The other possibility explored by some countries is to introduce quotas and limit consumption in this way. Doing so is possible, although quotas require the introduction of administrative systems such as user cards, which are costly and may generate illegal or informal redistribution systems of the product under quotas. Egypt has struggled with these problems for years and has yet to find a definitive solution for LPG.

Electricity subsidies have also their specificities. Most countries have now proceeded with gradual increases, and some countries (Morocco and Jordan) have instituted a reform of the tariff structure. The central problem of electricity subsidies relates to the production of electricity, which in many countries still relies on expensive heavy fuels as opposed to cheaper alternatives such as hydroelectric and natural gas power. The crisis of electricity subsidy of Jordan started when the country had to abandon the production of electricity with natural gas due to the cuts of imports from Egypt. Jordan had to switch to heavy fuels that almost quadrupled the cost of production of electricity. The costs quickly became a major liability for the Jordanian government. In these cases the main solution to the electricity subsidies problem is changing the source of energy used to produce electricity. It is also possible, however, to restructure tariffs in a way that are closer to the consumers' capacity to pay for electricity and reducing the consumer surplus, which is the difference between what consumers are willing to pay for a particular product and what they effectively pay on the market. There are some margins to do that in some countries, as tariffs blocks are obsolete and need to be rethought in the light of current consumption patterns. Small, transparent, and regular increases in the price of electricity is also a viable option that countries such as Morocco and Tunisia have experimented with successfully.

Several food subsidies remain in the MENA Region, and they are mostly subsidies on flour, bread, and sugar. The notable exceptions are Libya, which still subsidizes a wide set of food products, and Tunisia and Egypt which maintain food subsidies on essential consumption items. Where they exist, food subsidies can be high and similar in size to energy subsidies. The political will to remove these subsidies is low as these subsidies are important for the poor. Here the unresolved question is how to compensate the poor if subsidies are removed. MENA countries lack developed social protection systems and are unable to target the poor sufficiently well. The result is a tacit consensus between the government and the population for keeping food (mostly bread) subsidies in place. Quotas are already in place in some countries and could work in the direction of reducing subsidies in other countries, but introducing a quota system is administratively complex and may be expensive, especially if this is done for only one product. Where quotas are in place, as in Libya, one possibility is to reduce the quantity amount of the quota.

A Success Story?

Table 1.4 in Appendix summarizes and compares the main features of reforms across the eight countries considered. As already discussed, the MENA region offers a variety of experiences with subsidy reforms (non-reformers, gradual reformers, radical reformers or a mix of the two) in countries with different initial characteristics (net importer or net exporters of energy; upper middle-income or lower middle income) and which experienced different political changes (mild political changes or revolutions) during a relatively short period of time. In addition, the table compares the initial trigger of reforms; content of reforms by year; extent of reforms; the use of cash compensation; other parallel measures; use of indexation mechanisms; significant popular protests and public information campaigns. It is evident that no two countries can be considered similar if we compare all dimensions.

In such a context, what is a successful subsidy reform? This is a hard question to answer and, to some extent, it is a country specific question. The difficulty that countries face when making reforms are not equal and the measure of success should be somehow "weighted" by the objective difficulties that countries face. On the other hand, one can also use some objective measures of success such as the degree of subsidies elimination and rank countries according to this parameter alone. It is therefore useful to discuss success from both a relative and an absolute angle.

Using a relative perspective, the subsidy reforms that we observed in the MENA region between 2010 and 2014 can be regarded as a success story for several reasons. First, this period saw the major wave of subsidy reforms since independence. If we compare the scale and frequency of subsidy reforms during the 2010–2014 period with that of previous periods, it is evident that the latest period has seen a surge in reforms for the reasons already explained at the outset of this chapter. Second, this surge in reforms has occurred during a very complex period in social, economic and political terms. In 2010, no one predicted the social uprisings of 2011 and these uprisings have complicated subsidy reforms as compared to other world regions that enjoyed social stability. Social tensions resulted in political instability and economic declines that further complicated reforms. Yet, all countries went through some form of reforms with the notable exceptions of Djibouti and Libya. The government that emerged in Libya after the fall of Gaddafi inherited the most extensive and expensive subsidy system in the region and objectively faced a daunting task in reforming subsidies during a very volatile political period. Evidently, we cannot measure success in Libya with the same measure we use for countries like Morocco and Jordan, which managed to maintain internal stability during a difficult political period. Third, reforms occurred after a prolonged period of rising food and commodity prices and a global crisis that made populations very averse to any further price increase. If we consider these three factors alone against the actual reforms implemented, the region can be looked at as a success story overall.

There are also objective measures that can be used to measure success and these measures tell a somewhat different story. One of these measures is whether countries have permanently eliminated the use of subsidies for specific products. This implies lifting any kind of price control and leaving markets operating freely, or, for some products, have automatic price adjustment mechanisms that result in no cost for the government budget and no subsidies. Using this meter, only Morocco can claim to have made substantial progress over the past few years. Jordan probably follows in terms of success for petroleum products but in this country electricity subsidies remain extremely high and the major liability for the government budget. Subsidy reforms in Jordan cannot be looked at as a success until the cost of producing electricity will be brought under control. Egypt has made progress on some products like gasoline and LPG but price controls remain a prerogative of the government and subsidies remain very large for strategic products like food products and also LPG. Iran has implemented the largest subsidy reform in the region without lifting price controls, which resulted in a substantial reversal of reforms only four years after their launch. Tunisia implemented only mild reforms for products that did not suffer from major subsidies while did not touch some of the food products where subsidies are large. Djibouti's reforms are negligible also in the light of the fact that subsidies were very low to start with and administered in terms of tax exemptions. In conclusion and with one exception, objective measure of success show that the region cannot be held as a success story. As the section above has illustrated, the path towards complete elimination of subsidies is still long and we cannot exclude that some of the countries considered will rise subsidies in the future, particularly during periods of low oil prices.

Overall, we learned that reforms can occur in lower and upper middle-income countries and in net energy importer or exporter countries. These are not characteristics that distinguish reformers from nonreformers or good reformers from bad reformers, despite the similar global price shocks that these countries were exposed to. Similarly, reforms can occur during periods of high or low political instability, although political stability has clearly helped some countries such as Morocco and

Jordan while political instability made reforms impossible in Libya and very difficult in Yemen.

In the course of subsidy reforms the countries studied have shown to follow alternative strategies which converged only on selected choices. A piecemeal approach to reforms where products are considered one at the time and reforms are tailored to the characteristics of individual products was the path followed by all reformers. A gradualist approach where reforms are carried out over a period of time has been the dominant approach historically but some countries in particular points in time opted for radical reforms. Cash compensation has been used by some reformist countries but not by others with similar social outcomes. Public information campaigns specifically designed for subsidy reforms have been rare but sustained communication with the public on subsidies reforms has been the path followed by most countries.

What Next?

The book focused on a historic period (2010–2014) when oil prices were particularly high and many governments in the MENA region were forced to push through subsidies reforms because of the increasing budget constraints that subsidies entailed. Not surprisingly, the countries that requested support with subsidies reforms were prevalently net oil importers with the exceptions of Libya and Yemen, two countries that faced political instability which led to economic crises. Pressure for reforms was evidently weaker for the GCC countries where political stability was accompanied by higher budget revenues due to high oil prices.

Two years after the period covered in this book the situation has reversed. The price of crude oil per barrel declined from about US$105 in June 2014 to about US $28 in January 2016. This evidently changes the set of incentives for reforms that net oil exporters and net oil importers may have. Yet, there are good economic reasons for all countries to push through subsidy reforms during low oil prices. For net oil importers, while the budget and political pressure for reforms has diminished, a period of low oil prices is also the ideal period to remove subsidies and price indexation mechanisms because subsidies are low and the impact on prices and household welfare is minimized. For net oil exporters, low oil prices also provide a clear rationale to justify subsidy reforms via-a-vis populations that regard subsidies as an acquired right.

Whether these countries will use this window of opportunity is unclear. The recent period has seen a deceleration of subsidies reforms in the countries covered by this book if compared with the previous period. The GCC countries have effectively manifested increased interest for subsidy reforms but have not really moved on with any substantial reform. Moreover, oil prices have now started to rise again and they are currently around US$50 per barrel (March 2016). This window of opportunity may well come to an end with little progress on the front of subsidy reforms.

If we compare the period studied in this book with the most recent period, budget and political pressure seem more powerful incentives to reform than the cost of removing subsidies for the population. While the debate around pros and cons of subsidies reforms is prevalently economic, the impetus for subsidy reforms is driven by few economic factors such as oil prices and is prevalently political revealing the strategic importance that governments attribute to subsidies. In the years to come, we may therefore continue to observe erratic behavior towards subsidy reforms mostly driven by temporary political and budget considerations.

Acknowledgements The author is grateful to Vivien Foster, Gabriela Inchauste, Masami Kojima and Mustapha Nabli for useful comments on earlier drafts. All remaining errors are the sole responsibility of the author.

Appendix

See Table 1.4.

Table 1.4 Summary comparative table of subsidy reforms (2010–2014)

	North Africa				Middle East			
	Morocco	Tunisia	Libya	Egypt	Jordan	Yemen	Djibouti	Iran
Income level (World Bank Income Data)	Lower-middle	Upper-middle	Upper-middle	Lower-middle	Upper-middle	Lower-middle	Lower-middle	Upper-middle
Net energy importer/exporter (World Bank Energy Data)	Importer	Importer	Exporter	Exporter	Importer	Exporter	Importer	Exporter
Initial trigger of reforms	Removal of indexation mechanism, budget deficit	Budget deficit	n.a.	Budget deficit; change of regime	Budget deficit; pressure from IFIs	Budget deficit; IFIs pressure	n.a.	Budget deficit; Political strategy; International sanctions
Reforms 2010	n.a.	n.a.	No reforms	n.a.	n.a.	Prices on gasoline, diesel, and kerosene gradually increased by about 30%, and prices of LPG by 100%	No reforms	Major increase in food and energy prices

(continued)

Table 1.4 (continued)

	North Africa				Middle East			
Reforms 2012	Diesel prices increased by 14%, gasoline by 20%, and industrial fuel by 27%	Gasoline, Diesel, Electricity +7%	No reforms	Increases in gasoline prices	Increase in price of gasoline by 26% (June); Cut in subsidies and introduction of cash program (Nov.)	Gasoline prices increased by 66% and diesel and kerosene prices doubled	No reforms	Minor adjustments to the 2010 reform
Reforms 2013	Reactivation of price indexation for petroleum products	Gasoline, Diesel, Electricity +7%	No reforms	Electricity prices for households increased by 16%; increases in gasoline prices	Fuel indexation mechanism resumed	Diesel price unified across users, including the electricity sector	No reforms	Minor adjustments to the 2010 reform
Reforms 2014	Indexation of fuel oil; price increases for electricity, water, gasoline and diesel	Electricity +10% (2 rounds); Introduction of price indexation formula for gasoline	No reforms	Gasoline prices from LE 0.9 to LE 1.6 for 80 octane, from LE 1.85 to LE 2.6 for 92 octane, and from LE 5.75 to LE 6.25 for 95 octane; natural gas for cars from LE 0.45 to LE 1.1; diesel from LE 1.1 to LE 1.8. Prices for natural gas and fuel for commercial uses also increased significantly	Electricity tariffs increased	Full removal of subsidies with partial reversal. Prices of diesel and gasoline increased by a net 50 and 20%	No reforms	Minor adjustments to the 2010 reform

(continued)

Table 1.4 (continued)

	North Africa				Middle East			
Political changes (2011–2014)	Stable, new constitution and electoral system	Revolution, new constitution and political system	Revolution, political instability and civil war	Revolution, changes in governments	Stable, changes in governments	Political instability and civil war	Stable	Stable
Extent of reform	Piecemeal	Piecemeal	No reforms	Piecemeal	Piecemeal	Piecemeal	No reforms	Piecemeal
Pace of reforms	Gradual	Gradual	Nil	Gradual/radical	Radical	Gradual/radical	Nil	Radical
Cash compensation	No	Yes, poor	No	No	Yes, quasi universal	Yes, poor	No	Yes, quasi universal
Other parallel measures	Yes, fiscal consolidation	Yes, introduction of a low electricity tariff for poor households; increase in tax deductions, new social housing program	No	Yes, stable low electricity tariffs for the poor	No	No	No	Yes, housing reforms
Use of indexation mechanisms	Yes	Yes	No	No	No	No	Yes	No
Significant popular protests	No	No	No	No	No	Yes	n.a.	No
Public information campaign	Yes	No	No	No	No	No	n.a.	Yes

References

Coady, D., V. Flamini, and L. Sears. 2015. The Unequal Benefits of Fuel Subsidies Revisited: Evidence for Developing Countries, IMF Working Paper No. 15/250.

Devarajan, S., L. Mottaghi, F. Iqbal, G. Mundaca, M. Laursen, M. Vagliasindi, S. Commander, and I. Chaal-Dabi. Economic Monitor Corrosive Subsidies. Working Paper 2014. Washington, DC: World Bank.

EIA (Energy Information Administration). 2015. Department of Energy, Washington, DC. http://www.eia.gov/dnav/pet/pet_pri_spt_s1_m.htm.

Guillaume, D., R. Zytek, and M.R. Farzin 2011. Iran–The Chronicles of the Subsidy Reform. IMF Working Paper WP/11/167. Washington, DC: International Monetary Fund.

IMF (International Monetary Fund). 2014. Subsidy Reform in the Middle East and North Africa: Recent Progress and Challenges Ahead. Middle East and Central Asia Department. Washington, DC: IMF.

IndexMundi. 2015. http://www.indexmundi.com.

Kojima, M. 2013. *Reforming Fuel Pricing in an Age of $100 Oil*. Washington, DC: The World Bank.

Author Biography

Paolo Verme is a senior economist at the World Bank. A Ph.D. graduate of the London School of Economics, he was a visiting professor at Bocconi University in Milan (2004–09) and at the University of Turin (2003–10) before joining the World Bank in 2010. For almost two decades, he has served as adviser and project manager for multilateral organizations, private companies, and governments on labor market, welfare, and social protection policies. His research is widely published in international journals, books, and reports, and he has worked extensively on subsidies in the MENA Region and elsewhere. He is the coauthor of the subsidies simulation model SUBSIM (www.subsim.org).

Chapter 2
A Comparative Analysis of Subsidies and Subsidy Reforms in the Middle East and North Africa Region

Abdelkrim Araar and Paolo Verme

Introduction

As highlighted in Chap. 1, consumer subsidies in the Middle East and North Africa (MENA) Region are widespread. All of the countries in the Region administer energy subsidies, and most countries administer food subsidies on at least a few items. These subsidies are important for households in that they constitute a sizable part of household expenditure and represent an important share of governments' expenditure or forgone revenues. Consumer subsidies are also larger in this part of the world compared to other regions (Clements et al. 2013; Sdralevich et al. 2014) and they are more heterogeneous in many respects. The initial origins, types, profile, administration, and cost and beneficiaries of subsidies vary significantly across the countries of the MENA Region. This heterogeneity makes comparisons across countries more complex, but also provides an opportunity to derive lessons on subsidies and subsidy reforms.

This chapter aims to illustrate how the SUBSIM model can be used to analyze the impacts of consumer subsidies reforms and hence help guide policy reforms. Specifically, the chapter does this offering a standardized analysis of consumer subsidies in 2014. We use household budget survey data for five selected case studies and standardize the key variables for the analysis, including expenditure per capita on individual products and a basic set of household characteristics. We also update all surveys to 2014 using information on production, prices, and population

A. Araar (✉)
University of Laval, Quebec, QC, Canada
e-mail: aabd@ecn.ulaval.ca

P. Verme
The World Bank, Washington, District of Columbia, USA
e-mail: pverme@worldbank.org

P. Verme and A. Araar (eds.), *The Quest for Subsidy Reforms in the Middle East and North Africa Region*, Natural Resource Management and Policy 42,
DOI 10.1007/978-3-319-52926-4_2

growth and transform all values in purchasing power parity (PPP) using the latest round of the PPP survey (2011). We then use a version of the microsimulation model "SUBSIM," which is designed to make comparisons across countries, to provide a comparative distributional analysis of subsidies and simulations of subsidies reforms. This version of the software is designed to compare individual products across countries and allows researchers to see how any two countries compare in the distribution of subsidies and in the outcomes of subsidies reforms. In this way, we are able to simulate the same subsidy reforms in different countries and compare the outcomes across countries in terms of household welfare and government revenues.

The countries considered are Libya, Morocco, and Tunisia for North Africa and Djibouti and the Islamic Republic of Iran for the Middle East. The combined populations of these countries is 130 million or about 34% of the population of the MENA Region. The sample includes net oil exporters such as the Islamic Republic of Iran and Libya and net oil importers such as Morocco and Tunisia. It also includes low-income countries (Djibouti), low-middle-income countries (Morocco and Tunisia), and middle-income countries such as the Islamic Republic of Iran.

The products we consider are those that are the most relevant in terms of subsidies and those that are most frequently subsidized in the countries considered. These products are gasoline, diesel, liquefied petroleum gas (LPG), and electricity for energy products, and flour, bread, sugar, and vegetable oil for food products. The comparison of energy products could be done across all countries considered while the comparison of food products was possible only for selected countries. That is because for some countries like Tunisia it was not possible to gather all the necessary information while in other countries such as Djibouti some of the four food products considered were not subsidized.

The focus of the analysis is on direct effects only, as it was not possible to collect and standardize a sufficient number of input-output matrixes for a comparative analysis of indirect effects. The relative importance of indirect effects changes across products and income groups. It is high for products like gasoline and for richer quintiles and small for products like bread and for poorer quintiles. Therefore, results on welfare related to reforms on food products capture the greatest share of the total effect, but results on overall welfare related to energy products miss on an important share of the total impact of subsidies reforms. These indirect effects are reported in the country chapters that use input-output tables, but will not be discussed here.

Results show that the distribution and effects of subsidies are quite diverse across countries and products. Energy subsidies tend to be pro-rich in terms of absolute amounts (larger amounts accrue to richer households) but tend to be more important for the poor in terms of expenditure shares. Instead, food subsidies can be larger for the poor in absolute and relative terms. These findings do not apply everywhere, and the scale of these phenomena are different across countries and products. The welfare effect of a 30% reduction in subsidies can be important, especially if we consider the cumulated effect across products, but the cost of compensating the loss in welfare for the poorest is generally low as compared to the budget benefits of the reform. This leaves governments with some fiscal space for compensation of other groups such as the middle class.

This chapter is organized as follows. The next section illustrates the data and methods used for the analysis. The chapter then provides a comparative distributional analysis of subsidies and simulates subsidy reforms comparing the outcomes across countries.

Data and Analytical Approach

In the following sections, we describe the microdata used for the analysis and the baseline prices (subsidized products and unit subsidies) as of 2014, our baseline year. The HBS surveys, prices and methodology employed to update the data to 2014 are the same used for the country chapters. The updates were made using published IMF macroindicators for inflation and gross domestic product (GDP) per capita as well as population statistics (see Tables 2.11 and 2.12). The exercise that follows does not draw from the country chapters; rather, it re-estimates the distribution of subsidies and provides new simulations of subsidies reforms using the primary data files for each country and transforming expenditure into U.S. dollars ($) at purchasing power parity (PPP). This allows comparing subsidies and the outcome of subsidies reforms using a common currency.

Microdata

Table 2.1 shows the population statistics estimated directly from the surveys. These numbers are not identical to all country-specific population estimates, but they are very close. We can see that the sample of countries considered amounts to a total

Table 2.1 Baseline population and expenditure statistics, in US$ at PPP

Country	Population	Number of households	Per capita expenditures	Household expenditures
Djibouti	939,000	166,966	1,977	11,121
Iran, Islamic Rep.	77,969,000	21,909,116	7,477	26,609
Libya	6,213,000	991,549	1,983	12,424
Morocco	33,179,000	7,070,798	4,170	19,565
Tunisia	11,060,000	2,548,655	3,960	17,186
Total	129,360,000	32,687,084	3,913	17,381

Source World Bank estimations from Household Budget Surveys
Note PPP = purchasing power parity. Data on household expenditure per capita can be very different from data on GDP per capita and the cross-country ranking made according to these two criteria can be quite different. This is mostly explained by the fact that total household expenditure represents different shares of GDP across countries

population of almost 130 million people, approximately 34% of the population in the MENA Region in 2014. The total household expenditure for the countries considered is approximately $0.63 trillion-PPP per year, which amounts to $3,913-PPP per capita, per year, and $17,381-PPP per household, per year. This average hides differences across countries. The Islamic Republic of Iran is by far the country with the highest per capita expenditure ($7,477-PPP). Morocco, and Tunisia follow with approximately $4,000-PPP, and Libya and Djibouti come last with approximately $2,000-PPP. The sample of countries we have is representative of three groups of countries at different levels of economic development. We also have oil-producing countries and net exporters of oil, such as the Islamic Republic of Iran and Libya; non-oil-producing countries with some natural resources, such as Morocco; and non-oil-producing countries, such as Tunisia, which have little in the way of natural resources. Therefore, we have a certain diversity also in terms of natural endowments.

Baseline Prices and Subsidies

As a reference period for the analysis, we use the very early part of 2014 when oil prices and subsidies peaked at their highest levels. A major wave of subsidies reforms occurred in the MENA Region in 2014 but this chapter focuses on the extraordinary situation faced by MENA countries before the reforms. We are interested in the prices and subsidies existing in the MENA countries just before the reforms.

Table 2.2 shows the baseline prices and unit subsidies for energy products. For LPG, prices are the lowest for Libya and the Islamic Republic of Iran in that

Table 2.2 Energy unit prices and subsidies, in US$ at PPP (2014)

	Price	Subs.	Subs. (%)	Increase (%)	Price	Subs.	Subs. (%)	Increase (%)
	LPG (13 kg)				*Electricity* (kWh, *av.*)			
Djibouti	28.3	2.8	9.1	10				
Iran, Islamic Rep.	1.9	9.7	83.3	500	0.18	0.25	58.5	140.7
Libya	2.9	27.4	90.4	947	0.26	0.11	30.6	44
Morocco	10.4	20.7	66.6	199.8	0.21	0.15	42.3	73.2
Tunisia	9.8	20.9	68	212.7	0.11	0.63	85.4	583
	Gasoline (L)				*Diesel* (L)			
Djibouti	3	−0.1	−2		2.1	0.3	11.1	12.5
Iran, Islamic Rep.	0.5	2.3	83.3	500	0.4	2.3	84.8	557.1
Libya	0.2	1.6	87.7	714.7	0.2	1.6	88.1	740
Morocco	3.1	0	0		2.4	0.2	7.5	8.1
Tunisia	2.5	0.2	9.1	10	2.1	0.4	17.4	21.1

Source World Bank estimations from Household Budget Surveys
Note PPP = purchasing power parity

order and the highest for Djibouti. The highest shares of subsidies as a percentage of the free market price are in Libya and the Islamic Republic of Iran, the two oil-producing countries, with Libya's LPG subsidies reaching 90.4% of the full price. The percentage price increases that would be necessary to eliminate subsidies on LPG are remarkable. In Libya the price would have to be increased by 947% to eliminate subsidies and in the Islamic Republic of Iran by 500%.

It is interesting to see that in Djibouti, the poorest of the countries considered, the price of LPG is 15 times the price in the Islamic Republic of Iran, the richest country considered. This divergence is also striking because LPG is a product that is typically consumed by the poor and it is the most important among the poor. The claim that consumers' subsidies are a form of social protection schemes does not really hold if we observe data for LPG across countries.

Prices for electricity appear less diverse, but that can be explained by the way the prices are listed—in kilowatt hours (average across tariffs blocks). As a percentage of the free market price, electricity subsidies are the highest in Tunisia. The lowest subsidies are for Libya (30.6%) and Morocco (42.3%) but still high. To reach the market price, Libya would have to increase prices by 44%, an increase that would not go unnoticed by the population, and Tunisia would have to increase prices by 583%, a staggering figure.

Prices for gasoline and diesel are closer to the free market price for most countries except the Islamic Republic of Iran and Libya. The Islamic Republic of Iran and Libya in particular would have to raise prices of gasoline fivefold and more than sevenfold, respectively, to reach the free market price. For the Islamic Republic of Iran in 2014 this finding is remarkable given that this country went through a comprehensive reform of the subsidies system in 2010 that supposedly eliminated most subsidies and was costly in terms of cash transfers administered to the population in compensation of the subsidies removal.

For food (Table 2.3), the items considered are few, but we can see that subsidies can also be quite high. For flour, subsidies represent 91.3% of the free market price in Libya and almost 60% in the Islamic Republic of Iran. Libya has also the highest subsidies for bread, sugar, and vegetable oil, and the Islamic Republic of Iran has large subsidies on bread. Therefore, the oil-producing countries seem to be those that maintained the highest food subsidies. However, subsidies are also high in Morocco for flour and sugar, and in this country these products are universally subsidized and not subject to quotas.

A Distributional Analysis of Subsidies

As indicated in the overview to this book, all country case studies use the microsimulation model SUBSIM to provide a distributional analysis of subsidies and simulations of alternative subsidy reforms. The publicly available version of SUBSIM comes in two flavors, SUBSIM direct, which estimates direct effects

Table 2.3 Food unit prices and subsidies, in US$ at PPP (2014)

		Price	Subs.	Subs. (%)	Increase (%)	Price	Subs.	Subs. (%)	Increase (%)
		Flour (kg)				*Bread (kg)*			
Djibouti		0.759	0.053	6.5	7.0	n.a.	n.a.	n.a.	n.a.
Iran, Islamic Rep.		0.689	1.027	59.9	149.2	1.199	1.346	52.9	112.2
Libya		0.130	1.360	91.3	1044.4	0.054	1.334	96.1	2491.9
Morocco						n.a.	n.a.	n.a.	n.a.
	Flour1	1.197	0.168	12.3	14.0%				
	Flour2	0.479	0.342	41.7	71.5%				
		Sugar (kg)				*Vegetable oil (L)*			
Djibouti		0.865	0.061	6.5	7.0	1.422	0.171	10.7	12.0
Iran, Islamic Rep.		n.a.	n.a.	n.a.	n.a.	n.a.	n.a.	n.a.	n.a.
Libya		0.362	1.545	81.0	427.2	0.868	4.054	82.4	467.0
Morocco						n.a.	n.a.	n.a.	n.a.
	Sugar1	1.393	0.682	32.9	49.0				
	Sugar2	1.393	0.682	32.9	49.0				
	Sugar3	1.077	0.682	38.8	63.3				

Source World Bank estimations from Household Budget Survey
Note Subsidized flour and sugar in Morocco have different prices depending on varieties and forms; kg = kilogram; PPP = purchasing power parity

using Household Budget Survey (HBS) data only, and SUBSIM indirect, which uses HBS data and input-output matrixes to estimate direct and indirect effects.

This chapter uses a third version of SUBSIM, which is not yet publicly available and which is designed to provide comparative analyses of subsidies across countries. This version is similar to the SUBSIM direct version in that it automatically provides a set of results in Excel tables and graphs that can be readily used for analysis. The difference is that this version provides results for individual products across countries instead of results for individual countries across products. As part of the distributional analysis, we look first at the importance of subsidies and subsidized products for households. We then determine who are the main beneficiaries of subsidies, as well as the potential dilemmas for reforming subsidies.

When we talk about the importance of subsidized products, we should distinguish between *absolute* and *relative* importance. For absolute importance, we refer to the monetary values of subsidies or subsidized products in USD at PPP values. For relative importance, we refer to subsidies or subsidized products as a share of total household expenditure.

The Absolute Importance and Distribution of Subsidies

Table 2.4 compares the per capita expenditure of the four main energy and food products considered across countries in US$-PPP values. Looking at energy products and on average, households spend $19.7 per capita, per year on LPG, $85.5 on electricity, $54.2 on gasoline, and $9.5 on diesel. These amounts vary widely across countries. For example, Moroccans spend (in PPP values) the largest amount on LPG, electricity, and diesel. Libya has the lowest expenditure for electricity and one of the lowest for gasoline and diesel. As expected, because Libya has high subsidies and Morocco has low subsidies, it is clear that expenditures for crude oil products are partly driven by the level of subsidies. But other factors must be considered, including the desirability of these products and the exchange rate used in PPP values.

Subsidies on food are much less widespread in terms of countries and products. Libya has the largest variety of food subsidies, and a few other countries subsidize flour, bread, sugar, or vegetable oil, which are the four products that we analyze across countries. The largest subsidies go to flour and bread. The distinction between flour and bread is not always clear cut in the data. Some countries subsidize the price of flour for mills and then impose regulated prices on the sale of bread. What we observe in expenditure data are direct purchases of flour or bread on the part of households. Therefore, we need to estimate the flour subsidies received by households via the purchase of bread using conversion factors between these two products. As a consequence, the estimates on bread and flour should be taken with some caution. Sugar is also an important subsidized item in three countries, and vegetable oil remains subsidized in two countries.

The results on the distribution of subsidies across quintiles are very different depending on the product and the country (Fig. 2.1). Consider LPG first. In one country, the Islamic Republic of Iran, subsidies on LPG are progressive, meaning that poorer households get the largest dollar amounts of subsidies. But for all the other countries, subsidies on LPG are clearly regressive, as richer households get

Table 2.4 Per capita expenditure on subsidized products, in US$ at PPP/year

	Energy				Food			
	LPG	Electricity	Gasoline	Diesel	Flour	Bread	Sugar	Vegetable oil
Djibouti	1.8	95.1	36.9	n.a.	35.8	n.a.	51	29.2
Iran, Islamic Rep	10.6	83	102.8	0.6	12.6	163.7	n.a.	n.a.
Libya	4.4	26.4	26.8	0.5	9	30.1	17.9	46.6
Morocco	42.6	114.9	19.9	26.6	56.7	n.a.	26.8	n.a.
Tunisia	38.9	108.1	84.7	10.3	n.a.	n.a.	n.a.	n.a.
Average across countries	19.7	85.5	54.2	9.5	28.5	96.9	31.9	37.9

Source World Bank estimations from household budget surveys

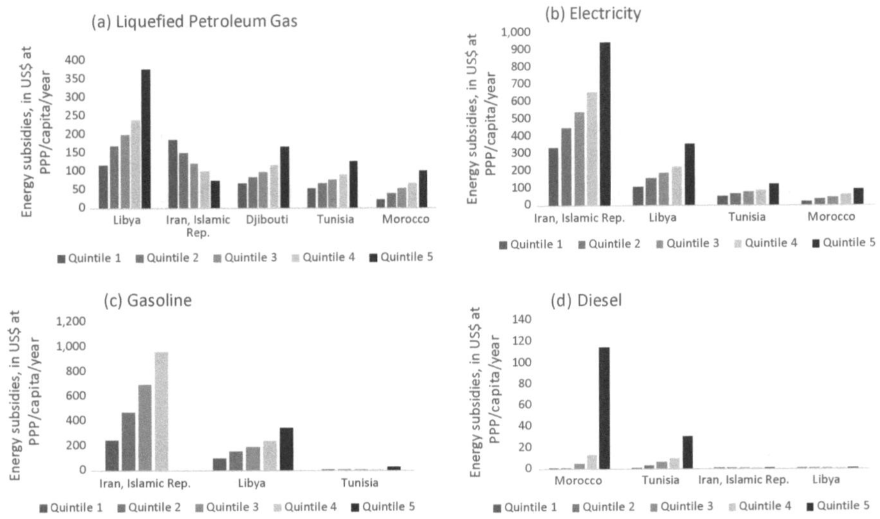

Fig. 2.1 Distribution of energy subsidies, in US$ at PPP/capita/year. *Source* World Bank estimations from household budget surveys

the largest amounts. Subsidies for LPG vary between a few dollars for the poorest quintile in Morocco to almost $400 for the rich in Libya. These amounts are significant, particularly for the poorest countries. However, we should not take for granted that subsidies on LPG are always prorich, as shown for the Islamic Republic of Iran.

Electricity subsidies are the most important in dollar amounts and exceptionally important in the Islamic Republic of Iran, where subsidies can reach up to $1,000-PPP per capita, per year for the richest quintile. Subsidies are less important in other countries but still nonnegligible, varying between a few dollars and more than $300-PPP per capita, per year. In the case of electricity, subsidies invariably favor the rich in absolute terms, as the largest amounts in dollar equivalents are taken up by the richest quintiles with no exceptions across countries. Clearly, oil-producing countries are those that offer the largest subsidies via electricity, probably because the need to produce electricity with cheaper fuels is less of a priority.

Also in the case of gasoline and diesel, subsidies are invariably prorich, with the largest dollar amounts taken up by the richest. The dollar amounts of these two products are relevant only in a few countries—the Islamic Republic of Iran and Libya for gasoline—that are either oil producers or endowed with natural resources. In these countries and for these products, it is evident that the dollar amounts across the distribution increase quickly as we move toward richer households, showing that the regressivity of these subsidies is steep and consistent across countries. Diesel is important only in Morocco and Tunisia and only for the top quintile.

The variety and amounts of food subsidies are much smaller than energy subsidies (Fig. 2.2). They are below $40-PPP for flour and oil and below $20-PPP for

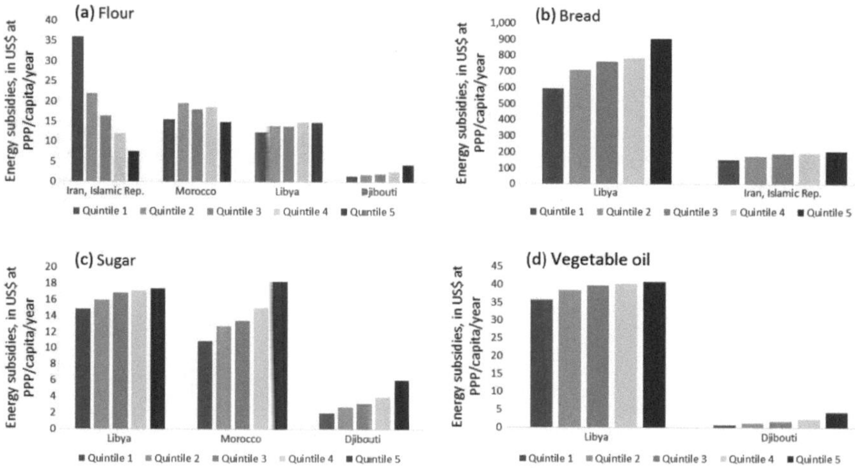

Fig. 2.2 Distribution of food subsidies, in US$ at PPP/capita/year. *Source* World Bank estimations from household budget surveys

sugar. The only significant subsidies are for bread in Libya and the Islamic Republic of Iran where the amounts can reach $900-PPP and $200-PPP, respectively, for the richest quintile, and the pattern is regressive. In general, larger subsidies accrue to richer quintiles with monotonic increases across quintiles. This pattern holds for sugar, bread, and oil for all countries and for flour in Libya and Djibouti, but not for Morocco and the Islamic Republic of Iran, where for flour subsidies are larger for poorer quintiles. Therefore, exceptions to the prorichness of subsidies may exist also for food products.

The Relative Importance and Distribution of Subsidies

Figure 2.3 illustrates the share of expenditure on total expenditure for the four energy products by country and by quintile. Starting with LPG, we see that Morocco and Tunisia have the highest shares of expenditure on LPG. These countries spend more in relative terms but less in absolute terms as shown in Fig. 2.1. We can also see that these shares decrease as we move toward richer quintiles. The richest quintile in the Islamic Republic of Iran spends less than 0.1% of total expenditure on LPG. The shares in other countries are lower than 0.5% for all quintiles. With the only exception of Djibouti, the share of expenditure on LPG decreases with richer quintiles.

The situation is rather different for electricity. We can see that the share of expenditure in Morocco is the highest for the third quintile whereas it decreases from the poorest to the richest quintiles for all other countries. This result depends on the type of tariff system in place and on the coverage of electricity. The countries

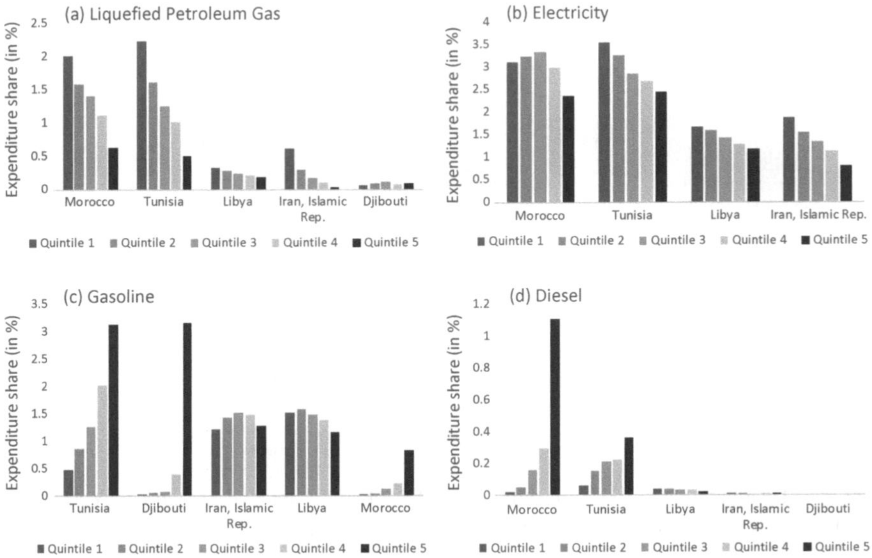

Fig. 2.3 Expenditure shares of subsidized energy products across countries and quintiles. *Source* World Bank estimations from household budget surveys

that show regular decreasing shares across the distribution tend to have almost universal coverage of electricity and mild progressive pricing, whereby higher blocks of consumption correspond to higher prices applied only to the marginal quantities. In Morocco the hump-shaped distribution could be due to the particular combination of increasing block tariffs (IBT) and volume differentiated tariffs (VDT) tariffs[1] and the size of the interblocks price increases. For electricity, therefore, it would be wrong to assume that the share of household expenditure is invariably more important for the poor, particularly because the poor benefit from very low tariffs.

For gasoline and diesel the distributional picture is fairly consistent, but opposite to LPG. Gasoline and diesel are disproportionally consumed by richer households. In Morocco car ownership is concentrated among richer households, and the consumption of these products among poorer households is confined to small quantities used for motorcycles or nontransport purposes. We see the shares of household expenditure on gasoline and diesel growing with richer quintiles as shown in Fig. 2.1 for almost all countries. The exceptions for gasoline are Libya

[1]IBT = increasing block tariffs, which means that consumers pay the marginal price on marginal quantities, for example, \$0.10 on the first 100 kWh of electricity consumed, \$0.15 cents on the consumption between 101 and 200 kWh, and so forth. VDT = volume differentiated tariffs, which means that consumers pay the marginal price on all quantities consumed, for example, \$0.10 if they consume less or equal to 100 kWh of electricity consumed, \$0.15 on all quantities consumed if they fall in the consumption block 101–200, and so forth

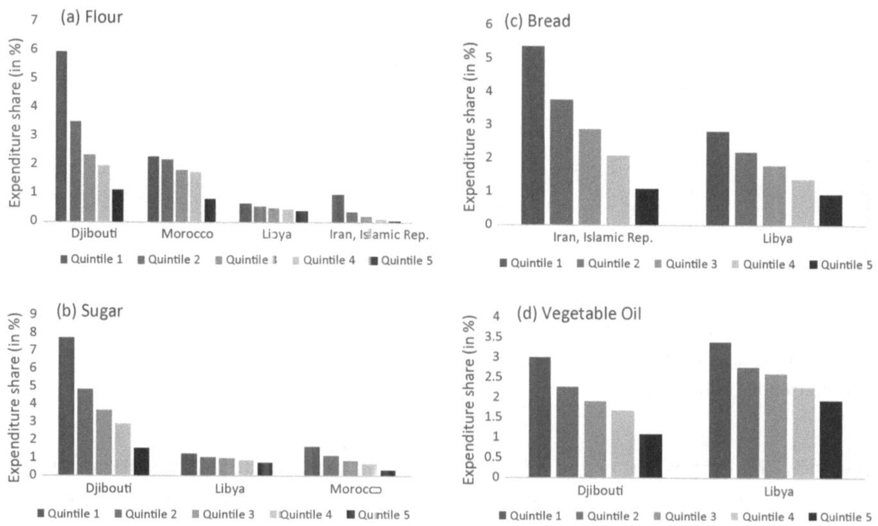

Fig. 2.4 Expenditure shares of subsidized food products across countries and quintiles. *Source* World Bank estimations from household budget surveys

and the Islamic Republic of Iran, two oil-producing countries where subsidies are high, public transport is limited, and the use of private transport is almost universal. Indeed, we can see that the distribution in these two countries are hump-shaped, with the largest expenditure relative to total expenditure borne by the middle class.

The consumption of diesel is much smaller in all countries, and in Djibouti the Islamic Republic of Iran, and Libya is negligible. These are the countries where diesel cars are scarcely available or not permitted. In countries that do consume some amounts of diesel, the share of expenditure invariably grows with richer quintiles.

For food products (Fig. 2.4), the situation is much simpler. For all products and in all countries, the household budget shares of expenditure on subsidized products is higher for poorer households and progressively lower for richer households, as we should expect. The decrease between quintiles is also very steep in general, particularly for flour and sugar in Djibouti and bread in the Islamic Republic of Iran. These products are evidently very important for the poor in these countries, representing up to 8% of total expenditure for the poorest quintile.

A Policy Dilemma

It should be clear by now that there is a certain trade-off between the share of expenditure on subsidized products in total household expenditure and the dollar amounts of subsidies received. To illustrate this trade-off, Fig. 2.5 plots these two dimensions across population percentiles for LPG in different countries. For most

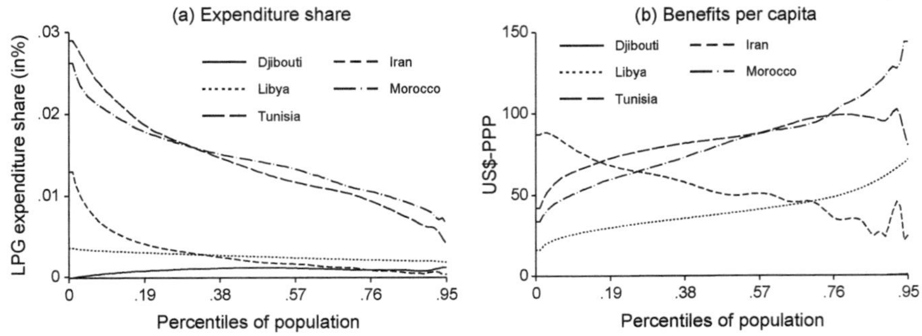

Fig. 2.5 Expenditure shares of LPG versus subsidies per capita. *Source* World Bank estimations from household budget surveys

countries, the curves are negatively sloped for the expenditure shares, meaning that poorer households spend a larger share of total expenditure on subsidized products than richer households (Fig. 2.5, panel a). Also in most countries, richer households receive larger amounts of subsidies in per-capita terms (Fig. 2.5, panel b). This rule is not, however, always true. For example, the data for LPG in the Islamic Republic of Iran show a negative slope in both graphs, demonstrating not only that this product is more important for poorer households but also that these households receive a larger amount per capita in subsidies than richer households. This is less evident for food products, such as flour (Fig. 2.6). We can see that although the share of expenditure is higher for poorer households as for energy products, the subsidies per capita are more pro-poor, particularly in the Islamic Republic of Iran. In Djibouti, however, subsidies on flour are prorich.

For most countries, this trade-off creates a dilemma. On the one hand, that subsidies are prorich would clearly speak in favor of eliminating subsidies with little consequences on welfare. On the other hand, these subsidized products can be relatively more important for the poor, even if subsidies are in place. The elimination of these subsidies would be felt more by the poor than by the rich with a

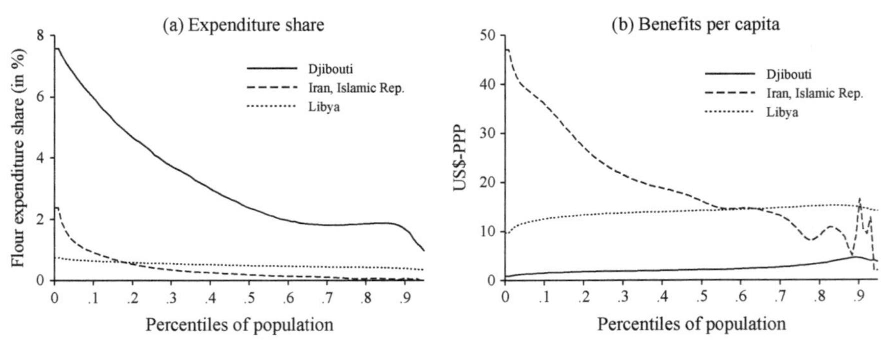

Fig. 2.6 Expenditure shares of flour versus subsidies per capita. *Source* World Bank estimations from household budget surveys

likely effect on poverty. As we saw, the trade-off does not necessarily apply to all countries; instead, it varies across products, and the size of the trade-off may be different across products and countries.

We should also note the structural relation between the values on the y-axes of the two panels in Fig. 2.5. Let p = unit free market price, s = unit subsidies, q = quantities, and y = total income. The y-axis of the panel a is then $(pq-sq)/y$ and the y-axis of panel b is sq. Income and quantities being equal, the higher the unit subsidy, the lower the expenditure share. Subsidies and quantities being equal, the higher is income, the lower is the share of expenditure. Because the unit market price and subsidy are set by the government and equal for all, the shape of the lines largely depend on the distribution of incomes in each country. Therefore, **knowledge of the household income or expenditure distribution is an essential prerequisite to prepare subsidies reforms**.

Simulations of Subsidies Reforms

In order to simulate comparable reforms across countries, we consider a flat reduction of unit subsidies by 30% across all products and all countries. We measure the impact of these reforms on household welfare, inequality, and the government budget in this order. We also consider the cost for the government of compensating the population to reach the prereform level of welfare. The implied changes in prices of the proposed simulations are large for most countries and products, which makes the standard linear approach to subsidies simulations inappropriate. We therefore model the demand function using Cobb-Douglas preferences.[2]

Welfare

Figures 2.7 and 2.8 show the impact on household welfare (measured in terms of household expenditure per capita). For each product in the figures we have two panels. The top panel illustrates the welfare impact in annual per capita US$-PPP terms. The bottom panel illustrates the welfare impact in terms of share of total household expenditure. Therefore, the top part of the figures is the absolute welfare effect, and the bottom part is the relative welfare effect.

For LPG, the greatest impact of this reform would be in Morocco, with a per capita impact per year of about $20-PPP on average. The smallest impact is in Djibouti, the poorest of the countries considered. It is also instructive to see that the distributions of these impacts can be regressive or progressive depending on the country. In the Islamic Republic of Iran, the impact is regressive all along the

[2]See www.subsim.org for more details on the SUBSIM model and its use.

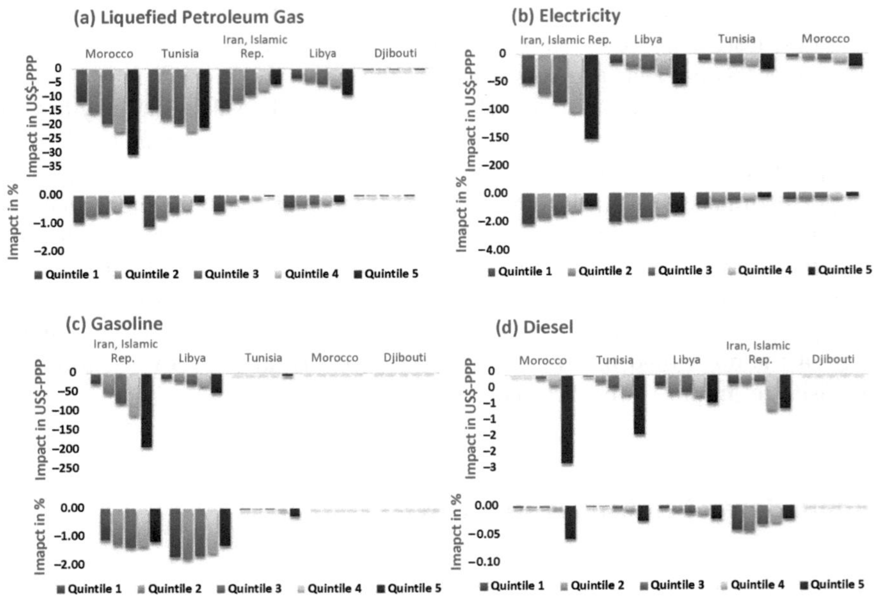

Fig. 2.7 Welfare impact of a 30% reduction in energy subsidies, in US$-PPP/capita/year. *Source* World Bank estimations from household budget surveys

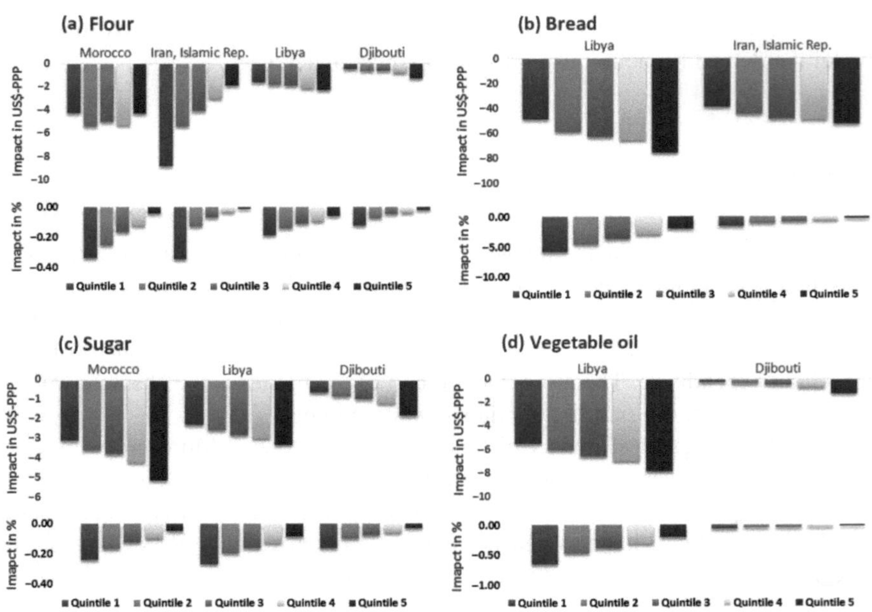

Fig. 2.8 Welfare impact of a 30% reduction in food subsidies, US$-PPP/capita/year. *Source* World Bank estimations from household budget surveys

distribution, with the highest per capita impact for the poorest quintile and the lowest impact for the richest quintile whereas they are progressive in all other countries. As these are dollar values, it is evident that the relative impact on household welfare is much greater for the poor than for the rich, as can be seen in the bottom part of the LPG figure, where it is clear that the welfare impact in terms of share of total expenditure is regressive in all countries.

For electricity, the welfare impact is quite large in all countries, with the Islamic Republic of Iran having by far the highest impact followed by Libya. In the Islamic Republic of Iran, the impact on the richest quintile is very high, about $150-PPP per person, per year. But because the richest quintiles are affected the most in absolute terms, this impact is progressive in all countries. This result is due to the tariff systems in place, which typically include low tariffs for the first or the first two tariffs' blocks and high tariffs for the last block. As the relation between electricity consumption and household welfare is quite linear in most countries, households in the richer quintiles are also the largest consumers of electricity. This finding is apparent in the difference between the bars for the fourth and fifth quintiles. As for LPG, the welfare impact is progressive in absolute terms, but regressive in relative terms (relatively to total expenditure). As shown in the lower part of the electricity figure, in all countries, the relative welfare impact is regressive.

Welfare impacts are also high for gasoline, especially for the oil-producing countries of Libya and the Islamic Republic of Iran. The average cost for households in the richest quintile in the Islamic Republic of Iran is about $200-PPP, a large amount even for a country that is the richest among those considered. For all countries, the welfare impacts are progressive because the poor do not own means of transport and therefore do not consume gasoline. The impacts on household welfare of diesel's reforms are very small as compared to the impact of other products. They are around $1-PPP per person, per year. Also for diesel, the impact is progressive in all countries considered. Contrary to LPG and electricity, the relative welfare impact is not necessarily regressive but mostly progressive or hump-shaped.

Figure 2.8 shows the welfare impact for food items. The relative welfare impact is unambiguously regressive for all products and countries. The absolute welfare impact can be progressive or regressive for flour, but is always progressive for

(a) Energy items (b) Food items

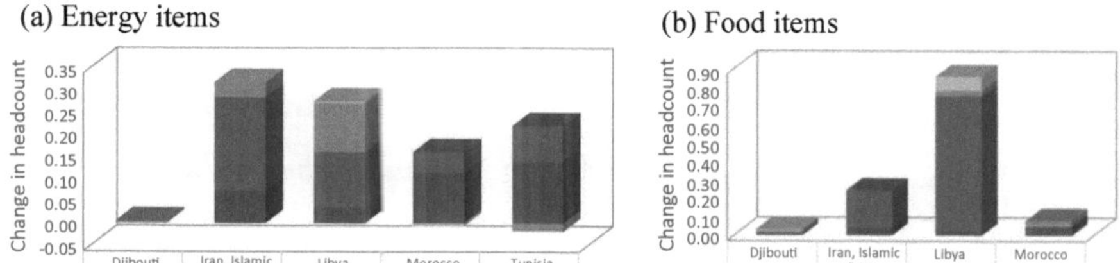

	Djibouti	Iran, Islamic Rep.	Libya	Morocco	Tunisia
Diesel	−0.0000	0.0003	0.0041	−0.0059	−0.0030
Gasoline	0.0044	0.0334	0.1098	−0.0000	−0.0158
Electricity		0.2103	0.1255	0.0459	0.0802
LPG	−0.0000	0.0724	0.0343	0.1135	0.1385

	Djibouti	Iran, Islamic Rep.	Libya	Morocco
Oil	0.01		0.08	
Sugar	0.02		0.03	0.03
Bread		0.20	0.73	
Flour	0.01	0.04	0.02	0.05

Fig. 2.9 Inequality impacts of a 30% reduction in subsidies. *Source* World Bank estimations from household budget surveys

bread, sugar, and oil. The largest impacts are observed for bread in Libya with close to $80-PPP per person, per year for the richest quintile.

Inequality

A reduction in subsidies implies a loss in welfare, but changes in inequality (measured in terms of changes of household expenditure per capita) can go in any direction depending on the distribution of expenditure and on the parts of the population that are most affected by the reforms. As is apparent in Fig. 2.9, the reduction in subsidies for energy products does not make much difference for inequality in any of the countries considered, with a maximum impact observed in the Islamic Republic of Iran for only one-third of one percentage point. These changes can also be positive or negative depending on the country, although it is clear that the changes are too small to be significant. The greatest increase in

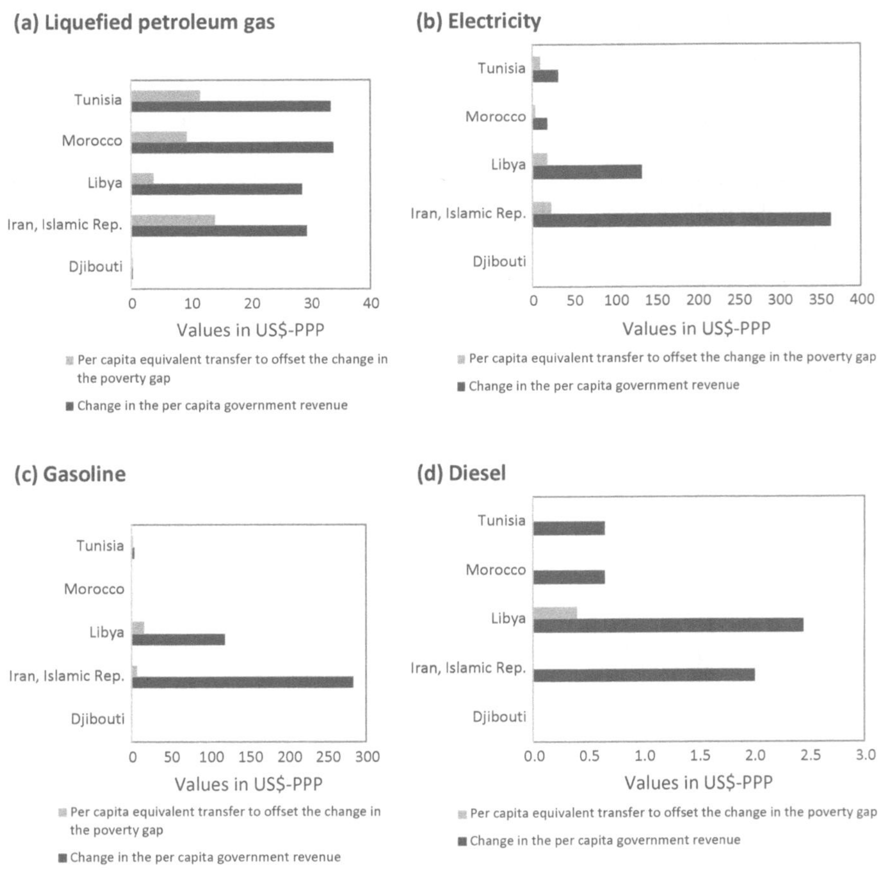

Fig. 2.10 Governments' revenue impact of a 30% reduction in subsidies on energy products, in US$-PPP/capita/year. *Source* World Bank estimations from household budget surveys

inequality is obtained in Libya if oil, sugar, bread, and flour subsidies are cut by 30%, but even in this extreme case, inequality would increase by less than one percentage point.

Government Budget

What are the gains in budget revenues? How much is required in cash transfers to offset the increase in the poverty gap determined by the reform? Figure 2.10 shows the increase in per-capita government revenue of a 30% reduction in subsidies. The graph also shows the necessary universal transfer required to offset the change in poverty gap resulting from the reforms. This amount can be considered as the minimum universal transfer to keep the poverty gap unchanged.

Government revenues are always much larger than the universal cost of compensation to bring the poverty gap back to its prereform level. It is also possible to target compensation and reduce further the cost to the budget, but governments that implemented large reforms in recent years, such as the Islamic Republic of Iran, have not followed that route. On the other hand, governments may want to compensate some of the non-poor, particularly the middle-class, to reduce the risk of political backlash in the aftermath of the reforms. This may rise substantially the cost of compensation but Fig. 2.10 shows that the space for maneuver to compensate beyond the poverty gap is quite large. Therefore, unless compensation benefits are extremely large and universal, reforming subsidies with compensation is most likely to reduce the overall cost of subsidies substantially.

For food items, in general, we observe that the impact is relatively low for the countries with limited subsidy programs, as is the case for Djibouti and Morocco. The picture is different for Libya, where the food subsidy program is very large. In this country and with a universal transfer designed to offset the poverty gap, the increase in per capita government revenue can be large but still below the overall gains in revenues determined by the reforms.

Conclusion

This chapter has provided a comparative analysis of the distribution of subsidies across the MENA Region and a comparative analysis of the welfare and budget effects of subsidies reforms considering a 30% reduction in subsidies. We used a special version of SUBSIM designed to make comparative analyses of subsidies reforms across countries in US$-PPP values. The purpose of the chapter was not to provide exact estimates of the impacts of reforms but to compare outcomes across countries and show how SUBSIM can be used for this purpose.

The population sample considered is large, almost 130 million people or 34% of the total population in the MENA Region in 2014. All data were actualized to 2014, and all expenditures transformed into US$-PPP values using the latest 2011 PPP conversion factor. The total household expenditure considered is approximately $0.63 trillion-PPP or 3,913 US$-PPP per capita, per year on average. The sample of countries covered includes low-income countries, low-middle-income countries and middle-income countries. The sample also includes net oil exporters as well as net oil importers.

We found that the size of subsidies does not necessarily relate to the needs of a population. In Djibouti, for example, the poorest of the countries considered in this chapter, the price of LPG is 15 times the price in the Islamic Republic of Iran, the richest country considered. Products such as LPG and electricity tend to have higher subsidies than gasoline. Food subsidies tend to be higher among net oil exporters, as the oil wealth is partly distributed to the population via food subsidies.

Subsidized products are quite important for the populations of the MENA Region. LPG can account for more than 2% of total expenditure as for the poorest quintile in Tunisia, and electricity can reach 3.5% of expenditure as for the poorest quintile in Tunisia. And products such as sugar can reach up to 8% for the poorest people in Djibouti. The importance of LPG decreases with welfare, but it increases for gasoline.

The consumption pattern of subsidized products partly explains who benefits from subsidies, and it is clear that the main beneficiaries can be very different depending on the product and country considered. For example, in the Islamic Republic of Iran, subsidies are progressive for LPG but regressive in all other countries, and electricity and gasoline subsidies are invariably regressive in that the majority of benefits in absolute terms accrue to richer households.

Comparing results on the importance of subsidized products and on the distribution of subsidies leads to an important policy dilemma. Subsidies may be very important for poor households, even though richer households receive the greatest share, which makes subsidy reforms complex from the perspective of public policies. A useful instrument to take decisions on subsidies is to compare the expenditure share curves by percentile of the expenditure distribution with the total subsidies per capita curves. Products and countries where both curves are positively sloped are the most promising for reforms because both the share of these products on household expenditure and the amount of subsidies are larger for the richer households.

Simulations of a 30% reduction in subsidies for all products showed that the welfare implications are important particularly for electricity and LPG where these reforms can reduce household welfare for the poorest quintiles by up to 2% for individual products and can reach 4–5% if we aggregate the impact for all products. Nevertheless, the impact on the poverty gap is small and the impact on inequality is negligible. Instead, the benefits to government budgets are quite large, even if countries decide to compensate households with a universal transfer that would offset the increase in the poverty gap. This result would suggest that countries have some fiscal space for compensating citizens beyond the poor.

Acknowledgements The authors are grateful to Shanta Devarajan and Mustapha Nabli for useful comments on previous versions of the chapter. All remaining errors are responsibility of the authors.

Annex 2.1

See Tables 2.5, 2.6, 2.7, 2.8, 2.9 and 2.10.

Table 2.5 Expenditure shares in energy products (percent)

	Djibouti	Iran, Islamic Rep.	Libya	Morocco	Tunisia
LPG					
Quintile 1	0.06	0.62	0.32	2.02	2.23
Quintile 2	0.09	0.3	0.28	1.58	1.61
Quintile 3	0.12	0.18	0.24	1.41	1.25
Quintile 4	0.08	0.1	0.21	1.12	1.02
Quintile 5	0.09	0.04	0.18	0.63	0.5
Population	0.09	0.14	0.22	1.02	0.98
Electricity					
Quintile 1	n.a.	1.86	1.66	3.11	3.55
Quintile 2	n.a.	1.53	1.58	3.25	3.27
Quintile 3	n.a.	1.33	1.42	3.34	2.85
Quintile 4	n.a.	1.13	1.28	2.99	2.68
Quintile 5	n.a.	0.8	1.17	2.35	2.44
Population	n.a.	1.11	1.33	2.76	2.73
Gasoline					
Quintile 1	0.03	1.22	1.52	0.01	0.47
Quintile 2	0.05	1.43	1.58	0.04	0.86
Quintile 3	0.08	1.52	1.49	0.12	1.27
Quintile 4	0.4	1.49	1.38	0.23	2.02
Quintile 5	3.16	1.28	1.16	0.83	3.13
Population	1.87	1.37	1.35	0.48	2.14
Diesel					
Quintile 1	0	0.01	0.04	0.02	0.06
Quintile 2	0	0.01	0.04	0.05	0.15
Quintile 3	0	0	0.03	0.16	0.21
Quintile 4	0	0.01	0.03	0.3	0.22
Quintile 5	0	0.01	0.02	1.11	0.36
Population	0	0.01	0.03	0.64	0.26

Source World Bank estimations from household budget surveys

Table 2.6 Expenditure shares in food (percent)

	Djibouti	Iran, Islamic Rep.	Libya	Morocco
Flour				
Quintile 1	5.95	0.95	0.63	2.29
Quintile 2	3.53	0.35	0.55	2.19
Quintile 3	2.35	0.19	0.48	1.81
Quintile 4	1.96	0.10	0.45	1.74
Quintile 5	1.12	0.03	0.37	0.79
Population	1.81	0.17	0.45	1.36
Bread				
Quintile 1	n.a.	5.4	2.85	n.a.
Quintile 2	n.a.	3.8	2.22	n.a.
Quintile 3	n.a.	2.9	1.80	n.a.
Quintile 4	n.a.	2.1	1.40	n.a.
Quintile 5	n.a.	1.1	0.94	n.a.
Population	n.a.	2.2	1.52	n.a.
Sugar				
Quintile 1	7.77	n.a.	1.23	1.68
Quintile 2	4.86	n.a.	1.05	1.16
Quintile 3	3.68	n.a.	0.99	0.86
Quintile 4	2.90	n.a.	0.88	0.67
Quintile 5	1.56	n.a.	0.76	0.34
Population	2.58	n.a.	0.90	0.64
Oil				
Quintile 1	3.02	n.a.	3.39	n.a.
Quintile 2	2.28	n.a.	2.76	n.a.
Quintile 3	1.91	n.a.	2.60	n.a.
Quintile 4	1.68	n.a.	2.28	n.a.
Quintile 5	1.10	n.a.	1.93	n.a.
Population	1.48	n.a.	2.35	n.a.

Source World Bank estimations from Household Budget Surveys

Table 2.7 Per capita subsidies in energy products, in US$-PPP

	Djibouti	Iran, Islamic Rep.	Libya	Morocco	Tunisia
LPG					
Quintile 1	66.5	185.1	116	23.3	52.1
Quintile 2	83.2	149.6	169.1	39.1	66.5
Quintile 3	96.9	122	200.5	52.9	76.8
Quintile 4	115.6	99.7	240.7	67.6	91.1
Quintile 5	165.6	73.2	377.5	100.3	125.5
Population	105.6	125.9	220.8	56.6	82.4
Electricity					
Quintile 1	n.a.	334.15	108.3	20.78	50
Quintile 2	n.a.	449.1	157.91	34.95	63.91
Quintile 3	n.a.	542.06	187.3	47.25	73.78
Quintile 4	n.a.	656.06	224.79	60.35	87.49
Quintile 5	n.a.	946.57	352.57	89.58	120.56
Population	n.a.	585.56	206.17	50.58	79.14
Gasoline					
Quintile 1	0	244.63	97.34	0	0.66
Quintile 2	−0.01	469.19	155.11	0	2.07
Quintile 3	−0.02	693.17	192.81	0	4.23
Quintile 4	−0.16	963.85	238.34	0	9.45
Quintile 5	−3.65	1685.58	343.1	0	27.76
Population	−0.77	811.22	205.33	0	8.83
Diesel					
Quintile 1	n.a.	0.28	0.31	0.25	0.8
Quintile 2	n.a.	0.32	0.5	1.03	3.48
Quintile 3	n.a.	0.24	0.47	4.67	6.6
Quintile 4	n.a.	1.19	0.58	12.97	9.94
Quintile 5	n.a.	1.11	0.76	114.33	30.43
Population	n.a.	0.63	0.52	26.64	10.25

Source World Bank estimations from household budget surveys

Table 2.8 Per capita subsidies on food, in US$-PPP

	Djibouti	Iran, Islamic Rep.	Libya	Morocco
Flour				
Quintile 1	1.5	36.0	12.3	15.5
Quintile 2	2.0	21.9	14.1	19.5
Quintile 3	2.0	16.5	13.9	18.0
Quintile 4	2.7	12.1	14.9	18.6
Quintile 5	4.3	7.6	14.8	14.9
Population	2.5	18.8	14.0	17.3
Bread				
Quintile 1	n.a.	152.7	594.9	n.a.
Quintile 2	n.a.	175.6	709.3	n.a.
Quintile 3	n.a.	190.9	760.4	n.a.
Quintile 4	n.a.	193.1	786.3	n.a.
Quintile 5	n.a.	205.7	903.1	n.a.
Population	n.a.	183.6	750.8	n.a.
Sugar				
Quintile 1	1.99	n.a.	14.9	10.9
Quintile 2	2.69	n.a.	15.9	12.7
Quintile 3	3.16	n.a.	16.8	13.4
Quintile 4	3.96	n.a.	17.1	15.0
Quintile 5	6.04	n.a.	17.3	18.2
Population	3.57	n.a.	16.4	14.0
Oil				
Quintile 1	0.77	n.a.	35.7	n.a.
Quintile 2	1.26	n.a.	38.4	n.a.
Quintile 3	1.64	n.a.	39.7	n.a.
Quintile 4	2.30	n.a.	40.3	n.a.
Quintile 5	4.26	n.a.	40.7	n.a.
Population	2.05	n.a.	39.0	n.a.

Source World Bank estimations from Household Budget Surveys

Table 2.9 Impact on welfare of 30% reductions in subsidies on energy products, in US$-PPP/capita

	Djibouti	Iran, Islamic Rep.	Libya	Morocco	Tunisia
LPG					
Quintile 1	0	−14.1	−3.6	−11.8	−14.5
Quintile 2	0	−11.5	−4.7	−15.5	−18
Quintile 3	0	−9.4	−5.5	−19.5	−19.6
Quintile 4	0	−7.7	−6.5	−22.2	−22.3
Quintile 5	−0.1	−5.6	−9.3	−30.5	−20.9
Population	−0.1	−9.7	−5.9	−19.9	−19.1
Electricity					
Quintile 1	n.a.	−52.6	−16.3	−5.3	−10.9
Quintile 2	n.a.	−71.2	−23.9	−8.7	−14.6
Quintile 3	n.a.	−86	−28.4	−11.8	−17.1
Quintile 4	n.a.	−104.1	−34.2	−15.1	−20.3
Quintile 5	n.a.	−151.1	−53.7	−22.9	−27.6
Population	n.a.	−93	−31.3	−12.8	−18.1
Gasoline					
Quintile 1	0	−27.7	−14.3	0	−0.2
Quintile 2	0	−53.3	−22.8	0	−0.6
Quintile 3	0	−78.9	−28.4	0	−1.2
Quintile 4	0	−109.8	−35.2	0	−2.7
Quintile 5	1.1	−192.8	−50.7	0	−7.9
Population	0.2	−92.5	−30.3	0	−2.5
Diesel					
Quintile 1	n.a.	−0.27	−0.35	−0.01	−0.05
Quintile 2	n.a.	−0.29	−0.57	−0.02	−0.21
Quintile 3	n.a.	−0.22	−0.54	−0.11	−0.4
Quintile 4	n.a.	−1.12	−0.67	−0.31	−0.61
Quintile 5	n.a.	−1.06	−0.87	−2.74	−1.86
Population	n.a.	−0.59	−0.6	−0.64	−0.63

Source World Bank estimations from household budget surveys

Table 2.10 Impact on welfare of 30% reductions in subsidies on food products, in US$-PPP/capita

	Djibouti	Iran, Islamic Rep.	Libya	Morocco
Flour				
Quintile 1	−0.5	−8.8	−1.6	−4.2
Quintile 2	−0.6	−5.4	−1.8	−5.4
Quintile 3	−0.6	−4.0	−1.9	−5.0
Quintile 4	−0.8	−3.0	−2.1	−5.2
Quintile 5	−1.3	−1.9	−2.3	−4.3
Population	−0.7	−4.6	−1.9	−4.8
Bread				
Quintile 1	n.a.	−39.0	−49.0	n.a.
Quintile 2	n.a.	−45.1	−59.0	n.a.
Quintile 3	n.a.	−49.1	−63.6	n.a.
Quintile 4	n.a.	−49.7	−66.1	n.a.
Quintile 5	n.a.	−53.1	−76.4	n.a.
Population	n.a.	−47.2	−62.8	n.a.
Sugar				
Quintile 1	−0.6	n.a.	−2.3	−3.0
Quintile 2	−0.8	n.a.	−2.5	−3.5
Quintile 3	−0.9	n.a.	−2.8	−3.7
Quintile 4	−1.2	n.a.	−2.9	−4.2
Quintile 5	−1.8	n.a.	−3.3	−5.1
Population	−1.1	n.a.	−2.7	−3.9
Oil				
Quintile 1	−0.2	n.a.	−5.5	n.a.
Quintile 2	−0.4	n.a.	−6.0	n.a.
Quintile 3	−0.5	n.a.	−6.6	n.a.
Quintile 4	−0.7	n.a.	−7.0	n.a.
Quintile 5	−1.3	n.a.	−7.8	n.a.
Population	−0.6	n.a.	−6.6	n.a.

Source World Bank estimations from household budget surveys

Annex 2.2

See Tables 2.11 and 2.12.

Table 2.11 International monetary fund macrodata

Country	Subject descriptor	Units	Scale	2006	2007	2008	2009	2010	2011	2012	2013	2014
Djibouti	GDP per capita constant prices	National currency	Units	108,169.33	110,567.48	113,800.2	116,269.69	117,047.07	118,946.39	121,307.84	123,904.68	127,752.04
	Inflation end of period consumer prices	Index		116.765	126.303	137.985	140.974	144.918	155.96	159.9	161.7	165.4
	Population	Persons	Millions	0.753	0.774	0.796	0.818	0.841	0.865	0.889	0.914	0.939
Iran, Islamic Rep.	GDP per capita constant prices	National currency	Units	25,057,736	26,360,340	26,426,030	26,651,480	27,983,292	28,773,649	26,584,071	25,743,492	25,787,180
	Inflation end of period consumer prices	Index		48	58.8	69.2	76.5	91.6	110.4	155.885	186.579	223.894
	Population	Persons	Millions	70.496	71.278	72.18	73.201	74.339	75.15	76	76.978	77.969
Libya	GDP per capita constant prices	National currency	Units	7358.255	7696.338	7774.212	7599.614	7864.235	3037.559	6120.156	5464.247	4963.839
	Inflation end of period consumer prices	Index		106.629	114.713	125.871	126.284	130.483	165.252	159.18	161.894	174.012
	Population	Persons	Millions	5.686	5.782	5.877	5.964	6.053	5.943	6.032	6.122	6.213

(continued)

Table 2.11 (continued)

Country	Subject descriptor	Units	Scale	2006	2007	2008	2009	2010	2011	2012	2013	2014
Morocco	GDP per capita constant prices	National currency	Units	17,680.617	17,961.779	18,760.908	19,443.461	19,938.567	20,714.095	21,053.161	21,787.614	22,416.684
	Inflation end of period consumer prices	Index		101.6	103.618	108	106.3	108.6	109.6	112.446	112.869	115.691
	Population	Persons	Millions	30.506	30.841	31.177	31.514	31.851	32.187	32.522	32.853	33.179
Tunisia	GDP per capita constant prices	National currency	Units	4367.983	4597.276	4756.819	4852.745	4943.176	4789.873	4914.562	4982.483	5066.098
	Inflation end of period consumer prices	Index		105.331	110.73	115.182	119.882	124.691	129.876	137.603	145.923	153.713
	Population	Persons	Millions	10.128	10.225	10.329	10.44	10.547	10.674	10.778	10.918	11.06

Source IMF world economic outlook database April 2014

Table 2.12 Macrodata, prices, and subsidies in local currency (2014)

Country	Year	Macrodata[a]			US$-PPP[b]	Price and subsidies in local currencies					
		Inflation	Population growth	GDP		LPG (13 kg)		Gasoline (1 L)		Diesel (1 L)	
						Price	Subsidy	Price	Subsidy	Price	Subsidy
Djibouti	2012	3.40%	5.60%	5.30%	**104.104**	2948.4	294.8	315	−6.3	215	26.875
Iran, Islamic Rep.	2013	20.00%	1.30%	0.20%	**8,565,406**	16,643	83,214.8	4000	20,000	3500	19,500
Libya	2008	38.20%	5.70%	−36.10%	**0.691**	2	18.9	0.15	1.072	0.15	1.11
Morocco	2007	7.10%	6.40%	19.50%	**4.178**	43.3	86.5	12.8	0	9.89	0.8
Tunisia	2010	23.30%	4.90%	2.50%	**0.753**	7.4	15.7	1.856	0.186	1.584	0.334

[a]IMF World Economic Outlook Database, April 2014, and *WDI*
[b]Updated to 2013 by the World Bank

References

Clements, B., D. Coady, S. Fabrizio, S. Gupta, T. Alleyne, and C. Sdralevich. 2013. *Energy subsidy reform: lessons and implications.* International Monetary Fund.

Sdralevich, C., R. Sab., Y. Zouhar, and G. Albertin. 2014. *Subsidy reform in the Middle East and North Africa. Recent progress and challenges ahead.* International Monetary Fund, Middle East and Central Asia Department.

Author Biographies

Abdelkrim Araar received his Ph.D. in economics from Laval University in 1998. He is a World Bank consultant and a resource member at the Partnership for Economic Policy (PEP) network. Abdelkrim has been involved in designing and conducting training activities, developing training material, and conducting fundamental research. He has provided theoretical and technical supports to many researchers, especially those in developing countries. He is the coauthor, with Paolo Verme, of the Stata SUBSIM package. Also he is the coauthor, with Jean-Yves Duclos, of the book *Poverty and Equity: Measurement, Policy and Estimation with DAD*, the DASP Stata package, and DAD software.

Paolo Verme is a senior economist at the World Bank. A Ph.D. graduate of the London School of Economics, he was a visiting professor at Bocconi University in Milan (2004–09) and at the University of Turin (2003–10) before joining the World Bank in 2010. For almost two decades, he has served as adviser and project manager for multilateral organizations, private companies, and governments on labor market, welfare, and social protection policies. His research is widely published in international journals, books, and reports, and he has worked extensively on subsidies in the MENA Region and elsewhere. He is the coauthor of the subsidies simulation model SUBSIM (www.subsim.org).

Part II
Country Case Studies

Chapter 3
An Evaluation of the 2014 Subsidy Reforms in Morocco and a Simulation of Further Reforms

Paolo Verme and Khalid El-Massnaoui

Introduction

Morocco's history with consumers' subsidies predates World War II. Over the years subsidies have fulfilled different functions, ranging from incentives to promote exports, to price stabilization mechanisms, to social protection policies. Irrespective of their role, consumers' subsidies continue to exist 73 years after their introduction, but they have been difficult to sustain. The global rise in commodities prices accompanied by the global rise in oil prices has turned consumers' subsidies in a major liability for the government's budget, becoming the main constraint to the current fiscal balance. This, in turn, has forced the government to reconsider subsidy policies, first by increasing prices of selected subsidized goods in 2012 and 2013, and then by undertaking a rather comprehensive reform in 2014, leading to a partial dismantling of the subsidy system.

This chapter evaluates the 2014 subsidy reforms by simulating the impact of reforms on household welfare, poverty, and the government budget. Using a household consumption survey and input-output tables, we estimate direct effects via changes in prices of subsidized products and indirect effects via changes in prices of nonsubsidized products. We also simulate the impact of the total elimination of subsidies to see the implications of completing the reforms initiated in 2014. In addition, we consider the costs and benefits of possible compensation mechanisms in cash. Two sections of the chapter set the framework for the reforms; first, the evolution of subsidies since their introduction; and second, the political

P. Verme (✉)
The World Bank, Washington, District of Columbia, USA
e-mail: pverme@worldbank.org

K. El-Massnaoui
The World Bank, Rabat, Morocco

P. Verme and A. Araar (eds.), *The Quest for Subsidy Reforms in the Middle East and North Africa Region*, Natural Resource Management and Policy 42,
DOI 10.1007/978-3-319-52926-4_3

economy of reforms. The latter explains what the major obstacles to further reforms may be.

This chapter is organized as follows: the first section covers the evolution of subsidies since their introduction. Following are sections that explain the baseline data, document the distribution of subsidies as of October 2014, describe the results of the simulations, and discuss the political economy of reforms. The final section offers conclusions.

The Evolution of Subsidies

The subsidy system in Morocco was created in 1941 to stabilize prices of consumers' products that had been rising strongly because of World War II.[1] To cope with the war effort, France was importing heavily from Morocco,[2] which contributed to higher domestic prices.[3] In response, the kingdom introduced a stabilization fund called *Caisse de Compensation* (CDC).[4] After the end of the war, the CDC continued to operate as an instrument to facilitate the entry of various French products into Morocco at competitive prices under the Open Entry regime.

After independence in 1956, the government continued to use the CDC to stabilize prices of selected commodities while extending its mission to helping all troubled sectors, mostly the craft, charcoal, cement, and fertilizers industries, along with selected firms exporting strategic products. Before 1974 the CDC was financially autonomous, with its resources coming from fees and taxes levied on sectors benefiting from its support, especially from the oil sector. Its financial balance was maintained through taxation, and the proceeds were used to support troubled sectors and stabilize prices of selected commodities.

The second oil shock of 1979 would lead the CDC into a fragile financial situation resulting in increasing budget transfers to cover its deficits. In 1986 the government introduced specific taxes on imported petroleum products, but the proceeds of these taxes were directly allocated to the state budget. This decision deprived the CDC from its most important source of revenues. From a financially autonomous instrument of equalization, the CDC turned into a subsidy fund relying mostly on the state budget. Nonetheless, the CDC was able to stabilize the burden on the budget over the period 1986–94 thanks to the removal of subsidies on

---

[1]Before 1941 there were six equalization funds to stabilize prices of sugar, steel, fuels, eggs, timber, and vegetables.

[2]Morocco was a protectorate of France until 1956.

[3]The main basic commodities targeted by the CDC during World War II include flour, bread, edible oil, charcoal, sugar, barley, corn, and milk.

[4]In the rest of the text, CDC will also be used to include the *Office National Interprofessionnel des Cereales et des Legumineuses* (ONICL). Created in 1973, the agency administers subsidies for soft wheat and flour.

selected commodities in accordance with the implementation of the structural adjustment programs of the 1980s.

Between the 1980s and mid-1990s, the government gradually proceeded with the liberalization of prices of a number of subsidized products, including milk, butter, fertilizers, cement, packaging of cooking oils, and jet fuel. For the remaining products, the government decided to reform subsidies gradually through their partial liberalization and simplification before their full liberalization. Among food products, after the liberalization of the cooking oils sector in November 2000, only flour and sugar remained subsidized. For petroleum products, a new pricing system was put in place in 2013 for gasoline, diesel, and fuel oil, allowing the transmission of international price changes to the domestic market. In 2014 the government removed subsidies for gasoline and fuel oil, followed by diesel. As of January 2015 subsidies are limited to flour, sugar, and liquefied petroleum gas (LPG). Annex 1 presents the main measures and reforms of the subsidy system since its creation. The following sections describe in more detail reforms for different sets of products.

Petroleum Products

The first substantial attempt to reform the subsidy system was launched in 1995 for liquid petroleum products. The reform established a price indexation system that linked domestic price changes to the fluctuations of corresponding quotations on the Rotterdam market. The system did not apply to LPG, for which the subsidy system continued to support fully its price differential. The fixing of prices for liquid petroleum products at the producers/importers level complied with the elements of the acquisition price structure set up in agreement with the main national refinery (SAMIR). The selling price to the public was revised monthly on the basis of the acquisition price and in accordance with the structure of the sale price agreed upon with the distributors (Tables 3.1 and 3.2).[5] In parallel to the implementation of the indexation system, other measures were taken, mostly consisting of the replacement of import duties paid on crude oil by a consumption tax and the exemption from taxes for certain sectors heavily dependent on fuel energy, such as fishing, air and maritime transport, and electricity production.

Against the backdrop of increasing global oil prices, the government decided in 2000 to suspend the use of the price indexation system. This decision was due to the increasing political and social cost for the government to continue passing the full changes in the global prices through to the local markets, given the impact on transport services and therefore on prices of basic commodities, and on competitiveness of the domestic enterprises.

[5]Note that the retail price for gasoline and diesel in 2013 were higher than the CIF border price. The difference is mostly explained by taxes. Therefore, subsidies are estimated net of taxes, which is a common practice. See, for example, IMF 2013.

Table 3.1 Pre-2013 reform selling price structure of liquid petroleum products, in DH per unit

	Gasoline	Diesel	Fuel Oil
	DH/L	DH/L	DH/t
FOB price	5.90	6.64	4715.58
Transport	0.09	0.10	156.83
Port taxes	0.02	0.02	12.79
Access cost	0.12	0.14	104.30
Parafiscal tax	0.02	0.02	12.21
Stock cost	0.11	0.13	110.00
CIF Border price, including tax and port handling fees	**6.26**	**7.04**	**5111.72**
CT	3.76	2.42	182.40
VAT	1.00	0.95	529.41
Duty Credit	0.02	0.01	2.92
Acquisition price, including taxes	**11.05**	**10.42**	**5826.45**
Fees and distribution margins	0.38	0.28	90.00
Subtotal 1	**11.42**	**10.70**	**5916.45**
Subtotal 2	**10.42**	**9.76**	**5387.03**
Equalization	0.88	0.11	0.00
VAT	1.13	0.99	538.70
Price adjustment account (Unit Subsidy)	**−0.85**	**−2.67**	**−849.11**
Wholesale prices, including VAT	**11.59**	**8.19**	**5076.63**
Premium for evaporation losses	0.06	0.04	n.a.
Correction for thermal changes in inventories	0.02	0.02	n.a.
Retail margin	0.32	0.26	n.a.
Retail price to the public, excluding VAT	**10.85**	**7.52**	n.a.
VAT	1.17	1.02	n.a.
Retail price to the public (regulated by govt.)	**12.02**	**8.54**	n.a.

Source CDC website
Note CIF = cost, insurance, and freight; CT = domestic consumption tax; DH/L = Moroccan dirham per liter; DH/t = Moroccan dirham per metric ton; FOB = free on board; n.a. = not applicable (fuel oil is sold on wholesale basis only); VAT = value added tax. Items in bold refer to totals or summary items.

Together with the suspension of the indexation system, the government seized the opportunity of the relative easing of global prices between 2001 and mid-2004 to correct some cost items in the price structure of petroleum products that with time had been unduly favorable to the producers, importers, and distributors of fuel products. In 2002 the government revised the price structure of petroleum products to simplify it. The government also reduced the coefficient of adequacy of the local refinery from 6.5 to 2.5%. This coefficient was reduced in response to the performance of crude oil processing by the local refinery that managed to make the needed investment to enhance its production capacity and efficiency, especially for the production of diesel. Following the modernization of the local refinery in 2009, measures were taken to adapt further the price structure through indexing the freight

Table 3.2 Example of the selling price structure of liquefied petroleum gas, in DH per kilogram

Items	Container > 5 kg	Container ≤ 5 kg
Acquisition price, taxes not included	**8299.3**	**8299.3**
Domestic consumption tax	46.0	46.0
VAT	834.5	834.5
Duty credit	3.6	3.6
Price for filling stations	**9183.4**	**9183.4**
Losses of filling process	183.7	183.7
Filling margin and costs	318.0	318.0
Special premium for inventory financing	30.0	30.0
Bulk transport provision	50.0	50.0
Capping of bottles	20.0	50.0
VAT	60.2	63.2
Sale price to distribution companies	**9845.3**	**9878.3**
Costs and margins of distribution companies	538.0	604.0
Costs and margin for stocking	387.5	450.0
Deduct VAT	894.7	897.7
Subtotal excluding VAT	**9876.1**	**10,034.6**
VAT (max)	987.6	1003.5
Compensation fund balance	−7726.2	−7954.7
Wholesale prices, VAT included	**3137.5**	**3083.3**
Retailers margin	195.8	250.0
Retail price	**3333.3**	**3333.3**

Source CDC website
Note DH = Moroccan dirham; VAT = value added tax. Items in bold refer to totals or summary items.

costs and replacing the coefficient of adequacy by a lump sum for the development of storage capacities. As the global oil price started to rise again strongly by mid-2004 and up until 2012, the government was forced to make several ad hoc partial upward adjustments to local prices of selected liquid petroleum products to reduce the growing pressure on the CDC and the budget. During this period, retail prices of LPG did not change (Table 3.3).

Table 3.3 Domestic annual average prices of main petroleum products

	2004	2005	2006	2007	2008	2009	2010	2011	2012	2013
Gasoline (DH/L)	9.18	9.85	10.54	10.26	10.75	10.32	10.18	10.18	11.35	12.23
Diesel (DH/L)	7.07	7.71	9.28	9.31	9.63	7.56	7.15	7.15	7.73	8.33
Fuel Oil (industrial) (DH/Ton)	2302	2595	3233	2887	3124	3032	3358	3678	4254	4666
LPG (DH/12 kg container)	40.00	40.00	40.00	40.00	40.00	40.00	40.00	40.00	40.00	40.00

Sources CDC and World Bank calculation, 2013
Note DH = Moroccan dirham; kg = kilogram; L = liter; LPG = liquefied petroleum gas

As the global price remained high in 2013, the government decided to reform the subsidy system starting on September 16 by first reactivating the price indexation mechanism to help reverse the deteriorating fiscal trend. The indexation concerned the main liquid petroleum products, namely gasoline, diesel, and fuel oil. The new system imposed a cap on the unit subsidies for the three products to be managed by the CDC, and the remaining price differential was to be passed through to domestic prices. The implementation of the price indexation system, helped by lower global oil prices, allowed reducing subsidies by almost 2% points of the gross domestic product (GDP) in 2013, resulting in lowering the fiscal deficit to 6% of GDP (from 7.3% of GDP in 2012).

On February 1, 2014, the government stopped supporting prices of gasoline and industrial fuel oil. As a consequence, as of June 1, 2014, fuel oil used for the production of electricity has been included in the indexation system, with related subsidies replaced by a direct lump-sum transfer to the National Electricity and Water Company (ONEE) for three years (2014–17). During this period, subsidies for fuel oil used to generate electricity are phased out as established by an agreement signed between the government and the ONEE. The agreement provides for gradual retail price increases of electricity over three years to match production prices to the sale prices, which will entail operational cost savings in addition to price rises of about 3.5% annually. Only the price of the first consumption bracket is maintained unchanged for household using less than 100 kWh per month.

Diesel has also been subjected to a gradual dismantling of its subsidies during 2014. To this end, the government decided to phase out unit subsidies to diesel from 2.15 Moroccan dirhams per liter (DH/L) in January to 0.80 DH/L in October 2014. Subsequently, the government removed diesel from its list of subsidized products as of January 2015. However, it decided to continue administering prices of liquid petroleum products through the implementation of the indexation mechanism up to the end of November 2015 when prices of all liquid petroleum products would be fully liberalized. Prices of these products would thereafter be subject to competition among the distributors. These actions have helped keep the subsidy outlays in line with their budgeted amounts while significantly reducing the vulnerability of the budget to international commodity price movements. These measures constitute major steps toward a comprehensive subsidy reform.

Sugar and Cooking Oil

Before 1996 the CDC subsidized sugar on the basis of the difference between the unit cost and the selling price declared by each production unit. With this system, the state had been implicitly funding all other operating and capital expenses of the concerned firms. For cooking oil, the CDC used a different method based on the average unit costs of the producing firms. This system favored larger producers at the expense of smaller units and led to inefficient use of public funds without necessarily benefiting consumers.

In 1996 the government launched the first phase of import liberalization for sugar and cooking oil. To keep the consumer prices to their levels before liberalization while encouraging firms to rationalize their production costs, the government introduced a lump-sum subsidy mechanism for the two products in July. The lump-sum subsidy to sugar concerned both local and imported sugar. Under this system, the importation of sugar and cooking oil was subjected to tariffs, the proceeds of which allowed the CDC to cover 75% of cooking oil subsidies and nearly 50% of sugar subsidies. The remaining price differential was borne by the state budget. In addition to customs duties, the government imposed other taxes on imports of both products. Taxation on sugar and cooking oil was meant to be an instrument of protection for domestic production, keeping the target border prices fixed. In 2000 prices of cooking oil were totally liberalized, leading to the suppression of the related subsidy system.

In 1999 the government forced certain industries, such as biscuit, chocolate, and soft drinks producers, to refund the lump-sum subsidy benefiting the sugar used as input in the production process. To maintain competitiveness of sugar-intensive national industries, the refund was abandoned in 2006, except for the soft drinks industry, which benefited from a reduced refund rate starting from 2008. In 2010 sugar exports under all its forms have been subject again to a refund of the allocated subsidy. The CDC continued to support sugar prices both directly through the consumer price, but also to the sugar industries through their main production inputs (beetroot and cane sugar). Sugar subsidies were still in place at the end of 2014.

Wheat and Flour

The government has been subsidizing flour since the creation of the CDC in 1941. It has also been protecting soft wheat produced locally for subsidized flour through high custom duties on imports. As consumption of flour and the associated subsidies started to increase rapidly, the government decided in 1988 to limit the subsidy allocated to soft wheat flour to a quota of 10 million tons per year. The 1996 liberalization phase also concerned soft wheat imports, but subjected the imports to an administered pricing mechanism at the border to protect domestic production. However, due to the surge in the price of wheat on the international market in 2007 and the need to meet the increasing demand for bread, imports of soft wheat for the production of liberalized flours benefited from import subsidies when prices exceeded the target price.

The high burden of subsidies stemming from the widening gap between domestic and international prices of wheat persuaded the government to take measures to reduce, albeit marginally, subsidies benefiting the low-cost national flour. To this end, it reduced the quota of subsidized flour to 9 million tons annually, while strengthening the control of production and delivery of subsidized flour and redeploying its distribution to targeted populations, mainly using poverty maps. The government further limited the subsidized flour's annual quota to 8.5 million tons starting from the second half of 2013. The reduction of the quota was limited to urban areas with a poverty rate below 10%.

Baseline Data

The distributional and simulation analyses that follow rely largely on household budget survey data. These data are collected occasionally in Morocco, and the last available survey is the 2007 Living Standards Survey (LSS). The first exercise before undertaking the distributional and simulation analyses that follow requires updating the information available in the 2007 data to 2014, the year we consider for the analysis. The 2007–14 extrapolations are based on demographic and economic estimates. Table 3.4 shows the reference statistics used for the extrapolation.

Based on the data presented in Table 3.4 and the subsequent update of the information available in the household budget survey, we reconstructed population and expenditure figures for the year 2014 (Table 3.5). The population of Morocco is estimated at 33.3 million including about 7.1 million families. Total household expenditure is estimated at 580.2 billion Moroccan dirham (DH), equivalent to DH 81,743 per household and DH 17,420 per capita. The average household size is estimated at 4.7 persons, but higher for poorer households. The first quintile (the poorest) spends about 12% of what the fifth quintile (the richest) spends on average. These extrapolations are not the exact figures available in macroeconomic statistics, but they represent good approximations considering that they are derived from household data and a rather old data set.

Table 3.4 Reference statistics, 2007–13

Source	Indicator	2007	2008	2009	2010	2011	2012	2013
1	GDP (current prices, bn DH)	616.3	688.8	732.4	764.3	804.2	850.6	909.4
1	GDP (real prices 1998, bn DH)	554.0	584.9	613.9	636.6	663.8	688.3	718.0
3	GDP growth (base 2007 = 100)	100.0	105.6	110.8	114.9	119.8	124.3	129.6
1	Govt. spending (current prices, bn DH)	185.2	219.2	227.7	243.8	277.4	277.0	294.9
2	Population (000)	30,841.0	31,177.0	31,514.0	31,851.0	32,187.0	32,522.0	32,853.0
3	Population growth (base 2007)	100.0	101.1	102.2	103.3	104.4	105.5	106.5
1	CPI (base 2006)	102.0	106.0	107.0	108.1	109.1	111.3	114.0
3	CPI (base 2007)	100.0	103.9	104.9	105.9	106.9	109.0	111.8

Sources 1. IMF 2014; 2. HCP Morocco; 3. World Bank estimates
Note bn = billion (1000 millions); CPI = consumer price index; DH = Moroccan dirham; GDP = gross domestic product

Table 3.5 Baseline population and expenditure data by quintile

Quintile	Population (m)	Number of households (m)	Household size	Total expenditures (m)	Total expenditures per capita	Total expenditures per household
1 (poorest)	6.66	0.98	6.8	34,789	5,223	35,362
2	6.66	1.19	5.6	58,543	8,789	49,105
3	6.66	1.36	4.9	82,599	12,398	60,946
4	6.66	1.57	4.2	118,540	17,794	75,382
5 (richest)	6.66	1.99	3.3	285,699	42,913	143,304
Total	33.30	7.10	4.7	580,169	17,420	81,743

Source World Bank estimations from household budget survey data
Note m = millions

A Distributional Analysis of Subsidies (October 2014)

The analysis presented in this chapter covers food products (sugar and flour), petroleum products (gasoline, diesel, and LPG), and electricity. The 2014 reforms included a change in the price structure of water for household consumers, and this change has implications for household welfare. However, water is not considered to be subsidized in Morocco, and for this reason water is not considered in this analysis.

The prices of subsidized products in October 2014 are described in Table 3.6 together with the unit subsidies and the unsubsidized prices. LPG, flour, and electricity are the products with the highest subsidies relative to the unsubsidized price, with LPG reaching 66.6% of the unsubsidized price. Households spend more than DH 47 billion on subsidized products, which represents 8.1% of total household expenditure. The largest expenditure item among subsidized products is electricity (16 billion). By far, the largest subsidies are for LPG, which alone costs the government about DH 11.8 billion, followed by electricity (6.4 billion) and flour (2.4 billion).

Figure 3.1 shows how important subsidized products are for households (panels a, c, and e, representing expenditure on subsidized products as a share of total expenditure) and how important are subsidies in individual terms (panels b, d, and f, representing subsidies per capita).

Starting from the food products (panels a and b), we can see that sugar and flour are both more important for the poor than for the rich (both curves are downward sloped in panel b). The poorest percentiles consume between 2% and 3% of total expenditure on these products, and the richest percentiles consume a tiny share of total expenditure. However, the data in panel b show that flour subsidies per capita are larger for the middle class than for the poor or the rich, and sugar subsidies favor the rich as higher subsidies per capita go to richer households.

Table 3.6 Subsidized products (October 1, 2014)

	Unit	Unit price	Unit subs.	Unsub. unit price	Unit subs. (% of unsub. price)	HH exp. on subs. products (DH bn.)	Total subs. (DH bn.)
Gas LPG	kg	3.330	6.654	9.984	66.6	5.9	11.8
Gasoline	L	12.800	0.000	12.800	0.0	2.8	0
Diesel	L	9.890	0.800	10.690	7.5	3.7	0.4
Sugar-piece	kg	5.820	2.850	8.670	32.9	2.5	1.2
Sugar-cube	kg	5.820	2.850	8.670	32.9	0.4	0.2
Sugar-granul.	kg	4.500	2.850	7.350	38.8	0.9	0.6
Flour-free	kg	5.000	0.700	5.700	12.3	5.6	0.8
Flour-nat.	kg	2.000	1.430	3.430	41.7	2.3	1.6
Electricity						16.0	6.4
0–100	kWh	0.9010	0.6600	1.5610	42.3	0.8	0.5
101–150	kWh	0.9689	0.5900	1.5589	37.8	0.8	0.5
151–200	kWh	0.9689	0.5900	1.5589	37.8	2.9	1.8
201–300	kWh	1.0541	0.5100	1.5641	32.6	4.6	2.2
301–500	kWh	1.2474	0.3167	1.5641	20.2	4.4	1.1
501 and more	kWh	1.4407	0.1200	1.5607	7.7	2.4	0.2

Sources Official bulletins no. 6222, January 16, 2014, and No. 6288, September 4, 2014, and CDC
Note bn = billion; DH = Moroccan dirham; HH = household; kg = kilogram; kWh = kilowatt-hour; L = liter

The pictures are different for petroleum products (panels c and d). Here the data show that LPG is an important item for the poorest and declines in importance for richer households, and although gasoline and diesel are not particularly relevant for the poor, they become increasingly relevant for the rich (panel d). In terms of subsidies per capita (panel c) the only important product is LPG, and this product is really prorich, meaning that richer households receive higher subsidies. Therefore, LPG is the most important subsidized product for the poor, but subsidies per capita are larger for the rich despite the poor having larger households. This is one example of inequitable distribution of subsidies.

The picture changes again if we look at electricity (panels e and f). The share of expenditure on electricity subsidies is declining, with poorer households consuming larger shares than richer households (panel e). Instead, in terms of subsidies per capita, electricity is pro-rich. Similarly to LPG, electricity is another product that appears to be particularly inequitable given the importance of this product for the poor and how the subsidies per capita favor the rich.

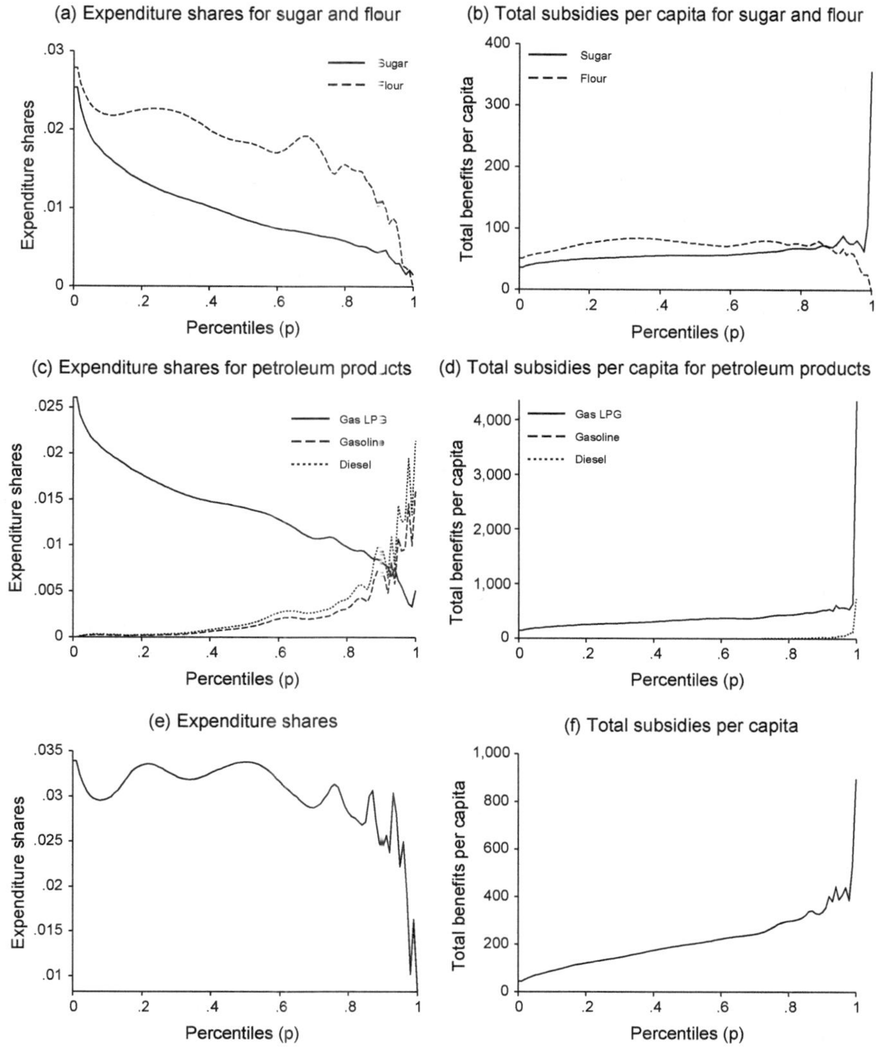

Fig. 3.1 Share of total expenditure on subsidized products and amount of subsidies per capita, by percentile. *Source* World Bank estimations from household budget survey data. *Note* The y-axes in panels **a**, **c**, and **e**, represent expenditure on subsidized products as a share of total expenditure. The y-axes in panels **b**, **d**, and **f**, represent subsidies per capita

Simulation of Subsidy Reforms

This section considers two sets of simulations. The first simulation focuses on the reforms carried out by the government of Morocco between January and October 2014. This simulation can be considered an *ex post* evaluation of the 2014 subsidy reforms. These reforms include the elimination of subsidies on gasoline in January, progressive increases in the price of diesel implemented between January and October, and changes to the electricity tariffs introduced in August.[6]

More precisely, the progressive increases in the price of diesel included four successive reductions of the unit subsidy from DH 2.15 per liter in January 2014 to DH 0.8 in October. The August reforms of electricity included an increase of the number of blocks from four to six. Tariffs have been adjusted, and starting from the third block, the tariffs' system has changed from increasing block tariffs (IBT) to volume differentiated tariffs (VDT).[7] Electricity billing includes a fixed cost for meter use and management. This cost is not included in the simulations for partially compensating underreporting of utilities' consumption and estimate quantities consumed from household data that are closer to reality.

The second set of simulations is the total elimination of subsidies based on October 2014 prices, the latest prices available at the time of writing. Table 3.7 provides initial and final prices for these simulations (October 1 unit price and unsubsidized price, respectively) as well as all price changes implied by the August 2014 reforms. Unit subsidies have been estimated using data on deficits published by the ONEE. For all simulations and products we use an own price-elasticity of 0.2.

The poverty lines used for all simulations are DH 2796/capita/year ($US 316) for rural areas and DH 4266/capita/year (US$ 481) for urban areas. These poverty lines have been estimated by updating the 2007 official poverty line for inflation. As they were in 2007, the poverty lines are quite low for a country like Morocco today and they provide a prereform poverty rate of only 4.15%. Keeping this poverty line is important for interpreting our results using the official poverty line. However, what is of interest for the simulations is the relative percentage change in poverty, which gives a better sense of the real impact of reforms on poverty. This percentage change will also be reported in the text.

Evaluation of the 2014 Subsidy Reforms

In this section, we simulate ex post the impact of the subsidies reforms that Morocco implemented between January and October 2014. The reforms include the elimination of the subsidies on gasoline, the progressive increases on the price of

---

[6]The elimination of subsidies on gasoline is based on the unit subsidies estimated by the government at the time of the January 2014 reform. It should be noted that the retail price for gasoline was higher than the import price (see Table 3.1) and that the difference is explained mostly by taxes on gasoline. Therefore, subsidies are estimated net of taxes, which is a common practice (IMF 2013). Also, the share of taxes in Morocco is lower than in countries like Italy or Germany where this share is well above 50% (OPEC 2014).

[7]Increasing block tariffs (IBT) apply when the tariff corresponding to a particular block affects only the latest block of consumption, while tariffs for the previous blocks of consumption apply to the previous blocks. Volume differentiated tariffs (VDT) apply when the tariffs corresponding to a particular block are applied to all quantities consumed up to that block.

Table 3.7 Baseline data for the simulation of subsidies reforms, direct effects

	Unit	January 1, 2014					October 1, 2014			
		Type of Tarification	Unit Price	Unit subsidy	Unsubsidized Unit Price		Type of Tarification	Unit Price	Unit subsidy	Unsubsidized Unit Price
Gasoline	L	Linear	12.020	0.780	12.800		Linear	12.800	0.000	12.800
Diesel	L	Linear	8.540	2.150	10.690		Linear	9.890	0.800	10.690
Electricity						**Electricity**				
0–100	kWh	IBT	0.9010	0.6600	1.5610	0–100	IBT	0.9010	0.6600	1.561
101–200	kWh	IBT	0.9689	0.5900	1.5589	101–150	IBT	0.9689	0.5900	1.559
201–500	kWh	IBT	1.0541	0.5100	1.5641	151–200	VDT	0.9689	0.5900	1.559
501 and more	kWh	IBT	1.4407	0.1200	1.5607	201–300	VDT	1.0541	0.5100	1.564
						301–500	VDT	1.2474	0.3167	1.564
						501 and more	VDT	1.4407	0.1200	1.561

Sources Official Bulletins No. 6222, January 16, 2014, and No. 6288, September 4, 2014
Note IBT = increasing block tariffs; kWh = kilowatt-hour; L = liter; VDT = volume differentiated tariffs

diesel, and the changes in electricity tariffs. Table 3.7 detailed the price increases and the restructuring of the electricity tariffs blocks relative to these reforms. These ex post simulations are useful in that Morocco has no new available microdata that can be used to evaluate the actual impact of the reforms. Even if these data were available, it would be difficult to isolate the impact of the reforms from the impact of other shocks, which makes ex post simulations of this kind a useful tool to evaluate reforms.

We divide the analysis into direct and indirect effects. Direct effects are estimated using household budget data only and are transmitted to households through price increases of subsidized products. Indirect effects are estimated by combining input-output data with household budget data. The indirect effects capture the impact that price increases on subsidized products have on the prices of nonsubsidized products and, through the latter, on household welfare.

Direct Effects

The total impact of the 2014 subsidies reforms on households is estimated at DH 3.2 billion or DH 95 per capita, per year. Table 3.8 breaks down the data by quintile and subsidized products. The impact rises with income groups from 0.12 billion for the poorest quintile to 1.84 billion for the richest quintile. The largest contributor is electricity with 2.4 billion. In terms of household welfare, the elimination of subsidies reduces welfare by about 0.5% on average, with the impact being larger for the richest quintile (−0.64%) as compared to the poorest quintile (−0.34%).

These reductions in welfare did not have a significant impact on poverty because the poor are not heavy users of gasoline and diesel, and the tariffs on electricity for this group (structure and prices) changed little. They also had an insignificant effect on inequality (Table 3.9). The 2014 reforms saved the government about 3 billion DH, assuming that the benefits of the average increase in prices due to the change in tariffs structure accrues to the government and not to producers or distributors (this is an implicit assumption of the model used for simulations). These savings come for the most part from the richest quintile and progressively less from the other quintiles. As there is no increase in poverty, there is also no need to provide a compensatory cash transfer.

Table 3.8 Direct welfare effects of the 2014 reforms, in DH million

Quintile	Electricity	Gasoline	Diesel	Total	Total (percentage of expend.)
1 (poorest)	−118.0	−0.3	−1.1	−119.4	−0.34%
2	−241.4	−1.4	−4.5	−247.3	−0.42
3	−366.5	−6.3	−20.6	−393.4	−0.48
4	−490.8	−17.6	−57.1	−565.5	−0.48
5 (richest)	−1182.0	−154.1	−502.7	−1838.8	−0.64
Total	−2398.7	−179.7	−586.0	−3164.3	−0.5

Source World Bank estimations using SUBSIM and household budget survey data

Table 3.9 Direct welfare and budget effects of the 2014 subsidies reforms

	Prereform	Postreform	Change
Welfare (per capita)	17,420.404	17,325.391	−95.014
Poverty (percent)	4.155	4.192	0.036
Inequality (percent)	42.433	42.381	−0.052
Subsidies (in millions)	10,371.180	7366.350	−3004.830

Source World Bank estimations using SUBSIM and household budget survey data

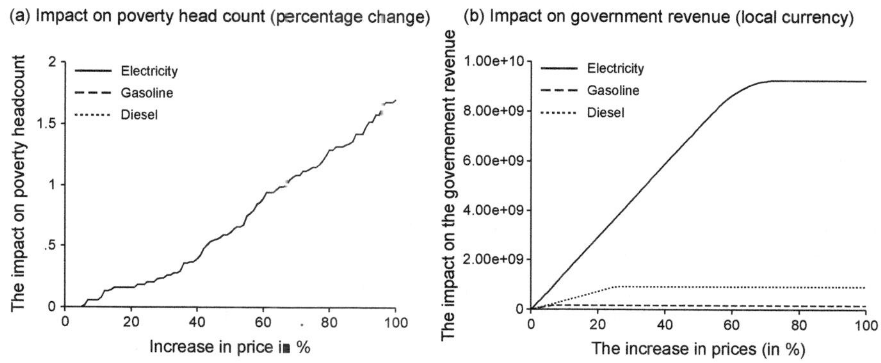

Fig. 3.2 Sensitivity of changes in poverty and government revenues to changes in prices. *Source* World Bank estimations using SUBSIM (subsidy simulation). *Note* The y-axis in panel **a** represents the change in poverty expressed in percentage points. The y-axis in panel **b** represents the gain in the government budget in local currency

The trade-offs between the gain in government revenues and the increase in poverty resulting from subsidies reforms are depicted in Fig. 3.2. Panel a shows the increase in poverty, and panel b the impact on government revenues of price increases between 1 and 100% for all products considered. From the standpoint of poverty, the only product that would have a real impact on the poverty head count is electricity for price increases above 30–40%. However, the reforms implemented in 2014 did not reach such price increases and did not affect the lower tariff block, which concerns the poor the most.

From the standpoint of government revenues, the most promising product is electricity. This sector results in government savings higher than those resulting from increasing prices on other products. Therefore, the government has taken the right decision in terms of increasing electricity tariffs and changing the type of tariffs (from IBT to VDT) for upper blocks and by increasing the number of blocks. In fact, by increasing the number of blocks, it is possible to achieve savings while respecting the household capacity to pay for electricity (consumer demand). Moreover, prices were increased particularly for those products that are poverty neutral (in terms of direct effects) such as gasoline and diesel.

Table 3.10 Indirect effects of 2014 reforms: baseline data

	Unit	Price January 1, 2014	Price October 1, 2014	Price increase (percent)	Average price increase	HBS sector	Corresponding I/O sector
Gasoline	L	12.02	12.80	6.49	11.15	Petroleum	D23-Oil refining
Diesel	L	8.54	9.89	15.81	11.15	Petroleum	D23-Oil refining
Electricity	kWh	1.02	1.04	2.10	2.10		E001 electric energy

Sources Official Bulletins No. 6222, January 16, 2014, and No. 6288, September 4, 2014, and World Bank estimations based on average prices for electricity
Note HBS = household budget survey; I/O = input/output; kWh = kilowatt hour; L = liter

Indirect Effects

The simulation of direct and indirect effects uses input and output (I/O) tables and household budget survey (HBS) data combined. The baseline data for the price shocks are in Table 3.10. With I/O tables it is not possible to simulate price increases by product or by tariff block given that the I/O tables are aggregated by sector. Therefore, we use averages across products belonging to the same sector or across tariffs blocks. As shown in Table 3.10, the shock to the petroleum sector is a price increase of 11.15%, which is an average of the price shocks applied to diesel and gasoline. The assumption here is that gasoline and diesel have a similar weight in the I/O oil refining sector and that they represent almost the totality of the sector. The price shock applied to electricity is 2.1%, which is an average price increase across tariffs blocks weighted by the number of households in each block.[8]

The most accurate estimates for direct effects remain those provided in the previous section, and we will disregard estimates of direct effects using I/O data. What is of interest here is the relative share of indirect effects over total effects. Using this share, one can then derive a better approximation of the real value of indirect effects using the direct effects values of the previous section.

Results of the simulations show that the relation between direct and indirect effects varies significantly across products and across quintiles (Table 3.11). If we simulate shocks for the two sectors independently we find indirect effects to be 87.79% of the total for petroleum products and 36.55% for electricity. The relative weight of indirect effects also differs across quintiles. Indirect effects on petroleum products are the quasi-totality of effects for the poorest quintile and they become 81.33% for the richest quintile. This is understandable because the poor consume very little gasoline and diesel. Instead, for electricity, indirect effects represent

[8]Note that the share of consumption in each block could also be used for weighting.

Table 3.11 Indirect effects of 2014 reforms, percent of total effects

Quintile	Petroleum	Electricity
1 (poorest)	99.55	30.10
2	98.87	30.31
3	96.48	30.52
4	93.43	33.89
5 (richest)	81.33	42.17
Total	87.79	36.55

Source World Bank estimations using SUBSIM

30.1% of total effects for the poorest quintile and this share increases to 42.17% for the richest quintile. That is because the coverage of electricity is very large in Morocco and many if not most of the poor consume electricity.

Complete Elimination of Subsidies

Recall that we are estimating the complete elimination of subsidies as of October 2014, after the 2014 reforms and when subsidies on gasoline had been already removed. Therefore, simulations concern petroleum products that still benefited from some subsidies and the food products that were not affected by the 2014 reforms. The products considered are LPG, diesel, sugar, flour, and electricity. The baseline data for these simulations are those in Table 3.6 (October 1, 2014).

Direct Effects

The total impact of subsidies removal on households is estimated at DH −23.6 billion or DH −707 per capita (Table 3.12). The impact rises with income groups from 2.7 billion for the lowest quintile to 7.3 billion for the highest quintile. By far, the largest contributor to this impact is LPG, which alone contributes for 11.8 billion, followed by electricity with 7 billion. In terms of household welfare, the elimination of subsidies reduces welfare by 4% on average, with the impact being almost three times as large for the poorest quintile (−7.8%) as compared to the richest quintile (−2.6%).

This reduction in welfare, in turn, created a significant increase in the poverty level from an estimated 4.2% before the reform to 5.6%. It should be noted that the low poverty level observed before the reform is a rough estimate based on the last available survey (2007) inflated to 2014 prices. Therefore, the poverty level is likely to be an incorrect estimate of the true poverty level in 2014. But what is of interest here is the relative change in poverty, which is estimated at more than 34%. This is a very large increase as compared to the initial poverty level. About a third of this increase is explained by the removal of subsidies on LPG alone. We can also observe an increase in inequality estimated with the Gini coefficient, from 42.4 to 43.4, a relative increase of about 2%. The removal of subsidies on products that are

Table 3.12 Direct effects on welfare of subsidies elimination, in DH million

	Quintile 1	Quintile 2	Quintile 3	Quintile 4	Quintile 5	Total
LPG	−1405.9	−1844.9	−2321.1	−2641.6	−3619.3	−11,832.8
Diesel	−0.6	−2.3	−10.5	−29.2	−257.2	−299.8
Sugar piece	−232.0	−253.4	−252.5	−254.5	−217.7	−1210.2
Cube	−0.1	−2.9	−9.6	−36.2	−129.7	−178.6
Granulated	−70.0	−97.4	−112.0	−125.8	−160.1	−565.4
Flour free	−33.6	−91.1	−138.0	−233.1	−291.9	−787.6
Natural	−397.2	−451.5	−363.1	−285.4	−123.4	−1620.6
Electricity	−579	−974	−1318	−1684	−2501	−7057
Total	−2719	−3718	−4525	−5290	−7301	−23,552

Source World Bank estimations using SUBSIM
Note LPG = liquefied petroleum gas

particularly associated with the rich, such as diesel, contributes to less inequality, but, on aggregate, inequality increases.

The elimination of subsidies would naturally save the government the equivalent of total subsidies or DH 23.6 billion. However, it is instructive to see what the cost would be to the government of providing a universal cash transfer to all households that would maintain the prereform poverty level unaltered. This amount is estimated at 12.0 billion and would result in government savings of 11.5 billion (Table 3.13). This amount should be considered as an upper bound for transfers. If the government is able to target cash transfers to the poor to compensate for their losses in subsidies revenues, the cost for the government would be much lower.

To better understand the trade-offs between the gain in terms of government revenues and the losses in terms of poverty increases of subsidies reforms, see Fig. 3.3. The data show the increase in poverty (panels a, c, and e) and the impact on government revenues (panels b, d, and f) of price increases between 1 and 100% for all products considered. Note that these price increases may not be realistic and even above the increases necessary to eliminate subsidies. The only purpose of this exercise is to show which product is the most promising in terms of positive impact on government finances while maintaining poverty low.

Concerning food products, increasing the prices of flour results in larger poverty increases as compared to sugar, but this is true only up to increases of about 40%.

Table 3.13 Direct effects of elimination of subsidies

	Prereform	Postreform	Change
Welfare (per capita)	17,420	16,713	−707
Poverty	4.16%	5.60%	1.44%
Inequality	42.43%	43.42%	0.99%
Subsidies	23,552 m.	0.000	−23,552 m.
Transfers	0	12,044 m.	12,044 m.
Total budget	23,552 m.	12,044 m.	−11,508 m.

Source World Bank estimations from household budget survey data

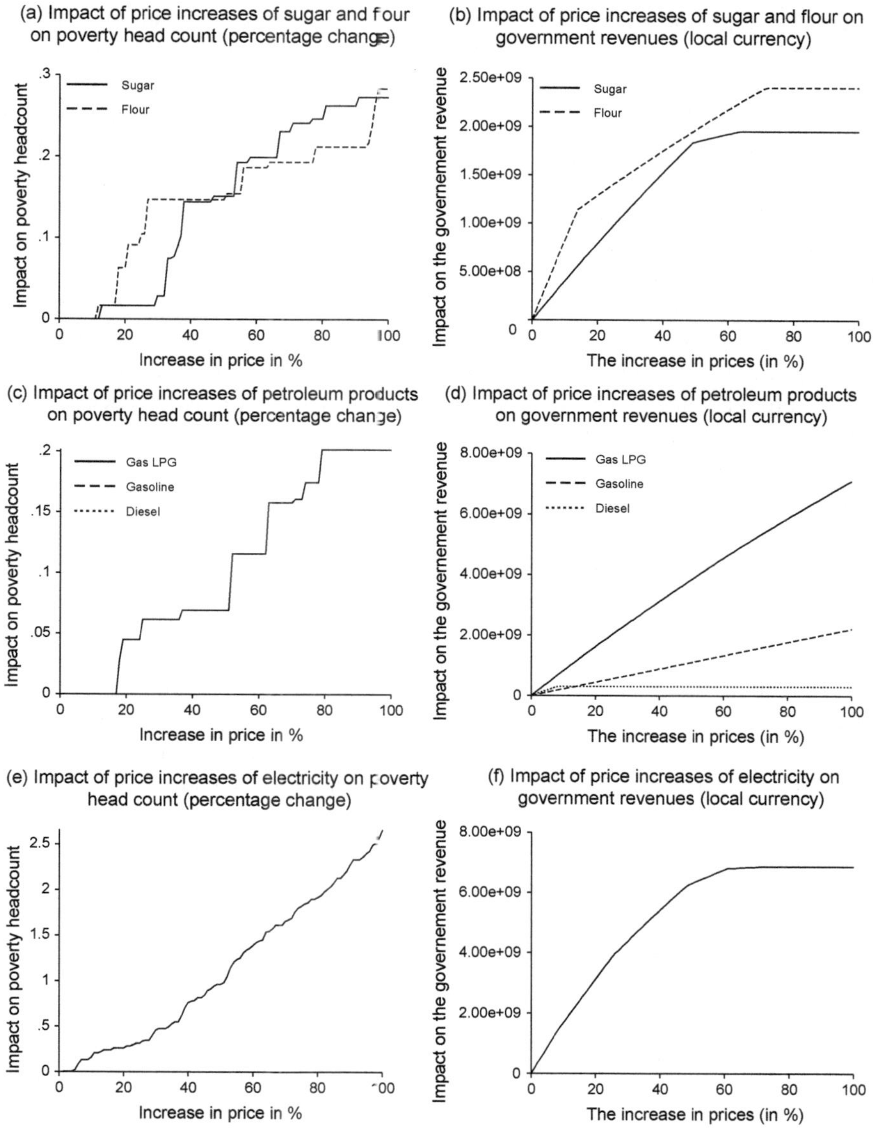

Fig. 3.3 Sensitivity of changes in poverty and government revenues to changes in prices. *Source* World Bank estimations using SUBSIM. *Note* The y-axes in panels **a**, **c**, and **e** represent the change in poverty expressed in percentage points. The y-axes in panels **b**, **d**, and **f** represent the gain in the government budget in local currency

After this threshold, it is sugar that increases poverty. In terms of government finances, increases in prices of flour provide more government savings than increases on sugar all along the price increasing spectrum. There is clearly a trade-off here. If the government increases prices of flour, it will gain more than it would by increasing prices of sugar, but the cost for poverty will also be higher than increasing prices for sugar. This is true up to price increases of 40%. After that, a good strategy is to continue increasing prices for flour while maintaining prices of sugar as sugar becomes more costly in terms of an increase in poverty and flour continues to be superior in terms of government savings.

Petroleum products (panels c and d) are simpler to interpret. The only poverty-increasing product is LPG given that poor households do not use diesel and that gasoline has no subsidies. Because increasing prices of gasoline and diesel further can increase government savings, it would be a good strategy to keep LPG subsidies while financing these subsidies with further increases in gasoline and diesel prices (from a purely poverty-savings perspective). However, we saw that LPG is prorich while panel d shows that the largest savings would be made with the increase in LPG prices. If we consider direct effects only (as we do in this section), increasing gasoline and diesel prices alone is not sufficient to fix government finances, and the government will have to address the large subsidies currently allocated to LPG.

The picture is even simpler with electricity (panels e and f). Increases in electricity prices are more promising for government savings than other products but they also have a much greater impact on poverty. What is noticeable here is that price increases of electricity beyond 60% bring very little additional government revenues (households start to consume much less), but poverty would continue to increase steadily. The reform of electricity subsidies therefore is quite complex and needs to take into account the elasticity of consumption to price increases as well as the tariffs' brackets. The price increases that are considered in reality—for example, the 2014 reform of electricity tariffs—are below 20%. This is the area of the graphs that is most of interest in Morocco today.

Indirect Effects

As a reminder, what we are considering is the elimination of subsidies in October 2014. By that time the subsidies for gasoline had been already removed, and this product will not be considered here. We also do not consider LPG and flour, assuming that these products do not have indirect effects. Although some enterprises may use LPG bottles and some large industrial bakeries may use subsidized flour, these effects are expected to be small. Household businesses such as small street restaurants and cafés and small bakeries run by households are captured in household consumption and therefore already accounted for in the direct effects. Instead, subsidized sugar, which is used as an intermediary product by the food industry, will be considered as well as diesel, which is used by commercial transport. In addition, we will consider the elimination of subsidies on electricity, as this sector functions as inputs to other sectors.

With input-output tables, price shocks can be applied only to sectors rather than individual products. For goods with linear pricing (gasoline and diesel), the price

Table 3.14 Baseline information of simulation of subsidies removal (indirect effects)

	Unit	Subsidized unit price	Unsubsidized unit price	Share in I/O sector (%)	Price increase (%)	HBS sector	Corresponding I/O sector
Diesel	L	9.89	10.69	38.6	3.12	Petroleum	D23-Oil refining
Sugar	kg	5.82	8.67	1.6	0.78	Food	A001-2 agriculture
Electricity	kWh	1.04	1.56	100	49.95	Electricity	E001 electric energy

Source World Bank estimates from baseline prices and household data
Note HBS = household budget survey; I/O = input/output; kg = kilogram; kWh = kilowatt hour; L = liter

shock for the sector (petroleum) is estimated as an average of the price shocks of gasoline and diesel resulting from the elimination of subsidies. For goods with nonlinear pricing (electricity), the price shock is estimated as the increase in average tariffs weighted by the number of households consuming in each block. Table 3.14 describes the price increases considered for the simulations.

Note that it is not possible to compare these simulations with the simulations on direct effects for various reasons: the simulations in this section do not cover all products simulated in the direct effects section; they include both direct and indirect effects; they consider a joint shock to different sectors; the impact is estimated on consumption items that are more aggregated than individual products as in the direct effects section; and for goods like electricity, we cannot simulate price shocks for individual tariffs' blocks with an I/O table. It is, however, possible to gauge the relative importance of indirect effects if simulations are run one at a time.

Consider diesel. This product is mostly consumed by commercial transport and only moderately by households. We should therefore expect shocks to this product to have large indirect effects and small direct effects. The elimination of subsidies on diesel would result in a price increase to the petroleum sector of 3.12%, and this increase has indirect effects that account for 87.8% of the total effects (Table 3.15). As predicted, indirect effects are much greater than direct effects for a product like diesel. If we consider instead a product like sugar, which is mostly consumed by households and we repeat the exercise, we find direct effects for only 2% of the total (recall also that industries using sugar as a production input have to reimburse the equivalent of the government subsidy).

Table 3.15 Indirect effects of subsidies elimination of selected products, percent

Quintile	Diesel	Sugar	Electricity
1 (poorest)	99.55	1.03	30.10
2	98.87	1.22	30.31
3	96.48	1.48	30.52
4	93.43	1.67	33.89
5 (richest)	81.33	2.84	42.17
Total	87.79	2.00	36.55

Source World Bank estimations using SUBSIM

The ratio of direct and indirect welfare effects changes very significantly across products and also across quintiles (Table 3.15). For diesel, indirect effects are almost 88% of the total, but for sugar they are only 2%. For electricity, indirect effects are estimated at 36.5% of total effects. An important difference also exists across quintiles. For diesel, the indirect effects are practically the only effects for the poorest quintile, but they become 93.4% for the richest quintile. For sugar, these shares are 1.03 and 2.84%, respectively, and for electricity they are 30.1 and 42.2%. These are gross estimates based on the price shocks described in Table 3.14. If the government should decide, for example, to change electricity tariffs for the production sector, the effects on household welfare may be very different.

The Political Economy of Reforms

The political economy of subsidy reforms in Morocco has been driven largely by the global prices of strategic commodities and by the increasing cost of subsidies to the state's budget. From an equalization fund with own resources sufficient to conduct its mission of stabilizing prices of basic commodities over short periods of time, the CDC transformed over the years into a permanent subsidy fund relying heavily on budget transfers. With rising world prices of basic commodities, especially of fuels, the burden on the budget of the subsidy system has grown increasingly heavy. Particularly burdensome is the cost of fuels, given that Morocco depends totally on imports. The share of fuels in total subsidies was relatively small before the first oil shock in 1974, but it rose steadily over time to reach almost 90% in 2012. With respect to GDP, subsidy outlays rose from less than 0.5% over the first decades after independence to almost 2% by end of the 1990s. As shown in Fig. 3.4, the trend in the amount of subsidies followed rather closely the international price of crude oil.

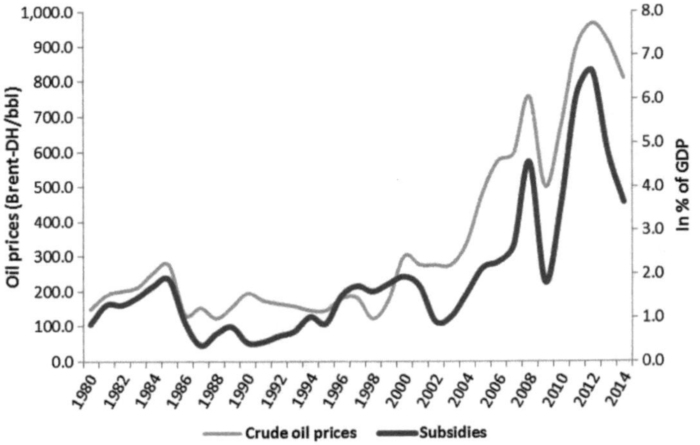

Fig. 3.4 Correlations of subsidies changes with oil prices. *Source* Ministry of Finance, CDC, and World Bank 2015. *Note* Oil prices are in DH/bbl (barrel); subsidies are in percentage of GDP

The first experience with the reform of liquid fuel subsidies implemented in 1995 helped to stabilize subsidies around 1.7% of GDP until 2000, when the systematic use of the indexation system was suspended. The removal of subsidies on cooking oil in 2000 and of jet fuel in 2005, together with the reform of the sugar subsidy system in 2006 and the price increases of liquid fuels, mitigated the impact on the budget between 2001 and 2007, but expenditures on subsidies continued to increase to reach 2.7% of GDP in 2007 because of the continued rise in oil prices over the period.

The 2008 financial crisis had limited direct effects on Morocco's economy, but the subsequent food and fuel price crisis had more serious repercussions. Subsidies reached a peak of 6.6% of GDP in 2012 when, for the first time, they became higher than budgetary investments. Over this period, subsidies explained most of the deterioration in the budget deficits (Fig. 3.5). Indeed, after two years of surpluses in 2007 and 2008, the budget experienced rising deficits peaking at 7.4% of GDP in 2012, the highest deficit since the early 1980s. The high budget deficits eroded all the fiscal space accumulated over the years. The resulting rapid increase in public debt was worrisome, jeopardizing the stability of the macroeconomic stance. Over the period 2008–12, public debt worsened by 13% points of GDP, reaching 60.3% of GDP in 2012.

It was the sharp fiscal crisis of 2012 that eventually forced the government to reform subsidies. The government reactivated the price indexation mechanism for fuel products, which helped cut subsidies by an impressive 24% (or almost 2% points of GDP) in 2013. This move, in turn, helped to reduce the budget deficit by 1.8% points of GDP. The full implementation of the fuel price-indexation mechanism and the subsidies reforms in 2014 contributed to cut further subsidies by almost 20% (or 1% point of GDP) by the end of the year. In addition, subsidies reforms were complemented by other fiscal consolidation measures. They included freezing higher wages and limits to new hires of civil servants to stop the rise of the

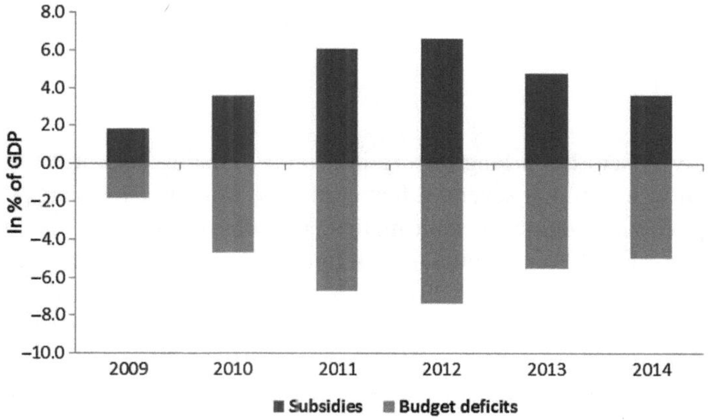

Fig. 3.5 Effects of subsidies changes on budget deficits, percent of GDP. *Source* Ministry of Economy and Finance 2009–14

public wage bill and improvements to the tax collection system through the extension of the tax base, harmonization of tax rates, and an effort to stop tax evasion. As a result, the budget deficit for 2014 was less than 5% of GDP as targeted by the 2014 budget law. The central government debt increased in 2014, but at a slower pace than in earlier years (66.4% of GDP compared to 63.9% of GDP in 2013).

Despite the government's commitment to deepen the subsidies reforms, addressing the remaining subsidies on LPG and flour seems uncertain over the short term, given the social and political cost. Indeed, unlike gasoline and diesel, which are mostly consumed by the nonpoor, the shares of LPG and flour are important in the consumption baskets of the poor and the low-middle class. Over the medium term, the government might proceed with a progressive reform of LPG subsidies given the weight of these subsidies on the budget. Because subsidies for LPG mostly benefit the nonpoor in absolute terms, the government is trying to find a way to reduce the number of beneficiaries. In this case, the depth of the LPG reform would depend on the size of the targeted population. Until this reform takes place, the government is considering limiting the use of LPG only to households and excluding the agriculture sector. It is also trying to put in place a restitution mechanism like that for sugar to allow recovering the subsidy amounts received by some service activities, such as restaurants and hotels that use LPG. As for flour, the government is trying to further improve its targeting to the poor, especially in rural areas.

The most recent decline in oil prices, which is being followed by price declines in major commodities, is both an opportunity and a constraint to further reforms. It is an opportunity because eliminating subsidies on the remaining subsidized petroleum products (LPG and diesel) results in a reduced impact on consumption prices. It is a constraint because low oil prices reduce the amount of subsidies and the pressure on the budget and therefore the political will to reduce subsidies further.

Conclusion

The subsidy system has a long history in Morocco, dating back to World War II. The system went through several different phases, from an export supporting system, to a price stabilization mechanism, to a pure subsidies system. The most recent evolution of oil and commodities prices forced the government to push through subsidies reforms in 2013 and 2014 with the elimination of subsidies on most products and the increase in prices on the remaining products, except for LPG, sugar, and flour.

The 2013 and 2014 reforms have been effective in reducing the budget deficit while protecting the most vulnerable parts of the population. The evaluation of the 2014 subsidy reforms has shown that the government has made a set of proper choices from a distributional and budget perspective. Subsidies have been eliminated on those products, such as gasoline, that favored the rich and affected poverty the least, and the reform of products that would hurt the poor the most, such as LPG, has been delayed. Electricity tariffs have been increased in a sensible way by raising the number of blocks (and therefore reducing the consumers' surplus) and by raising tariffs only on the upper blocks, protecting the poorest consumers. The 2014 reforms had important indirect effects, particularly for gasoline and diesel, and these reforms had an impact on poverty, although they did not seem to create a significant social backlash.

Further reforms, particularly for LPG, require more complex interventions that will probably imply some form of targeting mechanism to protect the poor. Starting from the situation that Morocco faced in October 2014, we modeled the total elimination of subsidies, which implied the removal of subsidies on LPG, electricity, flour, and sugar. Our estimations showed that the government can save an additional DH 23.5 billion in direct subsidies, but they also showed these measures would result in a significant increase in poverty. Some form of compensation to the poor may be necessary to push through the total elimination of all subsidies.

The latest global decline in oil prices has dramatically reduced the pressure for further reforms, but also provides an opportunity to lift subsidies during a period when doing so would result in minor price increases. Time will tell whether the government of Morocco will continue to push through with the announced gradual reforms for electricity and LPG, therefore exploiting the opportunity provided by low oil prices, or avoid taking any political risk linked to subsidies removal profiting from the decreased budget pressure.

Acknowledgements The authors are grateful to Abdoul Gadiry-Barry for preparing the data and to Jean-Pierre Chauffour for useful comments on the final draft. All simulations have been carried out with SUBSIM (see www.subsim.org)

Annex 3.1: Major historical landmarks of Morocco's subsidy system

Date	Measures/reforms
Prior to 1941	Six equalization funds (sugar, iron, fuel, eggs, wood, vegetables)
1941	Creation of the subsidy fund (Caisse de Compensation, CDC)
1941	Subsidies for flour, bread, edible oils, fats
1942	Subsidies for coal
1944	Subsidies for transportation of barley and corn
1945	Subsidies for sugar and canned milk, transportation of fresh milk
1946	Removal of subsidies for transportation of barley and corn Subsidies for farm equipment, seeds and fertilizers

(continued)

(continued)

Date	Measures/reforms
1947	One-time subsidies for cotton cultivation for one year
1948	One-time subsidies for wheat seed for farmers
1949	One-time subsidies for legume seeds
1949	Decision to cancel the CDC; decision not applied.
1952	Introduction of a policy of encouraging milk production by subsidizing cooperatives
1953	Creation of edible oils equalization fund
1955	Subsidies for petroleum products Premiums paid to the freezing of lamb Subsidies for industries of textiles, glassware, weaponry, tanneries, cold storage
January 1959	Reimbursement of export costs carried by certain handicrafts: slippers, wool carpets, hand-made carpets
1959	Subsidies to cover operating deficits of North African coal company
June 30, 1966	Removal of subsidies to export of handicrafts
1967	Creation of the BARS (procurement office of the Sahara) to be responsible for the logistics of administering subsidies for oil, sugar, and flour for the Saharan provinces
1971	Removal of subsidies for operating imbalances of North African coal company
August 1972	Subsidies to butter
September 1, 1973	Subsidy to milk producers
December 1, 1973	Subsidies to edible oils
1974	Subsidies to fertilizers Subsidies to packaging of edible oils Subsidies to jet fuel for charters and to the national air companies (RAM)
1975	Removal of subsidies to industries
April 28, 1975	Subsidies to cement
1977	Subsidies to jet fuel intended for cargo flights to transport perishable goods
1981	Subsidies on a year of diesel used by farmers
1982	Removal of subsidies for butter
1983	Removal of subsidies for milk, except milk powder
1986	Liberalization of cement prices
June 1989	Suppression of subsidies for edible oil packaging
July 1, 1990	Liberalization of the fertilizer sector
December 1994	Suppression of subsidies to jet fuel for the RAM and air transport companies
January 1995	Introduction of a system of price indexation of petroleum products
1999	Introduction of a restitution system for sugar subsidies benefiting industries
November 1, 2000	Removal of subsidies for edible oils

(continued)

(continued)

Date	Measures/reforms
2000	Suspension of the price indexation system for petroleum products
August 8, 2005	Suppression of subsidies allocated to jet fuel intended for cargo flights
February 28, 2006	Cancellation of the restitution system of sugar subsidies for industries of chocolate, biscuit, confectionery, ice cream, and milk derivatives, and factory-made pastries
March 7, 2006	Introduction of a lump-sum subsidy for raw sugar import
August 1, 2006	Suppression of subsidies to kerosene
June 1, 2008	Subsidies for diesel used by coastal fishing
December 31, 2008	Decrease in sugar refund rates for soft drink industries
2008	Subsidies to special fuel oil used in the generation of electricity by ONEE
July 2011	Subsidies for diesel used by high-sea fishing
July 1, 2012	Removal of subsidies of high-sea fishing
January 1, 2014	Subsidies to cover VAT on the cost of transportation of butane gas (LPG)
September 16, 2013	Resumption of the price indexation system for liquid petroleum products (gasoline, diesel 50 ppm, and industrial fuel oil)
February 1, 2014	Removal of subsidies to gasoline and industrial fuel oil
February 16, 2014	Progressive decrease each quarter of unit subsidy for diesel
May 29, 2014	Removal of subsidies for fuel oil used for generating electricity
January 1, 2015	Removal of subsidies to diesel

Source CDC

Note BARS = Bureau d'Approvisionnement des Régions Sahariennes; ppm = parts per million; RAM = Royal Air Maroc; VAT = value added tax

References

CDC (*Caisse de Compensation*). http://cc.gov.ma/.

HCP Morocco (High Commission for the Plan). www.hcp.ma.

IMF (International Monetary Fund). 2013. *Energy subsidies reforms: lessons and implications*. Washington, DC: International Monetary Fund.

Ministry of Economy and Finance. 2009–14. *Notes de Conjonctures, 2009–2014, Direction du Trésor et des Finances Exterieures*. Morocco.

OPEC (Organization of the Petroleum Exporting Countries). 2014. *Who gets what from imported oil?* www.opec.org, September.

Author Biographies

Paolo Verme is a senior economist at the World Bank. A Ph.D. graduate of the London School of Economics, he was a visiting professor at Bocconi University in Milan (2004–09) and at the University of Turin (2003–10) before joining the World Bank in 2010. For almost two decades, he has served as adviser and project manager for multilateral organizations, private companies, and governments on labor market, welfare, and social protection policies. His research is widely published in international journals, books, and reports, and he has worked extensively on subsidies in the MENA Region and elsewhere. He is the coauthor of the subsidies simulation model SUBSIM (www.subsim.org).

Khalid El-Massnaoui has been working with the World Bank since 2003 as a senior economist based in Morocco. He works mainly on macroeconomic, fiscal, and public sector management topics. He has also contributed to the discussions and analytical work on subsidy reform program in Morocco. He is currently the country economist for Libya. Prior to joining the World Bank, Khalid worked in the Ministry of Planning in Morocco since 1980, with a focus on macroeconomic and fiscal policies, modeling, and analysis. Khalid has a M.A. degree in applied economics from the University of Michigan, Ann Arbor (1989) and holds an engineer degree in statistics and applied economics from the Institut National de Statistiques et d'Economie Appliquée, Rabat, Morocco (1980).

Chapter 4
The Socioeconomic Impacts of Energy Reform in Tunisia: A Simulation Approach

Jose Cuesta, Abdel-Rahmen El Lahga and Gabriel Lara Ibarra

Introduction

Tunisia's improvements in monetary poverty have not translated into substantive reductions in disparities and unequal opportunities across individuals and regions. Poverty incidence declined from 35% in 2000 to 15% in 2010 (INS, BAD, and World Bank 2012). Rapid growth rates and generous universal subsidies, especially on energy, food, and transport, contributed to that successful poverty reduction, but did not have a similar effect on reducing inequalities. Despite the halving of poverty rates, the Gini coefficient fell only from 0.344 to 0.327 during the same period—a two percentage point effect 10 times smaller than that observed for poverty. Furthermore, drops in inequality were observed *within* regions, while inequality *across* regions increased leading to the concentration of extreme poverty in the typically less well-off western regions increased to 70% in 2010. In the midst of rapid economic growth and significant poverty reduction, the lack of equal economic opportunities may have contributed to the massive protests that ousted President Ben Ali from power in Tunisia and ignited political uprisings in other parts of North Africa and the Middle East (MENA).

Subsidies are integral to the story of growth, poverty, and disparities in the MENA Region, and Tunisia's tale is no different. IMF (2014) explains that the generalized price subsidies constitute a critical foundation of the social compact in MENA countries, acting as a deliberate cornerstone of social protection. However, those same subsidies can also introduce relative price distortions that typically

J. Cuesta (✉)
UNICEF Office of Research, Florence, Italy

A.-R. El Lahga
Université de Tunis, Tunis, Tunisia

G. Lara Ibarra
The World Bank, Washington, DC, USA

P. Verme and A. Araar (eds.), *The Quest for Subsidy Reforms in the Middle East and North Africa Region*, Natural Resource Management and Policy 42,
DOI 10.1007/978-3-319-52925-4_4

provoke the following situations: overconsumption and underinvestment in subsidized sectors, the crowding out of more productive investments, delays in economic diversification, weaker current accounts and increasing budget deficits, and adverse effects on health and the environment.

In Tunisia subsidies constitute a core aspect of its development model (World Bank 2013). Subsidies are pervasively present in critically productive sectors such as agriculture, energy, and tourism. The current social protection model relies on untargeted food and energy subsidies, which have been proven to be unequitable and increasingly expensive. As noted in the next section, subsidies represented some 7% of gross domestic product (GDP) in Tunisia in 2013, but the bottom 40% of the distribution captured only 29% of energy subsidies and 34% of food subsidies (World Bank 2014). This failure to protect the poorest is widely acknowledged in the country, including by the postrevolution government (Government of Tunisia 2014), and is generally believed to have contributed to past social tensions (World Bank 2013). There are also concerns in terms of governance and transparency. As illustration, there are no precise estimates of any hidden subsidies for oil and natural gas generated by the national oil company selling imported crude oil and natural gas at a fraction of international prices to state-owned companies (IMF 2014).

Fiscal and equity concerns have prompted the government of Tunisia to consider changes in its subsidy policy, particularly for energy. The new proposal forms part of a larger scheme of social protection reform that aims to improve the targeting of public spending. Detailed proposals have not yet been publicly discussed, but the government has announced its intention to partially remove electricity subsidies and completely eliminate other energy subsidies. In this context of uncertainty regarding subsidy reform by a recently elected administration, this chapter provides an analysis of the distributive impacts of a hypothetical subsidy reform similar to the reform the Tunisian government is considering.

This analysis follows an earlier distributional study of energy subsidies in Tunisia using SUBSIM, a subsidy reform simulation methodology developed by Araar and Verme (2012). This chapter, however, makes two contributions to the earlier analysis. First, it updates existing estimates (reported in World Bank 2013) by including the most recent structure of energy prices and the most recent proposal of subsidy changes considered by the Tunisian government. Second, this analysis includes a detailed simulation of the distributional effects of alternative compensating cash transfer schemes financed from the fiscal savings accruing from the subsidy reform.

To convey the implications of the reforms, the chapter starts with the evolution of energy subsidies in Tunisia. The next two sections provide an outline of the current structure of energy subsidies and report the most updated information on the socioeconomic patterns of energy subsidies; that is, how consumption, spending, and subsidy benefits of residential energy differ across different socioeconomic groups. Following is an analysis of the distributive impacts of a simulated subsidy reform that partially removes residential electricity subsidies and fully removes those of diesel, gasoline, and liquefied petroleum gas (LPG). It separates direct and indirect effects and reports both distributional and fiscal effects. The impacts of fiscally neutral policies are estimated using current and new targeting mechanisms to compensate for the immediate negative welfare effects following the hypothesized subsidy reform. The final section concludes with a review of the three proposed scenarios and their impacts on poverty and inequalities.

Evolution of Energy Subsidies in Tunisia

Tunisia has a long tradition of generous energy and food subsidies. Subsidies deliberately became the backbone of the country's new social protection strategies of the 1970s. At that time, advocates justified the universal subsidies because of the large size of the informal sector, the high levels of poverty, and the lack of information systems and registries to identify and target the poor. Energy subsidies have not been reformed in depth since that time. In the early 1980s, however, Tunisia went through a painful experience reforming its food subsidies. In 1983 food subsidies reached 3% of GDP, with reported significant leaks to the nonpoor. Overnight, the government announced the doubling of prices of cereals and their products, including bread, semolina, pasta, and couscous (IMF 2014). The rushed decision took the public by surprise, and after a month of widespread protests, the reform was abandoned. Later, during the Ali regime, the government did not attempt any in-depth reform of the subsidy systems in place since the 1970s, managing instead to maintain the generous system throughout both difficult and prosperous times. During 1991–93, the government launched a gradual reform on food subsidies, favoring foods largely consumed by the poor—such as lower-quality bread—and phasing out subsidies on foods consumed by the rich (IMF 2014). A well-timed awareness campaign coupled with increases in minimum wages and strengthening of other social protection programs helped improve the targeting and fiscal burden of food subsidies (IMF 2014).

During the final years of the Ali regime and the recent postrevolution period, the spending and composition of Tunisia's subsidies have notably changed (Fig. 4.1). During the last 10 years, the combined spending on energy, food, and transportation has more than tripled, rising from 2% of GDP in 2005 to 7% in 2013. Energy subsidies, in particular, increased fourfold during that period. Energy subsidies reached 4.7% of GDP in 2013, with sustained increases since 2010, reflecting the partial (rather than the full) pass-through of international oil prices to domestic prices sought by the government (IMF 2014). Regarding the composition of subsidies, during the postrevolution period, energy subsidies increased both in absolute and relative terms. As a result, energy subsidies went from one-third of total public subsidies prior to the revolution to about two-thirds in 2013. In contrast, food and other basic needs' subsidies have lost relative weight in the total subsidy bill despite having notably increased in absolute terms. With respect to other public expenditures, energy subsidies in Tunisia accounted for one-fifth of all public spending, or 7% of the GDP in 2013, the latest available figure. Because they are considered the backbone of the social protection strategy, it is not surprising that public spending on subsidies exceeds that of social assistance, health, and education, and individual programs for youth, children, or women (Fig. 4.2).

The changes in the composition and magnitude of subsidies reflect recent specific changes in the policy of energy subsidies. In effect, after the immediate and deliberate use of subsidies to appease postrevolution social tensions, the government of Tunisia began implementing a gradual strategy of subsidy reduction and improvement in public spending targeting. As reported by the IMF (2014), the prices of gasoline, diesel, and electricity increased by 7% in September 2012, followed by similar increases in March 2013. Energy subsidies to cement companies were halved in January 2014 and fully removed in June. Electricity tariffs on low- and medium-voltage consumers were increased in a two-step process, by 10% in January 2014 and another 10% in May. The government introduced a lifeline electricity tariff for households consuming less than 100 kWh per month in 2014. Also in January 2014 the government established a new automatic price formula for gasoline to align domestic price convergence to international prices over time, but without a smoothing mechanism or a clear calendar. In parallel, the government launched a new social housing program, increased income tax deductions for the poorest households, and committed to creating a unified registry of beneficiaries of social programs and to improving social spending targeting (to be finished in 2015). In addition, plans are also in the works to expand the current cash transfer program (PNAFN) to 250,000 beneficiaries and to reduce its exclusion errors.

This brief history of energy subsidies in Tunisia shows that the country is striving to achieve a difficult balance. That balance aims to improve fiscal and equity concerns by reducing subsidies, while also trying to appease social tensions by maintaining subsidies as a cornerstone of its social protection strategy. The transition administration has attempted to maintain that balance through a progressive reduction of subsidies that started well into the postrevolution period and by beginning an expansion of a social protection system less reliant on subsidies.

Not pursuing a more ambitious future energy subsidy reform would represent a big missed opportunity for Tunisian development. According to the IMF, Tunisia is the only country in the MENA Region that has made progress in most of the areas necessary for successful reform in both the MENA Region and elsewhere during the last 30 years (Table 4.1).[1] In effect, IMF (2014) argues that the changes observed in energy subsidies since 2012 have benefited from a gradual pace of adjustment and comprehensive coverage; that is, changes have affected all energy sources and have successively increased all energy prices. Because of fiscal and equity concerns, the Tunisian government supports the reversal of energy subsidies, a position also supported without reservation by international financial institutions. The transition government has included several compensation mechanisms to

[1]IMF (2014) analyzes 25 reforms of fuel and food subsidies in 15 countries across five continents between 1983 and 2012.

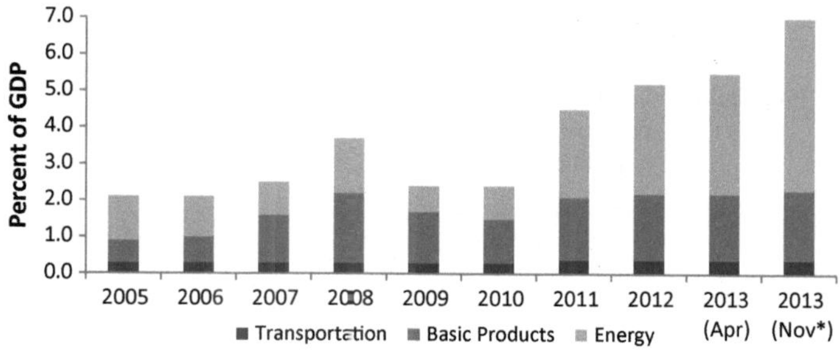

Fig. 4.1 Evolution of the composition and level of subsidies by type, 2005–13. *Source* World Bank calculations using data from Ministère des Finances, October 2013. *Note* Basic products refer to food products such as cereals, bread, sugar, and vegetable oil; * forecast

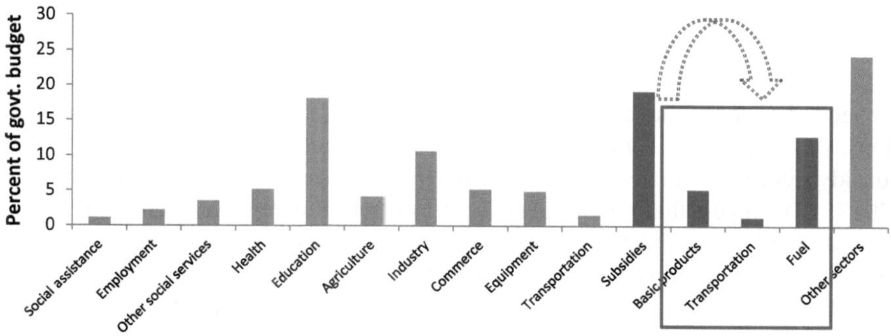

Fig. 4.2 Public spending by sector, including subsidies, percent of 2013 GDP. *Source* World Bank staff calculations using data from Tunisian Ministère des Finances, October 2013. *Note* Education includes all levels; subsidies refer to explicit subsidies; social assistance includes cash transfer programs and health cards; other social services includes programs and services of the Ministère des Affaires Sociales, de la Jeunesse, and de la Femme et l'Enfance; health does not include health insurance. Subsidies are further disaggregated into three categories, basic products, transportation, and energy

smooth the effect of the subsidies' removal. No other country in the MENA Region has initiated subsidy reforms of such breadth.

The progress made so far on multiple aspects of a successful reform raises the question of why a more decisive energy subsidy overhaul has not already taken place: the answer is that several factors are in play. First, even though the universal subsidy system was partly justified as a social protection mechanism, it was also designed to protect and strengthen the competitiveness of local firms by providing them with cheap energy sources. These noncompetitive enterprises, which employ unskilled workers and depend largely on government support through energy subsidies and generous tax exemptions, may not survive if subsidies are eliminated. World Bank (2014) provides a detailed account of the complex economic, financial, and governance factors associated with generalized subsidies across noncompetitive sectors of the Tunisian economy.

Table 4.1 Implementation status of most recent subsidy reforms in the Middle East and North Africa region

	Preparation	Gradual pace of adjustment	Breadth of reform	Consensus building and communication strategy	Role of partners	Mitigating measures
Egypt, Arab Rep.	✓	–	–	–	✓	✓
Jordan	✓	✓	✓	✓	✓	✓
Mauritania	✓	✓	✓	✓	✓	✓
Morocco	✓	✓	✓	✓	✓	✓
Sudan	✓	–	–	–	✓	✓
Tunisia	✓	✓	✓	✓	✓	✓
Yemen, Rep.	✓	–	–	–	✓	✓

Source IMF (2014, 48)

Second, reforms have not only economic, financial, and governance implications, but also marked welfare implications. Whether deliberately sought or not, subsidy reforms generate a pattern of winners and losers. Estimates by World Bank (2013, 17) suggest that a more decisive reform of all energy subsidies—along the lines currently conceived by the government of Tunisia—would have costly and increasing welfare impacts, around 3% of household consumption in the short run and about 5% in the long run.[2] Such impacts—without a careful compensating strategy—do not create a large demand for reform among those currently benefiting from those subsidies.

Third, the failed attempt in the early 1980s and the lack of legitimacy of the previous authoritarian regime made an overhaul of subsidies difficult. The generous subsidy system combined with mass recruitment in the public service and periodic revisions of wages were the principal mechanisms for maintaining, at least partially, social peace and stability during the past regime. Similarly, the need to maintain social stability in the onset of the postrevolution period also warned against a profound reform of the subsidy system, even though a national consensus in the face of the economic difficulties of 2011 emerged on the need to streamline subsidies' costs and ensure their fairness.

The final factor is the traditional lack of reliable and transparent estimates of the budgetary costs of subsidies, which further complicates the technical aspects of reforms, particularly a well-informed design of in-depth reform measures. For example, the actual budgetary cost (explicit subsidy) and the cost of inefficiency of refiners and electricity companies (implicit subsidies) are difficult to accurately

[2]The increasing effect on household consumption reflects the loss of production among non-competitive sectors of the economy that lose energy subsidies. See World Bank (2013) for a more detailed explanation.

estimate. According to World Bank (2013), implicit taxes from the generalized practice of the national oil company selling imported crude oil and natural gas at a fraction of international prices to state-owned companies may have exceeded two percentage points of GDP in 2012.

In this complex interplay of economic, fiscal, social, and political economy considerations, there is broad agreement on the need to reform the current system of energy subsidies. The next section provides a detailed outline of the current price, consumption, and subsidy structure.

Current Structure of Energy Subsidies in Tunisia

This analysis focuses on residential energy subsidies; that is, subsidies on electricity, gasoline, LPG, and diesel. As already noted, they constitute the lion's share of the total consumer subsidies funded by the government of Tunisia (two-thirds in 2013) and about 45% of the total consumption of energy among Tunisian households. These four energy subsidies are also among those that the government plans to reform.

The analysis will simulate the fiscal and distributive effects caused by changes in the current structure of energy prices and subsidies. The current structure was introduced in May 2014 and continues to be in effect at the time of this writing. The analysis uses consumption patterns in 2010 as reference because the household survey reporting households' energy spending—the 2010 *Enquête Nationale sur le Budget, la Consommation et les Conditions de Vie des Ménages* (ENBCV)—is the most recent available. The latest input-output matrix (I/O) for Tunisia is also for 2010. This I/O matrix enables estimation of the indirect effects of the reforms; that is, the effects on household consumption and spending accruing from the impacts that energy prices have on other productive sectors of the economy.

Household spending on energy and other products is then updated using successive rates of the annual consumer price index (CPI), GDP, and population growth to construct a distribution of energy spending for January 2014. The current energy tariff structures are applied to that distribution of household *spending* on energy to derive a distribution of household *consumption* on energy sources. It is on these distributions of spending and consumption constructed for 2014 that the subsidy reform is simulated and its distributive and fiscal effects estimated. The first step before beginning the simulation analysis is to look at a detailed outline of the current system of energy subsidies.

Structure of Residential Energy Prices

The current price structure for residential electricity consumption follows a two-tier system.[3] A different structure—the analysis of which is beyond the scope of this chapter—is applied to nonresidential users (which also differentiates between low- and high-tension use). Table 4.2 shows that for households consuming less than 200 kWh per month, a volume differentiated tariff (VDT) is applied to three consumption blocks and three distinctive prices apply: Tunisian dinar (TD) 0.075 per kilowatt hour, if consumption is 1–50 kWh; TD 0.108 per kilowatt hour (applied for all kilowatt hours consumed) if consumption is 51–100 kWh; and TD 0.140 per kilowatt hour if consumption is 101–200 kWh (also from the first kilowatt hour consumed). Households consuming more than 200 kWh per month are subject to an increasing blocks tariff (IBT) that includes multiple prices across different blocks of consumption. In this high-volume tier, TD 0.151 per kilowatt hour is charged for each of the initial 200 kWh consumed; TD 0.158 for each of the subsequent kilowatt hour in the 201–300 kWh block; TD 0.301 for the next 200 kWh block; and TD 0.501 per kilowatt hour for each of those kilowatt hours in excess of 500 kWh per month.

Based on this structure, both low-volume consumers—households consuming below 200 kW per month—and high-volume consumers face an increasing marginal cost from usage. High-volume consumers pay more than low-volume users for the first 200 kW and face increasing fees as their consumption rises. In this respect, the tariff structure is progressive: those consuming more pay higher marginal costs per kilowatt consumed. However, the pace at which marginal tariffs increase is not linear. If we take 50 kW increments in consumption, moving from a consumption level of 50–100 kW, the price of the second 50 kW is 44% higher than for the first tranche (from TD 75 to 108 millimes) among low-volume consumers. For those consumers moving toward the highest block of the second tier; that is, moving from 301–500 kW to the 501 plus kilowatt block, the residential tariff increase is TD 25% or 70 millimes. In short, nonlinear features (in terms of marginal prices per additional consumption) are combined across different segments of the two-tier system, making the system far from progressive in its entirety.

The pro-poor nature of the system depends on the concentration of consumers who are considered poor in the lower price blocks of each tier. In this light, the system falls short in benefiting the less well-off population: the concentration of poor consumers—specifically those in the bottom quintile of per capita household consumption—in the lifeline block is only 48% (Appendix 2). The share of consumers in the lifeline block rapidly declines for subsequent quintiles of the distribution. In turn, the concentration of consumers from the richest quintile ranges from 35 to 60% of all users in the high-volume consumption tier. Consumers from the

[3]The price structure described here became effective on May 1, 2014. The previous tariff structure, valid between January and April 2014, had slightly lower fees for the highest consumption block of the first tier, as well as for the second tier of residential consumption. Appendix 1 details the previous structure.

Table 4.2 Electricity tariff structure for low-tension residential consumers (valid since May 1, 2014)

Fee	Voltage (millimes/kVa/month)	Price of energy by monthly consumption bracket (millimes/kWh)					
		1–50	51–100	101–200	201–300	301–500	501+
Economic (1 and 2 kVa and consumption under 200 kWh)	500	75					
		108					
		140					
Economic (1 and 2 kVa and consumption over 200 kWh); normal (>2 kVa)	500	151			184	280	350
						250	295

Source Societé Tunisienne d'Eletricité et du Gaz 2014
Note Prices are in TD millimes and before taxes. kWh = kilowatt hour; kVa = kilo-volt-amperes or 1000 V amps

poorest quintile are hardly represented in the high-volume tier: only 3–6% of consumers belong to the poorest quintile. In other words, the poor represent a minimal proportion of consumers of the higher-volume tier, but more surprisingly, they are not the vast majority of beneficiaries of the lifeline price rates either.

The prices of other energy sources are not subject to differentiated price segments. The prices of gasoline, LPG, and diesel do not vary across consumption levels. The market price of gasoline is TD 1.67 per liter; the price of 0.2 diesel (containing 0.2% of sulfur) is TD 1.25 per liter; and a 13 kg cylinder of LPG costs TD 7.4 (or TD 0.57 per kg).[4] As indicated already for the case of electricity, the pro-poor measure of the distribution of those energy subsidies is determined by both the price structure and the extent to which these energy products are consumed by the poor. Yet the price structure is not progressive in marginal terms, because the price does not increase as consumption increases. In absolute terms, higher-volume consumers benefit from a higher public subsidy, making those subsidies not pro-poor.

Estimating Energy Subsidies

Most energy sources are publicly subsidized in Tunisia, but to different extents.[5] Based on the observed final—market—prices, price structures, international prices (of imported sources), and local production costs, it is possible to calculate shares of

[4]This type of cylinder is typically used by households. Larger cylinders of 25–35 kg are most frequently consumed in the hospitality/tourism industry.

[5]From a public finance perspective, the latest data available for both residential and nonresidential consumers in 2013 indicate that some 51% of total energy subsidies go to finance electricity subsidies; 23% to diesel; 15% to LPG; 6% to gasoline; 5% to crude oil; and 1% to kerosene (World Bank 2013).

subsidized prices for each energy source. Box 4.1 summarizes the methodology used to calculate to such shares.

Box 4.1: Estimating Shares of Subsidized Prices
For energy products consumed by the household—electricity, LPG, gasoline, and diesel—a subsidy level "S" for each product is estimated using the price-gap approach. According to this approach, a first price is calculated by adding to the international reference price (IP) all local taxes and domestic distribution costs. The resulting price is assumed to reflect the cost of efficient market supply, given the conditions and regulations of a given country and international prices. This price is called the *nonsubsidized price* (NP). Subsidies (S) are calculated as the difference between the estimated NP and the observed domestic sale price, or market price (DP): $S_i = NP_i - DP_i$, where *i* refers to each energy source for residential consumption. The subsidy rate SR_i for source *i* is the ratio of S_i to NP_i. In the case of Tunisia, domestic prices used in this analysis are from the Ministry of Finance, and the IPs were obtained from the Ministry of Industries (Direction Générale de l'Énergie) for electricity, LPG, gasoline, and diesel, respectively.

Sources Araar and Verme (2012); World Bank (2013).

Table 4.3 presents the rate of subsidized energy prices with respect to the observed market prices since May 2014. The rate of subsidized LPG prices is estimated at 68% of the nonsubsidized price. In other words, for every liter of LPG consumed at a final price of TD 0.570, some TD 1.220 have been subsidized from the estimated price of TD 1.790 (reflecting international reference prices). Likewise, a similar calculation shows shares of subsidized prices of 10% for gasoline and 21% for diesel. In the case of electricity, the subsidized rates for each block decrease with consumption. This is the case for the two-volume tiers. In fact, the two top consumption blocks of the high-volume tier—consumers of more than 300 kW per month—receive negative subsidies; that is, they are net contributors to the subsidies of consumers of lower-volume consumption. Consumers from the two levels of highest consumption end up paying a higher price than the international reference price plus taxes and distribution costs.

In the case of LPG, the latest available numbers are from 2013[6] (Table 4.4) and show a subsidy rate of 68%. In fiscal terms, these subsidies amounted to TD 749 million, 15% of all energy subsidies publicly transferred and 1% of GDP. Diesels (containing either 0.005 or 0.2% of sulfur) have subsidies between 16 and 26% of final prices, respectively, which represented 1.5% of GDP, 23% of energy subsidies, and TD 1146 million in 2013. The energy source most highly subsidized in terms of public spending was electricity, with 3.4% of GDP, 51% of all energy subsidies, and more than TD 2.5 billion a year (in 2013). Its subsidized

[6]Nevertheless, LPG prices have remained unchanged since February 2010.

Table 4.3 Estimated subsidy rates for energy sources in Tunisia (valid May 2014)

	Nonsubsidized price (NP_i), TD	Subsidy (S_i), TD	Subsidy rate ($SR_i = S_i/NP_i$), percent	Market price, ($DP_i = NP_i - S_i$), TD
Gasoline	1.856	0.185	10	1.670
LPG	1.790	1.220	68	0.570
Diesel	1.584	0.334	21	1.250
Electricity: Households consuming less than 200 kWh per month				
Electricity 0–50	0.268	0.193	72	0.075
Electricity 0–100	0.268	0.160	60	0.108
Electricity 0–200	0.268	0.123	47	0.140
Electricity: Households consuming more than 200 kWh per month				
Electricity 0–200	0.268	0.117	43	0.151
Electricity 201–300	0.268	0.084	31	0.184
Electricity 301–500	0.268	−0.012	−4	0.280
Electricity >500	0.268	−0.082	−31	0.350

Source World Bank staff calculations
Note DP_i = market price of each energy source *i*; kWh = kilowatt hour; NP_i = nonsubsidized price of the energy source *i*; S_i = subsidy of energy source *i*; SR_i = subsidy rate of energy source *i*; TD = Tunisian dinar

price share oscillated between 27 and 50%. The remaining 12% of energy subsidies were distributed among gasoline, kerosene, and heavy fuel.

At the level of residential spending for energy, other forms commonly utilized by households, such as charcoal, natural gas, or solid biofuels are not subsidized.[7] Within the household sector, solid biofuels constitute the main source of energy expenditure (42%), followed by LPG (18%), electricity (15%), and natural gas (10%). Diesels and gasoline are very low sources of energy expenditures. Also, as the next section shows, there are marked differences in consumption and spending by socioeconomic groups.

[7]In addition, the consumption of each energy source and, therefore, the ultimate beneficiaries of the subsidized prices vary substantially by sector, as shown in Appendix 3. Figures reported in Appendix 3 refer to 2012, the latest available for the composition of consumption within each sector, residential and nonresidential.

Table 4.4 Total public spending on energy subsidies, selected energy sources

Indicator	LPG	Gasoline	Diesel (50 ppm)	Diesel 0.2%	Electricity
Subsidy rate (percent)	68	15	16	62	27/50
Total consumption at sale price (TD million)	225	884	230	103	2169
Price increase estimated from elimination of subsidies (percent)	214	23	22	165	30
Expenditures					
Amount (TD million)	483	199	50	170	1671
As a percent of GDP	0.7	0.3	0.07	0.2	2.4
Amount estimated end of 2013 (TD million)	749	321	75	214	2569
As a percent of GDP	1	0.4	0.1	0.3	3.4

Source World Bank calculations using data from Ministère des Finances and Ministère de l'Industrie

Note All data are from April 2013 unless otherwise noted. April 2013 GDP in 2012 prices estimated at 70,400 million. *TD* Tunisian dinars; *GDP* Gross domestic product; *ppm* Parts per million

Socioeconomic Profile of Energy Subsidies

Previous sections have discussed the complex structure of energy prices (in terms of progressivity) and the estimated subsidy rates underlying current price structures. To determine the extent to which such price and subsidy structures lead to pro-poor welfare outcomes, the consumption of different socioeconomic groups, their expenditures, and their benefits from subsidies all need to be factored in. First, consumption and spending on energy will be disaggregated by socioeconomic group. This socioeconomic analysis covers both Tunisian individuals and households grouped by their consumption levels in quintiles. Quintile 1 refers to the poorest individuals and households, and quintile 5 refers to the richest.

Residential Consumption and Expenditures on Energy

Panels a and b in Table 4.5 show that *total* consumption of energy across quintiles varies by energy sources. Richer quintiles consume more energy, with significantly large differences for gasoline and diesel between these quintiles and the rest. Consumption by the richest two quintiles represents 80 and 90% of the consumption of diesel and gasoline, respectively. The poorest 40% consumes 2 and 8% of the total consumption of these two sources, respectively. For the other energy sources, the distribution of consumption across quintiles is not so skewed: the share

Table 4.5 Total residential energy consumption, by source and quintiles of household consumption

(a) Absolute terms

Quintile	Gasoline (million liters)	LPG (1000s tons)	Diesel (million liters)	Electricity (GWh)
1 (poorest)	1	80	1	587
2	5	99	4	761
3	18	107	8	881
4	54	122	12	1033
5 (richest)	213	114	37	1440
Total	292	521	63	4702

(b) Relative terms (in percent)

Quintile	Gasoline	LPG	Diesel	Electricity
1 (poorest)	0.3	15.3	1.6	12.5
2	1.7	18.9	6.8	16.2
3	6.3	20.5	12.9	18.7
4	18.7	23.4	19.4	22.0
5 (richest)	73.0	21.9	59.4	30.6
Total	100	100	100	100

Source World Bank calculations using SUBSIM (subsidy simulations)
Note GWh = Gigawatt hour

of the poorest two quintiles' consumption of LPG and electricity represents 45–52 and 28–34%, respectively.

Similarly, when it comes to the per capita consumption of energy, the data in Table 4.6 unequivocally confirm that the top consumption quintiles, the richest quintiles, consume much more than the poorest quintiles. Consumption differences are largest for gasoline, followed by diesel (panel a). On average, an individual from quintile 5 consumes 200 times more gasoline than someone from the poorest quintile. That ratio is still a whopping 38–1 in the case of diesel. Much narrower differences are observed for electricity and LPG. A richer individual consumes 4.5 times more electricity and 1.4 times more LPG than an individual from the poorest household. Individuals from quintile 4 consume more LPG on average than anyone else in the distribution. When the analysis is conducted for households—rather than individuals—(panel b) very similar ratios and distributions are observed, confirming results for individuals.

In terms of expenditures, Fig. 4.3 shows that the expenditure of energy represents between 5 and 6% of households' total spending. In other words, energy spending as share of household total spending is similar across socioeconomic groups, without marked differences across quintiles. Despite being small, these differences are still interesting. In fact, it is the households in the poorest and richest quintiles that spend a higher proportion of their budgets on energy (just over 6% of

Table 4.6 Per capita and per household consumption of subsidized energy, in quantity

(a) Consumption per individual				
Quintile	Gasoline (l)	LPG (kg)	Diesel (l)	Electricity (kWh)
1 (poorest)	0.46	36.50	0.45	37.41
2	2.30	45.35	1.95	49.59
3	8.45	49.08	3.70	61.23
4	25.02	55.99	5.58	86.58
5 (richest)	97.74	52.39	17.07	167.20
Total	26.79	47.86	5.75	80.40
(b) Consumption per household				
Quintile	Gasoline (l)	LPG (kg)	Diesel (l)	Electricity (kWh)
1 (poorest)	2.53	200.75	2.47	205.75
2	11.5	226.75	9.75	247.95
3	38.02	220.86	16.65	275.53
4	100.08	223.96	22.32	346.32
5 (richest)	342.09	183.36	59.74	585.2
Total	107.16	191.44	23	321.6

Source World Bank calculations using SUBSIM

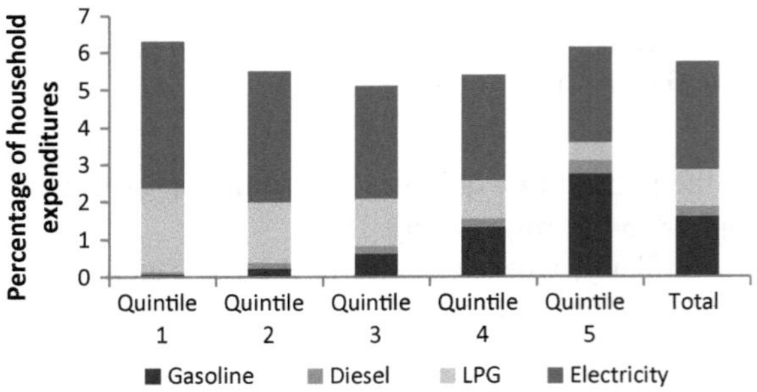

Fig. 4.3 Household expenditure on energy. *Source* World Bank staff calculations using SUBSIM (subsidy simulations)

their total spending). But while the poorest spent its largest share on electricity, the richest does so on gasoline.

Large differences become evident when absolute spending is compared across quintiles of the consumption distribution. Figure 4.4 shows that the richest individual spends more than 200 times per capita than a poor individual. Socioeconomic disparities in spending remain for diesel as well, but are notably reduced for electricity and LPG. In fact, spending on LPG is more uniform across all socioeconomic groups, between TD 20 and 29, and it is the fourth quintile that spends the most.

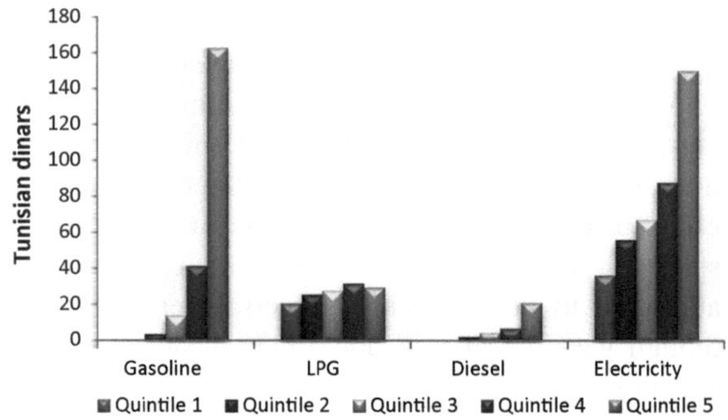

Fig. 4.4 Per capita expenditures on energy, in TD. *Source* World Bank staff calculations using SUBSIM (subsidy simulations). *Note TD* Tunisian dinar

Socioeconomic Distribution of Energy Subsidy Benefits

The distribution of monetized benefits accruing from subsidies is the result of a number of considerations: the degree of price progressivity, the pro-poor nature of the price structure, the share of subsidized price of final price, and the composition and total consumption by socioeconomic group. It is not surprising that energy subsidies are concentrated on LPG and electricity subsidies. Moreover, the concentration of benefits from these two sources is true for all consumption quintiles (Table 4.7, panel a). This finding implies that all of the poor, the bottom 40%, and richer individuals obtain most of their energy subsidies from LPG and electricity. In relative terms, LPG and electricity represent 53.3 and 40.4% of total subsidies, shares that for the poorest quintile increase slightly to 54.5 and 42.2% of their total energy subsidies, respectively. For the rest of the quintiles, subsidies from both sources also capture the lion's share of total benefits. The distribution of total benefits by socioeconomic group, however, also shows that energy subsidies—either universal or targeted—favor the rich. The poorest quintile captured the lowest

Table 4.7 Composition of subsidies received by residential consumers

	Distribution across each quintile (%)					Distribution over all quintiles	
Quintile	Gasoline	Diesel	LPG	Electricity	Total	Total (millimes TD)	Total (%)
1 (poorest)	0.1	0.2	54.5	42.2	100	178	14.9
2	0.4	0.7	56.6	42.3	100	213	17.9
3	1.4	1.1	55.1	42.4	100	237	19.9
4	3.8	1.5	55.7	39.0	100	267	22.4
5 (richest)	13.3	4.2	46.8	35.8	100	298	25.0
Total	4.5	1.8	53.3	40.4	100	1192	100

Source World Bank staff calculations using SUBSIM (subsidy simulations)
Note TD Tunisian dinar

share of all benefits associated with energy subsidies, 14.9%, and the richest quintile captured 25% (Table 4.7, panel b).

When analyzed in per capita terms, all energy subsidies are found to be regressive. The absolute amount of subsidy benefits increases as individuals and households become richer. Table 4.8 reports the distribution of subsidies benefiting each socioeconomic group. By and large, results reflect inequalities in the consumption of energy sources across quintiles. In fact, differences may not be attributed to the different—universal versus targeted—nature of subsidies. Even though gasoline, diesel, and LPG subsidies are all universal, their distributional effects vary. LPG is the energy source with the largest subsidy benefits in absolute and relative terms for the poorest quintile and the bottom 40%: in fact, the LPG subsidies received by the population as a whole represent close to 60% of all benefits obtained from energy subsidies. But that is also true for the richer quintiles. So, even though LPG is the most pro-poor—or rather, the least prorich energy source—it is not particularly progressive in terms of subsidy benefits. Moreover, electricity subsidies, with their complex interplay of progressive and regressive features, do not perform differently from the LPG universal subsidy. Electricity subsidies constitute the second largest source of subsidy benefits for Tunisians, around 35–45%, with shares decreasing as individuals become richer.

Table 4.9 reports the shares that energy subsidy benefits represent on total household spending. Consistent with previous results, LPG and electricity subsidies are the largest contributors to household expenditures, which in the case of the poorest quintile represent a substantive 8.8% of total expenditures. This share of subsidy benefits over total household spending decreases along with expenditure levels, up to 2.4% of total spending for households in the top quintile. Gasoline and diesel do not represent any substantive share of total spending, yet they are larger for the richest rather than for the poorest quintiles. For all households, these two sources of subsidies represent about 0.2% of the total 3.9% of household expenditures transferred from energy subsidies.

Table 4.8 Per capita energy subsidy benefits, in TD

Quintile	Gasoline	Diesel	LPG	Electricity	Total
1 (poorest)	0.09	0.15	44.53	36.99	81.76
2	0.43	0.65	55.33	41.42	97.82
3	1.57	1.24	59.88	46.06	108.74
4	4.65	1.86	68.30	47.85	122.67
5 (richest)	18.18	5.70	63.91	48.89	136.69
Total	4.98	1.92	58.39	44.24	109.53

Source World Bank staff calculations using SUBSIM (subsidy simulations)
Note TD Tunisian dinar

Table 4.9 Energy subsidy benefits as percentage of total household expenditure

Quintile	Gasoline	LPG	Diesel	Electricity	Total
1 (poorest)	0.0	4.8	0.0	4.0	8.8
2	0.0	3.4	0.0	2.6	6.0
3	0.1	2.7	0.1	2.1	5.0
4	0.1	2.2	0.1	1.5	3.9
5 (richest)	0.3	1.1	0.1	0.8	2.4
Total	0.2	2.1	0.1	1.6	3.9

Source World Bank staff calculations using SUBSIM (subsidy simulations)

Simulating the Distributional Impacts of a Subsidy-Reducing Reform

The government of Tunisia has announced its intention to remove all subsidies associated with gasoline, diesel, and LPG, and to increase the prices of each tranche of electricity for residential consumers (Jomaa 2014). As of this writing, however, the specific and detailed proposal on the timing, sequence, and compensatory measures was still being discussed internally. Nevertheless, any reform proposal raises the question of what the expected poverty and distributional effects of such changes might be. This section reports the estimated effects of the simulated subsidy reform, but first explains the methodology to estimate those effects. The discussion then turns to the additional distributional effects of expanding cash transfers using the fiscal savings generated by the subsidy reform.

A Methodological Note on Simulations

Given the preliminary stage of the policy discussion, the estimations consider two effects. One is the direct effect of price increases following the partial or full removal of subsidies. Direct effects have unequivocal impacts on individual and household budgets proportional to the increase in prices. No immediate changes in consumption are assumed, which is consistent with limited substitutability among energy sources in the short run (due to both technical and financial reasons and, presumably, individual preferences). Everyone consumes as before, but at higher prices. This result implies that individuals and households will have fewer resources to purchase other goods and services. For poorer households, these goods and services may include the necessary minimum consumption basket reflected in the poverty line. Changes in prices are therefore equivalent to a proportional increase in the poverty line faced by the household (weighted by its relative composition in the basic consumption basket). The second effect considered is the indirect impact: the changes on prices of goods that result from energy price changes. The indirect effect captures the change in relative prices for the rest of the economy and therefore on the prices of the other components of the consumption basket. Price changes across sectors are estimated by applying the price changes of energy to final products that use energy as an intermediary input. Using the a 2010 I/O table for Tunisia, constructed by the INS (*Institut National de la Statistique*), a simple approximation of such economy-wide changes following energy price subsidies can be calculated.[8]

The analysis draws from the distribution of consumption and spending reported in the 2010 Household Budget and Expenditure Survey, the most recent survey. The 2010 structures of consumption and spending are then updated to January 2014 using growth rates, population growth, and the CPI. It is on those distributions that simulations of a hypothetical reform in 2014 are conducted. In other words, the distributive effects of the 2014 reform are applied to the households—and their consumption patterns—existing in 2014. Therefore, the analysis assumes that consumption patterns and their drivers, such as preferences, in 2010 are a good proxy for 2014 consumption patterns. Finally, poverty status is defined in this exercise around the official poverty lines established by the INS (*Institut National de la Statistique*), BAD (*Banque Africaine de Développement*), and the World Bank (2012) as the monetized cost of a food basket that ensures minimum caloric needs, further adjusted by nonfood needs.[9]

Spending and Consumption Impacts

Table 4.10 applies the described methodology. Panel a presents the monetary impact of price increases resulting from the removal of subsidies for gasoline, LPG, and diesel, and the partial reduction in electricity subsidies. Final results from this simulation are disaggregated between direct and indirect effects. The average *total* impact of this set of interventions on per capita terms is TD 109. The largest effect on consumption comes from the removal of LPG subsidies, followed by diesel, electricity, and gasoline. In effect, about 62% of all the reduction in consumption comes from the elimination of LPG subsidies.

By type of effects, direct effects represent two-thirds of the total aggregated effect, and indirect effects, the remaining one-third. By energy source, socioeconomic patterns differ between direct and indirect effects. Among direct effects

[8]Due to limits on space, the full set of results is not presented here, but is available from the authors upon request.

[9]The monetary cost of the food basket defines the extreme poverty line. This line is also adjusted by differences in cost of living for cities (*grandes villes*), medium-sized towns (*petites communes*), and rural areas (*zones non-communales*). The extreme poverty line based on food needs is further adjusted by adding the average spending of extreme poor households on nonfood items to come up with a "low" poverty line and by adding the average spending of nonextreme poor households on nonfood items for setting the "high" poverty line. This exercise uses the upper poverty lines. INS, BAD, and World Bank (2012) provides a detailed description of the construction of the total consumption aggregate.

Table 4.10 Impact of the reform on total per capita expenditures (by energy source and quintile of consumption, in TD)

(a) Total effects					
Quintile	Gasoline	LPG	Diesel	Electricity	All
Quintile 1	−1.9	−47.3	−5.9	−5.5	−60.5
Quintile 2	−3.7	−60.7	−10.3	−8.7	−83.5
Quintile 3	−6.3	−67.7	−14.7	−11.1	−99.7
Quintile 4	−11.1	−79.6	−19.8	−15.0	−125.5
Quintile 5	−28.1	−85.8	−36.2	−27.0	−177.1
Total	−10.2	−68.2	−17.4	−13.5	−109.3
(b) Direct effects					
Quintile	Gasoline	LPG	Diesel	Electricity	All
Quintile 1	−0.1	−44.5	−0.1	−3.7	−48.4
Quintile 2	−0.4	−55.3	−0.7	−5.6	−62.0
Quintile 3	−1.6	−59.9	−1.2	−6.8	−69.5
Quintile 4	−4.7	−68.3	−1.9	−8.8	−83.7
Quintile 5	−18.2	−63.9	−5.7	−15.1	−102.9
Total	−5.0	−58.4	−1.9	−8.0	−73.3
(c) Indirect effects					
Quintile	Gasoline	LPG	Diesel	Electricity	All
Quintile 1	−1.8	−2.8	−5.7	−1.8	−12.1
Quintile 2	−3.3	−5.4	−9.7	−3.1	−21.5
Quintile 3	−4.7	−7.8	−13.4	−4.4	−30.3
Quintile 4	−6.4	−11.3	−18.0	−6.2	−41.9
Quintile 5	−9.9	−21.9	−30.5	−12.0	−74.3
Total	−5.2	−9.8	−15.5	−5.5	−36.0

Source World Bank staff calculations using SUBSIM (subsidy simulations)

(panel b), it is the effect of LPG that once again has the largest impact on household consumption (four-fifths of all direct effects), followed by electricity, gasoline, and diesel. In contrast, it is the removal of diesel subsidies that has the largest indirect effect on consumption (43% of total indirect effects), followed by LPG, electricity, and gasoline (panel c).

Among quintiles, the total impact of the reform increases among richer households, with the largest differences across quintiles observed for gasoline. The differences are less marked for diesel and electricity and relatively close for LPG. The increasing impact on consumption among richer quintiles is also observed for both direct and indirect effects.

In relative terms, the impact of the reforms averages 4.7% of households' expenditures (Fig. 4.5). The magnitude of the impact decreases with household expenditure levels. It progressively declines from 6.7% of the poorest households' expenditures to 3.1% of the richest households' expenditures. Similar to the case in absolute terms (that is, in TD terms), it is the LPG subsidy reform that brings the largest relative impact on households' expenditures: some 3.2% of all households' expenditures.

Estimates of the impacts on poverty and inequality show an increase of 2.69% points in the incidence of poverty, which represents an increase of 17% in the incidence of poverty. Table 4.11 shows a Gini coefficient increase of 0.61% points, or a 1.7% increase in the prereform levels of inequality. A large portion of those changes in poverty result from direct effects, both in poverty and in inequality, and LPG is the largest contributor to poverty and inequality deterioration.

The increases in poverty and inequality following the reduction of subsidies imply some TD 817.5 million in fiscal savings (Table 4.12). Fiscal savings accrue disproportionally from the removal of subsidies in LPG (77% of all fiscal savings) and electricity (13%). Furthermore, the savings accruing from the removal of subsidies affecting the poorest quintile represent some 13% of all fiscal savings, a share that increases across quintiles, so that the savings accruing from removed benefits to the richest group represent 28% of the total savings. These shares are very similar to the proportions of benefits from subsidies that each socioeconomic group captured prior to the reform (Table 4.7). Given that these simulations do not introduce behavioral effects (only direct and indirect effects are allowed), fiscal savings from the elimination of subsidies for the most part reflect the initial socioeconomic distribution of subsidies.

Compensating Interventions to Energy Subsidy Reforms

The final step is to assess the poverty and distributional effects of spending the total savings from the energy subsidy reform on poverty-reducing purposes. Once again, there is no clear guidance from the government of Tunisia on how these compensation programs will be implemented. For that reason, this analysis considers three hypothetical scenarios. Simulation 1 uses total savings to provide a universal transfer to each Tunisian. This scenario is called "universal transfer" because it includes a transfer to every Tunisian without discrimination. Simulation 2, or "current targeting," uses the current social assistance program, the subsidized health cards, as the targeting mechanism. This label does not intend to judge the current capacity of subsidized cards to reach the poorest. Instead, it simply indicates that no additional targeting efforts take place and that authorities use existing structures to channel all the savings accruing from energy subsidy reforms. Finally, in simulation 3, "perfect targeting," all the savings are distributed exactly to those who are poor after the reform. This is an unrealistic and idealistic scenario that describes a situation in which all the poor after the reform are perfectly identified and compensated on a per capita basis. It is idealistic because it assumes perfect and costless targeting; in other words, no additional resources are needed to identify the poor and distribute cash benefits to them. Although these three scenarios vary in terms of implementation feasibility, they are useful in this context where no detailed plans are announced. These results provide information on the boundaries of the

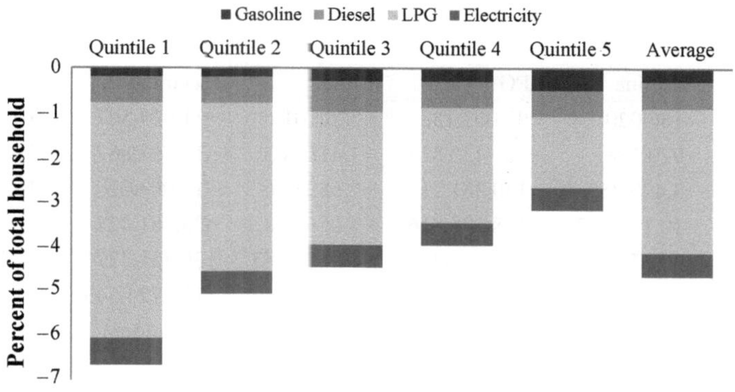

Fig. 4.5 Impact of reforms on households' expenditures. *Source* World Bank staff calculations using SUBSIM (subsidy simulations)

Table 4.11 Poverty and inequality impacts of energy reform

	Percentage points (pp)	Change in pp w/prereform		Percentage points (pp)	Change in pp w/prereform
Poverty prereform	**14.93**	–	**Gini prereform**	**35.81**	–
Gasoline	15.02	0.09	Gasoline	35.75	−0.06
LPG	16.84	1.91	LPG	36.43	0.62
Diesel	15.12	0.19	Diesel	35.82	0.01
Electricity	15.13	0.2	Electricity	35.83	0.02
Poverty postreform	**17.61**	**2.68**	**Gini postreform**	**36.42**	**0.61**
Misc. direct effect	–	1.95	*Misc. direct effect*	–	0.58

Source World Bank staff calculations using SUBSIM (subsidy simulations)
Note The reason that the prereform poverty and inequality rates are not the official rates for 2010 is that prices have all been updated for this specific exercise to 2013 prices, using growth rates and population growth rates. The poverty line has also been updated using CPI trends. Therefore, the starting point of this exercise is a poverty rate of 14.9 in 2013 rather than the 15.4% official estimate obtained in the 2010 original household budgetary survey. This adjustment enables comparisons across other countries analyzed in this book. However, the rest of the simulation exercise will be conducted using the 2010 household budgetary survey. A subsample of the 2010 survey is used and not the full sample of the original survey. In effect, it is a subsample of the original sample that is used to capture beneficiaries of the subsidized universal health care card. Even after re-weighting the subsample, the exact official poverty number of 15.4% could not be fully replicated—only a slim margin (15.3%). Similarly, the estimated prereform Gini of 36.5% differs slightly from the official 35.8% from the full sample (Table 4.13)

distributional effects of the reform—from no compensation following the reform to the complete use of fiscal savings from energy subsidy reform to reduce poverty under perfect targeting. The true impact of the reform and of feasible compensation

Table 4.12 Energy subsidy savings from the reform by source and quintile of consumption, in TD

Quintile	Gasoline	LPG	Diesel	Electricity	Total
1 (poorest)	−186,020	−97,003,152	−325,901	−11,624,507	−109,139,584
2	−929,258	−120,432,824	−1,418,063	−16,163,867	−138,944,016
3	−3,420,753	−130,381,216	−2,689,996	−19,003,020	−155,494,992
4	−10,129,942	−148,695,856	−4,054,068	−23,481,422	−186,361,280
5 (richest)	−39,575,064	−139,133,344	−12,414,583	−36,451,727	−227,574,720
Total	−54,241,036	−635,646,400	−20,902,610	−106,724,543	−817,514,560

Source World Bank staff calculations using SUBSIM (subsidy simulations)
Note TD Tunisian dinar

policies will lie somewhere in between. Table 4.13 summarizes the simulations' results.

These simulations indicate that the complete use of fiscal savings from the energy reform would not reduce postreform poverty levels by any significant amount with the current targeting mechanism or via universally benefiting the entire population (Table 4.13, simulations 2 and 1, respectively). The fiscal savings accruing from a universal transfer reform (simulation 2) would bring down postreform poverty levels by 2.5% points—or some 272,000 persons. Using the current health card targeting mechanism (simulation 1) would reduce postreform poverty by an additional percentage point, to 13.83% of the population. A perfect and costless targeting of fiscal savings (simulation 3) would lead to a postreform poverty incidence reduction of 12.5% points, up to 5.25% of the population. Despite the slash in poverty incidence, the fiscal resources freed from the current level of energy subsidies would not be sufficient to completely eradicate poverty in Tunisia. Neither would it be sufficient to make a notable dent on consumption inequality as measured by the Gini coefficient. The three compensation initiatives would fully reverse the initial increase in inequality following the subsidy reforms, but the reduction in inequality would by no means be large. The best results, accruing from the perfect targeting scenario, indicate gains of three percentage points in the Gini coefficient with respect to the postreform Gini. In relative terms, the compensation mechanisms simulated after the reform would improve inequality by less than 10%.[10]

[10]In effect, the three percentage point reduction in the Gini coefficient in simulation 3 implies an 8% reduction in the postreform Gini. The reductions in Gini from the other two simulations render even smaller relative improvements.

Table 4.13 Simulated poverty and inequality impacts of compensatory mechanisms after energy subsidy reform

	Fiscal cost of compensation	Average benefit transferred (rounded up)	Number of beneficiaries	Poverty (%)	Inequality (Gini 0–100 index)
Prereform	0	0	0	15.27	36.57
Baseline: subsidy reform with no compensation	0	0	0	17.84	37.18
Simulation 1: universal transfer after subsidy reform	TD 817.51 millimes	TD 75	10.9 million	14.87	36.29
Simulation 2: current targeting	TD 817.51 millimes	TD 264	3.1 million	13.83	35.46
Simulation 3: perfect targeting	TD 817.51 millimes	TD 420	1.9 million	5.25	34.22

Source World Bank staff calculations using SUBSIM (subsidy simulations)

Conclusion

Energy subsidies have played and continue to play a pivotal role in Tunisian social development policy making. Their fiscal implications are substantial, consuming about 5% of the country's GDP, and this analysis shows that their distributional impacts are considerable. But subsidies have also played an important role in appeasing social tensions. An overhaul of energy subsidies in Tunisia must strike a delicate balance to improve fiscal and equity considerations without increasing social tensions. The strategy followed so far has been one of progressive reduction of subsidies coupled with an expansion of the nonsubsidy elements of social protection. This chapter presents an analysis of the fiscal and distributive consequences of the still vaguely defined next step in that strategy: a uniform increase of 10% of electricity prices; a total removal of LPG, diesel, and gasoline subsidies; and alternative improvements in the current cash transfer system, which were announced at the end of 2014.

A review of Tunisia's residential energy subsidies helps us to understand the implications of the country's current strategy. In Tunisia, energy transfers are through a system of universal energy sources plus a complex multiblock price schedule for electricity that mixes progressive and regressive features. All in all, the energy price structure results in a regressive and prorich transfer system that produces a huge fiscal bill. Furthermore, the distributive impact of the system is heterogeneous, with LPG and electricity the most influential among poor (also among the nonpoor) consumers. This has to do with the price and subsidy structure, on the one hand, and differences in the consumption patterns across socioeconomic groups, on the other. Whether the subsidy is universal or targeted does not make much of a distributional difference in the current Tunisian context.

Although the Tunisian authorities have announced their intention to reform energy subsidies, policy is still in the planning stages, and final details remained unknown at the time of this writing. Limited information, however, points to a complete elimination of LPG, diesel, and gasoline subsidies, a uniform 10% increase in the price of electricity, and the introduction of compensation mechanisms to residential consumers. The present analysis simulates the immediate impacts of the increase in energy prices following the reform of subsidies and constructs several scenarios that simulate the poverty and inequality impacts of increasingly effective targeting mechanisms. Those targeting mechanisms make use of the total fiscal savings freed from the reform in energy subsidies to compensate consumers. In other words, the analyzed simulations of compensatory initiatives postreform are all fiscally neutral. They are also bold and ambitious because they assume that all fiscal savings from the energy reform would be fully invested back into poverty reduction. The scenarios are also unrealistic in that they assume no additional administrative costs. Still, they are useful to set the distributive limits that compensation measures will have after energy subsidies are reformed.

Results from simulations underscore two critical results. First, raising electricity prices to consumers and removing subsidies for other energy sources would immediately—that is, without behavioral responses from users—increase poverty by 2.5 points. Second, "easy" compensation mechanisms—that is, either universal or using current structures—will not bring substantive poverty reductions, even if the government channels the entire TD 817.5 million saved from the subsidy reform. Perfect and costless targeting would slash poverty incidence down to five percentage points. Yet while this ideal scenario would imply a huge reduction in poverty, it would still fall short of eradicating poverty, and inequalities would be reduced in more modest terms. Tunisia is still far from having such an ideal targeting system with comprehensive and updated lists of beneficiaries and minimal transaction costs. In addition, it should not be expected that all fiscal savings from the energy subsidy will be invested into poverty reduction. What becomes clear from the proposed simulations results is that bold reforms of energy subsidies need to be accompanied by equally bold improvements to the targeting schemes of public spending if both poverty and disparities are to be substantively reduced.

Appendix 1: Electricity Tariff Structure for Low-Tension Residential Consumers (January 1, 2014)

Fee	Voltage (millimes/kVa/month)	Price of energy by monthly consumption bracket (millimes/kWh)					
		1–50	51–100	101–200	201–300	301–500	501+
Economic (1 and 2 kVa and consumption under 200 kWh)	500	75					
		108					
		123					
Economic (1 and 2 kVa and consumption under 200 kWh); normal (>2 kVa)	500	136			157	240	330
						210	270

Source Société Tunisienne d'Electricité et du Gaz (2014)
Note kWh = kilowatt hour; kVa = kilo-volt-amperes or 1000 V amps

Appendix 2: Distribution of Monthly Electricity Consumption by Quintile

Consumer <200 kWh per month	Monthly consumption 1–50 kWh					Monthly consumption 51–100 kWh					Monthly consumption 101–200 kWh				
	Q1	Q2	Q3	Q4	Q5	Q1	Q2	Q3	Q4	Q5	Q1	Q2	Q3	Q4	Q5
Percent by quintile	48.1	19.2	12.9	11.6	8.2	32	25.5	20.1	13.7	8.7	15.9	20.5	23.2	22.6	17.9
Consumer >200 kWh per month	Monthly consumption 1–300 kWh					Monthly consumption 301–500 kWh					Monthly consumption +501 kWh				
	Q1	Q2	Q3	Q4	Q5	Q1	Q2	Q3	Q4	Q5	Q1	Q2	Q3	Q4	Q5
Percent by quintile	6.7	15.2	17.8	25.9	34.4	4.4	12.1	15.2	22.1	46.2	2.8	9.1	9.3	19.4	59.4

Source World Bank staff calculations using SUBSIM (subsidy simulations)

Appendix 3: Composition of Consumption of Energy Sources by Sector (2012)

See Fig. 4.6

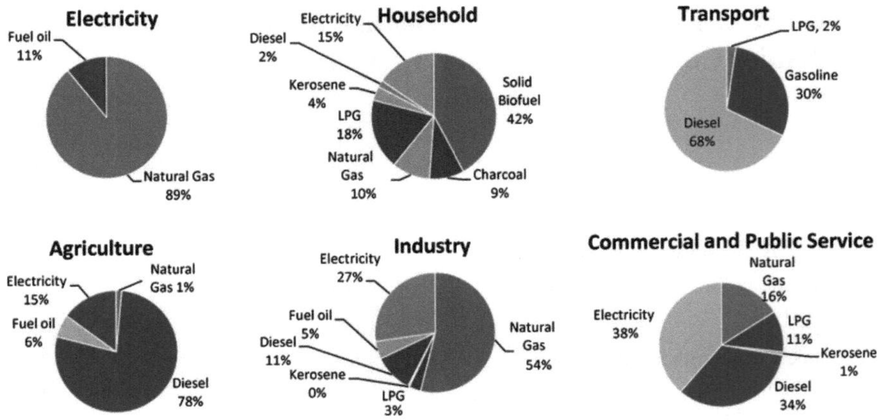

Fig. 4.6 Composition of consumption of energy sources by sector in 2012. *Source* World Bank (2013) with data from the International Energy Agency (2012). *Note* For nonresidential sectors, consumption of energy is an input for their production. For households, it is purely consumption

References

Araar, A., and P. Verme. 2012. Reforming subsidies: A tool-kit for policy simulations. Middle East and North Africa Region, Policy Research Working Paper 6148, World Bank, Washington, DC.

Government of Tunisia. 2014. *Reforme des subventions et du système d'assistance sociale; Organisation et Rôle des Groupes de Travail.*

IMF (International Monetary Fund). 2014. *Subsidy reform in the Middle East and North Africa: Recent progress and challenges ahead.* Washington, DC: Middle East and Central Asia Department, IMF.

INS (Institut National de la Statistique), BAD (Banque Africaine de Développement), and World Bank. 2012. Mesure de la pauvreté, des inégalités et de la polarisation en Tunisie 2000–2010. Tunis, l'Institut National de la Statistique.

Jomaa, M. 2014. Personne n'a le droit de bloquer les permis pétroliers. *Kapitalis*, September 4, http://www.kapitalis.com/kapital/24453-mehdi-jomaa-personne-n-a-le-droit-de-bloquer-les-permis-petroliers.html.

Société Tunisienne d'Electricité et du Gaz. 2014. Tables des Tarifs. Direction des Etudes et de la Planification.

World Bank. 2013. *Vers une meilleure equité: Les subventions energetiques, le ciblage, et la protection sociales en Tunisie*. Washington, DC: Policy Note.

World Bank. 2014. *The unfinished revolution: Bringing opportunity, good jobs, and greater wealth to all Tunisians*. Washington, DC: Development Policy Review, World Bank.

Author Biographies

Jose Cuesta is Chief of the Social and Economic Policy Unit at the UNICEF Office of Research and an affiliated professor at Georgetown University's McCourt School of Public Policy. Previously, he was a World Bank development economist and an assistant professor in development economics at the Institute of Social Studies in the Netherlands. He also worked as a research economist and social sector specialist for the Inter-American Development Bank, and as an economist for the UN Development Programme in Honduras. Cuesta's research interests revolve around poverty and conflict economics, specifically the distributive analysis of social policies; intrahousehold allocation; and social protection. He also studies the interaction among poverty, conflict, and culture. A Spanish national, he holds a PhD in Economics at University of Oxford. Cuesta has experience from a number of countries in Latin America, Asia, and Africa. He is currently an associate editor for the Journal of Economic Policy Reform.

Abdel-Rahmen El Lahga received his doctoral degree in economics from the University of Louis Pasteur, Strasbourg, France. He is currently Associate Professor of Economics at the University of Tunis, Tunisia. He is also a Research Associate at the Economic Research Forum (ERF, Egypt). His research fields are family economics and the analysis of inequality and poverty in the Arab World. AbdelRahmen is a Tunisian citizen.

Gabriel Lara Ibarra is an economist in the Poverty and Equity Global Practice. He is working on poverty issues and measurement, currently focusing on the Arab Republic of Egypt, Tunisia, and Djibouti and is collaborating on the data management program in Middle East and North Africa Region. Previously, Gabriel worked as a consultant in the Global Engagement Office, applying the inequality of opportunity methodology in Philippines, Russia, and Morocco, among other countries. His research interests include the welfare and distributional impacts of public policies, analysis and measurement of inequality, and household saving and financial behavior. He received his Ph.D. degree in economics from the University of Maryland.

Chapter 5
The Quest for Subsidy Reforms in Libya

Abdelkrim Araar, Nada Choueiri and Paolo Verme

Introduction

Libya has a long history with consumers' subsidies to cover food and energy products. Subsidies were first introduced in the early 1970s and continued with various degrees of coverage until the late 2000s when a first serious attempt to reform the system was launched. The reform process was quickly reversed shortly before the 2011 revolution in an attempt to reduce social discontent. That move could not stop the revolution, and it resulted in a major cost to the state budget during the postrevolution period already characterized by a declining economy and political instability.

Subsidies were not the only source of economic distortions in Libya under Muammar Gaddafi's rule, but the combination of subsidies and other distortionary policies deprived the Libyan economy of the fundamental set of incentives that drives a market economy and made both the population and private firms dependent on the state's support (Chami 2012; Charap 2013). Functioning markets are among the foundations of functioning democracies, and a reform of the subsidy system is a step forward in the direction of a functioning state. However, subsidy reforms are politically complex and economically costly for the population and cannot be implemented without a preliminary assessment of the reforms' implications.

A. Araar
University of Laval, Quebec, Canada
e-mail: aabd@ecn.ulaval.ca

N. Choueiri
International Monetary Fund, Washington, USA

P. Verme (✉)
The World Bank, Washington, USA
e-mail: pverme@worldbank.org

P. Verme and A. Araar (eds.), *The Quest for Subsidy Reforms in the Middle East and North Africa Region*, Natural Resource Management and Policy 42,
DOI 10.1007/978-3-319-52926-4_5

This chapter provides for the first time a distributional analysis of food and energy subsidies in Libya and simulates the impact of subsidy reforms on household well-being, poverty, and the government budget. We assess the benefit that different population income groups derive from subsidies, the social cost of subsidy reforms for the different segments of the population, and the government gain from increases in prices of subsidized goods. Information on the distributive incidence of subsidies and the social impact of reforms is essential to design compensation mechanisms that may accompany subsidy reforms and alleviate the burden of reforms for the poor. This chapter also provides some tentative estimates of the effect of cash compensations and some considerations on how subsidy reforms could be implemented.

Despite the focus on direct effects only, the results indicate that subsidy reforms would have a major impact on household welfare and government revenue. The elimination of food subsidies would reduce household expenditure by about 10%, double the poverty rate, and save the equivalent of about 2% of the government budget. The elimination of energy subsidies would have a similar effect in terms of household welfare but a larger effect on poverty; government savings would be almost 4% of the budget. The size of these effects, the weakness of market institutions, and the current political instability make subsidy reforms extremely complex in Libya. It is also clear that subsidy reforms will call for some sort of compensation in cash, a gradual rather than a radical approach, and a product-by-product sequence of reforms. This chapter offers an initial set of considerations that can be used by policy makers for preparing a reform plan.

This chapter is structured as follows: the next section presents an overview of Libya's food and energy subsidy program and its evolution. Following the overview is an introduction to the baseline data and assumptions made. The next two sections present the results for the distributive incidence of subsidies and reform simulations for food and energy subsidies. The concluding sections discuss the political economy of reforms, summarize the main findings, and consider possible future subsidy reforms.

Evolution of Subsidies

Libya's ample subsidy program dates back to 1971 when a national institute was created to oversee consumption of essential goods. The system covers a number of food and energy products, as well as public services (water, sanitation, education, and garbage collection), medicines, and animal feed. Subsidies are regulated by a compensation fund that determine prices with the objective of keeping essential consumption items at affordable prices and protect consumers from major global price shocks.

Since the early 2000s food subsidies have significantly increased, imposing a toll on the government budget. Data from Libya's Price Regulation Fund show that the nominal cost of food subsidies has increased from less than LD (Libyan dinar)172 million in 2001 to more than LD 2 billion (1 billion equals 1000 millions) in 2012. Over the years, the basket of subsidized goods has seen some variation, from a minimum of three products in 2009 to a maximum of 12 products after the 2011 revolution, with flour, semolina, and rice consistently subsidized since 2001. A process of subsidy reforms took place between 2005 and 2010, but at the outbreak of the revolution, these reforms were rolled back almost entirely. This move led to a significant increase in the cost of food subsidies from 1.1% of gross domestic product (GDP) in 2010 to 2% of GDP in 2012 (Table 5.1). As a share of government expenditure, food subsidies also doubled from 2 to 3.8% between 2010 and 2012. Flour, sugar, rice, vegetable oil, and semolina represent the lion's share of the cost of food subsidies to the government.

Food subsidies vary between 39 and 96% of the market price, and they are well above 80% for most products (Table 5.2). They are administered under a system of individual quotas regulated by the Ministry of Economy. Subsidized food products are made available in fixed per capita quantities at cooperatives throughout the country, except for subsidized flour used to bake bread which is distributed to bakeries directly. Quotas are identical for all individuals and have remained unchanged for more than a decade. The quantities are very generous and exceed an individual's nutritional needs.[1] As indicated in Table 5.2, these quantities generate about 4570 calories per person per day—more than double the level recommended by the World Health Organization (WHO) or the Food and Agriculture Organization (FAO). Initially, eight food products were made available under this system: flour, wheat, barley, rice, oil, sugar, tea, and salt. But the list gradually increased over the years to include items such as pasta, coffee, tomato paste, milk for children, and others.

Despite some attempts to control the food subsidy system, significant leakages and abuse are believed to occur. Individuals need to be members of a cooperative to be able to shop there. Because individuals are also able to buy these goods on the free market at liberalized prices, not all Libyans are cooperative members, particularly among wealthier households. Although there are no centralized membership records or other mechanisms to control "double-dipping," Libyan authorities estimate that the total number of cooperative members in the country exceeds the population size, suggesting that abuses of the quota system are widespread.

Energy subsidies were also introduced in 1971 and are currently administered by the National Oil Corporation under the authority of the Ministry of Oil. The subsidies cover five products: gasoline, diesel, liquefied petroleum gas (LPG), kerosene, and electricity. Between 1995 and 2000 subsidies on these products were already on the rise, increasing from around 234 million dinars in 1995 to 404 million in 2000 and with the largest subsidies accorded to diesel and electricity

[1]The quantities provided within the quota system are not negligible. For example, a family of four is entitled to the following quotas at subsidized prices each month: 8 kg of sugar, 800 g of tea, 4 kg of tomato paste, 6 L of vegetable oil, 10 kg of rice, 12 kg of flour, 4 kg of semolina, and 6 kg of pasta. These quantities are well above the total amount of calories necessary for a family of four for one month.

Table 5.1 Government expenditure on food subsidies, 2001–12 (LD millions)

Item	2001	2002	2003	2004	2005	2006	2007	2008	2009	2010	2011[a]	2012[a]
Wheat	12	99	−31	77	0	0	0	0	0	0	n.a.	n.a.
Flour	124	151	338	527	491	390	467	925	953	703	n.a.	n.a.
Sugar	11	22	39	44	55	54	107	0	0	0	n.a.	n.a.
Rice	8	52	46	104	101	108	97	141	236	187	n.a.	n.a.
Olive and other vegetable oils	−6	5	99	165	120	116	134	0	0	0	n.a.	n.a.
Tea	18	11	15	31	17	41	34	0	0	0	n.a.	n.a.
Tomato paste	9	9	16	0	0	0	0	0	0	0	n.a.	n.a.
Dry yeast	0	1	4	11	10	17	13	0	0	0	n.a.	n.a.
Evaporated milk	−7	3	56	147	0	0	0	0	0	0	n.a.	n.a.
Semolina	0	4	37	48	37	68	43	50	144	58	n.a.	n.a.
Miscellaneous	4	2	6	6	7	7	7	0	0	0	n.a.	n.a.
Pasta	0	0	0	42	0	0	0	0	0	97	n.a.	n.a.
Total	**172**	**357**	**625**	**1202**	**839**	**801**	**902**	**1117**	**1333**	**1046**	**1414**	**2046**
In percent of GDP										1.1	3.3	2
In percent of government expenditure										2	4.8	3.8

Source Data provided by Libya's Price Regulation Fund, obtained from the Central Bank of Libya

[a]Data for 2011 and 2012 are preliminary. For 2001–10, the breakdown refers to the Price Regulation Fund's operational balance, a proxy for the cost of subsidies to the government because the fund is responsible for buying the commodities on the international market and distributing them to cooperatives. A negative number therefore indicates an operational surplus for that particular commodity and year, which could be due to accumulated inventories from previous years

Table 5.2 Food subsidies and quotas, 2008–12

Item	Unit	Subsidized price (in LD)	Market price (in LD)	Subsidy (percent of the free market price) (%)	Quota enforced (per person per month)					Generated calories (per person per day)
					2008	2009	2010	2011	2012	
1 Flour for individuals	Kg	0.090	1.030	91	3.00	3.00	3.00	3.00	3.00	407
2 Flour for bakeries	Kg	0.040	0.960	96	12.00	12.00	12.00	12.00	12.00	1628
3 Yeast for bakeries	Kg	1.345	5.345	75	0.00	0.00	0.00	0.06	0.06	n.a.
4 Semolina	Kg	0.080	0.910	91	0.00	0.00	0.00	1.00	1.00	137
5 Rice	Kg	0.140	1.560	91	2.50	2.50	2.50	2.50	2.50	347
6 Sugar	Kg	0.250	1.320	81	2.00	2.00	2.00	2.00	2.00	1067
7 Tea	Kg	1.500	5.100	71	0.00	0.00	0.00	0.20	0.20	13
8 Pasta	Kg	0.200	1.390	86	1.50	1.50	1.50	1.50	1.50	206
9 Vegetable Oil	L	0.600	3.400	82	0.00	0.00	0.00	1.50	1.50	173
10 Tomato Paste	Kg	0.600	2.140	72	0.00	0.00	0.00	1.00	1.00	433
11 Milk for children	Kg	7.500	12.250	39	0.00	0.00	0.00	3.20	3.20	n.a.
12 Milk (condensed)	Kg	0.980	2.620	63	0.00	0.00	0.00	1.23	1.23	159

Sources Information provided by Libyan Authorities during World Bank missions; FAO (2003); World Bank staff calculations
Note kg = kilogram; L = liter; LD = Libyan dinar

Table 5.3 Energy prices and subsidies, 2013

	Subsidized price (LD per unit)	Market price (LD unit)	Subsidy (% of market price)
Gasoline (L)	0.150	1.072	86
Diesel (L)	0.150	1.110	86
Electricity (kWh)	0.020	0.156	87
LPG (L)	2.000	20.939	90
Kerosene (L)	0.090	1.089	92

Sources Libyan authorities and World Bank staff calculations
Note Market prices refer to first quarter of 2013. kWh = kilowatt hour; L = liter; LD = Libyan dinar

(Waniss and Karlberg 2007). The largest increases occurred during the 2000s before the revolution because of the inability of the regime to increase retail prices during the global rise in oil prices. Energy subsidies continued to increase after the revolution, reaching an estimated peak of LD 6.3 billion in 2012. Energy products are universally subsidized, at rates exceeding 85% of the products' market value (Table 5.3), with the highest subsidies provided for LPG and kerosene.

It is important to stress that estimates of subsidies in Libya vary significantly across sources. For example, government figures for 2012 indicated that the total amount for food and energy subsidies in 2012 was LD 9.5 billion, equivalent to about 9.2% of GDP,[2] while the IMF, by including estimates on electricity and other subsidies, reaches an amount of LD 14.8 billion or 13.8% of GDP (IMF 2013). These estimates vary in absolute terms and relatively to GDP. Absolute estimates vary partly because what is considered a subsidy is not fixed and partly on whether subsidies include or exclude administrative costs. Estimates of subsidies as percentage of GDP can also vary because GDP figures are themselves volatile estimates in Libya due to weak national accounts and the prominence of oil as a source of revenues. Despite these caveats, it is clear that consumers' subsidies in Libya are among the highest in the North Africa and Middle East (MENA) Region (Zaptia 2013).

Baseline Data, Assumptions, and Limitations

The analysis provided in this chapter is based on the 2007–08 Libyan Household Expenditure Survey (LHES), with all figures presented in the distributional and simulation analyses estimated at 2013 prices. This survey is the most recent household expenditure survey administered by the national statistical agency and

[2]Preliminary data on government spending in 2012 indicated that food, electricity, and other energy subsidies cost, respectively LD 2.1 billion, 1.1 billion, and 6.3 billion to the budget.

Table 5.4 Parameters used for the 2008–13 extrapolations

	2007	2008	2009	2010	2011	2012	2013
Gross domestic product (in billions of LD/constant prices)	44.5	45.7	45.3	47.6	18.1	36.9	44.4
Inflation (average percent change in CPI; base year 2003)	112.0	123.7	126.7	129.8	150.5	159.6	162.8
Population (in millions)	6.0	6.2	–	–	–	–	6.4

Sources IMF 2013 and Libyan authorities
Note CPI = consumer price index; LD = Libyan dinar

the only survey available in Libya today for this type of analysis. With 2007 as the starting point, data are projected from 2008 to 2013 using official population estimates and IMF estimates for inflation and real GDP growth for the period 2008–13 (Table 5.4).

This chapter focuses on the direct effects of subsidy reforms.[3] This is not a major constraint for the case of food subsidies, but is an important limitation for energy subsidies. Given that food subsidies in Libya are subject to a quota system, the share of subsidized food products that could be used in the production of other goods is likely to be negligible.[4] For example, although sugar can be an input to the production of many processed food products, the quota system in place makes it unlikely that sugar used in food production is actually bought at subsidized prices. We will therefore assume that indirect effects for food are relatively small.[5]

The treatment of bread in the analysis requires a number of assumptions. We have information on subsidized prices and quantities of flour (and yeast) for bakeries, both of which are supposed to be used in making bread, but we only have household expenditure data on bread. We translate the flour subsidy into a bread subsidy as follows. We estimate that 1 kg of bread requires 1 kg of flour, and given disparate prices of bread across bakeries in Tripoli we assume that a 100 g baguette is sold for 5 Libyan dirhams. Therefore, the price of a kilogram of bread is LD 0.5. We are therefore able to map the household expenditure on bread first into a quantity of bread (using the 5 dirhams per 100 g baguette) and then into a quantity

[3]Direct effects represent the impact of subsidies via subsidized products consumed by households. Indirect effects represent the impact of subsidies via nonsubsidized products consumed by households that use subsidized products as a production input.

[4]Anecdotal evidence suggests that because not all households actually take advantage of the quota system for their food purchases, some of the surplus subsidized food ends up being used as cattle feed or input to the production of sweets in bakeries for the case of sugar and flour. No data are available to quantify these observations, and if animal raising and bakeries are household activities, these effects would be captured in the direct effects estimations. A share of subsidized food products is reportedly smuggled and sold illegally in supermarkets, thereby depressing market prices. Some effect from removing subsidies on these products may filter through to market prices, but that effect is likely to be small.

[5]We note here that this paper's analysis does not capture the administrative costs of subsidies, which may be large given the system of quotas administered through cooperatives.

of flour, and present these information under the heading "Flour (bread)" in the chapter tables.

Although indirect effects are small in the case of food products, they are likely to be significant in the case of energy products. The reason is that energy subsidies in Libya are universal and very large in magnitude, and energy products are an important input in a number of production processes. Therefore, the effect of increasing energy prices on consumer prices is likely large, particularly if producers pass on the associated increases in production costs to consumers. However, input-output data for the Libyan economy were not available, and indirect effects could not be estimated.

The survey data suggest that Libyan households are large and their aggregate consumption is a low share of GDP (Table 5.5). Libya has a small population, estimated at just below 6.4 million and about 1 million households. Aggregate annual household expenditure is estimated at LD 12.5 billion, implying that annual expenditure per capita is about LD 1967. Households in the poorest two quintiles are large, at 9.5 and 7.4 members per household, respectively. On average, these household sizes are larger than those in neighboring countries. For example, household size in Morocco is 6.5 for quintile 1 and 5.9 for quintile 2, and in Tunisia these figures are 5.8 and 5.0, respectively. Aggregate household expenditure in Libya is only about 12% of GDP.[6] This number is atypical of the North African Region, where surveys indicate that household expenditure is usually around two-thirds of GDP; but it is not totally surprising when we look at comparative data for other oil rich countries such as Qatar, Saudi Arabia, and Algeria where household expenditure as percentage of GDP can vary between 11 and 35%.[7] Household final consumption is essentially a small fraction of output as a whole because oil dominates the economy (producing more than two-thirds of GDP). Only a small share of oil proceeds accrues to households via wages and public transfers, while a bigger share accrues through subsidies, which do not appear in actual expenditure.

In what follows, the incidence and impact analyses are presented separately for food products and energy products. The analysis is conducted separately because of the different subsidy systems (universal for energy but quota-based for food), which require a different setup for the subsidies simulation model. Also, differences in the relative importance of indirect effects call for a different approach to interpreting the results. The analyses that follow are based on SUBSIM, a subsidies simulation package produced by the World Bank (www.subsim.org).

---

[6]Although no data are available, hydrocarbons are believed to constitute about two-thirds of GDP in Libya, suggesting that estimated aggregate expenditure could be about 35% of nonoil GDP.

[7]See http://data.worldbank.org/indicator/NE.CON.PETC.ZS.

Table 5.5 Household statistics projected to 2013

Quintile	Population (persons)	Number of households	Average household size (persons)	Total expenditures (LD)	Average expenditures per capita (LD)	Average expenditures per household (LD)
1 (poorest)	1,936,699	203,399	9.5	1,842,216,192	951	9057
2	1,512,025	203,373	7.4	2,288,316,928	1513	11,252
3	1,264,391	203,346	6.2	2,580,271,872	2041	12,689
4	992,019	203,392	4.9	2,745,245,952	2767	13,497
5 (richest)	666,346	203,331	3.3	3,077,710,080	4619	15,136
Total	**6,371,480**	**1,016,842**	**6.3**	**12,533,761,024**	**1967**	**12,326**

Sources Libyan Household Expenditure Survey (LHES) 2007–08; Libyan authorities; and World Bank staff calculations

Food Subsidies

This section provides a distributional analysis of food subsidies to better explain who benefits from subsidies. It also provides a simulation of subsidies reforms to discover who would suffer the most from the partial or total removal of subsidies.

The Distribution of Food Subsidies

Food subsidies are relatively progressive, but a third of them do not reach households. In this section, we quantify the size of subsidies received by households at different income levels. The results suggest that food subsidies are relatively progressive in Libya, mostly thanks to the quota system by which they are administered. However, only about 65% of the budgetary costs of subsidies reach households. The difference is probably explained by "leaks" from the subsidy system, including waste from illegal resale of subsidized items outside of the quota system at near market prices and perhaps by administrative costs that cannot be clearly separated and accounted for.

Our estimates are an *upper bound* of the subsidies received by households. The reason is that the analysis is based on the assumption that all households purchase the entire amount of quotas to which they are entitled.[8] That assumption may not always be the case as some households may choose not to go to cooperatives to purchase products at subsidized prices—as is reported for a nonnegligible share of Libya's population (mostly middle- and upper-income tranches). In the absence of information on the share of households taking advantage of the quota system in their food purchases, it is more conservative to assume that households take the maximum advantage of the benefit available to them so as not to underestimate the impact of any reform on the population. This assumption also compensates for the nonobservable leakages due to "double dipping."

Households allocate about 9.3% (LD 1.2 billion) of their total expenditure on subsidized food products, if we consider the share bought under the quota system and the share bought at market prices (Table 5.6). About 22.2% of this amount is expenditure on quotas at subsidized prices, and the rest is on the same products bought on the free market. This finding may seem at odds with the fact that quotas provide generous quantities, but richer households are unlikely to shop at cooperatives, which administer quotas. Rich households may opt for better quality and more expensive products, and poorer households may also consume a share of better quality brands not available in the quota system. Indeed, for most of these food products, the market may offer several better quality options that may be preferred by the rich and poor alike. Also and more importantly, expenditure on

[8]We make that assumption when the survey provides no separate expenditure data for subsidized versus nonsubsidized quantities for a given product.

Table 5.6 Household expenditure on subsidized food products, in LD million

Food products	Q1	Q2	Q3	Q4	Q5	Total	Percent at subsidized prices
Flour	11.2	11.6	11.3	11.7	10.5	56.9	15
Flour-bread	3.6	3.3	2.9	2.4	1.9	14.1	100
Semolina	7.6	7.9	7.2	6.3	5.1	34.1	3.7
Rice	18.6	20.6	20.2	20.2	19.3	98.8	15.7
Sugar	21.3	23.5	23.2	23.3	21.8	113.1	21.7
Tea	17.9	20.2	20.0	19.4	19.1	96.6	12.6
Macaroni	33.4	34.8	33.3	32.1	29.8	163.5	11.4
Vegetable oil	58.0	60.9	61.4	59.1	55.4	294.8	18
Paste tomatoes	24.2	25.8	26.2	25.0	24.2	125.3	28.4
Milk for children	4.5	6.8	8.3	9.7	9.0	38.3	99.9
Milk (concentrated)	26.5	29.1	27.9	24.3	23.0	130.8	28.3
Total	227.0	244.5	242.4	233.4	219.0	1166.2	22.2
Percent of total expenditure	12.3	10.7	9.4	8.5	7.1	9.3	2.1

Sources Libyan Household Consumption Survey 2007–08; Libyan authorities; and World Bank staff calculations
Note Q = quintile, with 1 being the poorest, and 5, the richest

quotas is low because prices are low under the quota system as compared to the market prices. For some products, like flour-bread and milk for children, the total expenditure is only on quotas, and there are no purchases of these products at nonsubsidized prices. For products such as bread, which is also sold outside cooperatives, the quota system is not binding.

In terms of quantities, households consume approximately half of the food products via purchases made under the quota system at subsidized prices and buy the other half at market prices (Table 5.7). Given the larger size of poorer households and their greater reliance on quotas, the first and second quintiles consume products at subsidized prices in higher quantities than the richer quintiles. The share of products bought via the quota system varies from 30.6% for semolina to 100% for milk for children and flour for bread. Flour for bread and pasta are the subsidized products with the largest consumption. These products are basic staples for Libyans, and quotas for these products are larger than those for other products.

Poorer households spend a much greater share of total expenditure on subsidized food items than richer households. Indeed, while expenditure on food products at subsidized prices represents 9.3% of total household expenditure (Table 5.8) on average, this share is higher for the first (12.32%) and second (10.68%) quintiles and falls to 7.12 for the fifth quintile. The larger size of poorer households explains part of this observation. If we focus on quotas only (the share bought at subsidized prices), the first quintile'share is 3.61% against the fifth quintile share of 1.07%.

Table 5.7 Quantities of subsidized food products consumed, in kilograms or liters

	Q1	Q2	Q3	Q4	Q5	Total	Percent at subsidized prices (quotas)
Flour (kg)	35.4	31.7	29.2	26.0	19.6	141.9	66.9
Flour-bread (kg)	96.9	89.7	77.9	64.9	51.5	380.9	100
Semolina (kg)	12.8	12.6	10.9	9.0	6.7	52.0	30.6
Rice (kg)	39.1	37.2	34.2	30.0	24.0	164.3	67.5
Sugar (kg)	38.3	37.0	33.9	30.8	25.2	165.2	59.3
Tea (kg)	5.1	5.4	5.1	4.7	4.3	24.6	32.8
Macaroni (kg)	47.1	44.2	40.1	35.9	30.0	197.4	47.4
Vegetable oil (L)	37.8	35.3	33.0	29.2	24.2	159.6	55.5
Paste tomatoes (kg)	23.5	22.3	21.0	18.5	15.9	101.2	58.6
Milk for children (kg)	0.6	0.9	1.1	1.3	1.2	5.1	100
Milk (concentrated) (kg)	16.8	17.1	15.6	13.0	11.2	73.8	51.5

Sources Libyan Household Consumption Survey 2007–08; Libyan authorities; and World Bank staff calculations

Note kg = kilogram; L = liter; Q = quintile, with 1 being the poorest, and 5, the richest

Table 5.8 Percentage of spending on subsidized food in total expenditure

	Q1	Q2	Q3	Q4	Q5	Total	Total (quotas)
Flour	0.61	0.50	0.46	0.43	0.34	0.45	0.07
Flour-bread	0.19	0.15	0.11	0.09	0.06	0.11	0.11
Semolina	0.41	0.35	0.28	0.23	0.16	0.27	0.01
Rice	1.01	0.90	0.78	0.74	0.63	0.79	0.12
Sugar	1.16	1.03	0.90	0.85	0.71	0.90	0.2
Tea	0.97	0.88	0.77	0.71	0.62	0.77	0.1
Macaroni	1.81	1.52	1.29	1.17	0.97	1.30	0.15
Vegetable oil	3.15	2.66	2.38	2.15	1.80	2.35	0.42
Paste tomatoes	1.31	1.13	1.01	0.91	0.78	1.00	0.28
Milk for children	0.25	0.30	0.32	0.35	0.29	0.31	0.31
Milk (concentrated)	1.44	1.27	1.08	0.89	0.75	1.04	0.3
Total	12.32	10.68	9.39	8.50	7.12	9.30	2.07
Total (quotas)	3.61	2.63	2.08	1.65	1.07	2.07	–

Sources Libyan Household Consumption Survey 2007–08; Libyan authorities; and World Bank staff calculations

Note Q = quintile, with 1 being the poorest, and 5, the richest

The importance of food subsidies for poorer households is even more apparent when we look at the distribution of expenditure shares by population percentiles. Figure 5.1 plots the share of expenditure on food products at subsidized prices, relative to total expenditure, by population percentiles. The negative slopes indicate that poorer households devote a larger share of their total spending on food bought

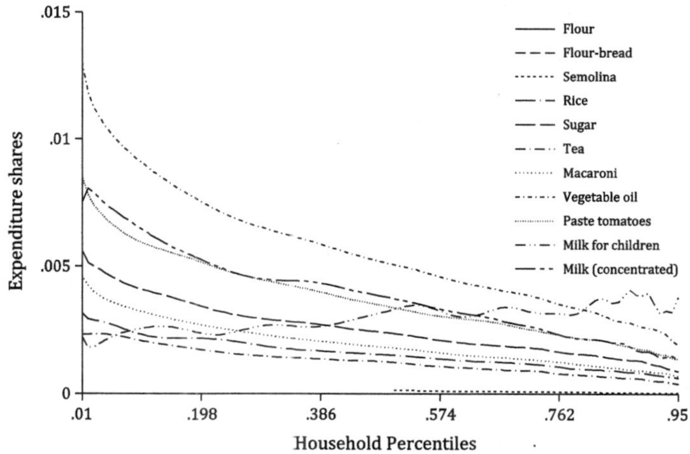

Fig. 5.1 Percentage of total household expenditure on food bought at subsidized prices (quotas only). *Sources* Libyan Household Consumption Survey 2007–08; Libyan authorities; and World Bank staff calculations

under the quota system than richer households (for all products except milk for children.) In other words, food is a larger component of the consumption basket of poorer households.

The poorest quintiles benefit the most from the monetary value of subsidies (Table 5.9), except for milk for children. This result sets Libya apart from other countries in the Region, where food subsidies tend to be slightly regressive because richer households consume more food overall and because subsidies are universal, unconstrained by a quota system.

The per capita data suggest that subsidies benefit all people equally, with the exception of flour used for bread and milk for children.[9] Figure 5.2 plots the total monetary value of food subsidies per capita on the y axis and the population percentiles on the x axis. The curves are flat, indicating everyone across the spectrum of the population derives the same monetary value from food subsidies. Again, this result is not surprising given that the quota system is established on a per capita basis, allocating the same quantity of food at subsidized prices to every individual regardless of the income bracket.

[9]Household sizes are different across quintiles, with poorer households also being the largest. It is therefore useful to also look at per capita estimates in addition to per household estimates to assess whether or not food subsidies are progressive.

Table 5.9 Value of food subsidies by quintile, in LD million

	Q1	Q2	Q3	Q4	Q5	Total
Flour	25.2	21.1	18.3	15.1	9.6	89.3
Flour-bread	89.4	82.7	71.9	59.8	47.5	351.2
Semolina	4.1	3.5	2.7	1.9	1.0	13.2
Rice	42.3	37.4	33.1	26.5	18.1	157.4
Sugar	29.2	25.3	21.4	17.4	11.3	104.6
Tea	8.2	7.2	6.1	4.6	3.0	29.1
Macaroni	32.3	26.9	22.6	17.9	12.0	111.7
Vegetable oil	70.7	59.3	50.9	40.2	27.1	248.3
Paste tomatoes	26.1	22.1	18.7	14.7	9.9	91.4
Milk for children	2.9	4.3	5.2	6.1	5.7	24.2
Milk (concentrated)	17.6	15.8	13.1	9.7	6.4	62.6
Total	348.0	305.6	264.1	213.8	151.6	1283.0

Sources Libyan Household Consumption Survey 2007–08; Libyan authorities; and World Bank staff calculations
Note Q = quintile, with 1 being the poorest, and 5, the richest

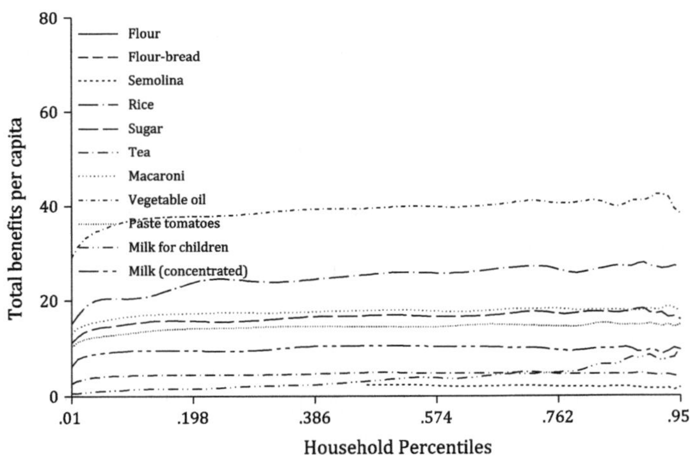

Fig. 5.2 Per capita benefits from food subsidies by product, in LD. *Sources* Libyan Household Consumption Survey 2007–08 Libyan authorities; and World Bank staff calculations

Simulation of Food Subsidy Reforms

This section simulates subsidy reforms and estimates the impact on household welfare and the government budget. We consider two scenarios: a 30% decrease in the subsidy for each product and the total elimination of all subsidies. Note that a 30% decrease in the subsidy on each product would result in a different price increase for each product. Table 5.10 reports the current subsidized price for each

Table 5.10 Prices, subsidies, and reform scenarios

	Initial price	Subsidy	Final price (scenario 1)	Final price (scenario 2)	Final price (scenario 2)/ Initial price
Flour	0.090	0.940	0.372	1.030	11.4
Flour for bread	0.037	0.922	0.314	0.959	25.9
Semolina	0.080	0.831	0.329	0.911	11.4
Rice	0.140	1.419	0.566	1.559	11.1
Sugar	0.250	1.068	0.570	1.318	5.3
Tea	1.500	3.597	2.579	5.097	3.4
Macaroni	0.200	1.194	0.558	1.394	7.0
Vegetable oil	0.600	2.802	1.441	3.402	5.7
Tomato paste	0.600	1.541	1.062	2.141	3.6
Milk for children	7.500	4.750	8.925	12.250	1.6
Milk	0.975	1.647	1.469	2.622	2.7

Source Libyan Household Consumption Survey 2007–08; Libyan authorities; and World Bank staff calculations

product under the quota regime, the unit subsidy, the price after a 30% reduction in subsidy (final price, scenario 1) and the price after the elimination of all subsidies (final price, scenario 2). The last price is equivalent to the market reference price we consider for each product.[10]

Eliminating all food subsidies (scenario 2) would result in exceptionally high price increases. The price of flour used in making bread would need to increase by almost 26 times to reach the market price, and prices of flour, semolina, and rice would need to increase more than 11 times. Even in the case of milk for children, the product with a price currently the closest to the market price, a 60% increase would be needed to match the market price—a significant price increase.

These price increases would affect the poor in greater proportion than the rich. The total monetary impact of a complete removal of subsidies (scenario 2) on households would be equivalent in magnitude to the total estimated monetary value of subsidies received by households, namely LD 1.3 billion (Table 5.11).[11] The total impact of a 30% reduction in subsidies (scenario 1) is estimated at LD 385 million. The impact would be regressive in that poorer households would be affected more than richer households, as indicated by the greater loss in per capita spending for lower quintiles (Table 5.12). This result is to be expected because food subsidies were shown to benefit the poor in greater proportion. For example, with an elimination of subsidies, the first quintile (the poorest 20% of the population) would bear a cost of LD 348 million. And at 18.9%, the decline in per capita

[10]Market prices were obtained from the Ministry of Economy dated for the first quarter of 2013.

[11]Note that these are upper bound estimates based on Laspeyres estimations.

Table 5.11 Aggregate monetary impact of subsidy reform on welfare, in LD million

	Q1	Q2	Q3	Q4	Q5	Total scenario 2	Total scenario 1
Flour	−25.2	−21.1	−18.3	−15.1	−9.6	−89.3	−26.8
Flour-bread	−89.4	−82.7	−71.9	−59.8	−47.5	−351.2	−105.4
Semolina	−4.1	−3.5	−2.7	−1.9	−1.0	−13.2	−4.0
Rice	−42.3	−37.4	−33.1	−26.5	−18.1	−157.4	−47.2
Sugar	−29.2	−25.3	−21.4	−17.4	−11.3	−104.6	−31.4
Tea	−8.2	−7.2	−6.1	−4.6	−3.0	−29.1	−8.7
Macaroni	−32.3	−26.9	−22.6	−17.9	−12.0	−111.7	−33.5
Vegetable oil	−70.7	−59.3	−50.9	−40.2	−27.1	−248.3	−74.5
Paste tomatoes	−26.1	−22.1	−18.7	−14.7	−9.9	−91.4	−27.4
Milk for children	−2.9	−4.3	−5.2	−6.1	−5.7	−24.2	−7.3
Milk (concentrated)	−17.6	−15.8	−13.1	−9.7	−6.4	−62.6	−18.8
Total	−348.0	−305.6	−264.1	−213.8	−151.6	−1283.0	−384.9

Source Libyan Household Consumption Survey 2007–08; Libyan authorities; and World Bank staff calculations
Note Q = quintile, with 1 being the poorest, and 5, the richest

Table 5.12 Per capita impact of subsidy reform (percent of per-capita expenditure)

	Q1	Q2	Q3	Q4	Q5	Total scenario 2	Total scenario 1
Flour	−1.37	−0.92	−0.71	−0.55	−0.31	−0.71	−0.21
Flour-bread	−4.85	−3.61	−2.78	−2.18	−1.54	−2.80	−0.84
Semolina	−0.22	−0.15	−0.10	−0.07	−0.03	−0.11	−0.03
Rice	−2.30	−1.63	−1.28	−0.97	−0.59	−1.26	−0.38
Sugar	−1.59	−1.10	−0.83	−0.63	−0.37	−0.83	−0.25
Tea	−0.44	−0.32	−0.24	−0.17	−0.10	−0.23	−0.07
Macaroni	−1.75	−1.18	−0.88	−0.65	−0.39	−0.89	−0.27
Vegetable oil	−3.84	−2.59	−1.97	−1.46	−0.88	−1.98	−0.59
Paste tomatoes	−1.42	−0.96	−0.73	−0.53	−0.32	−0.73	−0.22
Milk for children	−0.16	−0.19	−0.20	−0.22	−0.18	−0.19	−0.06
Milk (concentrated)	−0.96	−0.69	−0.51	−0.35	−0.21	−0.50	−0.15
Total	−18.89	−13.35	−10.23	−7.79	−4.93	−10.24	−3.07

Sources Libyan Household Consumption Survey 2007–08; Libyan authorities; and World Bank staff calculations
Note Q = quintile, with 1 being the poorest, and 5, the richest

spending of the lowest quintile if food subsidies were eliminated is nearly four times that of the highest quintile (4.9%). This would be a disproportionate cost for poorer households.

Table 5.13 Impact of subsidy reform on the government budget (Million LD)

	Q1	Q2	Q3	Q4	Q5	Scenario 1 total	Scenario 2 total	Scenario 2 (percent govt. expenditure)
Flour	13.7	11.4	9.9	8.2	5.2	48.5	89.3	0.1
Flour-bread	56.4	52.2	45.4	37.8	30.0	221.7	351.2	0.5
Semolina	2.2	1.9	1.5	1.0	0.6	7.2	13.2	0.0
Rice	22.8	20.2	17.9	14.3	9.8	84.9	157.4	0.2
Sugar	13.2	11.5	9.7	7.9	5.1	47.4	104.6	0.2
Tea	3.3	2.9	2.5	1.9	1.2	11.8	29.1	0.0
Macaroni	15.7	13.1	11.0	8.7	5.8	54.2	111.7	0.2
Vegetable oil	32.7	27.4	23.5	18.6	12.5	114.6	248.3	0.4
Paste tomatoes	10.7	9.0	7.7	6.0	4.0	37.5	91.4	0.1
Milk for children	1.0	1.4	1.8	2.1	1.9	8.1	24.2	0.0
Milk (concentrated)	6.7	6.0	5.0	3.7	2.4	23.9	62.6	0.1
Total	178.4	157.1	135.7	110.0	78.6	659.8	1283.0	2.0

Source Libyan Household Consumption Survey 2007–08; Libyan authorities; and World Bank staff calculations
Note Q = quintile, with 1 being the poorest, and 5, the richest

The direct impact on government expenditure from the complete removal of subsidies (scenario 2) would be equivalent to the total impact on household welfare, namely LD 1.3 billion—equivalent to 2.8% of government expenditure (Table 5.13).[12] Under a partial reduction of subsidies (30% in the case of scenario 1), the total impact on government expenditure would be greater than the impact on household welfare. Under scenario 1, the total impact on government expenditure would amount to LD 660 million, compared to LD 385 million for the impact on household welfare (Table 5.11). This difference is explained by the fact that when subsidies are not totally removed we have two potential causes for lower government expenditure, the first resulting from the increase in subsidized prices (which is equivalent in size to the impact on household welfare) and the second resulting from the reduction in quantities consumed by households at these higher subsidized prices. If subsidies were totally eliminated, this second effect would disappear given that no quantities would be sold at a subsidized price.

Should a gradual approach to reform be considered, measuring the government budgetary impact may help with the decision regarding the sequencing and size of subsidy reforms. Figure 5.3 traces, for each product, the impact of a proportional

[12]Estimates of the budgetary impact of alternative reform scenarios do not take into account savings from lower administrative costs of managing the subsidy program and from leakages of the subsidy program (e.g., smuggling).

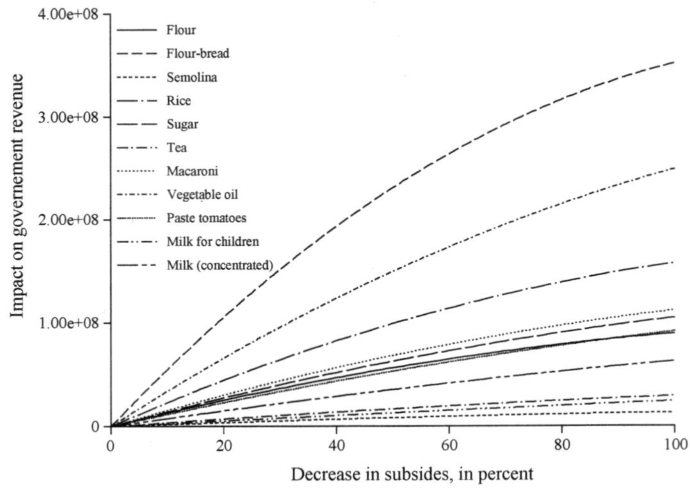

Fig. 5.3 Magnitude of decline in government expenditure under reform scenario 2, in LD. *Source* Libyan Household Consumption Survey 2007–08; Libyan authorities; and World Bank staff calculations

reduction in subsidy (shown in percent on the x axis) on government expenditure in absolute values (measured in LD on the y axis). The impact would differ across products because of different quantities consumed, different initial levels of subsidies, and different price changes associated with a specific subsidy reduction. The fastest decline in government spending would result from first reforming the subsidy on flour used in bread production and then that on vegetable oil. We note that the curves are not linear, implying decreasing marginal returns in terms of lower government spending should prices increase. This result is explained mainly by the importance of the decrease in consumed quantities in response to price increases.

Removing subsidies on food products would have a significant negative impact on poverty (Table 5.14). We estimate poverty in Libya based on both the international poverty line ($1.25 per day)[13] and an updated national poverty line (LD 966.26 per person per year).[14] Using the national poverty line, poverty is estimated

[13]We convert $1.25 to Libyan dinars using the 2009 purchasing power parity (PPP) exchange rate data (1 LD = $0.74-PPP, latest available data) and inflation for the period 2009–13. We find the equivalent universal poverty line for 2013 to be LD 821.42 per person, per year, which is lower than the national poverty line of LD 966.3 per person, per year leading to lower poverty rates.

[14]To estimate the national poverty line, we use the 2003 poverty line—which was estimated at LD 593.6 by staff of Libya's Office of Statistics but not endorsed officially—and CPI inflation between 2003 and 2013. This national poverty line estimate corresponds to LD 2.65 per day, or about $2 at the actual exchange rate. The national poverty line estimate represents 49% of the average per capita expenditure of households (LD 1967).

Table 5.14 Poverty impact of subsidy reforms

	International poverty line			National poverty line		
	Poverty level	Scenario 1 poverty change	Scenario 2 poverty change	Poverty level	Scenario 1 poverty change	Scenario 2 poverty change
Prereform	8.48	–	–	14.44	–	–
Flour	8.62	0.15	0.46	14.66	0.22	0.69
Flour-bread	8.91	0.43	1.63	15.06	0.61	2.38
Semolina	8.50	0.03	0.07	14.48	0.04	0.12
Rice	8.73	0.26	0.75	14.77	0.33	0.98
Sugar	8.59	0.11	0.45	14.72	0.28	0.75
Tea	8.53	0.05	0.14	14.50	0.06	0.17
Macaroni	8.64	0.16	0.56	14.72	0.28	0.85
Vegetable oil	8.77	0.29	1.36	14.88	0.44	1.81
Paste tomatoes	8.61	0.14	0.40	14.66	0.22	0.63
Milk for children	8.48	0.00	0.03	14.45	0.01	0.08
Milk (concentrated)	8.57	0.09	0.28	14.59	0.15	0.45
Postreform		2.02	8.11	17.26	2.82	9.58

Source Libyan Household Consumption Survey 2007–08; Libyan authorities; and World Bank staff calculations

at about 14.4% of the population. If food subsidies were eliminated, poverty would rise by about 2.8 percentage points under scenario 1 and by 9.6 percentage points under scenario 2. Price increases of flour (for bread), rice, and vegetable oil would contribute the most to a rise in poverty. Using the international poverty line would lead to a prereform poverty rate of 8.5% and a reform impact of 2.0 percentage points for scenario 1 and 8.1 percentage points for scenario 2.

Along with greater poverty, income inequality (approximated by expenditure) would rise from 30.2 to 33.2% following a complete elimination of food subsidies. This prediction is consistent with the finding that food subsidies are pro-poor. Note that inequality in Libya is very low: at 30.2%, the Gini coefficient is one of the lowest values in the MENA Region. For example, the latest Gini coefficient for Morocco estimated in 2007 was above 40%, and that for the Arab Republic of Egypt, where inequality is believed to be very low, was around 32% in 2011.

A cash transfer of LD 175 per capita per year targeted to the poorest quintile would be enough to keep poverty unchanged under the scenario of full subsidy elimination (Fig. 5.4). An increase in poverty from 8.5 to 16.5% implies that poverty remains concentrated in the bottom quintile following the price reform. Therefore, targeting that share of the population would be sufficient to maintain poverty unchanged at the prereform level. This targeted transfer system would cost the government LD 340 million per year. Given that savings from the price

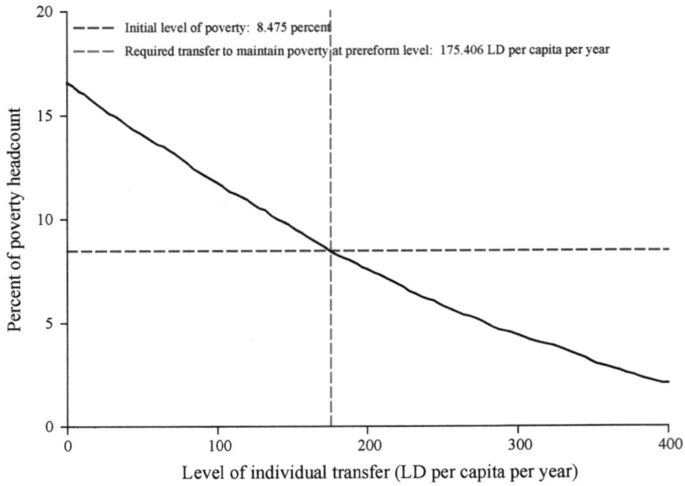

Fig. 5.4 Poverty impact of cash transfers to first quintile under food subsidy reform scenario 2 (international poverty line). *Source* Libyan Household Consumption Survey 2007–08; Libyan authorities; and World Bank staff calculations

increases would amount to LD 1.3 billion as calculated, the net gains to the budget from full subsidy elimination *and* cash compensation to the population in the first quintile of LD 175 per capita would be LD 943 million. If targeting the first quintile was not possible, extending that level of transfer to the entire population would raise the budgetary cost to LD 1.1 billion per year. In this case, total net gains to the budget from subsidy reform *and* cash transfers would be much lower, at LD 165 million per year.

The impact of subsidy reform on quantities consumed would also be significant (Table 5.15). It is useful to look at this impact because it gives an idea of the changes required in production and imports of food products bought via the quota system and to better understand the impact on government revenues. When compared to the initial quantities consumed under the quotas, changes would vary from −13.7% for milk for children to −62.3% for bread flour. The impacts are also quite flat across quintiles, although the impact on the first quintile would be lower for all products.[15]

[15]These results are entirely dependent on the choice we made regarding the point elasticity at market price and the shape of the demand curve. Other assumptions would lead to different results, and these findings should be taken with caution. Note, however, that the final results on household welfare are not affected by the choice of elasticity and demand curve as these estimates depend only on the initial expenditure and the price change (relative changes in quantities consumed of subsidized and nonsubsidized products do not affect the overall welfare effects given that we consider a hard budget constraint).

Table 5.15 Impact of subsidy reform on quantities consumed per capita (scenario 2)

Item	Unit	Q1	Q2	Q3	Q4	Q5	Total
Flour	Kg	−7.19	−7.69	−7.98	−8.37	−7.98	−7.73
Flour-bread	Kg	−31.19	−36.99	−38.42	−40.76	−48.18	-37.27
Semolina	Kg	−1.31	−1.45	−1.33	−1.19	−0.97	−1.29
Rice	Kg	−7.92	−8.97	−9.49	−9.69	−9.85	−8.96
Sugar	Kg	−5.55	−6.14	−6.23	−6.44	−6.26	−6.04
Tea	Kg	−0.36	−0.41	−0.41	−0.40	−0.38	−0.39
Pasta	Kg	−6.16	−6.58	−6.62	−6.67	−6.66	−6.48
Vegetable oil	L	−5.29	−5.68	−5.84	−5.87	−5.89	−5.64
Paste tomatoes	Kg	−2.78	−3.00	−3.05	−3.04	−3.04	−2.95
Milk for children	Kg	−0.04	−0.08	−0.12	−0.18	−0.25	−0.11
Milk (concentrated)	Kg	−1.42	−1.63	−1.61	−1.52	−1.50	−1.53

Source Libyan Household Consumption Survey 2007–08; Libyan authorities; and World Bank staff calculations
Note kg = kilogram; L = liter

Energy Subsidies

The benefits to households from energy subsidies are multiples of those derived from food subsidies—households in the lowest quintile derive 2.5 times more monetary benefit from energy than from food subsidies, and that ratio increases gradually to 6.5 times for the upper quintile.

The analysis in this section covers five energy products: gasoline, diesel, electricity, LPG, and kerosene. Gasoline is the main energy product used by the road transport sector for individuals—both in private cars and taxis, as there are no other means of public transportation. Diesel is consumed mainly by businesses (for transportation) and by the electricity generation company. Electricity and LPG are almost universally consumed. Half of the kerosene sold on the market goes to the air transport sector, and the rest is likely used by lower-income households as a substitute for electricity, but no data are available to corroborate the latter hypothesis.

The Distribution of Energy Subsidies

Gasoline and electricity represent the bulk of energy consumption and, together with other energy products, are heavily consumed by the rich. Gasoline and electricity take up more than 90% of household energy consumption, which corresponds to the same share of government spending on subsidies. Subsidies for these two products are clearly regressive in absolute terms. An individual in the upper quintile benefits 3.5 times more from subsidies on electricity and gasoline than an individual in the bottom quintile. That ratio is 2.8 and 2.7 for diesel and LPG, respectively.

Table 5.16 Household expenditure on energy products, in LD million

Quintile	Gasoline	Diesel	Electricity	LPG	Kerosene	Total
1 (poorest)	28.9	0.7	29.9	5.7	0.3	65.4
2	34.9	0.7	34.0	5.9	0.5	76.0
3	36.1	0.6	34.2	5.7	0.5	77.1
4	36.2	0.6	33.1	5.5	0.6	76.0
5 (richest)	33.6	0.7	35.8	5.2	0.6	75.9
Total	169.6	3.3	167.1	28.0	2.5	370.5

Source Libyan Household Consumption Survey 2007–08; Libyan authorities; and World Bank staff calculations

Table 5.17 Share of energy expenditure in total household expenditure, in percent

Quintile	Gasoline	Diesel	Electricity	LPG	Kerosene	Total
1 (poorest)	1.57	0.04	1.62	0.31	0.01	3.55
2	1.53	0.03	1.49	0.26	0.02	3.32
3	1.40	0.02	1.33	0.22	0.02	2.99
4	1.32	0.02	1.21	0.20	0.02	2.77
5 (richest)	1.09	0.02	1.16	0.17	0.02	2.47
Total	1.35	0.03	1.33	0.22	0.02	2.96

Source Libyan Household Consumption Survey 2007–08; Libyan authorities; and World Bank staff calculations

Households' direct benefits from energy subsidies are close to LD 2.5 billion, which represents only about a third of the total cost to the budget of energy subsidies.[16] Given the extremely low subsidized prices, energy products represent a very small share of household expenditure—about 3% of total expenditures, equivalent to LD 370 million (Table 5.16). Gasoline and electricity represent the greatest share, while expenditure on kerosene is very low. The share of household spending on energy products is slightly higher for poorer households (3.6%) relatively to richer households (2.5%). The share of expenditure on LPG shows the largest difference across quintiles (Table 5.17), suggesting that it is used more intensely by poorer households.

Compared to other countries in the North Africa Region, the share of expenditure on energy products in Libya is more homogeneous across quintiles. This finding corroborates the result we found in analyzing food subsidies, namely that the income distribution in Libya is comparatively more flat, with lower inequality, compared to other countries in the Region. Particularly striking is the distribution of gasoline and diesel expenditure. The poorest quintile of households spends on gasoline 85% of what the richest quintile spends and twice as much for diesel. Indeed, data on car ownership from the household survey confirm that most

[16]The budget data do not include administrative costs associated with the subsidy system.

Table 5.18 Percentage of households that own cars, by quintile and number of cars

Quintile	0 car	1 car	2 cars	3 cars	4 cars	5 cars	Total
1 (poorest)	6.25	12.17	1.32	0.17	0.08	0.00	20
2	4.64	13.54	1.51	0.29	0.03	0.00	20
3	4.87	13.62	1.26	0.21	0.04	0.00	20
4	4.69	13.86	1.16	0.24	0.04	0.01	20
5 (richest)	5.35	13.63	0.83	0.16	0.03	0.00	20
Total	25.8	66.81	6.09	1.06	0.22	0.01	100

Source Libyan Household Consumption Survey 2007–08; World Bank calculations

Table 5.19 Household consumption of energy products (in millions of units)

Quintile	Gasoline (L)	Diesel (L)	Electricity (kWh)	LPG (15 kg bottle)	Kerosene (L)
1 (poorest)	192.4	4.8	1496.2	2.8	3.0
2	232.9	4.9	1700.9	2.9	5.2
3	240.6	3.7	1710.9	2.9	5.7
4	241.2	4.0	1654.9	2.8	6.7
5 (richest)	223.7	4.7	1791.3	2.6	6.9
Total	1130.8	22.1	8354.2	14.0	27.4

Source Libyan Household Consumption Survey 2007–08; Libyan authorities; and World Bank staff calculations

households in Libya own at least one car and that the share of nonowners, 25.8% (Table 5.18), is rather homogeneously distributed across quintiles. This finding, which is atypical for countries at similar levels of per capita income, is likely explained by the very low cost of gasoline and the availability of cheap old cars.[17]

Highly subsidized prices have led to excessive consumption of energy products in Libya. The household survey data imply that households consume an estimated 1.13 billion liters of gasoline per year, equivalent to about 177 L per capita (Table 5.19).[18] To put that into context, we have extracted comparable data from the World Bank database on energy consumption for Libya and other countries in 2010.[19] These data suggest that per capita gasoline consumption in Libya in 2010 was 281 L, which is far greater than the household survey data imply, much higher than per capita consumption in Italy (225 L) or France (159 L) for that year, and far higher than the world average (187 L). Per capita gasoline consumption in Algeria, another oil producer, is reported at 96 L in the World Bank's database. These

[17]Anecdotal evidence suggests that the stock of cars in Libya is quite old. Many low-income people drive run-down cars and keep doing so because of cheap gasoline and the lack of alternative transportation means.

[18]The authorities had budgeted for 4.47 billion liters of gasoline to be sold on the market in Libya in 2013.

[19]See http://data.worldbank.org. The data were converted from kilograms to liters on the basis that 1 L of petrol weighs 0.711 kg.

statistics all point towards significant gasoline overconsumption in Libya. The same conclusion holds when comparing electricity consumption in Libya to that of other countries.

Figure 5.5 confirms that the expenditure share of energy products is low for both the poor and rich, although the share is higher for the poor, which is shown by the negative slope of some of the curves depicted in the figure. The differences between quintiles are not perceptible for diesel and kerosene partly because these products are consumed in very small quantities but also because these products follow a different pattern across quintiles. The share of kerosene expenditure in total expenditure in particular is flat across quintiles.

Households derive substantial benefits from energy subsidies. We estimated the total value of direct energy subsidies received by households at LD 2.5 billion (Table 5.20)—6.7 times higher than total household expenditure on these products.

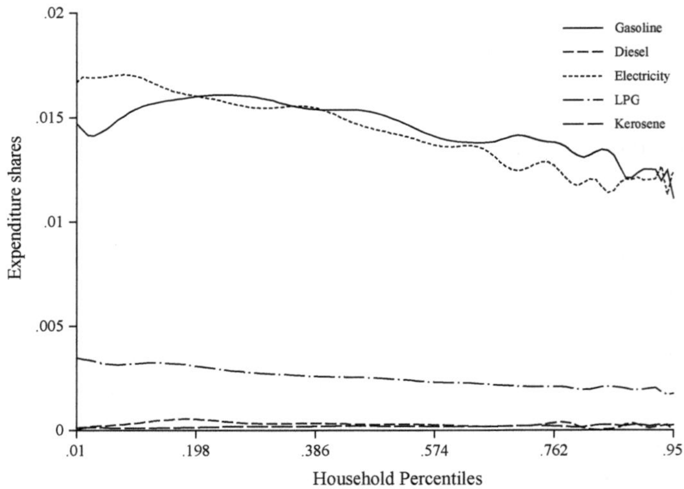

Fig. 5.5 Household spending on energy products, as share of total household expenditure. *Sources* Libyan Household Consumption Survey 2007–08; Libyan authorities; and World Bank staff calculations

Table 5.20 Energy subsidies, in LD million

Quintile	Gasoline	Diesel	Electricity	LPG	Kerosene	Total
1 (poorest)	177.4	4.6	203.5	53.6	3.0	442.0
2	214.8	4.7	231.3	55.4	5.2	511.4
3	221.8	3.6	232.7	54.1	5.7	517.8
4	222.4	3.8	225.1	52.5	6.7	510.4
5 (richest)	206.3	4.5	243.6	49.5	6.9	510.8
Total	1042.6	21.2	1136.2	265.2	27.4	2492.5

Sources Libyan Household Consumption Survey 2007–08; Libyan authorities; and World Bank staff calculations

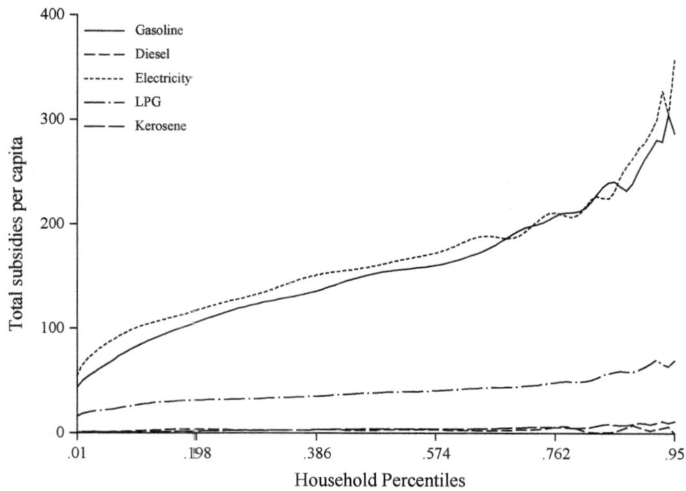

Fig. 5.6 Per capita benefits accruing from subsidies on energy products, in LD. *Sources* Libyan Household Consumption Survey 2007–08; Libyan authorities; and World Bank staff calculations

About LD 1 billion of this total derives from gasoline and LD 1.1 billion from electricity. These numbers underscore the significant share of subsidy incorporated in energy prices in Libya: on average, the government should increase energy prices by 670% to reach market levels and eliminate subsidies.

Energy subsidies in Libya are regressive (in absolute value), or pro-rich, which can be seen by looking at the distributional analysis on a per capita basis. Figure 5.6 shows per capita subsidies (y axis) across population percentiles (x axis) for each subsidized energy product. All curves are positively sloped, which indicates that richer households receive higher amounts of subsidies per capita. The regressive feature of energy subsidies is less pronounced for the cases of kerosene and diesel, consistent with the proposition that these products are consumed more intensively by the poorer population. This feature is most pronounced for gasoline and electricity, the two products whose subsidies generate the biggest cost to the government budget.

Simulations of Energy Subsidy Reforms

Energy subsidy reforms are expected to have a significant direct impact on households. Consistent with gasoline and electricity being the main energy products consumed by households, we find that reducing subsidies on these two items would have a far larger impact on household real income and poverty, as well as on the government budget, than reducing subsidies on other energy products. Presumably, the impact on productive sectors would also be large. Given the considerable price adjustments necessary to eliminate subsidies and the consequent impact on household welfare, a gradual approach to subsidy reform would be preferable, even if a cash compensation scheme is put in place.

As in the case of food subsidies, we simulate two scenarios: a 30% cut in subsidies for each product and a 100% decrease (total elimination) of subsidies. Recall that a 30% cut in subsidies would result in a different price increase for each product because prices vary across products. Table 5.21 reports for all energy products considered the initial subsidized price, the unit subsidy, the price following a 30% reduction in subsidy (final price, scenario 1) and the price after the elimination of all subsidies (final price, scenario 2). The last price is equivalent to the market reference price that we consider for each product.

The elimination of subsidies (scenario 2) would lead to exceptionally large price increases. The price of kerosene would need to rise 12.1 times to match the market price; that of gas LPG would need to rise by a factor of 10.5; and those of gasoline, diesel, and electricity would need to rise by seven or eight times. Gasoline, the product with a price currently the "closest" to market price, would still undergo a price increase of 7.15 times to match the market price. These gaps are the largest observed between subsidized and market prices in North Africa and Middle East Region and represent a real challenge for reform.

The direct cost of a complete elimination of subsidies to households is estimated at LD 2.5 billion (Table 5.22), equivalent to the total amount of direct subsidies received by households. This is a very large sum, representing almost 20% of total

Table 5.21 Two scenarios of energy subsidy reform, LD per unit

Energy product	Initial price	Subsidy	Final price (S1)	Final market price (S2)	Final price (S2)/ initial price
Gasoline	0.15	0.92	0.47	1.07	7.15
Diesel	0.15	0.96	0.48	1.11	7.40
Electricity	0.02	0.14	0.06	0.16	7.80
LPG	2.00	18.94	8.28	20.94	10.47
Kerosene	0.09	1.00	0.42	1.089	12.10

Sources Libyan authorities and World Bank staff

Table 5.22 Welfare direct effects, in LD millions

Quintile	Gasoline	Diesel	Electricity	LPG	Kerosene	Total
1 (poorest)	−53.2	−1.4	−61.0	−16.1	−0.9	−132.6
2	−64.4	−1.4	−69.4	−16.6	−1.5	−153.4
3	−66.5	−1.1	−69.8	−16.2	−1.7	−155.3
4	−66.7	−1.1	−67.5	−15.8	−2.0	−153.1
5 (richest)	−61.9	−1.3	−73.1	−14.9	−2.1	−153.3
Total (scenario 1)	−312.8	−6.4	−340.9	−79.6	−8.2	−747.7
Total (scenario 2)	−1042.6	−21.2	−1136.2	−265.2	−27.4	−2492.5

Sources Libyan Household Consumption Survey 2007–08; Libyan authorities; and World Bank staff calculations

household expenditure. A 30% reduction in subsidies on each product would cost households LD 0.75 billion. These costs would be rather evenly distributed across quintiles with the exception of the first quintile, which would bear a much lower cost than the rest. The quintile that would bear the greatest cost is the third. In per capita terms, removing subsidies would cost more to the upper quintiles, as expected given the result that energy subsidies are regressive. Nonetheless, because energy expenditure represents a higher share of total expenditure for the poor, the per capita loss of the lower quintiles represents a larger share of their total per capita spending (Table 5.23), although the difference is not as stark as we found it to be in the case of food subsidy reforms.

Eliminating all energy subsidies (scenario 2) would create direct savings of LD 2.5 billion to the government budget—the same amount as the total direct value of subsidies to households (Table 5.24). This amount is equivalent to 3.83% of total government expenditure. The removal of gasoline subsidies alone could create direct savings of 1.6% of government expenditure, and the removal of subsidies on electricity about 1.75% (Table 5.24). A 30% reduction in subsidies on all products (scenario 1) would create LD 1.22 billion in direct savings to the government

Table 5.23 Per capita welfare direct effects, as percentage of total welfare (scenario 1 and 2)

Quintile	Gasoline	Diesel	Electricity	LPG	Kerosene	Total
1 (poorest)	−2.89	−0.07	−3.31	−0.87	−0.05	−7.20
2	−2.82	−0.06	−3.03	−0.73	−0.07	−6.70
3	−2.58	−0.04	−2.71	−0.63	−0.07	−6.02
4	−2.43	−0.04	−2.46	−0.57	−0.07	−5.58
5 (richest)	−2.01	−0.04	−2.37	−0.48	−0.07	−4.98
Total scenario 1	−2.50	−0.05	−2.72	−0.63	−0.07	−5.97
Total scenario 2	−8.32	−0.17	−9.06	−2.12	−0.22	−19.89

Sources Libyan Household Consumption Survey 2007–08; Libyan authorities; and World Bank staff calculations

Table 5.24 Reduction in government expenditure, in LD

Quintile	Gasoline	Diesel	Electricity	LPG	Kerosene	Total
1 (poorest)	84.3	2.2	101.4	27.9	1.6	217.4
2	102.0	2.3	115.3	28.8	2.8	251.2
3	105.4	1.7	116.0	28.1	3.0	254.2
4	105.6	1.8	112.2	27.3	3.6	250.5
5 (richest)	98.0	2.1	121.5	25.7	3.7	251.1
Total scenario 1	495.3	10.1	566.4	137.8	14.7	1224.4
Total scenario 2	1042.6	21.2	1136.2	265.2	27.4	2492.5
Percent of govt. expenditure (scenario 2)	1.60	0.03	1.75	0.41	0.04	3.83

Sources Libyan Household Consumption Survey 2007–08; Libyan authorities; and World Bank staff calculations

budget, which is more than one-third of the decline in spending under the 100% reduction scenario (scenario 2). As explained for the case of food subsidies, with a partial reduction in subsidies we have two sources of reduced government spending, the first resulting from higher subsidized prices and the second resulting from lower quantities consumed by households at these higher prices. If subsidies were totally eliminated, this second effect would disappear given that no quantities would be sold at a subsidized price.

Reforming gasoline and electricity prices would bring the greatest savings to the government budget. Figure 5.7 illustrates, for each energy product, the direct impact on government expenditure (measured on the y axis in LD) versus a percentage reduction in subsidy (x axis). The values that correspond to 30 and 100% reductions are the same as those reported under the two scenarios in Table 5.24. For all products, government expenditures are a decreasing function of subsidy reduction. The marginal returns to reducing subsidies would diminish as prices get closer to market levels, because fewer and fewer quantities would be bought at subsidized prices given fixed household expenditure levels.

Energy subsidy reforms could have a substantial impact on poverty. A 30% reduction in subsidies, assuming unchanged consumption patterns, would increase poverty (measured by the national poverty line) by four percentage points, from 18.5 to 22.5% (Table 5.25). The increase in poverty following a total elimination of subsidies would be significantly higher, at 17.7 percentage points, resulting in a postreform poverty rate higher than 36%. These projections are commensurate with the magnitude of price adjustments that would be needed under either reform scenario. The products that would explain most of the rise in poverty under the two scenarios are gasoline and electricity. The rise in poverty would also be

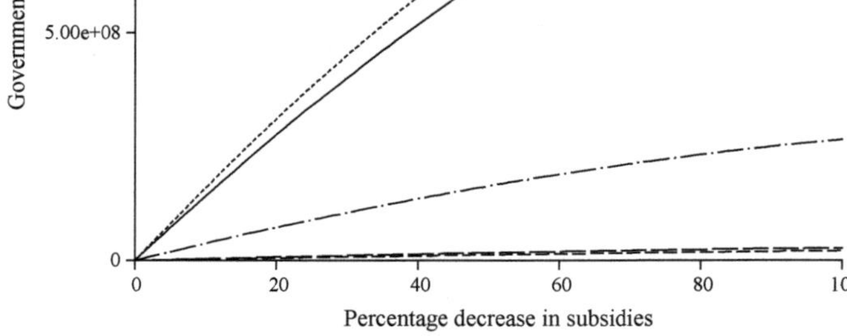

Fig. 5.7 Magnitude of decline in government spending following reform scenario 2, in LD. *Source* Libyan Household Consumption Survey 2007–08; Libyan authorities; and World Bank staff calculations

Table 5.25 Impact of energy subsidy reform on poverty (head count index)

	International poverty line			National poverty line		
	Poverty level	Scenario 1 poverty change	Scenario 2 poverty change	Poverty level	Scenario 1 poverty change	Scenario 2 poverty change
Prereform	8.475	n.a.	n.a.	14.44	n.a.	n.a.
Gasoline	9.306	0.83	4.01	16.16	1.72	6.77
Diesel	8.509	0.03	0.11	14.49	0.05	0.22
Electricity	9.687	1.21	5.25	15.97	1.53	6.47
LPG	8.674	0.20	0.84	14.83	0.39	1.49
Kerosene	8.502	0.03	0.06	14.47	0.03	0.06
Postreform	11.156	2.68	13.19	18.46	4.02	17.67

Sources Libyan Household Consumption Survey 2007–08; Libyan authorities; and World Bank staff calculations

accompanied under scenario 2 by a rise in inequality, estimated at 3.1 percentage points. These estimates are among the highest when compared with those for other countries in the Region such as Morocco, Tunisia, Egypt, or Jordan, in part because of the higher level of subsidies in Libya compared to these countries.

A number of factors can help attenuate the negative impact of energy subsidy reform. A gradual and sequenced approach to energy subsidy reform, across products and across time, would help to make room for simultaneously working on improving public service delivery, so that households and productive sectors are able to gradually adjust to the new economic realities. Moreover, the poverty impact of energy subsidy reform discussed here is purely monetary and therefore does not take into consideration inevitable substitution patterns that would result when a reform is introduced. Such substitutions would be greatly facilitated if the reform were gradual and accompanied by complementary measures to provide other options for citizens in terms of services, for example, more efficient electricity production or the introduction of public transportation networks.

The impact of subsidy reform could also be attenuated through cash transfers. A transfer of LD 243 per capita per year targeted to the first quintile would be sufficient to restore poverty to the prereform level of 8.5% under the scenario of full subsidy elimination and using the international poverty line of USD 1.25 per person per day (Fig. 5.8). This targeted transfer system would cost the government LD 471 million per year. Alternatively, because poverty would jump by almost 18 percentage points if all energy subsidies were eliminated, the government may decide to target the transfers to the first two quintiles. The per capita amount required to bring poverty back to 8.5% in this case would be LD 245, costing the government LD 845 million per year. Yet another possibility to restore poverty to the prereform level would be a universal transfer of LD 243 per capita per year, costing the government

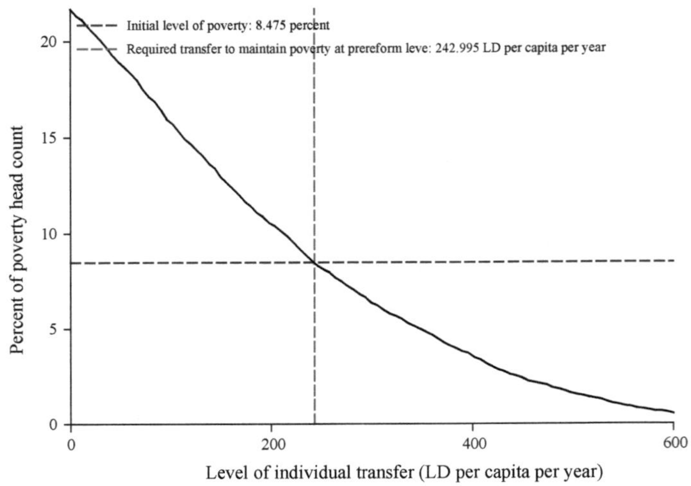

Fig. 5.8 Poverty impact of cash transfers to first quintile under energy subsidy reform S2. *Source* Libyan Household Consumption Survey 2007–08; Libyan authorities; and World Bank staff calculations

Table 5.26 Impact of energy subsidy reform (scenario 1) on quantities consumed

Quintile	Gasoline (liter)	Diesel (liter)	Electricity (kWh)	LPG bottle (15 kg)	Kerosene (liter)
1 (poorest)	−48.1	−1.2	−424.4	−0.9	−1.0
2	−58.3	−1.3	−482.4	−0.9	−1.7
3	−60.2	−1.0	−485.3	−0.9	−1.9
4	−60.3	−1.0	−469.4	−0.9	−2.3
5 (richest)	−56.0	−1.2	−508.1	−0.8	−2.3
Total (scenario 1)	−282.8	−5.6	−2369.5	−4.4	−9.3
Total (scenario 2)	−454.2	−9.0	−3843.2	−6.6	−14.4

Sources Libyan Household Consumption Survey 2007–08; Libyan authorities; and World Bank staff calculations

LD 1.5 billion annually. Given that direct savings from the price increases would amount to LD 2.5 billion (Table 5.24), the net gains to the budget from full subsidy elimination *and* cash compensation to the population in the first quintile of LD 243 per capita would be about LD 2 billion. If targeting the first quintile is not possible, extending a transfer of LD 243 per person per year to the entire population—sufficient to maintain poverty at 8.5%—would reduce the net gains to the budget from subsidy reform *and* cash transfers to about LD 1 billion per year.

Energy price increases would also be expected to reduce consumption (Table 5.26).[20] Based on our assumptions, a 30% reduction in energy subsidies would reduce the quantities of energy products consumed by 46% for electricity, 52.7% for kerosene, and 40% for gasoline and diesel. The estimated impact on quantities would also vary across quintiles. For kerosene, for example, the impact would be greater for richer households, but for other products such as diesel and LPG the impact would be the greatest for the second quintile.

The Political Economy of Reforms

Attempts at subsidy reforms were made during the decade that preceded the revolution, but they did not last. In the early 2000s, following the removal of international sanctions, Libya embarked on a reform path to modernize and open up its economy (Vandewalle 2011), and cutting subsidies seems to have been an important part of that program (Wahby 2005). Despite widespread opposition among the population, the government proceeded with the reform, raising fuel, diesel, and electricity prices in 2005 and completely liberalizing the price of some food products. By 2006 only four food products were still subsidized: flour, rice, semolina, and pasta. In 2007 the government also eliminated the subsidy on pasta, and to compensate the population tried to put in place a transfer system of 4 dinars per capita, per month. The government, however, was unable to dispense this cash transfer. Still, subsidies remained restricted to flour, rice, and semolina until early 2011 when Gaddafi, in an attempt to quell the revolutionaries' demands, extended food subsidies back again to 12 items.

The political economy of the Gaddafi period was entirely driven by the leader's decisions, and these decisions served budget interests or short-term political objectives. The post-Gaddafi period has been characterized by internal conflicts among various factions that participated in the revolution and by a very volatile political environment, making reforms difficult to implement and the possibility of a public debate on subsidy reforms almost impossible. High oil and gas prices that characterized the period between the revolution in 2011 and the first half of 2014 helped to boost government revenues, but the internal conflict over natural resources limited the possibility to exploit oil reserves to their full potential. The most recent slump in the price of crude oil, which began in June 2014, and the continued internal instability are contributing to increase the pressure on government finances while keeping subsidy reforms difficult to implement from a political

[20]These results are entirely dependent on the choice we made regarding the point elasticity at market price and the shape of the demand curve. Underlying our analysis are demand curves that depict the same elasticity for all households but differ in elasticity across products, with the difference depending on the gap between market price and subsidized price. For energy products, we assumed a point elasticity of −0.5 at the free market price. This estimate and a linear demand curve function are then used to estimate the point elasticity at the subsidized price.

perspective. Libya therefore remains the most extreme of the cases in the MENA Region in terms of the size and variety of subsidies, in terms of weight of subsidies on the government budget, and in terms of lack of reforms, and it will be very unlikely to see a reform of the subsidies system anytime soon.

Despite this very complex environment, reforming subsidies remains an important question for the Libyan government. In February 2013 the Ministry of Economy conducted a survey of a sample of 931 adult citizens aged 18 to 95 living in 25 cities. The University of Tripoli analyzed results and found that about 70% of the respondents were in favor of a policy that would eliminate subsidies and replace them with cash transfers, although only 28% thought that compensation via cash subsidies should be targeted to the poor only. Libyans believed that they are entitled to subsidies as a means to distribute national wealth to most citizens, but they would trade low subsidized prices for a cash benefit.

The government announced several times the intention to reform subsidies. In April 2014 it made public the intention to introduce smart cards for the purchase of fuels and stated the intention to eliminate subsidies within three years. In July 2014 it committed to substitute goods and fuel subsidies for cash subsidies by January 2015. According to the *Libya Herald* it was the first time in Libya's history that such a move was promised, and this in spite of the political instability (Zaptia 2013). Yet, at the time of this writing, no substantial reform had been implemented, and political instability was deteriorating further.

Summary and Recommendations

This chapter provided a food and energy subsidy incidence analysis as well as an impact analysis for two alternative reform scenarios for Libya. The results provide information for each subsidized good in terms of the subsidy's impact on household welfare and on poverty. This section briefly reviews the key findings and discusses the main issues that would still need to be addressed for a more comprehensive picture of subsidy incidence and reform analysis.

Food subsidies save households some 10% of annual expenditure and eliminating them would have a significant effect on poverty. Table 5.27 summarizes the results of the food subsidy analysis. Household expenditure loss would reach 3.1% under scenario 1 and 10.2% under scenario 2. The incidence of subsidies would drop from 10.2% in the prereform scenario to 7.4% under scenario 1 and zero under scenario 2. Subsidy reform would reduce government spending by about 1% under scenario 1 and 2% under scenario 2 (but additional savings from lower administrative costs and less waste/smuggling would also materialize). The poverty impact would be particularly stark: depending on the poverty line used, poverty would rise from 8.5 (or 14.4%) to 10.5% (or 17.3%) under scenario 1 and to 16.6% (or 24%) under scenario 2. Inequality would also rise.

Although food subsidies are relatively progressive, a significant share, about 35% of government spending on these subsidies, is wasted, which would support a move to replace them with cash transfers. This chapter's analysis can provide

Table 5.27 Summary of aggregate results for cuts in subsidies

	Prereform	Scenario 1 (30% reduction in subsidies)	Scenario 2 (elimination of subsidies)
Total real household expenditure (LD bn)	12.53	12.15	11.25
Household expenditure loss in real terms (% of prereform)	n.a	−3.1%	−10.2%
Total subsidies(LD bn)	1.23	0.9	0
Incidence of subsidies (% of total expenditure)	10.2%	7.4%	0
Change in govt. spending following reform (LD bn)[a]	n.a.	−0.66	−1.28
Savings to the govt. following reform (% of govt. expenditure)[a]	n.a.	1.0%	2.0%
Poverty head count (%, international poverty line)	8.5%	10.5%	16.6%
Poverty head count (%, national poverty line)	14.4%	17.3%	24.0%
Inequality (%, Gini)	30.2%	31.0%	33.2%

Sources Libyan Household Consumption Survey 2007–08; Libyan authorities; and World Bank staff calculations

[a]Estimates exclude savings from reduced waste, smuggling, and administrative costs

bn = billions

Table 5.28 Per capita monetary value of food subsidies, in LD/capita/year

	Q1	Q2	Q3	Q4	Q5	Total
Flour	13.0	13.9	14.5	15.2	14.5	14.0
Flour-bread	46.1	54.7	56.8	60.3	71.3	55.1
Semolina	2.1	2.3	2.1	1.9	1.5	2.1
Rice	21.8	24.7	26.2	26.7	27.1	24.7
Sugar	15.1	16.7	16.9	17.5	17.0	16.4
Tea	4.2	4.8	4.8	4.7	4.5	4.6
Macaroni	16.7	17.8	17.9	18.0	18.0	17.5
Vegetable oil	36.5	39.2	40.3	40.5	40.7	39.0
Paste tomatoes	13.5	14.6	14.8	14.8	14.8	14.3
Milk for children	1.5	2.8	4.1	6.2	8.5	3.8
Milk (concentrated)	9.1	10.5	10.4	9.7	9.6	9.8
Total	179.7	202.1	208.8	215.5	227.5	201.4

Sources Libyan Household Consumption Survey 2007–08; Libyan authorities; and World Bank staff calculations

Note Q = quintile, with 1 being the poorest, and 5, the richest guidance for the size of cash transfers that would compensate for food subsidy reform. One can look for guidance in the estimates of the per capita monetary value of subsidies received by the various quintiles of the population (Table 5.28). For example, under a scenario of full subsidy elimination, maintaining the poverty rate constant at 8.5% is feasible if a per capita transfer of LD 175 per year is allocated to the population in the first quintile. If the objective is rather to compensate the population falling in the first quintile for the totality of their loss, the transfer could be LD 180 per capita, again granted only to the population in that group. And if the objective is to compensate the average member of the population (a way to address in part the needs of the middle class in a compensation scheme), cash transfers could amount to, for example, 201 LD per year, per person, which is the average monetary value that a Libyan person derives from food subsidies today.

The above examples dealt with eliminating all subsidies in one step but, alternatively, another possibility may be to sequence the reform over products and over time. Price liberalization could start with items, such as semolina, that are likely to have a small impact on households and move onto bigger ticket items over time.[21] This approach may be easily followed in Libya because it was implemented in the past between 2007 and 2010 with only three food items subsidized, flour, rice, and semolina. Yet another possibility, given the generous caloric content of the quotas, could be to start reducing the quantities of all food items under the quota system gradually before eliminating subsidies altogether at a later point in time.[22]

Energy subsidies save households about 26% of annual expenditure, and their elimination would also significantly impact poverty. Table 5.29 summarizes the aggregate results for an analysis of energy subsidies. Household expenditure loss would reach 6% under scenario 1 and 19.9% under scenario 2. These amounts are larger than those for food subsidies, given the larger subsidized component underpinning energy prices in Libya today, compared to that in food prices. Subsidy reform would reduce government spending by about 1.9% under scenario 1 and 3.9% under scenario 2. The impact would, however, be only a *partial impact* on the government budget because factors such as indirect effects and effects on productive sectors are not incorporated in the analysis, nor are other factors such as smuggling. The impact on poverty would be high with a rise in poverty from 8.5% under the international poverty line (or 14.4% under the national line) to 11.2% (or

[21]A caveat to our analysis is that it does not take into consideration the nutritional consequences of food subsidy reform. Such an analysis may be needed before arriving at a view on how small the impact is on households particularly if the reform is not accompanied by cash transfers.

[22]The current basket of subsidized products provides more than twice the amount of adult calories intake as recommended by WHO or the FAO. If we consider that children make up the majority of household members in poor households of six to seven people, the amount of calories allocated within the quota system may be between two and three times the calories needed. This finding would justify a reduction in quotas based on the level of individual calorific needs. Quotas could be cut by half, for example, which would be equivalent to reducing food subsidies by half, saving more than 1 percent of government spending.

Table 5.29 Summary of aggregate results for the case of energy subsidies

	Pre-reform	Scenario 1 (30% reduction in subsidies)	Scenario 2 (Elimination of subsidies)
Total real household expenditure (LD bn)	12.53	11.79	9.29
Household expenditure loss in real terms (% of prereform)	n.a.	−6%	−19.9%
Total subsidies (LD bn)	2.49	1.74	0
Incidence of subsidies (% of total expenditure)	19.9%	14.8%	0
Change in govt. spending after reform (LD bn)	n.a.	−1.22	−2.49
Savings to the govt. after reform (% of govt. expenditure)[a]	n.a.	1.9%	3.9%
Poverty head count (%, internat'l poverty line)	8.5%	11.2%	21.7%
Poverty head count (%, nat'l poverty line)	14.4%	18.2%	30.4%
Inequality (% Gini)	30.2%	30.8%	33.4%

Source Libyan Household Consumption Survey 2007–08; Libyan authorities; and World Bank staff calculations

[a]Estimates exclude savings from reduced waste, smuggling, and administrative costs. bn = billion

18.2%) under scenario 1 and to 21.7% (or 30.4%) under scenario 2. This rise in poverty would also be accompanied by a rise in inequality of 3.2 percentage points.

Clearly, energy subsidy reform would have a huge impact on the Libyan economy, which calls for gradualism. Full liberalization would imply price increases of between 7 and 10 times the existing prices, in a context where alternatives (such as more efficient production processes for electricity or public means of transportation) are not available. It would therefore seem imperative that energy subsidy reform be planned in stages, with a product-by-product approach, gradually liberalizing them over a number of years, and along with significant improvements in service delivery in related areas (electricity, transport, and so forth.). This approach would help improving efficiency and contributing to lower energy consumption. For the electricity sector in particular, it would be important to first improve performance at all levels of production and distribution while tariffs are slowly increased.

Although more analysis is needed to develop a suitable subsidy reform plan, this chapter suggests a number of broad recommendations. The complete elimination of all subsidies in one stroke with no compensation to households could result in a sharp increase in poverty and could affect the middle class severely and lead to social unrest.[23]

[23]This chapter's analysis does not take into account new transfers enacted by the government in 2013 (such as transfers to heads of households and transfers for minors). A complete picture of the impact of subsidy reform on poverty and the middle class will require including these in the assessment.

A radical approach to subsidy reforms in Libya during this particular historical period is not advisable.

A less drastic approach would be to reduce subsidies in sequential steps over an extended period of time. Morocco and Tunisia have followed this approach, achieving significant budget savings without social unrest. It is also advisable to implement reforms one product at a time starting with the products that affect the poor the least. Other considerations may be important as well, for example, the importance of not delaying reforms where substantial waste is clearly established. Other things being equal, this approach would suggest starting with petroleum products rather than food products and with gasoline rather than LPG. This chapter provides information that helps making choices on priority products based on the importance of each product for different groups of households.

The elimination or reduction of subsidies would also call for targeted cash transfers. Compensation could be provided to the bottom 20 or 40% of households in the form of coupons or cash transfers. Such reforms could result in significant budget savings and no increases in poverty. The difficulty of this approach resides in the better targeting of households, and specific systems would need to be in place to ensure that such targeting is operationally feasible. If the country does not develop such effective systems, targeted subsidies may result in substantial waste of resources. A universal transfer is a second best option, but would still reduce the burden on government expenditure.

This chapter provided only part of the information required to put in place subsidy reforms. Much more work and preparation will be needed to prepare a feasible reform agenda. In particular, a few areas stand out for further work. First, it will be important to assess, in the context of the existing formal and informal support mechanisms in Libya, whether a new cash transfer system is really needed to compensate for subsidy reform and for what product. Second, if a transfer is needed, the next question is how best to introduce it in the context of existing social safety nets and/or what reforms to these safety nets are needed to support subsidy reforms. Also, actual mechanisms to disburse the transfers might need to be created and may be costly. Third, a strategy for phasing out the transfers may also be needed, particularly if targeting cannot be achieved. Fourth, broad consultation needs to be conducted with all sectors affected by the reform to address any negative impacts. Beyond the impact on households, energy subsidy reforms will probably have significant impact on producers, and such impact will need to be assessed and factored in the reform. Fifth, a communication strategy in Libya would seem to be even more important than in other countries given the size and sensitivity of subsidies and the current political fragility. These aspects are all beyond the scope of this study but need to be tackled in preparing for subsidy reforms.

Acknowledgements The authors thank the Libyan authorities for the information, comments, and advice provided throughout the study. In particular, we thank the staff at the Ministry of Economy, Ministry of Finance, Ministry of Planning, and the Central Bank who provided excellent support during the various missions to Tripoli. The World Bank country and regional teams provided essential logistical support and various World Bank staff contributed with comments and advice. They are Marouane El Abassi, Bernard Funck, Khalid El-Massnaoui, Fanny Missfeldt-Ringius, Maria Vagliasindi, and Heba Elgazzar. Any errors are the sole responsibility of the authors.

References

Chami, R. 2012. *Libya Beyond the Revolution: Challenges and Opportunities.* International Monetary Fund. http://www.imf.org/external/pubs/ft/dp/2012/1201mcd.pdf.

Charap, J. 2013. Note on Subsidy Reform in Libya. IMF Country Report No. 13/151, Washington, DC: International Monetary Fund.

FAO (Food and Agriculture Organization). 2003. Food Energy: Methods of Analysis and Conversion Factors. Food and Nutrition Paper 77, ftp://ftp.fao.org/docrep/fao/006/y5022e/y5022e00.pdf.

IMF (International Monetary Fund). 2013. Libya: Selected Issue. IMF Country Report. 13/151, Washington, DC: International Monetary Fund.

Vandewalle, D. 2011. Libya: Post-War Challenges. African Development Bank Economic Brief, September. http://www.afdb.org/fileadmin/uploads/afdb/Documents/Publications/Brocure%20Anglais%20Lybie_North%20Africa%20Quaterly%20Analytical.pdf.

Wahby, E. 2005. Libya: Economic Reforms Anger Citizens. Carnegie Endowment, June 20. http://carnegieendowment.org/files/Wahby.pdf.

Waniss, O., and E. Karlberg. 2007. *The Libyan Economy: Economic Diversification and International Repositioning*. Berlin, London: Springer.

Zaptia, S. 2013. The IMF and the Vexing Issue of Reforming Subsidies: Ramifications for Libya. *Libya Herald*, Tripoli. http://www.libyaherald.com/2013/04/17/the-imf-and-the-vexing-issue-of-reforming-subsidies-ramifications-for-libya/.

Author Biographies

Abdelkrim Araar received his Ph.D. in economics from Laval University in 1998. He is a World Bank consultant and a resource member at the Partnership for Economic Policy (PEP) network. Abdelkrim has been involved in designing and conducting training activities, developing training material, and conducting fundamental research. He has provided theoretical and technical supports to many researchers, especially those in developing countries. He is the coauthor, with Paolo Verme, of the Stata SUBSIM package. Also he is the coauthor, with Jean-Yves Duclos, of the book *Poverty and Equity: Measurement, Policy and Estimation with DAD*, the DASP Stata package, and DAD software.

Nada Choueiri is advisor to the deputy managing director/chief administrative officer at the International Monetary Fund. A Ph.D. graduate of the Johns Hopkins University, she joined the IMF in October 1998 and served in various positions in the Research Department, Middle East and Central Asia Department, European Department, and Communications Department before joining the Office of the Deputy Managing Director as an advisor. During 2013–14, while on leave from the IMF, she spent two years at the World Bank's country office in Rabat, Morocco, where she served as lead economist for Algeria and Libya.

Paolo Verme is a senior economist at the World Bank. A Ph.D. graduate of the London School of Economics, he was a visiting professor at Bocconi University in Milan (2004–09) and at the University of Turin (2003–10) before joining the World Bank in 2010. For almost two decades, he has served as adviser and project manager for multilateral organizations, private companies, and governments on labor market, welfare, and social protection policies. His research is widely published in international journals, books, and reports, and he has worked extensively on subsidies in the MENA Region and elsewhere. He is the coauthor of the subsidies simulation model SUBSIM (www.subsim.org).

Chapter 6
Energy Subsidies and the Path Toward Sustainable Reform in the Arab Republic of Egypt

Sudeshna Ghosh Banerjee, Heba El-laithy, Peter Griffin, Kieran Clarke and Mohab Hallouda

Introduction

Energy subsidies have existed in developing countries for a long while. Traditionally, subsidies were put in place to enhance access to modern energy services, protect the poor against high and fluctuating energy prices, foster industrial development, smooth consumption levels, and contain inflationary pressures. In spite of these intentions, energy subsidies have not fulfilled their purpose in many ways. International experience suggests that such subsidies come with significant economic, social, and environmental costs in the form of a high fiscal burden on government budgets, inequity in subsidy delivery to different income groups, and making fossil fuels more attractive compared to other lower carbon options (Fattuah and El-Katiri 2012).

In the Arab Republic of Egypt subsidies, primarily in food items, have been prevalent for many years. Since the British withdrawal in 1956, subsidies were imposed on a large group of items—food, transport, housing, energy, health care, soap, and cigarettes—to create a system of social assistance in the absence of an administrative machinery to transfer wealth. Attempts to reduce or remove the system are politically sensitive and have often met with widespread resistance, for example, the 1977 riots in Egyptian streets following President Anwar Sadat's decision to cut food subsidies (Rohac 2013). Along with food, energy subsidies have been the mainstay in Egypt's budget for decades. Following a downward turn in economic performance following the January 2011 revolution, energy subsidies

S.G. Banerjee (✉) · P. Griffin
World Bank, Cairo, Egypt

H. El-laithy · M. Hallouda
Cairo University, Giza, Egypt

K. Clarke
International Institute for Sustainable Development, Winnipeg, Canada

P. Verme and A. Araar (eds.), *The Quest for Subsidy Reforms in the Middle East and North Africa Region*, Natural Resource Management and Policy 42,
DOI 10.1007/978-3-319-52926-4_6

have emerged as a prominent fiscal burden as the country undergoes a historic sociopolitical transition.

This chapter presents the evolution of prices and subsidies in the historical context, provides a glimpse of stakeholder views regarding subsidy reforms, and analyzes the direct and indirect impacts of subsidy reforms on one of the most important stakeholders—the households. The analysis presented here draws from work carried out under technical advisory services provided to Egypt's Ministry of Petroleum in 2013–14 (prior to the comprehensive subsidy reforms announced in July 2014) on two intertwined components: direct and indirect impacts of subsidy reform scenarios and communications strategy to support subsidy reforms. A multisectoral team from the World Bank, supported by consultants, carried out this task. The World Bank-developed software SUBSIM (subsidy simulation) was used to analyze the scenarios of impact of subsidy reforms on households.

Scale of Subsidies

Egypt's fuel basket contains six items—liquid petroleum gas (LPG), gasoline, diesel, heavy fuel oil (HFO), kerosene, and natural gas. Among them, consumption of natural gas is the highest and has reported the maximum increase between 2002 and 2013 more than four times (Fig. 6.1). Natural gas is followed by diesel and fuel oil in consumption.

Since 1990 the retail price of fuels has been raised incrementally, particularly after 2003. In real terms, with nominal prices deflated by the annual gross domestic product (GDP) deflator, (WDI 2014) prices generally show a declining trend except for fuel oil. In 2012 a whole slew of price measures were implemented, particularly in a group of energy-intensive industries and fuel for electricity generation.

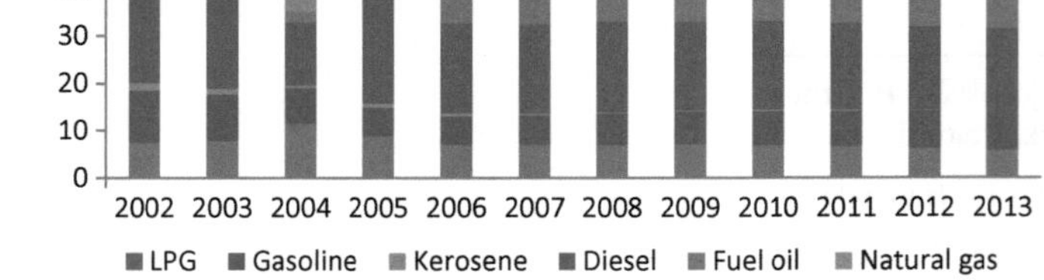

Fig. 6.1 Consumption of fuels. *Source* Ministry of Petroleum 2014

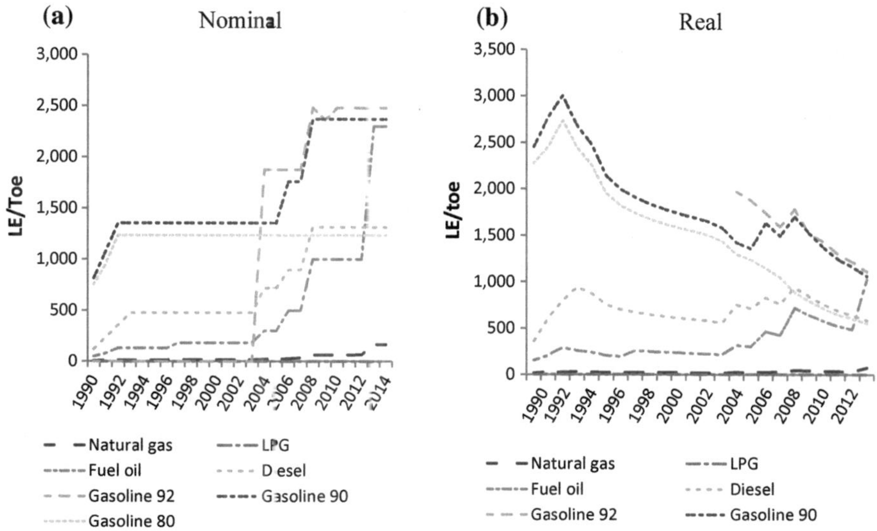

Fig. 6.2 Nominal and real changes in energy prices, 1990–2014. **a** Nominal **b** Real. *Source* Ministry of Petroleum 2014. *Note* LE = Egyptian pound; TOE = Tonne of oil equivalent

Even LPG prices that had remained frozen for 21 years experienced a substantial increase from 4 Egyptian pounds (LE) per cylinder to LE 8 per cylinder in 2013 (Fig. 6.2).

On July 5, 2014, the government of Egypt (GoE) took a significant step forward and announced price changes in many categories of fuels and electricity (Tables 6.1 and 6.2). Except for LPG, the prices of all fuels increased. The GoE estimated subsidy savings of LE 51 billion of which LE 27 billion will be allocated to health, education, and social protection programs. Around the same time, the GoE announced its intention to phase out subsidies over the next five years. The GoE projected a price path for electricity for annual changes until a minimal cross-subsidy (primarily for households) begins in 2019 (Table 6.2).

This journey toward price rationalization stems from the ballooning fuel subsidies since 2002, growing at a compound annual growth rate of 26% between 2002 and 2013. Their share in the government budget increased from 9% in 2002 to 22% in 2013, and their share in Egypt's GDP increased from 3 to 7% in the same period (Fig. 6.5). Among the fuel products, diesel subsidies in particular increased dramatically over this period, while the share of LPG and natural gas declined. Fuel subsidies remained a substantial component of the government budget in fiscal 2013/14. Diesel, LPG, and gasoline account for close to four-fifths of fuel subsidies, but represent only a third of the overall fuel consumption (Fig. 6.3).

Following the July 5 reforms, the average cost recovery rose from 30 to 36%. Among the fuels, the cost recovery performance of LPG is the worst, standing at 7% (Fig. 6.4, panel a). The mismatch between the cost of LPG and the domestic

Table 6.1 Fuel prices in July 5, 2014, subsidy reforms

Product	Unit	Sector	Old price	New price
Natural gas	$/mmBtu	Iron, copper, aluminum, glass, ceramics	4	7.00
		Fertilizer, petrochemicals	4	4.50
		Cement	6	8.00
		Brick, engineering, chemicals, food, medicines, fabric	4	5.00
		Electricity, BOOT	1.1	3.00
	LE/M^3	Cars	0.45	1.10
		Residential 1	0.4	0.40
		Residential 2	1	1.00
		Residential 3	1.5	1.50
		Bakeries	0.14	0.14
Gasoline	LE/L	80	0.9	1.60
		92	1.85	2.60
		95	5.75	6.25
Fuel oil	LE/Ton	Food industry	1000	1400
		Cement	1600	2250
		Electricity	2300	2300
		Others	1500	1950
Diesel	LE/L	All sectors	1.1	1.80
		66% of tourism sector	1.1	1.80
LPG	LE/C	Residential	8	8
		Commercial	16	16

Source Ministry of Petroleum 2014
Note BOOT = Build, Own, Operate, Transfer; C = cylinder; L = liter; LE = Egyptian pound; M^3 = cubic meter; mmBtu = 1 million British thermal units

Table 6.2 Electricity prices in July 5, 2014, subsidy reforms

Residential (PT/kWh)	Old price	Proposed price
up to 50	5	7.5
51–100	12	14.5
0–200	–	16
201–350	19	24
351–650	29	34
651–1000	53	60
Above 1000	67	74
Commercial (PT/kWh)	Old price	Proposed price
0–100	27	30
0–250	41	44
251–600	53	59
601–1000	67	78
Above 1000	72	83

Sources Ministry of electricity and new and renewable energy
Note kWh = kilowatt hour; PT = piastre

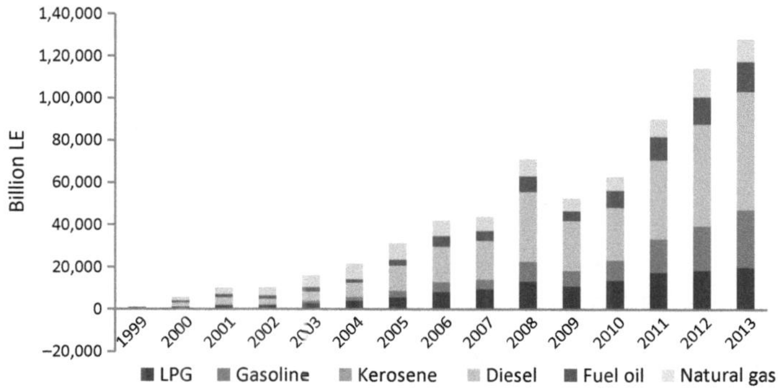

Fig. 6.3 Evolution of fuel subsidies, in LE billion. *Source* Ministry of Petroleum 2014

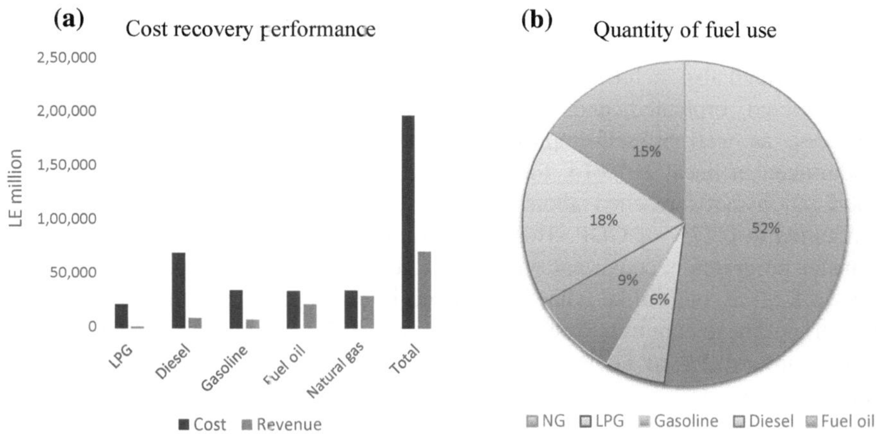

Fig. 6.4 Fuel subsidies, fiscal 2014. **a** Cost recovery performance. **b** Quantity of fuel use. *Source* Ministry of Petroleum 2014

retail price has been widening. A little more than half of LPG is imported, and the international prices have risen over time. The weighted average cost of LPG, including both the domestic and international quantities, was $756/ton in 2013. The retail price had been frozen at LE 2.5 per cylinder for almost two decades since 1991, but going up in 2013 to LE 8 per cylinder. This change is equivalent to a tripling of the sale price from LE 200 per ton to LE 640 per ton, which is equal to $91 per ton. At the other end is natural gas, where the cost recovery performance is the highest at 85%, and it makes up a little more than half of total fuel consumption in Egypt.

Fuel subsidies, comprising 7% of GDP in estimates undertaken in fiscal 2013/14, were greater than the government's combined estimated expenditures in health and education in the same period, which constituted 5% of GDP (Fig. 6.5). Fuel subsidies also dwarf other elements of Egypt's social safety net (SSN) system in the

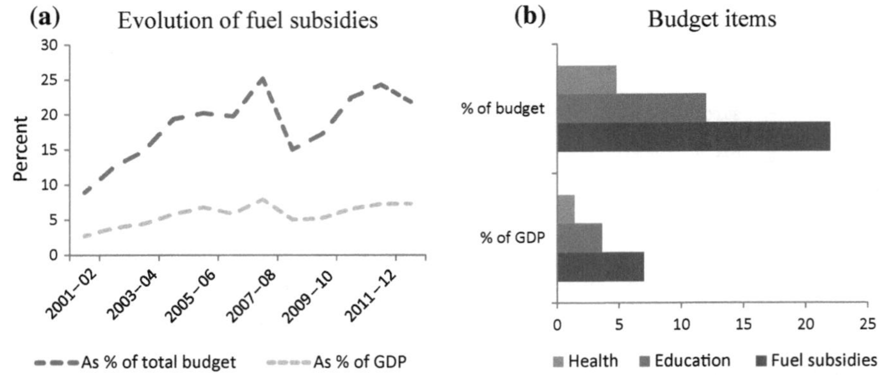

Fig. 6.5 Fuel subsidies, percentage of GDP, and percentage of budget. **a** Evolution of fuel subsidies **b** Budget items. *Source* Ministry of Finance, Ministry of Petroleum 2014

budget, which also includes direct cash transfers to the poor; social care services for the disabled, orphaned, and vulnerable persons; skill building and employment services, as well as self-employment training and microlending. In estimates undertaken in fiscal 2013/14, food subsidies corresponded to about 2% of GDP, food ration cards reached about 0.5% of GDP, and cash transfers to the poor amounted to 0.17% of GDP. This allocation between food and fuel subsidies and transfer programs is consistent with trends observed in the Middle East and North Africa Region, but unlike what is practiced in a comparable group of developing countries. These countries' spending on overall SSN, including subsidies, is much lower (around 2% of GDP) and is more evenly divided between subsidies and transfer programs (Silva et al. (2012).

The highest volume of subsidies goes to the most energy-intensive sectors. Among them, electricity generation and transportations sectors receive the maximum amount of subsidies, with each receiving around 20% of the total energy subsidies in estimates undertaken in fiscal 2013/14 (Fig. 6.6). Depending on the sector, energy subsidies apply to different energy products. The electricity sector's subsidies mainly originate from natural gas and fuel oil use, and transportation sector subsidies are from the consumption of subsidized diesel and gasoline.[1] Households received about 17% of the subsidies directly in the same period, mainly from LPG and to a lesser extent from the consumption of electricity and natural gas. For other sectors, subsidies to diesel are the main sources of energy subsidies, with manufacturing also receiving fuel oil subsidies. Service sectors also received small natural gas subsidies.

[1]In the CGE model, household consumption of gasoline is treated as a transportation service expense.

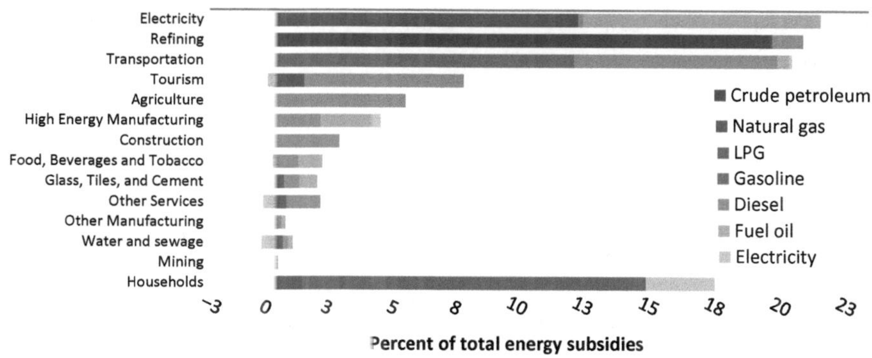

Fig. 6.6 Distribution of energy subsidies by sectors and energy products. *Source* World Bank (2014)

How Do the Key Stakeholders Perceive Subsidy Reforms?

Since the Egyptian revolution in early 2011, various ministers and prime ministers in different governments have discussed the issue of energy pricing and the need for subsidy reform, and they have put forward a number of tentative policy plans. Before the July 2014 announcement of subsidy reform, numerous statements were made emphasizing that current subsidy arrangements are wasteful and a "bad deal" for the poor. These statements have, in turn, started a public discussion on the issue of subsidy reform in traditional media and online.

Comprehensive stakeholder analysis was undertaken as part of the advisory services component on communications strategy to understand the knowledge, attitudes, and concerns of Egyptians regarding energy subsidies and the process of subsidy reform, as well as the self-perceived impacts of this process on key stakeholders. Tools employed for this analysis include a large-scale household survey of more than 2000 households to examine their energy use, knowledge of energy subsidies, attitude toward reform, perceived impacts of reform, and level of information on consumption patterns. The researchers broke down the results by income, age, education, and region. They analyzed focus group discussions on attitudes to and impacts of energy subsidy reform with small transport operators, small agricultural producers, the "youth," and a variety of small- and medium-size enterprises (SMEs), including energy-intensive SMEs. The researchers also conducted structured interviews with policy makers, business leaders, and industry representatives to assess the attitude to and appetite for energy subsidy reform in key sectors and among sectoral leaders. Stakeholder mapping assessed the importance of various stakeholders in Egyptian public life to the debate on energy subsidy reform according to likely power, interest, and influence in this process.

Two-thirds of Egyptians believe energy prices are high (Fig. 6.7). In people disaggregated by age and income, this perception is apparent in about 75% of

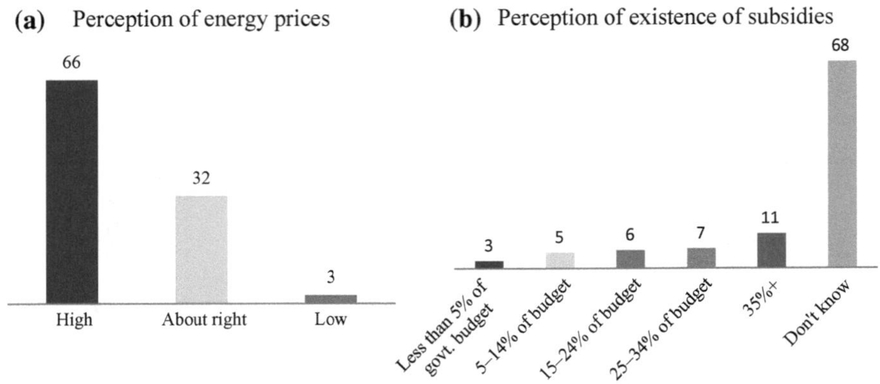

Fig. 6.7 Household perception on energy prices and subsidies (% of sample). **a** Perception of energy prices. **b** Perception of existence of subsidies. *Source* World Bank (2014)

people under age 30, and in about 75% of lowest-income group people (earning less than LE 500 per month). Sixty-eight percent of households did not know the extent of subsidy expenditure by the government when presented with options as to the relative size of current subsidies. Only around 20% of respondents estimated correctly or overestimated. Knowledge of the size of subsidy expenditure was correlated with education and income: only 29% of households in the richest income bracket said they did not know the scale of subsidies, compared to 81% of the poorest households. The survey did not disaggregate by age or region on this question.

When respondents were informed of the size of energy subsidy expenditure, however, close to 75% said that subsidies were not a good use of public money, with richer, older, and more educated households especially concerned about this use of public funds. This result suggests that it will be more difficult to convince poorer and less-educated households of the wastefulness of energy subsidies, although this task could be easier given the general feeling of the profligacy of subsidy spending. When asked why they thought subsidy expenditure was not a good use of public money, the most popular response among households was that subsidy benefits "go to the wrong people," suggesting a good knowledge of the limitations of subsidy targeting and that the distributional issues with current subsidy policy should be stressed in communications seeking to build support for reform.

When asked how potential subsidy savings should be spent, 55% of households listed health as an area in which expenditure should be increased following reform, and 43% of households listed education as another. Only 17% of respondents listed targeted income support to the poor as a better alternative to energy subsidies. In fact, only 24% of the very poorest households said savings from reform should be transferred to targeted income support for the poor. This finding reflects a general lack of support for a redistributive spending policy, which that was also evident in the results of other survey questions.

Clear evidence of resistance to reform also emerged in the household survey. Households are suffering under current economic conditions, and they are concerned that they will not be able to cope with significantly higher energy prices. Close to 80% of households said that they could afford a maximum 5% increase in energy prices. And, despite poor energy service provision, only about half of households were willing to pay higher energy prices for greater reliability of energy supply, and most of these were wealthier households. This theme emerged repeatedly in the focus group discussions. Small businesses are also under severe economic hardship, making energy subsidy reform difficult to manage or support.

A preliminary political economy analysis and stakeholder mapping exercise point to the interest and influence of various Egyptian social interest groups on energy subsidy reform. This research will identify key groups and potential sources of opposition and support for reform that will need to be strategically managed through communications. Different social interest groups are divided according to whether they are political entities, businesses, or consumers/civil society and then are subdivided based on the categories most frequently found in the secondary literature. These categories may sometimes overlap, but are still useful for analytical purposes. In creating the matrix, for each social interest group:

- *Interest* is scored based on how much the stakeholder is likely to welcome the prospect of fuel subsidy reform, owing to both material and ideological factors, ranging from 1 (strongly opposed) to 5 (largely neutral) and on to 10 (strongly in favor). Some actors may react based less on the issue itself than on the potential it offers to mobilize in pursuit of other goals, which are noted in Fig. 6.8.

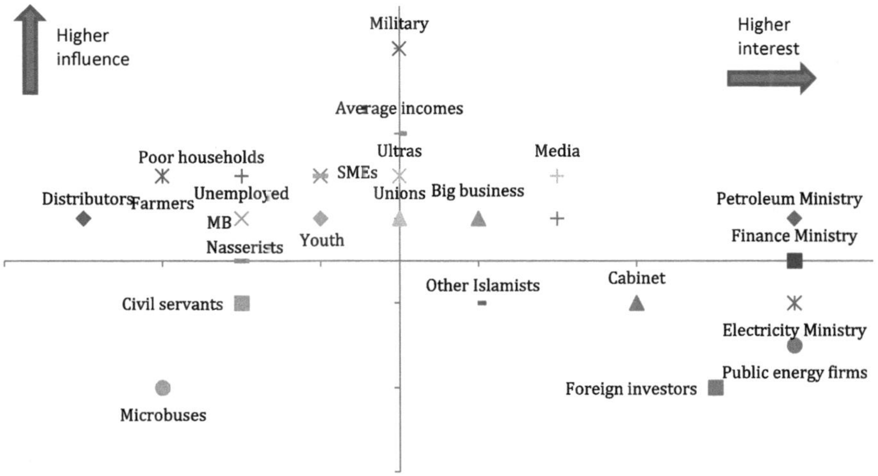

Fig. 6.8 An influence-interest matrix vis-à-vis subsidy reform for key Egyptian stakeholders. *Source* World Bank (2014). *Note* The scoring methods used for the indicative matrix are intuitive rather than systematic. *MB* Muslim Brotherhood; *SMEs* small- and medium-size enterprises

- *Influence* is a multidimensional concept, including political influence at the elite level, access to means of mass communication, financial resources, perceived legitimacy, propensity to engage in violence, and raw numbers. These various factors are combined into a rough measure, ranging from 1 (largely sidelined) to 10 (highly influential) (Fig. 6.8).

The key social interest groups are those in the "low interest" section of the matrix, especially those with both low interest and high influence, who have the potential to become influential opponents of reform, and a few in the low-influence category who may need special protection and guidance. Because the latter group could easily be manipulated by the former, both categories should be a particular target for communications work. These key groups include:

- *Average-income and low-income households* are proportionally the hardest hit by subsidy cuts, and those most able to express their displeasure. It will be vitally important to explain the rationale and the mitigating measures in terms they understand.
- *Small businesses and farmers* are also disproportionately vulnerable. They may need to be advised on how more reliable energy supplies and higher growth will benefit them, as well as what interim support (e.g., microcredit, assistance with a revised business model) is available. Some sectors (e.g., *agriculture, microbuses*) may be more vulnerable than others, and these could be identified for a tailored approach.
- *Youth and the unemployed* combine to form a nexus of dissatisfied and disempowered people who are the most likely to engage in street protests. Innovative means of communication are likely to be needed to reach them.
- *Unions and leftists/Nasserists* are ideologically predisposed to oppose subsidy reform, in the absence of effective mitigation measures, because of its effect on the poor. That said, the benefits of energy subsidies accrue disproportionally to richer households. A compelling case can be made to leftist advocates and unionists that energy subsidy reform can be a pro-poor policy that seeks to undermine the "rich welfare," which is based on a flawed and untargeted welfare mechanism.

The emphasis on all these groups, which is suggested by stakeholder mapping, tends to be supported by analysis from the household survey. For example, the youth tend to have much lower confidence in government than older groups. Low- and average-income households tend to have less awareness of the extent of government subsidisation of energy consumption and tend to consider energy prices already too high.

The potentially difficult groups will require management and engagement through communications to undermine their opposition to reform, but other groups are natural allies in the process of subsidy reform. Within the influence-interest matrix (Fig. 6.8), these groups have a high interest in subsidy reform. The business elite, wealthy consumers, the energy sector, and certain parts of the higher levels of the Egyptian government bureaucracy have both high interest and high influence in this process. These social interest groups should be engaged early in the process of subsidy reform to leverage and utilize their energies in building support for reform. Building partnerships with prominent, respected, and influential natural allies will be crucial in communicating the government's key messages supporting reform in the current context of low government credibility.

Household Use of and Spending on Energy

Electricity and LPG are the most commonly used fuels in households, as evinced from the nationally representative Household Income Expenditure and Consumption Survey (HIECS) in 2012. The HIECS contacts 24,000 households covering all governorates to collect information on the annual consumption of 300 different goods and services, including household direct fuel and electricity consumption. Electricity access is universal, but the level of use increases significantly with income. Monthly average consumption of energy in the richest quintile is at least double that of the consumption of households in the poorest quintile.[2] The average monthly electricity consumption across the entire population is 234 kWh. Use of gasoline progressively rises with income quintile, forming one-fourth of their total fuel consumption. For the poorest, electricity and LPG comprise the energy basket, and the use of any other fuel is negligible (Fig. 6.9).

LPG is almost universally used for cooking in rural areas and by two-thirds of the households in urban areas. The LPG distribution system is chaotic and informal, which directly affects the quality of service delivery for households. The retail price is artificially depressed at LE 8 per cylinder, but it can go up to LE 50–60 per cylinder during months of shortages. Natural gas, as the alternative to LPG for cooking, is prevalent in the higher-income quintiles and in urban areas. Gasoline and fuel oil, mainly used as transport fuels, are mostly consumed by the higher-income quintiles. Natural gas for cooking and transport fuels has been gaining users. The share of households using natural gas for cooking increased from 10% in 2005 to 19% in 2013, and the share of households using wood/coal and liquid fuel fell during this period. The share of households using transport fuels grew from 11 to 23% during the same period.

On average, households spend about 3% of their budget on energy. Although energy spending increases with income, the share of the budget spent on energy is similar in rural and urban areas and across income quintiles. Electricity represents the largest share, accounting on average for more than 50% of the energy budget. Households in the richest quintile spend a larger proportion of their income on

[2]Households are ranked according to their per capita consumption and grouped into five equal groups from the poorest to the richest Average per capita consumption for each of the five quintiles are LE 2795; LE 3845; LE 4878; LE 6216; and LE 11,708, respectively.

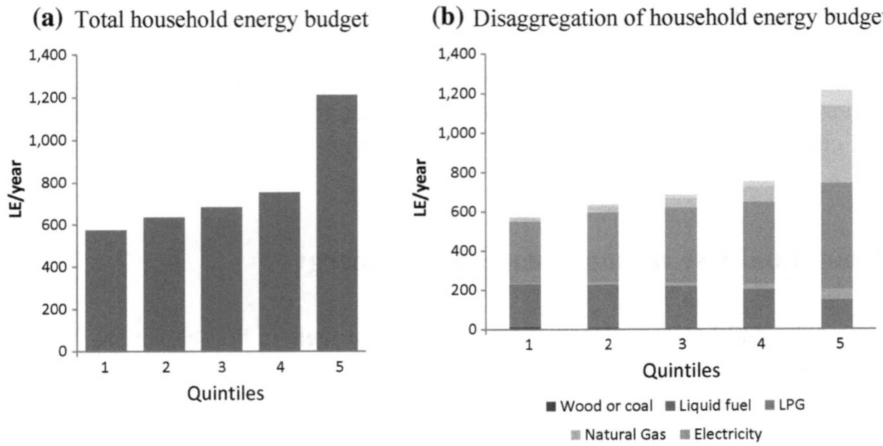

Fig. 6.9 Household annual average energy expenditure. **a** Total household energy budget. **b** Disaggregation of household energy budget. *Source* HIECS 2012. *Note* HIECS = Household income expenditure and consumption survey

transportation fuels compared to households in poorer quintiles. In contrast, households in poorer quintiles spend more of their income on LPG than households in richer quintiles (Fig. 6.10).

Distribution of Direct Subsidies Among Households

Products consumed by richer households, such as diesel and regular gasoline, have traditionally been the most heavily subsidized, followed closely by LPG and electricity. Natural gas subsidies are the lowest per household. Distribution of subsidies is skewed toward the rich, with estimates undertaken in fiscal 2013/14 suggesting that the richest quintile receives 36% of the total energy subsidies. In contrast, the poorest quintile receives an estimated 12% of total energy subsidies. All types of energy subsidies are regressive: the richest quintile receives the highest benefits, especially for gasoline, diesel, and natural gas. For example, the overall share of energy subsidies accruing to the poorest 20% of the households was 12% in the 2014 estimates, but was as little as 3% for natural gas and 1.6% for gasoline. LPG subsidies are the most evenly distributed.

The richest quintile receives three times as much subsidy as poorest quintile. Total direct household energy subsidies amounted to LE 1726 per annum or almost 7% of total household annual consumption in fiscal 2013 (Fig. 6.11). Subsidies are highest for gasoline followed by LPG, and natural gas subsidies are by far the lowest in the household portfolio. The amount of subsidy received by a household increases with expenditure and therefore income quintile: the richest quintile received about LE 690 per capita of energy subsidies, and the poorest quintile

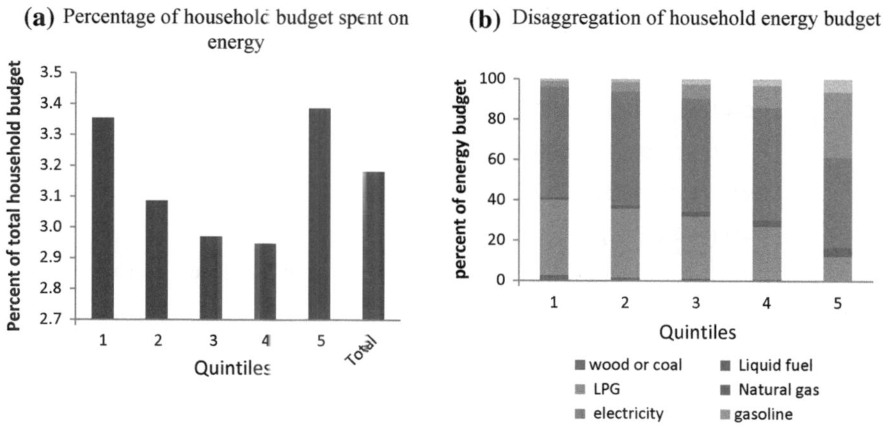

Fig. 6.10 Household spending on energy items. **a** Percentage of household budget spent on energy. **b** Disaggregation of household energy budget. *Source* HIECS 2012. *Note* HIECS = Household income expenditure and consumption survey

received on average LE 232. Nevertheless, as a proportion of total income, subsidies are more important for the poorest quintile, representing 8% of household expenditure, but amounting to 6% of household expenditure for the richest quintile.

LPG subsidy reduction would directly impact the poorest quintile the most, whereas gasoline subsidies removal would mainly affect the richest quintile. For the poorest quintile, the LPG subsidy accounts for 60% of total energy subsidy, followed by electricity with 36%. In contrast, the LPG subsidy represents only 25% of total energy subsidy received by the richest quintile, and gasoline and electricity account for 41 and 31%, respectively (Fig. 6.12). Gasoline subsidies are most inequitably distributed among the fuels (Fig. 6.13). If gasoline subsidies are eliminated, fuel subsidies will be reduced by 40% for the richest quintile and by only 3% for the poorest quintile. On the other hand, if the LPG subsidy is eliminated, 60% of benefits from fuel subsidies will be removed from the poorest quintile.

Energy products are consumed directly through household consumption of these products and indirectly through household consumption of other goods and services that use fuel products as inputs. Therefore, the *total* welfare effect[3] of higher fuel prices—or lower fuel subsidies—on household real expenditure depends both on the *direct effect* of higher prices for energy products consumed by households and on the *indirect effect* arising from higher prices for other goods and services consumed by households to the extent that higher energy costs are passed on to consumer prices.

The analysis of the direct effect on households is estimated through SUBSIM from the 2013 HIECS. The analysis of indirect effect draws from the computable

[3]Welfare is measured by total energy expenditure.

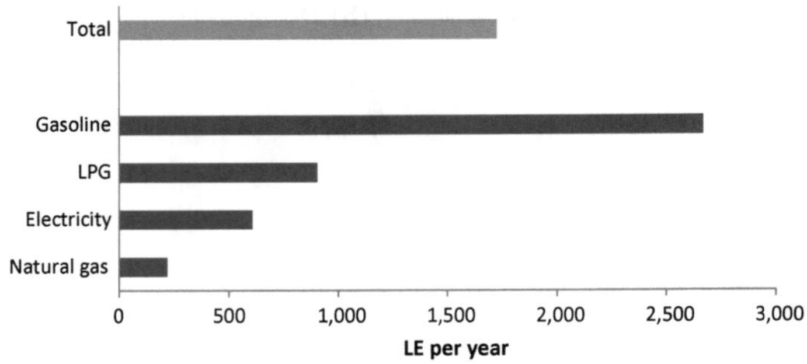

Fig. 6.11 Distribution of household subsidies among fuels. *Source* HIECS 2014. *Note* HIECS = Household income expenditure and consumption survey; LE = Egyptian pound

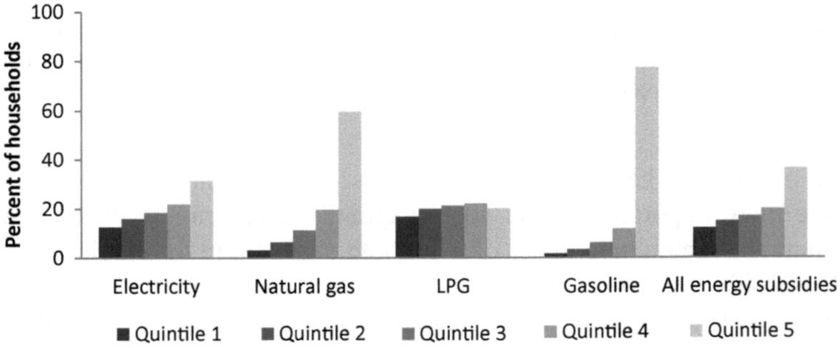

Fig. 6.12 Distribution of subsidies by quintiles. *Source* World Bank (2014)

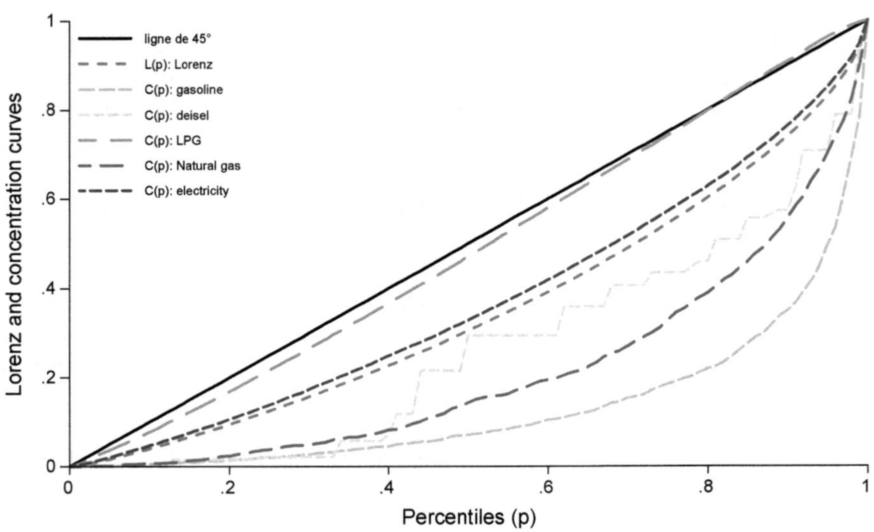

Fig. 6.13 Progressivity in the distribution of benefits. *Source* World Bank (2014). *Note* Lorenz curve is a reflection of cumulative percentage of total national income (or some other variable). It is plotted against the cumulative percentage of the corresponding population

general equilibrium (CGE) model for Egypt underpinned by the social accounting matrix (SAM), representing 56 sectors of the economy, including 11 energy sectors. The SAM has 10 types of households—including five quintiles by urban and rural location—each supplying two types of factors, capital and labor. SAM describes the flow of payments from final demand institutions to production activities and the flow of payments of production factors from activities to institutions, as well as any transfers between institutions.

The incidence of the welfare effect can be analyzed by examining how the magnitude of the effect of price change varies across different household groups; in other words, by calculating the average real expenditure loss for each quintile as a percentage of consumption. In addition to the real expenditure effects of the energy price increase, inequality measures, poverty incidence, and the poverty gap are considered. The poverty gap measures how far below the poverty line is the income of the poor on average.

At the baseline situation (before the announcement of July 5, 2014, reforms), the total annual expenditure was LE 5967, the poverty rate was 26.3%, the poverty gap was 5.2%, and the Gini coefficient[4] was 29.8. Any changes in the scenarios presented in this section will be measured from this baseline situation. The scenarios are, first, a 25% increase in all fuel prices and, second, the July 5 increase in fuel prices. A situation of cost recovery, particularly for diesel, gasoline, and fuel oil, is also simulated.

Considering a 25% increase in all fuel prices, the direct impact on per capita consumption would be a reduction by 1.22%. The per capita expenditure of the poorest quintile falls by about 1.58%, and by 1.12% for the richest quintile. For the poorer quintiles, the decline results largely from the removal of subsidies on LPG cylinders. In contrast, for the richest quintile households, most of the decline in per capita expenditure is driven by higher gasoline prices. Price changes in LPG had the largest impact on well-being especially for the poor, resulting in a decline of 1.31% for the poorest quintile, but only 0.37% for the richest quintile (Table 6.3).

Consequently, the direct impact on poverty incidence is an increase of 1.13 percentage points, from 26.3 to 27.4% of the population (Table 6.4). The poverty gap increases by about 6%. The largest adverse impact on welfare is driven by LPG price increases (0.9 percentage points), accounting for 82% of the overall poverty increase of this scenario, as LPG consumption accounts for a large share of the poor household budget. LPG is followed by electricity, where the subsidy reform contributes to 10% of poverty increase. Because natural gas is mainly consumed by well-off households, increased prices of natural gas have minimal impacts on poverty indicators.

As a result of consumption patterns of energy products by different quintiles, a rise in LPG prices has an increasing inequality impact as well as electricity (with

[4]Gini coefficient is represented by the area between the Lorenz curve and the line of equality. The coefficient varies between 0, which reflects complete equality and 1, which indicates complete inequality.

Table 6.3 Impact of price change on well being, in percentage of annual household budget

Quintile	Gasoline	Diesel	LPG	Natural gas	Electricity	Total
1 (poorest)	−0.05	−0.00	−1.31	−0.00	−0.21	−1.58
2	−0.08	−0.00	−1.10	−0.01	−0.18	−1.36
3	−0.12	−0.01	−0.95	−0.01	−0.17	−1.25
4	−0.18	−0.00	−0.77	−0.01	−0.15	−1.11
5 (richest)	−0.63	−0.01	−0.37	−0.02	−0.11	−1.12
Total	−0.32	−0.00	−0.74	−0.01	−0.15	−1.22

Source World Bank (2014)

Table 6.4 Impact of price change on poverty

	Prereform	Change to postreform	Prereform	Change to postreform	Prereform	Change to postreform
	Poverty incidence		Poverty gap		Gini index	
Total	26.3	1.13	5.21	0.33	29.82	0.08
Gasoline	26.36	0.07	5.23	0.01	29.69	−0.14
Diesel	26.29	0	5.21	0	29.82	0
LPG	27.23	0.94	5.48	0.27	30.02	0.2
Natural gas	26.3	0.01	5.22	0.00	29.82	0
Electricity	26.4	0.11	5.26	0.04	29.85	0.02

Source World Bank (2014)

smaller magnitude), and natural gas, gasoline, and diesel have a decreasing inequality impact. When LPG or electricity prices increase, the poorest quintile exhibited the largest declines in per capita expenditure compared to other quintiles, but these households experienced the smallest deterioration in their well-being when natural gas, gasoline, and diesel increased.

To mitigate the adverse impact, the government may compensate the poorest two quintiles for their real expenditure losses. Such compensation amounts to LE 56 per person, per year. In the scenario involving this mitigation transfer, per capita expenditure of households declines by about 0.84% on average. It rises by about 0.09% for the bottom quintile and declines by more than 1% for other quintiles. Consequently, poverty increases only by 0.45 percentage points.[5]

Considering the price changes in the July 5 subsidy reforms, this scenario is considered without mitigation. The reason is that the potential recipients of the government's increased funding of health and education are not identifiable. Direct expenditure losses amount to LE 36 per person, per year (Table 6.5). This scenario refers to energy products consumed mainly by nonpoor households; therefore, income losses are larger for the richest quintile (LE 97). The poorest quintile also

[5]Direct impact resulted in increase in poverty by 0.19 percentage points.

Table 6.5 Impact on per capita well being (annual household budget)

Quintile	Gasoline	Diesel	Natural gas	Electricity	Total
1 (poorest)	−0.97	−0.01	−0.37	−11.16	−12.51
2	−2.20	−0.03	−0.88	−14.53	−17.63
3	−4.13	−0.11	−1.71	−16.99	−22.94
4	−7.98	−0.08	−2.93	−20.35	−31.34
5 (richest)	−54.06	−0.26	−9.24	−32.95	−96.51
Total	−13.87	−0.10	−3.03	−19.20	−36.19

Source World Bank (2014)

Table 6.6 Reform, poverty head count, and Gini index

	Poverty level	Change in poverty	Standard error	*p*-value	Gini index	Variation in Gini	Standard error	*p*-value
Prereform	26.290	–	–	–	29.82	–	–	–
Gasoline	26.353	0.065	0.025	0.011	29.72	−0.10	0.01	0.00
Diesel	26.290	0.000	0.000	0.000	29.82	−0.00	0.00	0.20
Natural gas	26.309	0.019	0.012	0.103	29.81	−0.01	0.00	0.00
Electricity	26.637	0.426	0.057	0.000	29.85	0.02	0.00	0.00
Post reform	26.801	0.511	0.062	0.000	29.73	−0.09	0.01	0.00

Source World Bank estimates

suffers from deterioration in their living standards, mostly resulting from higher electricity prices (LE 11).

As a result of implementation of this scenario, the poverty rate is expected to rise from 26.3 to 26.8% (Table 6.6). As the price reforms do not touch LPG, which constitutes a substantial proportion of the household energy basket, the direct poverty impact is moderate. However, households are affected indirectly, particularly by the rise in the price of transportation fuels. Indirect and substitution impact on poverty are larger than direct impact, as increased gasoline prices are passed through prices of services, especially transportation. All prices are pushed up because of the increase in transportation prices. This scenario exhibited small improvements in inequality resulting from increases of gasoline, diesel, and natural gas, which is mainly consumed by the better-off. Therefore, indirect and substitution impacts on poverty are larger than direct impacts, as increased gasoline prices are passed through services prices, especially transportation. The relatively strong welfare impacts of reform demonstrate the central importance of putting in place social protection and compensation mechanisms to mitigate the impacts of reform on the poorest citizens—mechanisms that can start simple and become more sophisticated and targeted over time as data collection and institutional capacity are enhanced. This approach is especially important if the general public is to accept necessary ongoing price increases in Egypt.

To the credit of the government of Egypt, following the 2014 reforms, certain measures were indeed put in place to dampen the immediate effect of higher energy prices on consumers, particularly the poor. To ensure that energy price increases did not translate into higher prices for staple goods, the government has frozen the prices of publicly distributed bread, rice, sugar, tea, flour, and oil. In anticipation of reduced energy subsidies, in June 2014 the government expanded the food subsidy system, discounting the price of 20 new products, including meat, chicken, fish, detergents, pasta, certain staple vegetables, butter, and other dairy products. Nevertheless, these kinds of mitigation measures will need to evolve and be enhanced in advance of further energy price reform.

A cost recovery scenario is simulated for gasoline, diesel, and fuel oil, allowing these products to trade at market (cost recovery) prices. In this scenario consumption losses amount to LE 243 per person, per year. This scenario involves energy products directly consumed mainly by nonpoor households. Income losses are larger for the richest quintile, but the poorest also suffer from deterioration in their living standards, mostly resulting from the indirect impact of price increases of all goods and services. Poverty rates increase by only 0.3% as a result of direct impact. Moreover, income distribution improves (Gini coefficient declines by 1.75%) as consumption percentage loss for nonpoor is higher than the poor.

Conclusions

The government of Egypt has embarked on a comprehensive subsidy reform program with an announced price reform trajectory in electricity markets and a similar intention for liquid fuels. This is a bold and welcome first step, but for Egypt's subsidy burden to become more manageable, further price appreciation will likely be necessary. For example, the price of LPG—the most highly subsidized of energy products in Egypt and used extensively by poorer households—was not revised in the July 2014 reforms. From a political perspective, ongoing price increases may be difficult given the current economic circumstances and that consumers have already expressed some frustration at those already in place. Successful and sustainable energy subsidy reform in Egypt will continue to require three key elements: an effective, gradual, and thoughtful price appreciation strategy for different energy types that consider the user profiles for each energy type; the expansion and creation of social protection mechanisms to mitigate the impacts of reform on the poor; and effective communication to build public support for reform.

In terms of pricing, the direct welfare effects of energy subsidy reform on the poor are felt strongly through higher prices for fuels that they consume in large quantities, such as LPG and household electricity, and the indirect effects of reforms on the poor are expressed less through consumption of other fuels and more through their consumption of other goods and services, especially transportation services. This profile of energy consumption and of the direct and indirect impacts of reform has informed, and should continue to inform, energy pricing plans into the future.

No matter how well-considered price reform strategies are, there will necessarily be impacts on the poor (and indeed all energy consumers) resulting from reform. Mitigating the impacts of subsidy reforms will likely require a relatively small amount of fiscal resources, but effective targeting to the poor and vulnerable is currently difficult given the limited scope of national social protection systems. Many favor the creation of a national cash transfer system, starting with a universal registry of the poor, which would be the cornerstone of a cash compensation mechanism and should be prioritized. In the meantime, the government should consider other short-term measures that can be rolled out to minimize the impact of energy subsidy reform (if and when this process occurs), as occurred in 2014 with the changes to the food subsidy system. There are a wealth of policy options to achieve this, from the provision of vouchers for key goods consumed by the poor, to price controls for certain nonenergy staple goods. International experience in subsidy reform is illustrative of the interventions that are likely to be successful in this regard.

The communications efforts for the July 5 reforms were rather weak. Moving forward with subsidy reforms will require a sustained and consistent communications effort to inform Egyptians about subsidies, help them understand the benefits of moving away from the subsidy regime, and make them aware of the spending on health and education from subsidy savings. The government also needs to continuously monitor the media for public sentiments regarding subsidy reforms, conduct polls to understand the people's pulse, and build alliances with prominent Egyptians to promote awareness on subsidies and greater consensus on the need for subsidy reforms.

Finally, the government will need to deliver tangible results in terms of improved public services provision. The often-repeated rationale for energy subsidy reform is that it will provide the fiscal space to deliver better public services, including investment in education, health, and infrastructure, all of which are sorely needed. The government has stated that LE 21 billion of the total saving of LE 51 billion from the current reforms will be channeled directly into health and education. Egyptian consumers who have been affected by higher energy prices will demand that their sacrifices result in a tangible change in the way the government provides essential services for them. Delivering noticeable, timely improvements in service provision, in the context of general fiscal consolidation, should therefore be a priority of Egypt's macroeconomic policy in the short to medium term. Communication and transparency will be key to achieving this objective.

References

Fattouh, B., and L. El-Katiri. 2012. *Energy and Arab economic development.* Arab human development report, United Nations Development Program. http://www.arab-hdr.org/publications/other/ahdrps/ENGFattouhKatiriV2.pdf.

Household Income and Expenditure, and Consumption Survey. 2012, 2014. Available from Central Agency for Public Mobilization and Statistics (CAPMAS), Cairo.

Rohac, D. 2013. *Solving Egypt's subsidy problem.* Cato Institute, policy analysis no. 741. http://www.cato.org/publications/policy-analysis/solving-egypts-subsidy-problem.
Silva, J., V. Levin, and M. Morgandi. 2012. *Inclusion and resilience: the way forward for social safety nets in the Middle East and North Africa.* World Bank: Washington D.C.
WDI (World Development Indicators). 2014. Available at http://data.worldbank.org/data-catalog/world-development-indicators.
World Bank. 2014. Policy brief: energy subsidy reforms in Egypt. Report prepared for technical advisory services to Ministry of Petroleum, Arab Republic of Egypt. Unpublished draft. World Bank, Washington, DC.

Author Biographies

Sudeshna Ghosh Banerjee is a Lead Energy Specialist in the Energy and Extractives Global Practice at the World Bank Group. She has worked on energy and infrastructure issues in the South Asia and Africa departments in both operations and analytic assignments. She focuses on project economics, monitoring, and evaluation, and on a broad range of energy sector issues including energy access, energy subsidies, renewable energy, and sector assessments. She holds a Ph.D. in public policy from the University of North Carolina at Chapel Hill and M.A. and B.A. degrees in economics from Delhi University.

Heba El-laithy is a professor of statistics at Cairo University's Faculty of Economics and Political Science. She is a key expert for microdata analysis and socioeconomic and social impact evaluation for development programs. Dr. El-laithy has a strong background in statistical analysis. She received her Ph.D. degree from Sussex University. She is a key poverty and inequality expert, who has contributed her expertise to several poverty assessments and poverty alleviation program evaluations in the Arab Republic of Egypt, Lebanon, Syria, and the Republic of Yemen, authoring and co-authoring seminal reports on poverty, inequality, poverty alleviation, and social safety net development in the World Bank's MENA Region and the UN's ESCWA Region for governments, research centers, and national and international organizations such as Social Fund for Development, the World Bank, and many others. Dr. El-laithy has published papers on issues including the gender dimension of poverty, social risk management, and monetary poverty, multidimensional poverty, and food security. She designed, prepared manuals, and delivered training course on measuring monetary and nonmonetary poverty, gender statistics, human development indicators, inequality, and targeting mechanisms. She led the team for developing the poverty map for Egypt, using the Household Income, Expenditure, and Consumption Survey 2012–13 and the Population and Housing Census 2006. Recently, she participated in designing targeting mechanisms for new cash transfer programs for the Ministry of Social Solidarity, based on geographical targeting and proxy means testing.

Peter Griffin is a macroeconomist and modeler. In more than 40 countries, he has developed and implemented CGE (computable general equilibrium) and econometric models for analyzing and demonstrating impacts of energy subsidy reforms as well as other major policy reform initiatives. Currently he is working as a consultant to the World Bank conducting an economy-wide impact assessment of the energy subsidy reforms agenda in the Arab Republic of Egypt. Additionally, he is a consultant for the government of Turkey and World Bank's Public Finance Review, analyzing the impacts and effectiveness of public finance measures undertaken over the last decade, as well as developing proposal for new fiscal measures in support of sustained growth in Turkey.

Kieran Clarke works for the International Institute for Sustainable Development's (IISD) Global Subsidies Initiative, where he manages in-country work programs—chiefly in India, Vietnam, and the Arab Republic of Egypt—promoting energy subsidy reform and supporting governments with this process. Prior to joining IISD, Kieran worked over several years in energy and climate change policy for the Australian federal government, latterly as executive international energy adviser. Kieran has also worked for the Organisation for Economic Co-operation and Development (OECD) in Paris in the International Energy Agency's South Asia Outreach Program. Kieran has undertaken consultancies on energy policy for the Earth Institute in New York and for Ghana's Ministry of Environment, among others. His postgraduate studies in applied economics and public administration were undertaken at Columbia University, New York, and Sciences Po College, Paris.

Mohab Hallouda is a senior energy specialist in the Energy and Extractives Practice of the World Bank. He graduated from the Faculty of Engineering-Cairo University in 1983, where he also received his M.S. degree. He received his Ph.D. from North Carolina State University in 1992. He spent two years as visiting faculty in the United States and Germany. He is a professor in the Electric Power and Machines Department, Cairo University, and has worked and conducted research and development programs with industries and utilities on power quality, energy efficiency, motor drives, and renewable energy. He coordinated the work on energy efficiency codes and standards and labels for the Energy Efficiency Improvement and Greenhouse Gas reduction project for five years. He has directed the Information and Communication Technology (ICT) trust fund for development. Hallouba has been with the World Bank since 2007, managing conventional, renewable, and energy efficiency programs as well as energy policies and reform. His primary areas of specialization are clean energy, power quality, and local development.

Chapter 7
Energy Subsidies Reform in Jordan: Welfare Implications of Different Scenarios

Aziz Atamanov, Jon Jellema and Umar Serajuddin

Introduction

As political unrest spread across the Arab world, Jordan faced an adverse economy as well. Fundamental to the economic challenge was high and rising energy prices, already heavily subsidized for consumers. With the government intent on staving off emerging unrest through a series of measures, buffering consumers from increased energy prices being a key action, fiscal costs mounted. By 2012 subsidies on petroleum products alone were about 2.8% of the gross domestic product (GDP) and 8.8% of government expenditures. At the same time, political unrest disrupted the supply of natural gas from the Arab Republic of Egypt, and Jordan had to abruptly switch to using imported oil products (heavy fuel oil and diesel) to produce electricity. The cost of producing electricity increased several folds. As the higher cost was not passed on to the consumers, National Electric Power Company (NEPCO), bore all the increases in fuel prices and accumulated debt as a result. At approximately 17% of government expenditures and 5.5% of GDP in 2011, the new prices doubled the amount of the petroleum subsidies.

Even for a country with a history of universal subsidies, the suddenness and immensity of the fiscal burden were remarkable. Facing strong fiscal pressures of the unsustainably large subsidies, in November 2012 the government decided to remove the subsidies for high quality gasoline, diesel, and kerosene and reduce the subsidies on liquefied petroleum gas (LPG). To compensate households for the price increases, the government introduced a large-scale cash transfer program to households earning less than 10,000 Jordanian dinars (JD) a year, covering about two-thirds of households. This major policy decision was carried out in the middle of a volatile political atmosphere. All the same, reform efforts were incomplete, and the government continues to contemplate how to reduce electricity subsidies, which

A. Atamanov (✉) · J. Jellema · U. Serajuddin
World Bank, Washington, DC, USA
e-mail: aatamanov@worldbank.org

P. Verme and A. Araar (eds.), *The Quest for Subsidy Reforms in the Middle East and North Africa Region*, Natural Resource Management and Policy 42,
DOI 10.1007/978-3-319-52926-4_7

surpass the fiscal burdens imposed by the petroleum subsidies. Much like the 2012 petroleum subsidies reform, the government could implement far-reaching reforms by reducing electricity subsidies and combining the cuts with a targeted cash transfer. Yet, it has been difficult for the government to put in place such a measure, despite the quite successful removal of petroleum subsidies.

One reason for the hesitation in further reforms is perhaps that the question of "who gets what, when, and how"[1] from reform has no clear answer. The costs and benefits of potential reforms are not well understood, especially for electricity, where the pricing may often appear opaque even to policy makers. This chapter attempts to shed light on the distributional and fiscal impacts of reform options, focusing on petroleum and electricity subsidy reforms. Understanding the impacts of the petroleum subsidy reforms can inform alternative reform options for electricity subsidies.

The chapter is organized as follows. It starts with the evolution of subsidies in Jordan since the 2000s. The distributional impacts of reform would depend on how important the subsidized items are to consumers in terms of their expenditures on those items. The next section discusses this question from the perspective of richer and poorer households. The distributional impacts of reform would depend not only on how much consumers spend on the subsidized items but also on the extent of price changes. The following two sections simulate direct and indirect impacts of potential reform scenarios across the income distribution. From this discussion, the chapter moves on to considering how reforms are weighed down by vexing political economy constraints. In Middle East and North Africa (MENA) countries, universal subsidies have been in place as part of the governments' role in ensuring stability in the lives of the people, and doing away with them is not straightforward.

Evolution of Subsidies

As in other countries in the MENA Region, the government of Jordan has traditionally provided universal subsidies to consumers and producers of petroleum products, electricity, water, and food. With the government continuing to insulate the population from spikes in global commodities and food prices, the subsidies experienced sharp increases. In 2005 the government was spending more than JD 600 (British) million on food and oil subsidies alone, about 17% of total government expenditures. The magnitude of the subsidies rose and fell with international price changes, but they remained a challenge for the government.

Jordan's consumer subsidies have a long history, with food price subsidies dating back to the 1960s. Starting with wheat and sugar, over time a host of food items were subsidized. By the early 1990s most food prices were liberalized with the exception of wheat, which has continued to be subsidized despite occasional

[1]Quote from Harold Laswell's seminal work *Politics: Who Gets What, When, and How.*

attempts at reform. The government's attempt to remove the wheat subsidies (with prices almost trebling from JD 0.075 per kilogram to JD 0.25 per kilogram), resulted in widespread social discontent and erupted in "bread riots" in 1996 (Lamis and Schwedler 1996). Although the increase was scaled back, the retail price almost doubled in 1996 and was subsequently accompanied with a cash transfer program to compensate the poor. Since then, wheat prices have remained fixed in nominal terms. Consumers today also receive water at subsidized rates. In this chapter, we focus on petroleum products and electricity because of their relative importance to Jordanian households and the government.

Subsidies on Petroleum Products

Before 2003 Jordan received oil from Iraq at below market prices, and the government passed on part of these savings to consumers. After 2003 Jordan's savings from this source declined, and at the same time international prices went up (World Bank 2009). Between 2002 and 2008 world energy prices increased by more than threefold, and world food prices doubled (Fig. 7.1). The government was forced to increase prices on petroleum products in 2005 and again in 2006, but it still kept prices below international levels. Consequently, in 2005 government spending on petroleum subsidies alone reached 5.8% of GDP (Coady et al. 2006).

In the face of serious fiscal strain, the government phased out cash subsidies on petroleum products between 2008 and 2010 (Table 7.1). For the first time prices were at the international level (LPG was still partially subsidized), and a rapid drop in petroleum subsidies followed—from 2.5% of GDP in 2007 to 0.3% in 2009. At the same time the government compensated households in the form of salary

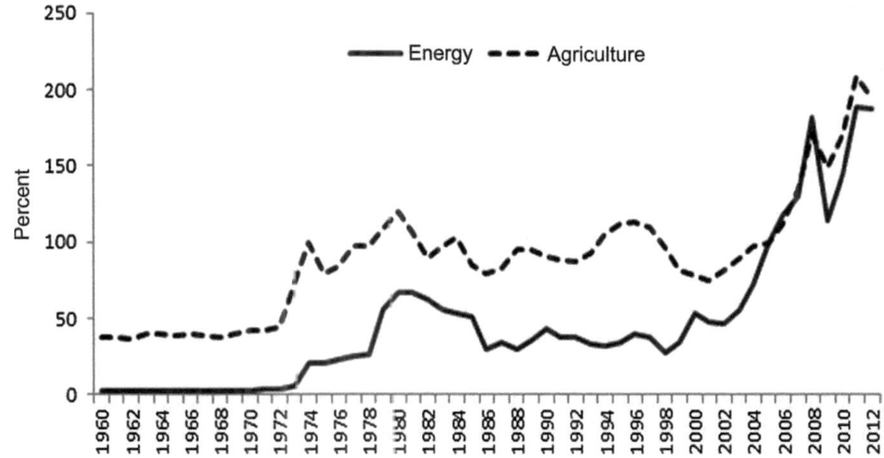

Fig. 7.1 World energy and agriculture price trends, 1960–2012, *Source* Araar et al. (2013); figures based on the World Bank commodity prices database (Index, 2005 = 100%)

Table 7.1 Jordan: Changes in petroleum subsidies, 2007–12 (in JD million)

	2007	2008	2009	2010	2011	2012
Budgetary petroleum subsidies	306	197.9	42.9	88.2	571	626
Nominal GDP at market prices	12,131	15,593	16,912	18,762	20,477	22,230
Petroleum subsidies (% of GDP)	25	13	0.3	0.5	2.8	2.8
Petroleum subsidies (% of budget expenditures)	6.8	3.8	0.9	1.6	8.4	8.8

Source Araar et al. (2013). *Note* GDP = gross domestic product; JD = Jordanian dinar

increases for public and private sector employees and military personnel. At the very end of 2010, however, as oil prices reached US$ 90 a barrel, the government discontinued the monthly petroleum price adjustments and reintroduced petroleum subsidies. By 2012 petroleum subsidies were at 2.8% of GDP or close to 9% of the government budget.

Facing fiscal pressure again, in June 2012 the government increased the price of premium octane gasoline (octane 95) by about 26%. However, as octane 95 accounted for only about 10% of the gasoline consumption of Jordan's transport sector, this move proved inadequate to address the government's fiscal burdens. The government then launched the major reforms of November 2012, when subsidies on petroleum products were cut drastically and an extensive cash transfer program was instituted. This program has continued till the present and will be described in more detail.

Subsidies on Electricity

The production and distribution of electricity in Jordan are in the hands of the private sector, and transmission is in the hands of the public sector. Prior to 2006 the entire electricity system was under the public sector. In 2002 a new electricity law was passed to open the system to the private sector. In 2006 the privatization process was initiated, and by 2008 two independent power producers entered the market. Today there are four major private (or almost private) production companies and three main private distribution companies (JEPCO, IDECO, and EDCO). The transmission company, NEPCO, a public shareholding company, purchases all its energy from the producers and resells it to the distributors. Verme (2011) provides a more detailed discussion of this arrangement. The sale price from the production companies to NEPCO is established by bilateral contracts. These contracts specify that NEPCO is responsible for the purchase of the fuel necessary for the functioning of the power stations. The sale price from NEPCO to the distribution companies and the tariffs for consumers are established by the government's Energy and Minerals Regulatory Commission (EMRC).

The existing structure of the electricity system implies that all financial risks are borne by NEPCO. The four private producers companies are insulated from the risks associated with changes in fuel prices, as the cost of fuel is borne by NEPCO as stipulated in the NEPCO-production companies agreements. The three private distribution companies are insulated from price increases by the tariff system in place, which guarantees a positive return to distribution companies.

In the 2000s electricity generation in Jordan relied mostly on Egyptian gas and heavy oil, with the former accounting for 80–85% of inputs. Electricity is produced almost entirely with fuels, and alternative sources of production, such as hydro or solar power, are absent. The price of heavy oil almost doubled in February 2008, but Egyptian gas was heavily subsidized at about 50% below international market prices (World Bank 2009). Between 2008 and 2009 NEPCO managed to maintain positive balances, but at the end of 2010 the company reported a debt of more than JD 200 million. Then, due to disruptions of gas supply from Egypt in 2011, the cost of producing electricity in Jordan increased several times over. The producers had to switch to expensive diesel and heavy fuel oil, the use of which in the fuel mix reached 80% in 2012 from 29% in 2010. As the increased costs were not passed onto the final consumers, NEPCO assumed the burden of increases in fuel prices and began running monthly deficits of an estimated JD 100 million, which amounted to JD 1.2 billion annually (5.5% of GDP in 2011). This enormous fiscal burden on the government was one of the main reasons the government has stated its intention to follow fiscal consolidation plans in the context of an International Monetary Fund (IMF) program known as the stand-by arrangement (SBA).

Distribution of Subsidies

This section describes the distribution of expenditures on subsidized products and the distribution of subsidies across households in Jordan based on the 2010 Household Expenditures and Income Survey (HEIS), the most recent flagship consumption survey conducted by Jordan's Department of Statistics (DOS). As the survey is outdated, all expenditures were inflated to 2013 prices using nominal GDP per capita growth rates.[2]

Petroleum Products

Households in Jordan spent an estimated JD 856 million on subsidized petroleum products such as kerosene, LPG, gasoline (octane 90 only), and diesel in 2013

[2]WBOPENDATA Stata ado (Azevedo 2011) was used to retrieve information on GDP per capita from the *WDI* database as of September 3, 2014.

Table 7.2 Household expenditures on subsidized petroleum products, in JD million

Quintile	Kerosene	LPG	Gasoline	Diesel	Total
1 (poorest)	7	27	21	0	55
2	9	33	55	0	98
3	12	38	91	1	141
4	12	45	139	2	199
5 (richest)	14	63	251	35	363
Total	55	206	557	38	856

Source World Bank calculations based on extrapolated HEIS 2010 data
Note HEIS = Household Expenditures and Income Survey; population quintiles based on spatially adjusted consumption per capita before the reform

Table 7.3 Expenditure on subsidized petroleum products relative to total expenditures, in percent

Quintile	Kerosene	LPG	Gasoline	Diesel	Total
1 (poorest)	0.7	2.4	1.9	0.0	5.0
2	0.6	2.0	3.4	0.0	6.0
3	0.6	1.8	4.3	0.0	6.6
4	0.4	1.6	4.8	0.1	6.9
5 (richest)	0.2	1.1	4.4	0.6	6.4
Total	0.4	1.5	4.1	0.3	6.4

Source World Bank calculations based on extrapolated HEIS 2010 data. *Note* HEIS = Household expenditures and income survey; population quintiles based on spatially adjusted consumption per capita before the reform

(Table 7.2). Expenditures on gasoline account for about two-thirds of this amount, followed by LPG (24%), kerosene (6%), and diesel (5%). Wealthier households spend larger amounts on subsidized petroleum products than poorer households.

Expenditures on gasoline and diesel are relatively more important for wealthier households, and LPG and kerosene are relatively more important for less-affluent households (Table 7.3). Households in the wealthiest quintile spend an estimated 4.4% of their total expenditures on gasoline, and the poorest quintile spends only 1.9%. Conversely, the poorest quintile households spend 2.4% of their expenditures on LPG, and the wealthiest quintile spends 1.1%. Budget shares of each product can be clearly seen in Fig. 7.2 plotted over population percentiles ranked by consumption per capita. The positive slope means higher shares of the product in the total budget of the wealthier population. Petroleum products as whole account for an estimated 6.4% of total household expenditures, with the poorest quintile households spending 5% of their total expenditures on these products and the richest quintile spending 6.4%.

In terms of actual amounts spent on subsidized products, richer households far outspend poorer households. The poorest quintile was spending seven times less on subsidized petroleum products than the richest quintile (6% of total national expenditures versus 42% as shown in Fig. 7.3), which indicates that wealthier

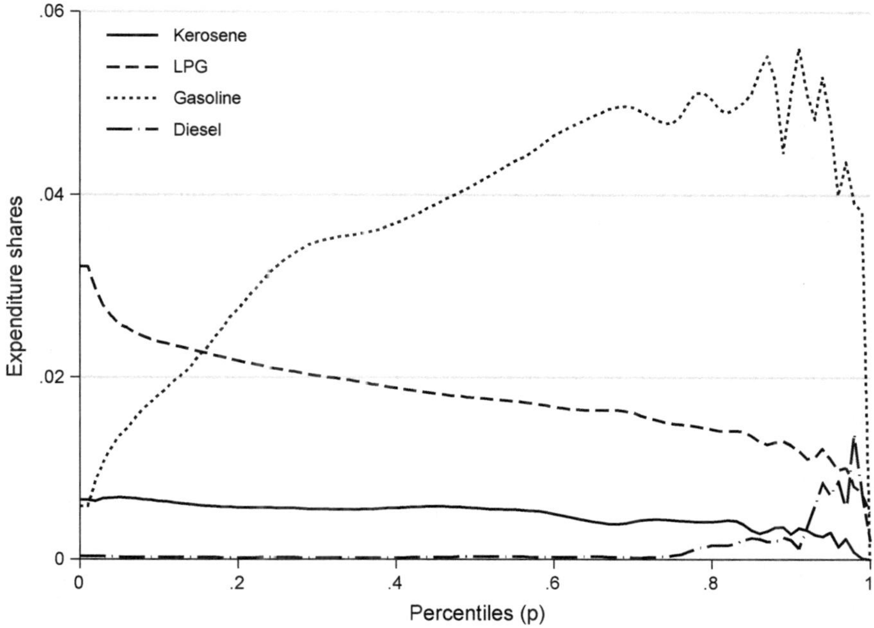

Fig. 7.2 Expenditure on subsidized petroleum products relative to total expenditures, in percent, *Source* World Bank calculations based on extrapolated HEIS 2010 data

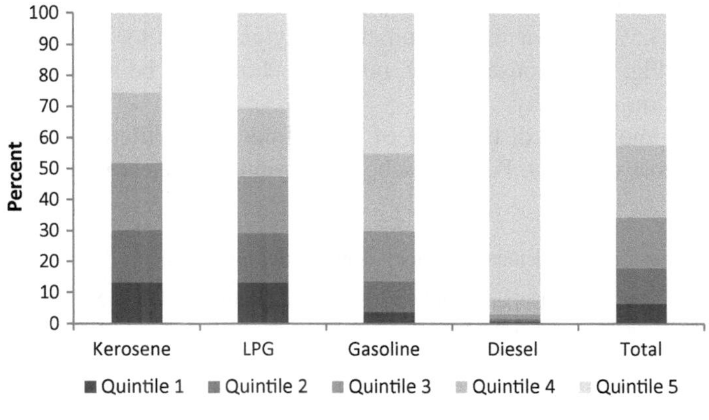

Fig. 7.3 Shares of total expenditures on subsidized petroleum products by quintiles, in percent, *Source* World Bank calculations based on extrapolated HEIS 2010 data, *Note* HEIS = Household expenditures and income survey; population quintiles based on spatially adjusted consumption per capita before the reform; Quintile 1 = poorest

households received higher per capita subsidies than poorer households. Table 7.21 shows that for all products, per capita subsidies are lower for poor households, particularly for gasoline and diesel.

Electricity

Jordan divides electricity usage—kilowatt hours—into seven tariff brackets. According to the latest revision made in August 2013, electricity tariffs range from JD 0.033 per kilowatt hour for the lowest consumption bracket (1–160 kilowatts per hour, per month) to 0.259 JD per kilowatt hour for the highest consumption bracket (1000+ per kilowatt hour per month), with households paying progressively higher amounts only on the incremental consumption of the higher brackets.

Table 7.4 shows the tariffs, mean annual expenditures on electricity, and the number of households for each tariff bracket. More than half of all households in Jordan consume electricity between 301 and 500 kilowatt hours per month. These households spend an estimated JD 270 on electricity per year. Hardly any households consume in the lowest tariff bracket (of less than 160 kilowatt hours per month), and the same is true for the highest tariff bracket (of more than 1000 kilowatt hours per month).

Household expenditures on electricity in Jordan are substantial and more important for poor households in terms of budget shares. Households spent an estimated JD 359 million on electricity in 2013 (using extrapolated data from HEIS 2010), an amount higher than that spent on LPG, diesel, and kerosene combined, but lower than expenditures on gasoline. Households from the lowest quintiles spend less on electricity in absolute terms. Households from the poorest quintile spend about a little less than a third on electricity than the wealthiest quintile (annually about JD 30 per capita compared to JD 105 for the wealthiest quintile). The budget shares of electricity are higher among the poorest households, who spend about 3.5% of their budgets on electricity compared to 2.4% for the richest households (Fig. 7.4). Consequently, poor households can be highly vulnerable to higher tariffs on electricity.

Table 7.5 shows the distribution of households with different electricity consumption across quintiles. Poor households consume less electricity and as a result

Table 7.4 Parameters to calculate electricity consumption in Jordan

Brackets: kWh/month	2014 tariff, JD	Upper bound consumption, yearly (JD)	Mean annual consumption on electricity, JD	No. of HH	Percent of HH
1–160	0.033	63	54	8967	1
161–300	0.072	184	136	355,443	29
301–500	0.086	391	270	620,619	51
501–600	0.114	528	448	127,452	10
601–750	0.152	801	631	80,494	7
751–1000	0.181	1344	986	26,901	2
>1000	0.259		1828	4673	0

Source World Bank calculations based on extrapolated HEIS 2010 data, *Note* HEIS = Household expenditures and income survey; HH = households; JD = Jordanian dinar; kWh = kilowatt hour. Population quintiles based on spatially adjusted consumption per capita before the reform

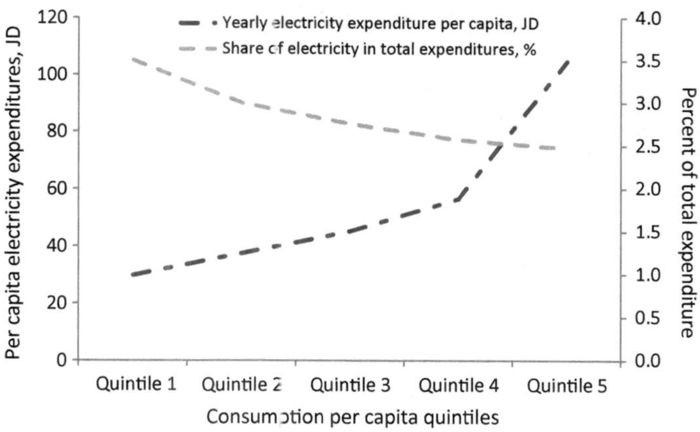

Fig. 7.4 Annual expenditure on electricity, by quintile

Table 7.5 Distribution of households by tariff brackets and consumption per capita across quintiles

Brackets: kWh/month	Consumption per capita quintiles					Average
	1	2	3	4	5	
1–160	1	0	0	1	1	1
161–300	41	35	29	25	15	29
301–500	52	55	55	51	40	51
501–600	5	6	10	14	17	10
601–750	1	3	4	7	17	7
751–1000	0	0	1	2	8	2
>1000	0	0	0	0	2	0
Total	100	100	100	100	100	100

Source World Bank calculations based on extrapolated HEIS 2010 data and official information,
Note HEIS = Household expenditures and income survey; kWh = kilowatt hours; household quintiles based on spatially adjusted consumption per capita before the reform

pay lower tariffs. Forty-one percent of the poorest households consume 161–300 kilowatt hours per month compared to 15% among the wealthiest households. Nevertheless, the relationship between electricity consumption and welfare is not perfect. Some rich households have low electricity consumption, and some poor households have high electricity consumption; this result may be partially attributed to richer households having smaller households.

Direct Impact of Simulation of Subsidies Reform

All simulations in this chapter are based on Jordan's 2010 HEIS, a nationally representative survey that the DOS used to produce official welfare aggregates and poverty estimates. Even though the reforms chosen for simulation were implemented in 2012, the analysis here refers to 2013.[3] Extrapolations between 2010 and 2013 are based on adjustments for economic growth (GDP per capita nominal) and the consumer price index (CPI) for inflation. Household and population weights were updated to reflect population size in 2013.[4]

Estimates of demand elasticity with respect to price are necessary to model consumer responses to price change. Given limitations of having only cross-sectional household data with no variation in individual petroleum product prices across households, we used an own price elasticity of −0.3 to simulate changes in quantities consumed.[5]

Petroleum Products

Simulations for petroleum products are based on price changes largely mimicking the real reform that occurred in November 2012. The price of gasoline (octane 90) rose by 14%, and diesel and kerosene prices increased by 33%. The price increases were meant to fully eliminate subsidies on these items. The highest increase was for LPG gas cylinders, with a unit price increase from JD 6.5 to JD 10, or by 53.8%. Despite this large increase, LPG continued to be subsidized. In this chapter, we decided to simulate the full removal of petroleum subsidies and therefore simulated for the full removal of LPG subsidies as well—the only difference of our simulation from real subsidies reform introduced in November 2012.

---

[3]SUBSIM simulates short-term effects, and November 2012 reforms were expected to kick in early in 2013.

[4]GDP per capita growth and population size are taken from *World Development Indicators,* while CPI is based on official country numbers if different from *WDI* numbers. GDP per capita growth is used to inflate consumption, while CPI is used to inflate the poverty line. This procedure gives a poverty incidence of 13% for 2013 (lower than the official poverty estimate of 14.4% for 2010). Exact numbers used are shown in Table 7.22.

[5]SUBSIM calculates quantity using updated expenditures into 2013 prices and prices of similar period. There is a risk of disparity between quantities from the household budget survey and utilities records (Lampietti et al. 2007). Disparity may stem from data quality and usage of the current tariffs instead of effective tariffs applicable to the period of data collection in the survey.

However, in case on Jordan this issue does not seem to be very important. First, electricity tariffs changed between 2010 and 2013 only for the top three brackets with less than 5% of population. Second, the consumption pattern changes based on elasticities anyway and the tariffs changes occurred in Jordan are a second order issue. Third, we compared estimated quantities across the HBS and administrative sources and the differences are reasonable and within the range we would expect given the different sources.

Table 7.6 Pre- and postreform prices of petroleum products, in Jordanian dinar

	Prereform prices[a]	Unit subsidy	Prices after removal of subsidies[b]	Increase, %
Gasoline (octane 90)	0.7	0.1	0.8	14
Kerosene	0.52	0.170	0.685	33
Diesel	0.52	0.170	0.685	33
LPG	6.5	8.8	15.3	135

Source Araar et al. (2013), [a]As of October 2012, [b]As of November 2012, except LPG

Using historical data from Saudi Aramco's contract price on butane and propane, World Bank energy specialists estimated the "efficient" LPG price to be about US$ 1428 per ton. This estimate implies JD 15.3 per cylinder to be the final LPG unit price without any subsidy (Kojima 2014).[6]

Two scenarios are used for simulation (Table 7.6). In the first scenario, we simulate the full removal of subsidies without any compensating measures by the government. In the second scenario, subsidies reform is combined with the actual cash transfer program that accompanied the petroleum price increases. The cash transfer targets resident Jordanian households (with the households being the unit of reference) with yearly incomes not exceeding JD 10,000. The transfer amounts to JD 70 per person per year, for up to a maximum of six individuals per household (Araar et al. 2013).

Scenario 1: Subsidy Cuts Without Cash Transfers

The simulation reveals that the full removal of subsidies on petroleum products would on average lead to an estimated 2.9% drop in consumption per capita of households (Table 7.7). For the poorest quintiles, the drop will be higher (3.8%). The adverse impact on the poor results mainly from increased LPG prices. The increases in gasoline and kerosene prices have tiny impacts, and the increase in diesel price has no impact on consumption. When all households are considered, LPG and gasoline are the two main products to affect household consumption.

Poverty would be expected to increase by 1.6 percentage points—from 13% in 2013 to 14.6% after subsidy removal—accompanied by increases in the poverty gap and in inequality. The overwhelming increase in poverty is caused by LPG prices, which is not surprising given its high share in the budget of poorest households and the large increase in its price (Fig. 7.2; Table 7.8). The poverty gap, measuring how far poor are from the poverty line on average or depth of poverty,

[6]Masami Kojima is a lead energy specialist at the World Bank.

Table 7.7 Impact on the per capita well-being of removing petroleum subsidies

Quintiles, consumption per capita	Prereform, JD	Postreform impact on per capita well-being, JD					Change in per capita consumption, %
	Total expenditures per capita	Kerosene	LPG	Gasoline	Diesel	Total	
1 (poorest)	843	−2	−28	−2	0	−32	−3.8
2	1240	−2	−34	−6	0	−42	−3.4
3	1624	−3	−39	−10	0	−52	−3.2
4	2198	−3	−47	−15	0	−65	−3.0
5 (richest)	4336	−4	−65	−27	−9	−104	−2.5
Total	2048	−3	−42	−12	−2	−59	−2.9

Source World Bank calculations based on extrapolated HEIS 2010 data, *Note* HEIS = Household expenditures and income survey; JD = Jordanian dinar; population quintiles based on spatially adjusted consumption per capita before the reform

Table 7.8 Impact of petroleum subsidies removal on poverty, poverty gap, and inequality

	Poverty head count, %		Poverty gap		Gini coefficient	
	Level	Change	Level	Change	Level	Change
Prereform	13.0	–	2.44	–	33.66	–
Kerosene	13.0	0.0	2.47	0.02	33.68	0.03
LPG	14.3	1.3	2.83	0.39	34.00	0.35
Gasoline	13.1	0.1	2.47	0.02	33.61	−0.04
Diesel	13.0	0.0	2.44	0.00	33.61	−0.05
Postreform	14.6	1.6	2.89	0.45	33.94	0.28

Source World Bank calculations based on extrapolated HEIS 2010 data
Note HEIS = Household expenditures and income survey

would have increased as well, with LPG being the main contributor. Finally, inequality is expected to increase modestly, as reflected by a slightly higher Gini coefficient.

Scenario 2: Subsidy Cuts with Cash Transfers

In the second scenario we simulate the impact of petroleum price increases on well-being if the government initiates a compensatory cash transfer program to Jordanian households with annual incomes below JD 10,000.

As can be seen in Tables 7.9 and 7.10, if perfectly targeted, the cash transfer offsets the negative impact of higher prices of subsidized products for the bottom 40% of the population. Consumption per capita would in fact grow by 1.6% for the poorest quintile, although on average consumption per capita would decline by

Table 7.9 Impact of petroleum subsidy reform and cash transfer on per capita well-being

Quintile	Prereform	Postreform		
	Total expenditures, per capita	Total expenditures, per capita	Impact on per capita well-being, JD	Change in per capita consumption, %
1 (poorest)	843	857	14	1.6
2	1240	1244	3	0.3
3	1624	1611	−13	−0.8
4	2198	2166	−32	−1.5
5 (richest)	4336	4253	−83	−1.9
Total	2048	2026	−22	−1.1

Source World Bank calculations based on extrapolated HEIS 2010 data, *Note* HEIS = Household expenditures and income survey; population quintiles based on consumption per capita before the reform

Table 7.10 Impact of petroleum subsidy reform and cash transfer on poverty and inequality

Scenario	Poverty level, %	Change in poverty, pp	Poverty gap, %	Change in poverty gap, pp	Gini coefficient	Change in Gini coefficient, %
Prereform	13		2.4		33.66	
Postreform: no cash transfers	14.6	1.6	2.9	0.4	33.94	0.8
Postreform: cash transfer perfectly targeted	12.4	−0.6	2.2	−0.2	33.08	−1.7

Source World Bank calculations based on extrapolated HEIS 2010 data, *Note* HEIS = Household expenditures and income survey; pp = percentage points

1.1%. Poverty would be expected to fall by 0.6 percentage points from 13 to 12.4%. The depth of poverty would decline by an impressive 0.2 percentage points, and inequality, as measured by Gini coefficient, would fall by 1.7%.

Impact of the Petroleum Products Reform on Government Revenue

Removing subsidies on petroleum products without compensation would generate an increase in government revenues by JD 389 million per year (Table 7.11). More than 70% of the increased revenues would come from higher LPG prices, and 20%

Table 7.11 Impact of petroleum subsidy elimination on government revenue, in JD million

Quintile	Kerosene	LPG	Gasoline	Diesel	Total
1 (poorest)	2	37	3	0	42
2	3	45	8	0	56
3	4	51	13	0	68
4	4	61	20	1	86
5 (richest)	5	85	36	12	137
Total	18	279	80	13	389

Source World Bank calculations based on extrapolated HEIS 2010 data, *Note* HEIS = Household expenditures and income survey; population quintiles based on consumption per capita before the reform

would come from gasoline. Higher revenues from LPG are associated with the much higher increase in prices for LPG compared with that for gasoline (135% vs. 14%). The removal of kerosene and diesel subsidies will generate only modest increases in revenues. As the subsidies were prorich in nature, with their removal, richer households would contribute proportionally more to the increased revenues: the poorest quintile accounts for only an estimated 11% of the increase in revenues, compared to 35% by the richest quintile.

The cost of the cash transfer program launched by the government was about JD 320 million a year. This cost was in fact higher than the revenues generated to the government *from households* from the actual reforms the government had carried out in November 2012. Although additional savings to the government were generated from consumers other than households, the cash transfer program appeared costly in the sense that it overcompensated a majority (almost 70%) of Jordanian households (Araar et al. 2013). The reform option we simulated in this chapter estimates the revenues/cost savings generated from households' use of petroleum products (JD 389 million) to be higher than the cash transfer cost but still appear to be quite generous as it overcompensates almost half the population. To put matters in perspective, only JD 206 million are needed to maintain the prereform poverty rate if transfers are universal. If transfers are perfectly targeted to the poorest quintile, only JD 41 million would be needed to bring poverty to its prereform level. The design of the cash transfer program implemented in November 2012, along with a detailed discussion of options for improvement, can be found in Araar et al. (2013).

Electricity

Three Scenarios for Electricity Tariffs Reforms

Three scenarios are explored in simulating the impact of reforms in electricity tariffs (Table 7.12). The first scenario assumes no change in the tariff policy and simply applies tariffs planned for implementation in 2015. According to this scenario, tariffs will increase slightly for consumers from the top fifth, sixth, and seventh brackets. The second scenario lays out the most radical reform, implying a full removal of subsidies. Within this scenario we present two reform options. According to the first one—labeled "flat" reform—tariffs for all consumers become flat, in other words, equal to the cost recovery level at JD 0.164 per kilowatt hour. This option implies a huge burden on the poorer households with the lowest electricity consumption because their prices were the lowest. The second subscenario—labeled "progressive" reform—mimics the first subscenario in terms of the *average* impact on well-being, but uses a completely different approach to tariff increase.[7] Under this subscenario, the burden of subsidies elimination is disproportionately placed on the shoulders of the richest households, who experience the highest increase in electricity tariffs. Given that scenario two is quite severe—leading to a more than doubling of prices for many brackets—and likely very difficult to implement, we simulate a third scenario with a "quasi-progressive" increase in tariffs for all consumers and keeping tariffs on the first two brackets subsidized.[8] This scenario, however, does not fully eliminate the electricity subsidies.

Applying 2015 tariffs has little negative impact on the per capita well-being of households. Given small increases in tariffs that are focused mostly on rich consumers, expenditures per capita are expected to decline on average by JD 0.6 or about 0.03% (Table 7.13) Such a decline would bring no changes in poverty and poverty gap measures.

Full removal of subsidies, however, will have a considerable impact on economic well-being. Replacing subsidies with a flat tariff rate is expected to reduce consumption per capita on average by JD 72.5 or by 3.6%. The negative impact is expected to be the strongest for the poorest households, with the bottom quintile experiencing on average a 5.7% reduction in per capita consumption. The negative burden on the poorest households can be reduced if a progressive increase of tariffs is applied. In this case, the negative impact would be less pronounced for the poor, even though the average household consumption would drop by the same amount. Nevertheless, both subscenarios are quite severe and would be difficult to implement. A semiprogressive increase in tariffs leading to a smaller reduction in subsidies, as depicted in scenario 3, is perhaps more realistic; the relative impact on households across the distribution would be almost equal, with a 1.2% reduction per capita on average (Table 7.14).

Full elimination of subsidies has the strongest negative impact on poverty and inequality. In particular, poverty is expected to increase by 2.4 percentage points, the poverty gap by 0.7 percentage points, and inequality by 1.9% (Table 7.15).

---

[7]Strictly speaking the second subscenario does not fully eliminate subsidies because consumers from the first block continue to be subsidized, and tariffs on others are not raised by enough to offset this subsidy.

[8]People in the third bracket also may be subsidized if their consumption in the third bracket is low.

Table 7.12 Three scenarios for electricity tariff reforms

kWh per month	Current tariff 2014	Subsidy	Scenario 1 2015 tariffs		Scenario 2 full elimination of subsidies				Scenario 3 Semiprogressive increase in tariffs	
					Flat		Progressive			
			Final	%	Final	%	Final	%	Final	%
1–160	0.033	0.113	0.033	0.0	0.146	341.5	0.056	70.0	0.036	10
161–300	0.072	0.074	0.072	0.0	0.146	102.3	0.144	100.0	0.09	25
301–500	0.086	0.06	0.086	0.0	0.146	69.4	0.232	170.0	0.146	69
501–600	0.114	0.032	0.114	0.0	0.146	27.8	0.365	220.0	0.228	100
601–750	0.152	0	0.175	15.1	0.146	−3.9	0.502	230.0	0.304	100
751–1000	0.181	0	0.209	15.5	0.146	−19.3	0.615	240.0	0.362	100
>1000	0.259	0	0.285	10.0	0.146	−43.6	0.907	250.0	0.518	100

Source Official tariff instructions replacing electricity tariff instructions, June 17, 2012, *Note* Subsidies are calculated based on 2012 cost recovery tariff from NEPCO (2012)

Table 7.13 Impact of 2015 tariffs on economic well-being

Quintile	Impact, JD	Impact, %
1 (poorest)	−0.02	0.00
2	−0.05	0.00
3	−0.15	−0.01
4	−0.31	−0.01
5 (richest)	−2.48	−0.06
Total	−0.60	−0.03

Source World Bank calculations based on extrapolated HEIS 2010 data, *Note* HEIS = Household expenditures and income survey; JD = Jordanian dinar; population quintiles based on consumption per capita before the reform

Table 7.14 Different scenarios for electricity tariff reforms

Quintile	Total consumption per capita	Scenario 2 full elimination of subsidies				Scenario 3 semiprogressive increase in tariffs	
		Flat		Progressive			
		Impact, JD	Impact, %	Impact, JD	Impact, %	Impact, JD	Impact, %
1 (poorest)	843	−49	−5.8	−33	−3.9	−10	−1.1
2	1240	−59	−4.7	−42	−3.4	−13	−1.0
3	1624	−66	−4.1	−54	−3.4	−18	−1.1
4	2198	−78	−3.5	−71	−3.2	−24	−1.1
5 (richest)	4336	−109	−2.5	−157	−3.6	−58	−1.3
Total	2048	−72	−3.5	−72	−3.5	−24	−1.2

Source Official tariff instructions replacing electricity tariff instructions, June 17, 2012, *Note* JD = Jordanian dinar; population quintiles based on consumption per capita before the reform

Table 7.15 Impact of electricity subsidy reform and cash transfer on poverty and inequality

	Poverty level, %	Change, pp	Poverty gap, %	Change, pp	Gini coefficient	Change, %
Prereform	13.0		2.4		33.66	
Postreform: Scenario 1: 2015 tariffs	13.0	0.0	2.4	0.0	33.64	−0.04
Postreform: Scenario 2: full elimination of electricity subsidies, flat	15.4	2.4	3.2	0.7	34.28	1.9
full elimination of electricity subsidies, progressive	14.7	1.7	2.9	0.5	33.66	0.0
Postreform: Scenario 3: semiprogressive increase in tariffs	13.5	0.5	2.6	0.1	33.59	−0.2

Source World Bank calculations based on extrapolated HEIS 2010 data, *Note* HEIS = Household Expenditures and Income Survey; pp = percentage points

Table 7.16 Impact of electricity subsidy reform on government expenditures, in JD million

Quintile	Scenario 1, 2015 tariffs	Scenario 2, full elimination of subsidies		Scenario 3, semiprogressive
		Flat	Progressive	
1 (poorest)	−0	−64	−44	−14
2	−0	−77	−55	−19
3	−0	−87	−66	−25
4	−0	−102	−82	−33
5 (richest)	−3	−143	−144	−71
Total	−4	−473	−391	−162

Source World Bank calculations based on extrapolated HEIS 2010 data, *Note* HEIS = Household expenditures and income survey; JD = Jordanian dinar; population quintiles based on consumption per capita before the reform

Planned tariffs for 2015 will not have negative impact, but a semiprogressive increase in tariffs will lead to a moderate (0.5 percentage points) increase in poverty. This reform will, however, have a rather equalizing impact on distribution reducing the Gini coefficient by 0.2%.

Impact of Electricity Reform on Government Revenue

The largest savings from electricity reform will come from the second scenario, assuming full elimination of subsidies. The government can save the largest amount (estimated at JD 473 million) from full removal of subsidies under the scenario of flat tariffs (Table 7.16). This reform, however, will also have the largest impact on poverty as shown in Table 7.15. To get to the prereform poverty and poverty gap levels, around JD 319 million will be required. Therefore, the net gain will be JD 158 million. Under the progressive subscenario, the costs of the transfer to compensate the poor will be smaller and the government will save about JD 174 million. In the third scenario with semiprogressive increase in tariffs, overall gain from higher tariffs will be JD 162 million. From this amount, JD 70 million have to be transferred back (assuming universal transfer) to bring poverty to prereform level and leaving the government with JD 92 million (Table 7.17).

Indirect Impact of Simulation of Subsidies Reform

Petroleum Products

The chapter now turns to the simulation of indirect effects of the rise in petroleum product prices combining a Jordanian input-output (I/O) table with HIES data. The

Table 7.17 Impact of electricity subsidy reform on government expenditures, correcting for measures, in JD million

	Prereform	Postreform				Change[a]			
		Scenario 1	Scenario 2		Scenario 3	Scenario 1	Scenario 2		Scenario 3
			Flat	Progressive			Flat	Progressive	
Subsidies	477	473	3	86	315	−4	−473	−391	−162
Transfers[b]	0	1	316	217	70	1	316	217	70
Total budget	477	473	319	303	385	−3	−158	−174	−92

Source World Bank calculations based on extrapolated HEIS 2010 data, *Note* HEIS = Household expenditures and income survey; population quintiles based on consumption per capita before the reform. [a]Negative values mean reduction in government expenditures or savings. [b]Universal transfers assumed

Table 7.18 Expected producer price increase in Jordanian fuel sector

Product	Price increase, pre- to postreform period (%)[a]	Expected share in total industry fuel consumption (%)	Expected magnitude of producer price increase in fuel sector
Gasoline	14	21	2.9
Diesel	33	32	10.5

Sources Araar et al. (2013); Jordan Petroleum Co. LTD. annual report 2012; World Bank calculations, *Note* See Table 7.6 for prices

Table 7.19 Direct and indirect impacts on well-being of removing petroleum subsidies

Quintile	Diesel			Gasoline		
	Total direct (JD)	Total indirect (JD)	Share of indirect in total (%)	Total direct (JD)	Total indirect (JD)	Share of indirect in total (%)
1 (poorest)	0	3	100	2	0.9	30
2	0	5	100	6	1	17
3	0	6	100	10	2	14
4	0	8	100	15	2	12
5 (richest)	9	13	60	27	4	12
Total	2	7	77	12	2	14

Source World Bank calculations based on extrapolated HEIS 2010 data and the Jordan 2010 input/output table. *Note* HEIS = Household Expenditures and Income Survey; JD = Jordanian dinar

baseline data for the producer price shocks are in Table 7.18. The Jordan I/O Table (2010) does not have disaggregated-by-type petroleum product statistics. Therefore, to capture the likely impact on economy-wide prices (of petroleum product subsidy removal), we use disaggregated production figures from the state-owned refinery as an expectation proxy of the industry-wide petroleum-product mix. The gasoline shock to the petroleum sector is a price increase of 2.9%, which is equal to the change in price in gasoline (from Table 7.6) multiplied by gasoline's expected share (20.6%) in industry's total petroleum product usage. Similarly, the diesel shock—at 10.5%—is equal to the change in price in diesel multiplied by diesel's expected share in industry's fuel mix.[9]

Results of the simulations (Table 7.19) show that the relation between direct and indirect effects varies significantly across products and across quintiles. For example, indirect effects are approximately 77% of the total for diesel but only 14%

[9]The indirect impacts on households of these two producer price changes are calculated separately and independently, and holding fixed all other controlled producer prices—including those of the other petroleum products. Industry is not expected to use significant amounts of LPG or kerosene.

for gasoline.[10] The difference is directly attributable to household consumption patterns. Even though the diesel price increase is more than three times larger than the gasoline price increase and economy-wide prices rise more after the diesel subsidy is eliminated, households purchase so little diesel that they are almost unaffected directly. Any impact from higher diesel prices arrives indirectly through an increase in the price of the household consumption basket.

For gasoline, the relative weight of indirect effects is also different across quintiles. The total indirect effect of the gasoline subsidy removal falls from about a third of total effects in the first quintile to about 12% for the upper quintile. This is understandable as the wealthiest quintile spends more than 10 times as much on gasoline directly as does the poorest quintile (see Fig. 7.3).

Electricity

The simulations for indirect effects of electricity subsidy removal, similar to the petroleum product subsidy reform, were carried out by linking the Jordan I/O table to the HIES data.[11] In average magnitude, the producer price shocks in the electricity sector are equivalent to a household-consumption–weighted average of the household price shocks (Table 7.12).[12]

Simulation results indicate that the indirect effects of electricity price changes vary significantly by household rank (Table 7.20). In absolute magnitude—in other words, in terms of JD—the indirect effects are approximately five times greater for the richest quintile than for the poorest. The reason is primarily that richer households have consumption baskets weighted more heavily with nonfood, electricity-intensive goods and services. Poorer households, in contrast, have consumption baskets weighted toward food, the production of which is not as electricity intensive.

Results also indicate that the relation between direct and indirect effects varies significantly by the electricity subsidy elimination scenario. For example, in scenario 2.I, indirect effects are about a third of the total for the poorest households and close to half of the total for the richest households. In this scenario households consuming the highest electricity volumes see the smallest relative postreform electricity price increases, so it makes sense that the direct effect rises slowly across expenditure quintiles. In scenario 3 price increases are higher for higher volume users (richer quintiles), so the quintile-wide relationship between direct and indirect

[10]The most accurate estimates for direct effects remain those provided in the previous section, and we will disregard estimates of direct effects using I/O data. What is of interest here is the relative share of indirect effects over total effects.

[11]The indirect impacts on households of these price changes are calculated holding all other controlled producer prices fixed.

[12]See Table 7.23 and accompanying text in Box 7.1 for more details on the construction of the block- and consumption-weighted average electricity tariffs.

Table 7.20 Direct and indirect impacts on well-being of removing electricity subsidies

Quintiles, consumption per capita	Scenario 2.I, flat			Scenario 3		
	Total direct (JD)	Total indirect (JD)	Share of indirect in total (%)	Total direct (JD)	Total indirect (JD)	Share of indirect in total (%)
1 (poorest)	49	21	30	10	4	26
2	59	31	34	13	5	29
3	66	41	38	18	7	28
4	78	54	41	24	9	28
5 (richest)	109	102	48	58	17	23
Total	72	50	41	24	8	26

Source World Bank calculations based on extrapolated HEIS 2010 data and the Jordan 2010 input/output table. *Note* HEIS = Household expenditures and income survey

effects is reversed: direct effects rise more quickly across expenditure levels than do indirect effects. In scenario 3, indirect effect shares are smaller for the richest quintile than for the poorest quintile.

The Political Economy of Reforms

The simulations indicate that the current subsidy system provides valuable assistance to the poor, but at the same time are prorich and inefficient. Eliminating subsidies and compensating the poor and vulnerable with a direct cash transfer would be a more effective form of social protection. Subsidy reform, however, is a politically sensitive issue. A major reform of the bread subsidy in 1996 involving the complete elimination of the price support and its replacement by a cash transfer was rapidly overturned following widespread social unrest and what came to be known as "food riots." Thus, even as the government is burdened by high subsidy costs, its reform efforts are hampered by political economy considerations.

The opposition to subsidy reform appears particularly strong in Jordan and Egypt, especially when compared with Lebanon and Tunisia (Fig. 7.5). Data from the MENA SPEAKS (Social Protection Evaluations of Attitudes, Knowledge, and Support) survey, indicate that about 56% of Jordanians were opposed to subsidy reform on any consumer item, be it electricity, food, petroleum products, or water (Silva et al. 2013). In all countries, the (self-identified) lower-middle-income group is slightly less likely to oppose subsidy reform than the upper-middle and wealthy group, and in three of four countries the lower-middle-income group is slightly more willing to consider subsidy reform than the self-identified poor.

However, of those willing to consider subsidy reform (in the MENA SPEAKS survey's Jordan sample), diesel was the most frequently cited candidate for reform, followed by subsidy on bread (Fig. 7.6). Electricity and LPG subsidies, which are much larger, appear to be even more politically sensitive than bread subsidies: only

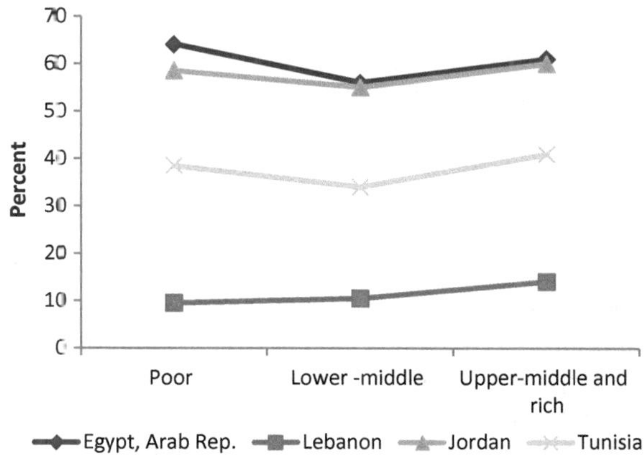

Fig. 7.5 Opposition to reform consumption subsidy on any product, *Source* Silva et al. (2013) calculations using the MENA SPEAKS survey, *Note* MENA SPEAKS = Social protection evaluations of attitudes, knowledge, and support

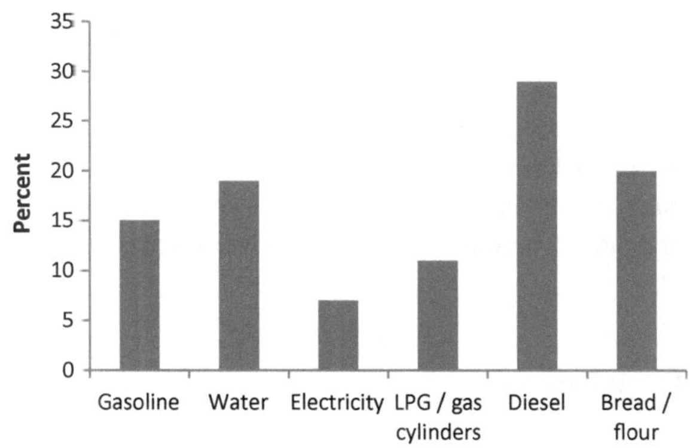

Fig. 7.6 Preferred product for inevitable subsidy removal, *Source* Silva et al. (2013) calculations using the MENA SPEAKS survey, *Note* SPEAKS = Social protection evaluations of attitudes, knowledge, and support

11% of respondents were open to LPG subsidy removals, and a paltry 7% were willing to consider electricity reforms. These figures underscore the challenges the government faces. In fact, the government appears to be sensitive to such concerns, and the November 2012 reforms did not fully eliminate LPG subsidies but did eliminate the subsidies on other petroleum products. It is interesting that the opposition to reforming expensive and regressive energy subsidies is stronger than opposition to food subsidies, which tend to be less regressive. A likely explanation for this finding is the relative importance of these energy products in the people's consumption baskets.

These numbers raise the question as to how the November 2012 petroleum reforms went into effect without any significant public unrest. Silva et al. (2013) synthesize the vast literature in social protection to summarize the strategies that underscore successful reforms. First and foremost, they mention timing as the key to the success or failure of reforms. More specifically, they argue that it is easier to generate support behind a reform during a crisis, a situation that aptly characterizes Jordan. The population appeared to sense that Jordan was in fiscal crisis and petroleum subsidy removals were inevitable. Moreover, from initial episodes of hope, the social unrest eventually generated fear of violence, heightened by the experiences of neighboring Egypt and the Syrian Arab Republic. The subsidy reforms were likely aided by the strong aversion to the political and social instability that vocal opposition had the potential to generate.

Compensation of losers from reform also played a role in the reform's apparent success. Although fiscal constraints often make it challenging for a government to provide direct compensation, the November 2012 reforms were accompanied by a generous cash transfer designed to fully compensate the bottom 70% of Jordanians for the losses suffered from the removal of subsidies. The cash transfer in fact appeared to overcompensate a large portion of the population (Araar et al. 2013). The speed with which the transfer took place is also a factor in the reform's apparent success. The petroleum price hikes were announced on November 12, and within the next few weeks a large number of people started receiving the cash compensation.

In enacting future reforms, the government can learn from its own experience. One concern arose regarding the targeting efficiency of the cash program accompanying the 2012 subsidy reforms (see, e.g., Araar et al. 2013). The government itself has taken measures to improve the targeting, specifically by setting up the National Unified Registry (NUR) database to better target beneficiaries for future cash compensation programs. Tackling electricity subsidy reform, however, appears to be daunting for the government because of its sheer scale.

Conclusions

This chapter examined the distributional and fiscal implications of petroleum and electricity subsidy reforms. Both subsidies are prorich in nature, and in absolute monetary terms, richer households benefit more than poorer households as their consumption levels are higher. These universal subsidies are costly and inefficient because a majority portion of the total subsidies "leaks" to the nonpoor households, and significant amounts actually leak to the richest quintile households. The analysis, however, also suggests that the poorer segments of the population benefit quite substantially from the subsidies and removal of subsidies would impose economic hardship on these groups.

Nevertheless, as the government wishes to strike a balance between protecting its population from price increases and ensuring fiscal prudence, a move away from the universal subsidies system appears imperative. This move would require a considered analysis of both technical and political economy considerations. A generous cash transfer can be put in place to help build broad-based public support for reforming universal subsidies, but the government needs to target these transfers well through developing a sound social protection system.

Finally, it is important to note that although this chapter has presented several findings, the scope of analysis was necessarily constrained by time and data availability. The focus was limited to a microanalysis of household-level impacts.

A more comprehensive analysis would involve broader sectors of the economy (such as nonhousehold users of petroleum products and electricity), and involve a political economy and stakeholder analysis to identify who would gain and who would lose from reform and how.

Annex 7A

See Tables 7.21 and 7.22

Table 7.21 Per capita benefit through subsidies (in currency)

Quintile	Kerosene	LPG	Gasoline	Diesel	Total
1 (poorest)	2	28	2	0	32
2	2	34	6	0	42
3	3	39	10	0	52
4	3	47	15	0	65
5 (richest)	4	65	27	9	105
Average for all products	3	43	12	2	59

Source World Bank calculations based on extrapolated HEIS 2010 data, *Note* HEIS = Household expenditures and income survey; population quintiles based on consumption per capita before the reform

Table 7.22 Parameters used for extrapolation of expenditures, poverty line, and weights to reflect year 2013

Year	CPI index, base 2010	GDP per capita growth index, 2010 base	Population (millions)
2010	1.00	1.00	6.05
2011	1.04	1.07	6.18
2012	1.09	1.12	6.32
2013	1.15	1.19	6.46

Source WDI 2014; and Jordanian Department of Statistics. *Note* CPI = consumer price index; GDP = gross domestic product

Annex 7B

Box 7.1: Construction of Weighted Price Increase on Electricity

Construction of kilowatt per hour (kWh)-weighted price increases (Table 7.23) are calculated by multiplying the price increases for a particular bracket (available from Table 7.13) by the kilowatt hour electricity consumption in that bracket (available from Table 7.3) and then taking a weighted average of those by-bracket price increases. So under Scenario 2.I, for example, a household consuming in the third bracket (at 301–500 kWh per month) would see its expenditure go up by 160 * 342% for its first 160 kWh; by 140 * 102% for its next 140 kWh consumed; and by 138 * 69% for its next 138 kWh consumed, where 138 kWh is the mean consumption in the third bracket (according to the Jordan HIES 2010) for a household in which total monthly electricity consumption falls into the third bracket range. Taking a kWh-weighted average of those three price increases yields a total price increase of 180% for such a household.

Consumption-weighted price increases (Table 7.23) are calculated by multiplying the kWh-weighted price increases for a particular bracket by the share of households whose monthly electricity consumption falls into that bracket's range (available from Table 7.4). So under scenario 2.I, for example, the share of households whose monthly consumption falls in the third bracket is 51%; multiplying that share by the total kWh-weighted price increase for consumption in the third bracket yields 0.91, or a 91 percentage point contribution to the total kWh-weighted, consumption-weighted price change.

Total price increases in electricity are a simple sum of the consumption-weighted price increases. As such, total electricity price increases are a kWh-weighted, consumption-weighted average of by-bracket price increases, where the by-bracket price increases are those stated in Table 7.13.

Table 7.23 Construction of electricity price increases under subsidy reduction scenarios

Brackets, kWh/month	Scenario 2.I		Scenario 3	
	kWh-weighted price increase	Consumption-weighted price increase	kWh-weighted price increase	Consumption-weighted price increase
1–160	3.4	0.02	0.10	0.00
161–300	2.5	0.72	0.16	0.05
301–500	1.8	0.91	0.33	0.17
501–600	1.5	0.15	0.47	0.05
601–750	1.2	0.08	0.57	0.04
751–1000	0.87	0.02	0.67	0.01
>1000	0.65	0.00	0.73	0.00
Total		1.89		0.32

Source Jordanian department of statistics
Note HEIS = Household Expenditures and Income Survey

References

Araar, A., E. Le Borgne, U. Serajuddin, and P. Verme. 2013. "An Assessment of the Jordan 2012 Petroleum Subsidies Reform and Cash Compensation Program." World Bank Report 79837. World Bank, Washington, DC.

Azevedo, J. P. 2011. "WBOPENDATA: Stata module to access World Bank databases." Statistical Software Components S457234, Boston College Department of Economics. http://ideas.repec.org/c/boc/bocode/s457234 html.

Coady, D., M. El-Said, R. Gillingham, K. Kpodar, P. Medas, and D. Newhouse. 2006. "The Magnitude and Distribution of Fuel Subsidies: Evidence from Bolivia, Ghana, Jordan, Mali, and Sri Lanka." International Monetary Fund Working Paper WP/06/247.

Kojima, M. 2014. Personal communication, August 28.

Lamis, A., and J. Schwedler. 1996. Bread Riots in Jordan. *Middle East Report* 201: 40–42.

Lampietti, A., G. Banerjee, and A. Branczik. 2007. *People and Power: Electricity Sector Reforms and the Poor in Europe and Central Asia*. Washington, DC: World Bank.

NEPCO (National Electricity Company). 2012. Amman, Jordan.

Silva, J., V. Levin, and M. Morgandi. 2013. *Inclusion and Resilience: The Way Forward for Social Safety Nets in the Middle East and North Africa*. MENA Development Report, Washington, DC: World Bank.

Verme, P. 2011. "Electricity Subsidies and Household Welfare in Jordan: Can Households Afford to Pay for the Budget Crisis?" Background paper for the Jordan Poverty Reduction Strategy.

World Bank. 2009. *Hashemite Kingdom of Jordan: Poverty Update*. Volume II: Appendices. World Bank Report 47951-JO. World Bank, Washington, DC.

WDI (*World Development Indicators*). 2014. September 3. World Bank, Washington, DC.

Note: HEIS = Household Expenditures and Income Survey; population quintiles based on spatially adjusted consumption per capita before the reform.

Source: World Bank calculations based on extrapolated HEIS 2010 data.

Note: HEIS = Household Expenditures and Income Survey; JD = Jordanian dinar; population quintiles based on spatially adjusted consumption per capita before the reform; Quintile 1 = poorest.

Author Biographies

Aziz Atamanov is an economist at the World Bank working on poverty and inequality issues in the Middle East and North Africa Region. His areas of interest include poverty and inequality analysis, international migration, and social protection. Aziz is also engaged in regional work on microdata management, harmonization, and visualization. He holds a Ph.D. degree in development economics from Maastricht University.

Jon Jellema is an applied policy research economist currently working in Southeast Asia, Africa, and the Middle East. He has led or contributed to reports, publications, and analyses on, among other things, the redistributive effects of fiscal policy, the poverty- and vulnerability-reducing impacts of social assistance and social protection systems, and experimental and quasi-experimental impact evaluations of both community-level and household-level transfers. Jon received his Ph.D. from the University of California, Berkeley.

Umar Serajuddin is a senior economist-statistician at the Development Data Group of the World Bank. He currently leads the Development Data Group's Socio-economic and Demographic data team. His main interests are poverty, inequality, labor markets, and social protection. He has also worked as a poverty expert in the South Asia and the Middle East and North Africa Regions of the World Bank.

Chapter 8
Energy Subsidies Reform in the Republic of Yemen: Estimating Gains and Losses

Aziz Atamanov

Introduction

The Republic of Yemen is one the poorest countries in the Middle East and North Africa (MENA) Region, with a gross domestifc product (GDP) per capita of around US$3959 in purchasing power parity (PPP) terms in 2013. The country went through a range of internal shocks, including civil war in 1994 and political unrest in 2011. In 2015 President Abd-Rabbu Mansour Hadi and the government resigned after a new spate of violence in the capital San≪ayn≫a, and at present the country is at high risk of full-fledged sectarian conflict. The average economic growth rates were not exceeding 1.5% during the 10 years (2000–10) preceding the crisis in 2011, which led to a huge drop in real GDP by almost 13% (IMF 2014). Sluggish economic performance was accompanied by deteriorating social indicators and access to public services. Poverty is estimated to have increased from 35% in 2005 to 54% in 2011. Unemployment reached an unprecedented high of 35% in 2011 (World Bank 2012).

Oil production and oil export revenues play a crucial role in the Republic of Yemen and compensate for the underperforming sluggish economy, but at the same time the country has become vulnerable to changes in oil output and oil prices. Oil reserves and products were declining, with severe fiscal implications exacerbated by the presence of generous fuel and electricity subsidies in the form of fixed domestic prices.

For illustration, domestic prices on gasoline (super) and diesel were below the price of crude oil in 2012, as shown in Fig. 8.7, indicating the high level of subsidies (GIZ 2012–13). Subsidies accounted for 7.2% of GDP in 2013 (IMF 2014). They absorbed a large part of fiscal revenues and crowded out urgently needed social expenditures. The government spent on fuel subsidies almost as much

A. Atamanov (✉)
World Bank, Washington, DC, USA
e-mail: aatamanov@worldbank.org

P. Verme and A. Araar (eds.), *The Quest for Subsidy Reforms in the Middle East and North Africa Region*, Natural Resource Management and Policy 42,
DOI 10.1007/978-3-319-52926-4_8

as on education, health, and social protection combined in 2009 (Breisinger et al. 2011). Subsidies benefited mostly the rich and created incentives for smuggling, corruption, and inefficient use of fuel.

Falling hydrocarbon revenues and the increasing fiscal deficit in 2014 urged the government to adjust fuel prices and initiate subsidies reform. Gasoline, kerosene, and diesel prices increased by more than 50% in August 2014, leading to mass protests in the capital San≪ayn≫a. The government had to partially reinstate the fuel subsidies on gasoline and diesel. Currently, official fuel prices are at about 70% of the international level, and there is a plan to fully eliminate subsidies in 2015.

This chapter explores the distributional and fiscal impacts of different reform options, including the increase in prices in August and focusing on fuel and electricity subsidies. Using the 2005 Household Consumption Survey, updated to 2013 prices, this chapter demonstrates how different groups of the population benefit from subsidies and how the costs of reforms are distributed among the groups. The chapter also discusses the gains to the government from removing subsidies and political economy issues.

Evolution of Subsidies

The state dominates the oil and gas sector in the Republic of Yemen and is involved in all parts of the oil and gas chain, including oil production, refining, distribution, and marketing of petroleum products. Private companies are involved in upstream oil exploration and production activities, the filling and distribution of liquefied petroleum gas (LPG) bottles, and the distribution of petroleum products. The state is also a major player in the electricity market. After unification of the country in 1990, the Public Electricity Corporation (PEC) was established. The PEC is a sole public utility with a mandate for the generation, transmission, distribution, and sale of electricity in the country (World Bank 2005).

Subsidizing fuel products and electricity goes back to unification. The size of fuel subsidies has changed over time, reflecting changes in international fuel prices, exchange rates, consumption patterns, and domestic prices. As shown in Fig. 8.1, the share of government expenditures on subsidies varied from 14% in 2008 of GDP to 7.2% in 2013. At the same time, the share of revenues from hydrocarbon products was declining steadily from 29% in 2006 to 12% in 2013 (IMF 2010, 2014).

Fuel subsidies put a strain on fiscal balance, accounting for 22% of the government budget in 2009.[1] Spending on fuel subsidies is almost identical to the overall amount of budget expenditures spent on health, education, and social protection. For example, the share of health in total expenditure was about 3.5%, and

[1]Electricity production benefits from fuel subsidies because the Public Electricity Corporation purchases mazut, diesel, and natural gas at subsidized prices compared to domestic and international prices (Vagliasindi 2014).

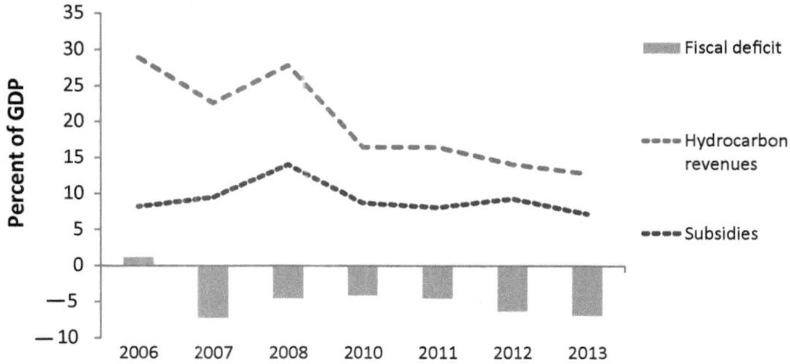

Fig. 8.1 Hydrocarbon revenues, subsidies, and fiscal deficit, in percent of GDP. *Source* IMF (2010, 2014). *Note GDP* gross domestic product

the share of social protection was about 2.7% in 2009. Increasing costs of fuel subsidies crowded out public investment program in infrastructure, which was crucial for long-term growth, economic diversification, and sustainable poverty reduction (Breisinger et al. 2011).

The government made many attempts to increase fuel prices to improve its fiscal position (Box 8.1), but the situation did not improve. The fiscal deficit was still high, approaching 7% of GDP in 2013 (Fig. 8.1). With a substantial decline in oil revenues and fuel shortages, in 2014 the situation became unsustainable. The population did not have access to fuel products at subsidized prices, and black market prices outpaced international prices. The government decided to fully eliminate subsidies on three products in August: gasoline, kerosene, and diesel. Kerosene and diesel prices were expected to increase by 100%, and gasoline by 60%. In the wake of violent public protests, the government was dissolved, and subsidies were partially reinstated on diesel and gasoline. Prices on gasoline increased by 20% and diesel by 50% (retail prices after the August reform are shown in Fig. 8.2). The government's plan to fully eliminate subsidies on fuel products, including LPG, in 2015, was stymied by civil war.

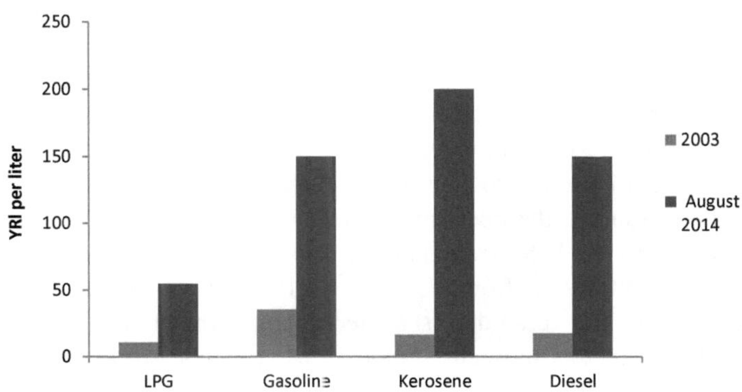

Fig. 8.2 Retail prices on fuel products, 2003 and 2014. *Source* IMF (2010, 2014). *Note GDP* gross domestic product; *YRl* Yemeni rial

Box 8.1: Changes in Fuel Prices and Mitigating Measures from 1995 to 2012

The government of the Republic of Yemen increased fuel prices by 75% in 1994, but benefits from this increase were wiped out by a huge depreciation of the local currency. The second increase in 1995–96 affected gasoline, diesel, kerosene, and LPG prices, but again in dollar terms prices remained at 1994 level. The third increase in prices took place in 2004 and affected only diesel prices. Overall, these reforms did not achieve the intended goal to remove the gap between domestic and international prices on fuel products.

Initiated by the IMF and the World Bank, the next subsidies reform started in 2005 to maintain fiscal sustainability in light of falling oil reserves. The government increased fuel prices by about 130% on average, and new prices coincided with reforms in the taxation system. The violent protests that followed this reform forced the government to adjust the price increase, but prices still remained higher than they were before the reform. International commodity prices then increased, canceling out the initial success in price adjustments.

Prices on gasoline, diesel, and kerosene were gradually increased by about 30%, and prices of LPG by 100% in 2010. In 2011–12 the government increased the price of gasoline by 66% and doubled the prices of diesel and kerosene. These increases in prices were not accompanied by public protests in 2010 and 2011.

The most recent reform took place in July and September 2014. This reform, which aimed at fully removing fuel subsides and initially increased prices by 60–90%, was launched earlier (July) than planned (October), without an adequate public campaign as advised by the International Monetary Fund (IMF) and the World Bank (among others). As a result, the reform was partially reversed in September, under the pressure from sectarian groups and popular protests.

The country's Social Welfare Fund (SWF) was established in 1996 to provide transfers to the poor. It has expanded from 100,000 beneficiaries in 1996 to 1.5 million in 2013. The fund has the most comprehensive database of the poor and vulnerable population in the Republic of Yemen. The success in compensating the negative impact of subsidies reform was limited. Increasing monthly benefits and streamlining the application process took three years to be approved after the 2005 subsidies reform. In contrast, the coverage of the programs increased by half after the 2010 reforms. No mitigating measures were introduced during the 2011–12 reform episodes. Reforms in 2014 were also launched before a compensation scheme was designed and funded; the operation to help in this endeavor (funded by the World Bank and the U.S. Treasury) was approved in December 2014.

In addition to transfers from the SWF, the Republic of Yemen has a Public Works Project that provides short-term employment and support for small-scale contractors through a labor-intensive public works program.

Source Part of this box is based on IMF 2013.

To mitigate potential adverse impacts of higher fuel prices on the poor, the government planned to increase the allocations for the Social Welfare Fund (SWF) by 50% starting in the last quarter of 2014 (IMF 2014). The World Bank is helping the government to improve the coverage and targeting of benefits.

Distribution of Subsidies

This section describes distribution of subsidies across households in the Republic of Yemen based on the 2005 Household Budget Survey (HBS), the most recent survey conducted by the country's Central Statistical Office and the World Bank.[2] Descriptive and simulation analysis is done using SUBSIM software.[3]

Baseline Data

Because the country's household budget survey used in this study is outdated, all information has been updated to 2013 prices.[4] In particular, expenditures were inflated using nominal GDP per capita growth rates. The poverty line was inflated by the growth in consumer prices. Weights were also rescaled to reflect the change in the population size between 2005 and 2013. All input data is presented in Table 8.1. After updating expenditures and the poverty line, the extrapolated poverty rate turned out to be 49.8% in 2013. This number is close to estimates in other studies that also documented substantial increases in poverty in the Republic of Yemen due to the economic and political turmoil in the considered period of time (World Bank, UN, EU, and IDB 2012).

Reconstructed population and expenditure figures for 2013 are shown in Table 8.2. Total household expenditures are estimated to be around 5.271 billion Yemeni rials (YRls), which is equivalent to YRls 203,976 per capita. Households from the poorest quintiles have larger household sizes, and the richest households spent about six time higher amounts than households from the poorest quintile.

The analysis in this chapter covers four products: liquefied petroleum gas (LPG), gasoline, diesel, and electricity. The December 2014 unit prices and unit subsidies for the four products are shown in Table 8.3. From the perspective of total expenditures, households spend almost equal amounts on LPG, gasoline, and electricity. Nevertheless, electricity is the most subsidized product. The unit subsidy

[2]A new household budget survey is in the field in the Republic of Yemen, and the plan is to have welfare aggregate in the middle of 2015.

[3]SUBSIM is freely available to download from www.subsim.org.

[4]Updating to 2014 prices would be preferable, but would require finalized information on prices, population, and GDP per capita growth, which were not available at this writing.

Table 8.1 Reference statistics, 2005–13

Source	Indicator	2005	2006	2007	2008	2009	2010	2011	2012	2013
1	GDP, per capita (YRl billion)	159,313	181,981	240,764	279,782	259,695	298,151	285,127	288,241	316,554
1	GDP growth (base 2005)	100.0	114.2	151.1	175.6	163.0	187.1	179.0	180.9	198.7
2	Population (000)	20,140	20,662	21,539	22,198	22,864	23,584	24,312	25,066	25,843
2	Population growth (base 2005)	100.0	102.6	106.9	110.2	113.5	117.1	120.7	124.5	128.3
2	CPI (base 2005)	100.0	110.8	119.6	142.3	150.0	166.8	199.4	219.1	243.1

Sources: *1* WDI; *2* Central Statistical Office. *Note CPI* consumer price index; *GDP* gross domestic product; *000* thousand

Table 8.2 Baseline population data and expenditure by quintiles, in Yemeni rials

Quintile	Population	Number of households	Household size	Total expenditures	Total expenditures per capita	Total expenditures per household
1 (poorest)	5,174,505	577,032	9.0	412,463,398,912	79,711	714,802
2	5,165,212	599,262	8.6	619,873,042,432	120,009	1,034,395
3	5,166,950	648,383	8.0	813,628,260,352	157,468	1,254,857
4	5,167,864	718,895	7.2	1,095,255,457,792	211,936	1,523,526
5 (richest)	5,168,179	897,907	5.8	2,330,065,895,424	450,849	2,594,996
Total	25,842,708	3,441,479	7.5	5,271,286,448,128	203,976	1,531,692

Source World Bank calculation based on extrapolated HBS 2005. *Note HBS* household budget survey

Table 8.3 Subsidized energy products, December 2014

Product	Unit	Unit price	Unit subsidy	Unsub. unit price	Unit subsidy (% of unsub. price)	HH Expenditures on subs. products (YRl billion)	Total subsidies (YRl billion)
LPG	kg	109.1	47.7	156.8	30.4	60.3	26.4
Gasoline	L	150.0	32.5	182.5	17.8	63.5	13.8
Diesel	L	150.0	40.0	190.0	21.1	0.9	0.2
Electricity						54.7	319.3
0–200	kWh	6.9	57.6	64.5	89.3		
201–350	kWh	12	52.5	64.5	81.4		
351–700	kWh	14.1	50.4	64.5	78.1		
701+	kWh	19	45.5	64.5	70.5		

Sources World Bank calculation based on extrapolated HBS 2005. Unit subsidies and prices are provided by Amir Althibah from the Yemen World Bank country office. *Note HBS* household budget survey; *HH* households; *kg* kilogram; *kWh* kilowatt hour; *L* liter. Unit price for electricity is a weighted average for urban and rural areas: 0.7 weight is for urban areas and 0.3 weight is for rural areas

accounts for about 80% of the unsubsidized unit price (cost recovery price) with households having low electricity consumption being subsidized the most. As a result, the most costly program for the government is associated with electricity subsidies, which is not surprising given that electricity production is based on highly subsidized mazut—a heavy low-quality fuel oil, which can also become diesel.[5] In 2014 about YRl 320 billion were spent on electricity subsidies compared to YRl 26.4 billion spent on LPG and YRl 13.8 billion spent on gasoline.

Subsidies on diesel are very small, but only because we consider only the diesel and gasoline expenditure spent on private cars. Wealthy farmers spend substantial amounts of gasoline on agriculture and water pumps, but these expenditures are not in included in welfare aggregate and not reflected here.

Given the information presented, one may hypothesize that changes in prices on electricity can generate substantial changes in government revenues and have the strongest impact on households' well-being if fully eliminated. The incidence of subsidies across the distribution can help to clarify this in the next section.[6]

[5]For illustrative purposes, the subsidy on mazut used for electricity was higher than 4.5 times than retail price. Overall, the cost recovery price is about 0.3 cents per kwh, which is much higher than usually considered adequate to cover most of capital costs of 0.08 cents per kwh (Kamives et al. 2005).

[6]Expenditures on diesel and gasoline were obtained from data private cars' weekly diaries. To separate them into expenditure on diesel and gasoline we used information on road sector gasoline and diesel consumption in the Republic of Yemen in 2009 from www.tradingeconomics.com. According to this website, diesel consumption in the country was 43 kiloton of oil equivalent, and gasoline consumption was 1,530 kiloton of oil equivalent in 2009. Using information on prices, share of diesel expenditures was about 1.4%, and it was applied to fuel expenditure on private cars from household budget survey.

Distribution of Subsidies

This section describes the importance of subsidies for households across the four products considered. Figures 8.3 and 8.5 show expenditure on subsidized products as shares of total expenditures.[7] The household distribution of expenditures (in percentiles) is depicted on the x-axis; the poorest percentiles are on the left and the richer percentiles are on the right of the figures. The y-axis depicts expenditures on subsidized products. The curves with a negative slope imply that expenditures on subsidized products are more important for poor households than for rich households, and a positive slope implies that rich households spend higher shares of their budgets on subsidized products than do the poor. The amounts of subsidies in per capita terms across the distribution are shown in Figs. 8.4 and 8.6. This information is complementary to the information provided in Figs. 8.3 and 8.5 showing explicitly which group—rich or poor—receives the highest subsidies.

Households spend slightly larger shares of their budgets on fuel products other than electricity (Figs. 8.3, panel a, and 8.4, panel a). In particular, Yemeni households spend on average 1.04% of their budgets on electricity compared to 1.14% on LPG and 1.2% on gasoline. In terms of the distribution, gasoline and electricity play a more important role in the budgets of rich households. The poorest households spend only 0.2% of their expenditures on gasoline compared to 1.7% among the richest households. LPG, in contrast, is the only product with a slightly negative slope of the curve, meaning that it plays a slightly more important role for the poor than for rich households.

The data on subsidies per capita across the distribution (Figs. 8.3, panel b, and 8.4, panel b) show that subsidies for all products favor the rich. The subsidies per capita on electricity are seven times higher for the richest households compared to the poorest; for gasoline and diesel the gap is 50 times higher.[8] Even for LPG, which is the least prorich among selected products, subsidies per capita for the richest quintile are three times higher than subsidies per capita for the poorest quintile.

A final observation from Figs. 8.3 and 8.4 is that, overall, the electricity subsidies per capita are much higher than the subsidies on fuel products. On average, households in Yemen receive YRl 12,356 in annual electricity subsidies, which is much higher than those they receive from fuel subsidies: YRl 1020 for LPG and YRl 532 for gasoline.

[7]Figs. 8.3 and 8.5 were replicated for fuel products, including kerosene, and based on August 2014 prices. Results are shown in the annex. The role of fuel products in household budget does not change. The only important addition is that kerosene was more important for the poor than for the rich and subsidies on this product were pro-poor.

[8]It is also important to remember that many poor households in the Republic of Yemen do not have access to electricity.

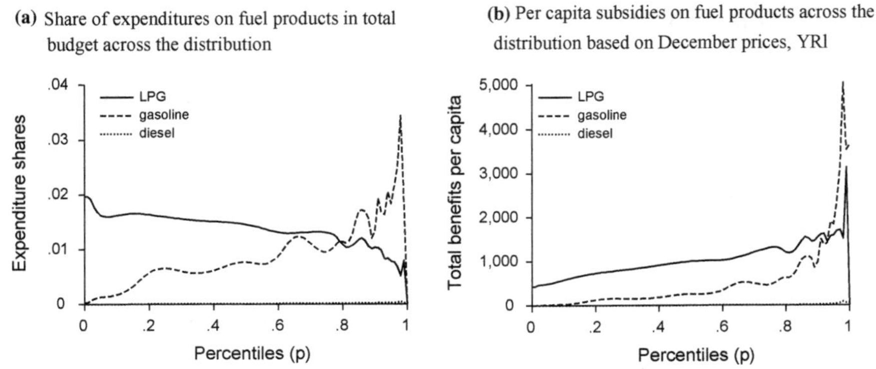

Fig. 8.3 Share of expenditures and per capita subsidies on fuel products across the distribution. **a** Share of expenditures on fuel products in total budget across the distribution. **b** Per capita subsidies on fuel products across the distribution based on December prices, YRl. *Source* World Bank calculation based on extrapolated HBS 2005. *Note HSB* Household Budget Survey

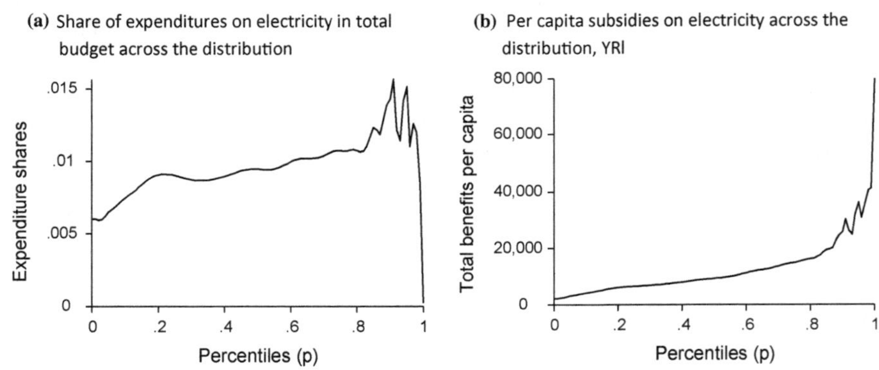

Fig. 8.4 Share of expenditures and per capita subsidies on electricity across the distribution. **a** Share of expenditures on electricity in total budget across the distribution. **b** Per capita subsidies on electricity across the distribution, YRl. *Source* World Bank calculation based on extrapolated HBS 2005. *Note HBS* household budget survey

Simulation of Subsidies Reforms

The purpose of the simulations in this section is to inform the current debate on subsidies in the Republic of Yemen by showing results for different scenarios. The main scenario is common to all chapters of the book: it implies the total elimination of subsidies and is based on December 2014 prices. This scenario provides an upper bound of the effects of this reform on the government budget and on household welfare. Simulations are done separately for fuel products and electricity.

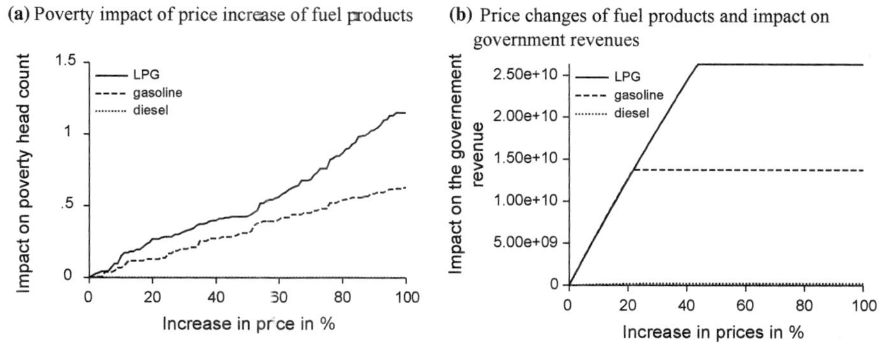

Fig. 8.5 Impact of price increase on poverty and government revenues. **a** Poverty impact of price increase of fuel products. **b** Price changes of fuel products and impact on government revenues. *Source* World Bank calculation based on extrapolated HBS 2005. *Note HBS* household budget survey

In this chapter we focus only on direct effects of subsidy reform, which are the price and quantity changes that apply to the final consumer when subsidies on final products are changed. Simulation of indirect impact on prices of other goods was not possible due to the lack of input-output tables. Estimates of demand elasticity with respect to price are necessary to model consumer responses to price change. Given the limitations of having only cross-sectional household data with no variation in individual petroleum product prices across households, we used an own-price elasticity of −0.2 to simulate changes in quantities consumed.

Fuel Products

Tables 8.4 and 8.5 provide initial and final (unsubsidized) prices of fuel products for two simulation scenarios. The first scenario simulates the impact of the actual reform conducted in August 2014. Under this scenario, unit prices are the August

Table 8.4 Scenario 1 for fuel subsidies reform, August 2014 reform

Product	Unit	Unit price, August 2014	Cost recovery price	Scenario 1, August 2014 reform	
				Unit price	Change, %
Gas LPG	kg	109.1	156.8	109.1	0
Gasoline	L	100.0	182.5	150.0	50
Diesel	L	125	190.0	150.0	20
Kerosene	L	100	200	200.0	100

Source Unit subsidies and prices are provided by Amir Althibah from Yemen World Bank country office. *Note kg* kilogram; *L* liter

Table 8.5 Scenario 2 for fuel subsidies reform, full elimination

Product	Unit	Unit price, December 2014	Scenario 2, full removal	
			Unit price	Change, %
Gas LPG	kg	109.1	156.8	43.7
Gasoline	L	150.0	182.5	21.7
Diesel	L	150.0	190.0	26.7

Source Unit subsidies and prices are provided by Amir Althibah from Yemen World Bank country office. *Note* Cost recovery prices for this simulation are shown in Table 8.3. *kg* kilogram; *L* liter

Table 8.6 Impact of fuel subsidies reform in August 2014 on poverty and inequality

	Prereform	August 2014 reform	
		Postreform	Change
Welfare (per capita)	203,976	202,667	−1309
Poverty (%)	49.8	50.2	0.4
Inequality (%)	35.9	36.0	0.1
Subsidies (in millions)	77,055	42,530	−34,524
Transfers (in millions)	0	24,524	24,524
Total budget (in millions)	77,055	67,054	−10,001

Source World Bank calculation based on extrapolated HBS 2005

2014 prices, with the expectation of increasing 100% for kerosene, 20% for gasoline and 50% for diesel. Prices on LPG did not change.

For the second scenario we simulate the full removal of subsidies based on December 2014 prices after the August reform. This is the main scenario to inform policy makers about the potential impact of the full removal of subsidies planned for 2015. As can be seen for gasoline and diesel, prices as of December 2014 were not so far from cost recovery. Full elimination of subsidies will imply increase in prices on diesel by 27%, on gasoline by 22%, and on LPG by 44%.

Simulated impacts of fuels subsidies reform on poverty, inequality, and government revenues are presented in Tables 8.6 and 8.7. Table 8.6 shows the simulated impact of partial subsidies reform conducted in August 2014. Consumption per capita is expected to drop by 0.6% on average with the negative impact being again strongest for the poorest households (−1.1%) as compared to the richest quintile (−0.5%). The increase in poverty will be about 0.4 percentage points, and inequality would increase by 0.1%.

The most negative impact on the poorest households comes from increasing prices on kerosene, and the richest households are most affected by higher prices on gasoline. For illustration, consumption per capita is supposed to drop by 1.1% for the poorest quintile, and 96% of this decline comes from increasing prices on kerosene. In contrast, kerosene accounts only for 31% of overall decline in consumption for the richest 20% of the population, and the rest of the negative impact comes from higher prices of gasoline (Table 8.12).

Table 8.7 Impact of full elimination of subsidies on poverty and inequality based on December 2014 prices

	Prereform	Full elimination of subsidies	
		Postreform	Change
Welfare (per capita)	203,976	202,414	−1562
Poverty (%)	49.8	50.3	0.5
Inequality (%)	35.9	35.9	0.0
Subsidies (in millions)	40,356	0	−40,356
Transfers (in millions)	0	31,631	31,631
Total budget (in millions)	40,356	31,631	−8726

Source World Bank calculation based on extrapolated HBS 2005

The August subsidies reform is estimated to save the government about YRl 34.5 billion if the population is not compensated for its losses. If universal subsidies were provided, government savings would shrink to YRl 10 billion.

Full elimination of subsidies would reduce consumption per capita by 0.7% on average with the impact being relatively equal across quintiles. The poor are more affected by higher prices on LPG, while the negative impact from subsidies removal on gasoline is more pronounced for the richest households (Table 8.13). This result is consistent with higher role of LPG for budgets of poor households.

Poverty will increase by 0.5 percentage points after full elimination of subsidies, which could save the government about YRl 40.4 billion (Table 8.7). If universal transfers are provided to keep the prereform level of poverty, most of the savings from subsidies reform would be required for this purpose, and overall savings for the government would be around YRl 9 billion instead of YRl 40.4 billion. If the government is able to target cash transfers to the poor to compensate for their losses in subsidies revenues, the costs would be slightly lower: YRl 29 billion instead of YRl 32 billion.

The trade-off between increases in poverty and government revenues for planned subsidies reform can be seen in Fig. 8.5 across two main fuel products. In particular, Fig. 8.5, panel a, shows increases in poverty by price increases between 1 and 100%. Figure 8.5, panel b, shows the impact on government revenues of price increases between 1 and 100%. Not all price increases are realistic and some can be well above the increases necessary to eliminate subsidies. The only purpose of this exercise is to show which product is the most promising in terms of positive impact on government finances while keeping poverty low.

Consistent with larger shares in poor household budgets and high per capita subsidies, increasing prices on LPG have a stronger impact on poverty compared to gasoline, but at the same time they generate higher savings for the government. Government revenues stop growing after the price of gasoline increases by more than 20% and on LPG by more than 40% because they will reach the cost recovery level.

Table 8.8 Old and new proposed tariffs for electricity, by tariff brackets

Tariff brackets	Old tariffs and blocks		Scenario 1, full removal	Scenario 2, gradual increase with three brackets		Scenario 3, gradual increase with six brackets	
	Unit	Unit price	Unit price	Tariff brackets	Unit price	Tariff brackets	Unit price
0–200	kWh	6.9	64.467	0–200	9	0–200	9
201–350	kWh	12	64.467	201–700	19	201–240	17
351–700	kWh	14.1	64.467	701+	30	241–280	19
701+	kWh	19	64.467			281–340	35
						341–460	40
						461+	55

Source Current tariffs are provided by Amir Althibah from the Yemen World Bank country office.
Note kWh kilowatt hour. Unit price for electricity is a weighted average for urban and rural areas: 0.7 for urban and 0.3 for rural areas

Electricity

The Republic of Yemen uses an increasing block tariffs (IBT) system for electricity. This system implies progressive tariffs that charge a higher marginal price per kilowatt hour (kWh) for higher levels of energy usage. The four electricity brackets differ between urban and rural areas. For simulation purposes, an average weighted tariff was constructed (70% for urban and 30% for rural areas).

Three different scenarios have been selected to simulate the impact of electricity subsidies reforms (Table 8.8). The first scenario simulates full removal of subsidies. The second scenario simulates the impact on poverty and inequality of a new tariff structure with three brackets and progressive tariffs. The last scenario keeps the same tariff for the lowest bracket as in the second scenario, but extends the number of brackets to six (see also Fig. 8.9). Increasing the number of brackets is expected to reduce the consumer surplus and increase revenues for the system without a substantial increase in poverty.[9]

Full removal of electricity subsidies leads to a huge increase in tariffs, with the highest increase for households with the lowest consumption of electricity. This result happens because prereform tariff structure was progressive, with the lowest tariffs for households at lower energy usage, and the change means the final price is flat for all households. The overall impact of full elimination of electricity subsidies on poverty is substantial, but still less than one could expect given the magnitude of the increase in prices because of the low share of expenditures on electricity in total household budgets, especially for the poor. Consumption per capita will drop by 6% on average, and poverty will increase by 4.8%. Inequality will also increase

[9]Issues with practical implementation of extending the number of brackets are beyond the scope of this paper.

Table 8.9 Impact of electricity subsidies reform on poverty and inequality

	Prereform	Scenario 1, full removal		Scenario 2, three brackets		Scenario 3, six brackets	
		Postreform	Change	Postreform	Change	Postreform	Change
Welfare (per capita)	203,976	191,620	−12,356	203,099	−877	201,835	−2.141
Poverty (%)	49.8	54.6	4.8	50.1	0.3	50.4	0.7
Inequality (%)	35.9	36.1	0.2	35.9	0.0	35.7	−0.2
Subsidies (millions)	319,314	0	−319,314	263,574	−55,740	237,040	−82,274
Transfers (millions)	0	237,828	237,828	16,820	16,820	39,345	39,345
Total budget (millions)	319,314	237,828	−81,486	280,395	−38,919	276,385	−42,929

Source World Bank calculation based on extrapolated HBS 2005. *Note HSB* household budget survey

significantly by 0.2% because the increase in tariff is the highest for the poorest households with lowest consumption of electricity.

Full removal of subsidies is not a feasible option for policy makers to consider; instead, gradual and progressive increases in tariffs can be a more realistic scenario. Progressive electricity tariffs assume a direct relation between household welfare and electricity consumption. Indeed, there is a positive relationship between household expenditures and expenditure on electricity (Fig. 8.12).

As shown in Table 8.9, a progressive increase in tariffs has a weaker negative impact on welfare compared to full removal of subsidies. In particular, having three brackets and progressive increase in tariffs in scenario 2 will increase poverty only by 0.3% and will generate about YRl 39 billion in government revenues after universal transfers. If the government wants to increase its gains from reform, the option of having six brackets with more progressive tariff scales will create a slightly higher increase in poverty (0.7%) and will bring higher savings—YRl 43 billion. Note that scenarios 2 and 3 will both reduce inequality because the increase in tariffs is highly progressive.

Compared to the impact of fuels subsidies reform, the negative impact on poverty from higher prices on electricity is comparable to the negative impact of higher prices on LPG (Fig. 8.6, panel a, vs. Fig. 8.5, panel a). However, the government can save more from electricity subsidies reforms because the amount of electricity subsidies per capita is higher than subsidies on fuel product (Fig. 8.5, panel b, vs. Fig. 8.6, panel b).

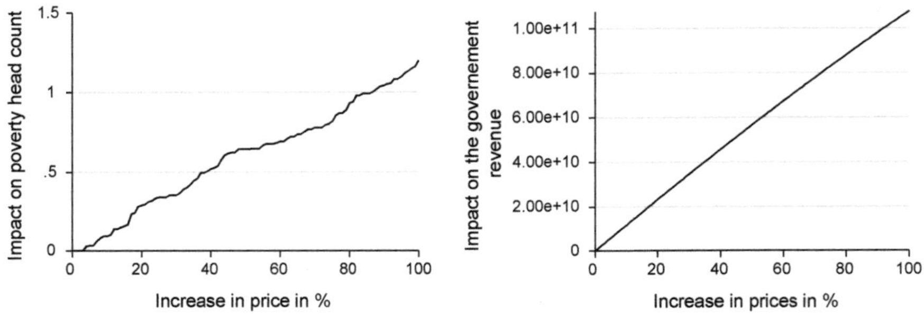

Fig. 8.6 Impact of price increase on poverty and government revenues. **a** Poverty impact of price increase of electricity. **b** Price changes of electricity and impact on government revenues *Source* World Bank calculation based on extrapolated HBS 2005. *Note HSB* household budget survey

The Political Economy of Reforms

Once adopted, subsidies are hard to remove. Usually countries have to conduct reform by piecemeal changes with constant reversals. Fear of loss of economic rents and political power are common factors behind reluctance to reform subsidies (Commander 2012). The Republic of Yemen was not an exception. In at least two occasions, increases in fuel prices caused violent public protests that led to a reversal of reforms. In this section, we discuss the factors affecting reform paths and try to identify the lessons learned.

Modern Republic of Yemen was established in 1990 by uniting the Arab Republic of Yemen (YAR) and the People's Democratic Republic of Yemen (PDRY). The state-society social contract was very different under the two former states. Lack of resources made the population in YAR (north) unite along tribes, while in the PDRY (south) the state was much stronger and controlled by one party. Oil rents and political patronage allowed political powers to unite the country, changing the voice of different religious, regional, and tribal groups. One result was that elite groups captured the key sectors of the economy and less-powerful groups could benefit either from fuel subsidies or from the illegal trade of subsidized products. The patronage system created by petroleum products made the reform of subsidies on these same products politically very complex (World Bank 2005; Salisbury 2011).

Falling oil production after 2000 and the poor performance of non-oil sectors shrank the resource base and contributed to the evolving political, social, and economic crises that culminated in the 2011 protests and the departure of President Ali Abdullah Saleh in 2012. The United Nations and the Gulf Cooperation Council have helped to bring about a peaceful transition in the Republic of Yemen, but the situation is still very fragile and has not yet been resolved.

The success of subsidies reform depends on timing, institutional capacity, communication campaigns, and the overall micromanagement of reforms. In the Republic of Yemen, the failure of the 2005 subsidies reform seems to be associated with bad timing because it coincided with tax reforms. The compensation scheme designed to accompany price increases could not work because it took almost three years to increase the size of benefits. If the cash transfer program had been implemented on time, it could have reduced the opposition to reforms and increased the likelihood of success.

The increase in energy prices in 2010 and 2011 happened in the context of abrupt changes in supply and retail prices in the black market higher than international prices. An effective public campaign kept the public informed the public about the benefits of reforms to ensure adequate supply (IMF 2013). As a result, these episodes of subsidies reforms were not accompanied by public protests and violence.

Given that the amount of subsidies depends on international commodity prices and that subsidy is a politicized topic, international organizations proposed a system of automatic fuel prices adjustment. Such a measure may help to depoliticize the process of energy pricing, avoid drastic changes in domestic prices, and allow governments to preserve and increase the savings from a subsidy reform when international prices go up (IMF 2014).

Conclusions

The Republic of Yemen is going through a very difficult political and socioeconomic crisis, and the current level of subsidies makes the fiscal situation unsustainable. The country partially removed subsidies on fuel products in 2014 and planned to fully eliminate subsidies in 2015. This chapter explored the distributional and fiscal implications of fuel and electricity subsidy reforms in Yemen.

Electricity is the most subsidized product and accounts for the largest share of overall subsidies. In contrast, in terms of share of total expenditures, gasoline and diesel are relatively more important. The distributional analysis shows that only kerosene subsidies are pro-poor, and that subsidies for other products are prorich, meaning that richer households benefit more from these subsidies compared to poorer households. Nevertheless, poor households still spend substantial shares of their budgets on subsidized products, which implies that the removal of subsidies would impose economic hardship on these households.

In particular, the simulation shows that increases in prices on gasoline, kerosene, and diesel in August 2014 are expected to increase poverty by 1.3 percentage points and reduce household consumption by 3%. Further removal of the remaining subsidies on LPG, diesel, and gasoline planned for 2015 is expected to generate a slightly less negative impact increasing poverty by 1.1 percentage points.

Full removal of subsidies on electricity is not a feasible option to consider. The huge increase in tariffs, especially for poor households, would increase poverty by 4.6%. A more realistic reform would be a progressive increase in tariffs partially removing electricity subsidies, which is expected to increase poverty either by 0.4 percentage points (using three brackets) or by 0.7 percentage points (using six brackets). One benefit of having more brackets is higher government revenues, which are estimated to be almost identical to savings from the full removal of subsidies.

In terms of the political economy of subsidies reform, several important lessons can be learned from the Republic of Yemen's experience in reforming subsidies. The successful implementation of subsidies reforms depends crucially on the right timing and a sound compensation scheme with targeted benefits. In addition, adequate public campaigns are needed to inform the public about the benefits of reforms. Finally, introducing automatic adjusting mechanisms of domestic prices to international commodities prices by law may reduce the politicians' ability to manipulate prices.The author thanks peer reviewer Guido Rurangwa (senior country officer) and Paolo Verme (task team lead) for their useful comments and suggestions on how to improve the chapter. The author also thanks Lire Ersado, Jianping Zhao, and Amir Mokhtar Althibah for their advice and help.

Annex

See Figs. 8.7, 8.8, 8.9, 8.10, 8.11 and 8.12; Tables 8.10, 8.11, 8.12 and 8.13.

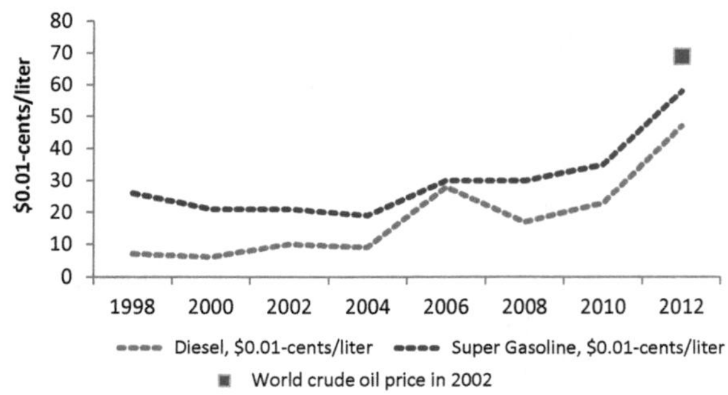

Fig. 8.7 Retail prices on diesel and super gasoline in the Republic of Yemen compared to the price of crude oil in the World Market, 2012. *Source* GIZ (2012–13)

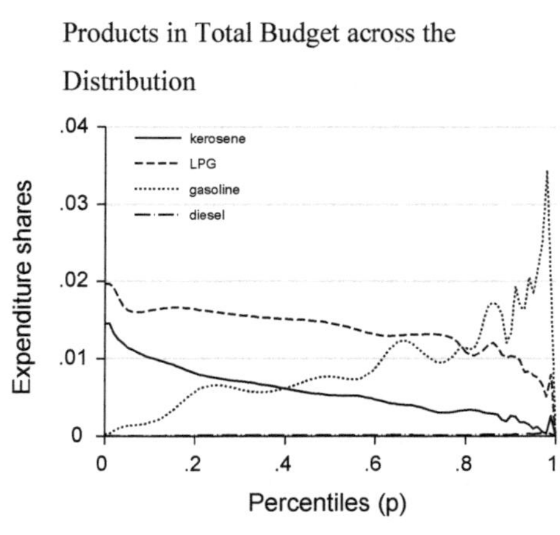

Fig. 8.8 Share of expenditures on fuel products in total budget across the distribution. *Source* World Bank calculation based on extrapolated HBS 2005. *Note HSB* household budget survey

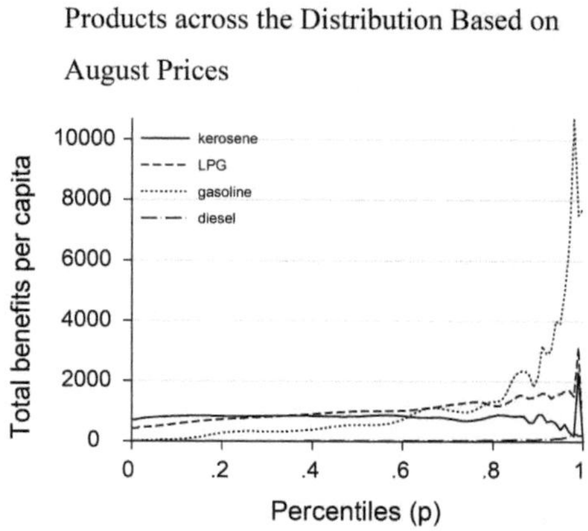

Fig. 8.9 Per capita subsidies on fuel products across the distribution based on August prices. *Source* World Bank calculation based on extrapolated HBS 2005. *Note HSB* household budget survey

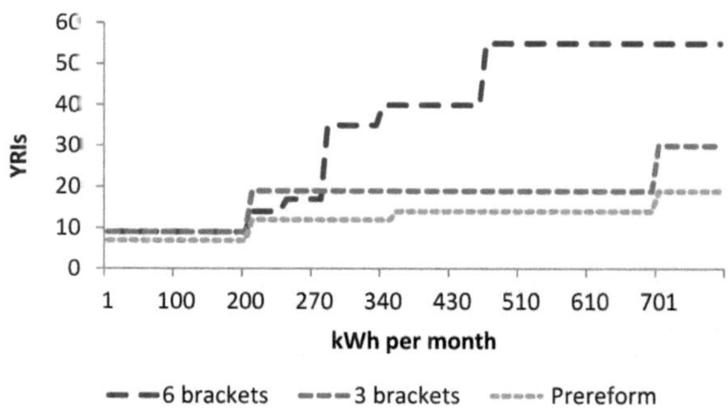

Fig. 8.10 Different electricity tariff structures, in Yemeni rials. *Source* World Bank compilation. *Note kWh* kilowatt hour; *YR* Yemeni rial (color figure online)

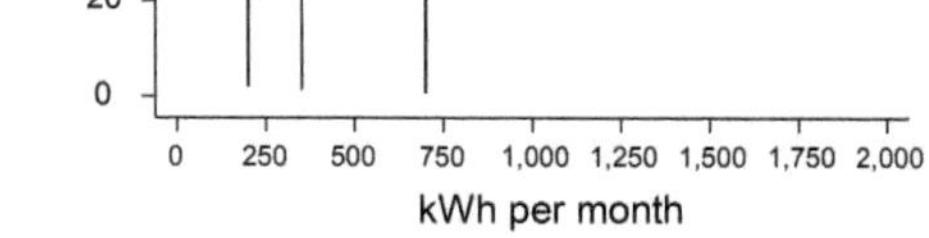

Fig. 8.11 Distribution of households by tariff brackets. *Source* World Bank calculation based on extrapolated HBS 2005. *Note HSB* household budget survey; *kWh* kilowatt hour

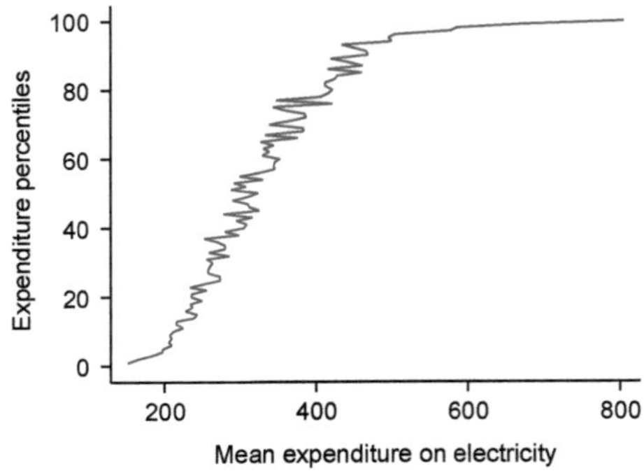

Fig. 8.12 Expenditures on electricity versus total consumption per capita. *Source* World Bank calculation based on extrapolated HBS 2005. *Note HSB* household budget survey; *kWh* kilowatt hour

Table 8.10 Annual per capita consumption of fuel products, in quantity

Quintile	LPG (kg)	Gasoline (liter)	Diesel (liter)
1 (poorest)	12.15	4.24	4.82
2	17.17	19.42	7.73
3	20.99	28.63	17.60
4	24.84	63.60	47.10
5 (richest)	31.78	211.74	152.83
Total	21.39	65.52	46.01

Source World Bank calculation based on extrapolated HBS 2005. Note: *HSB* household budget survey

Table 8.11 Annual per capita consumption of electricity, in kWh

Quintile	Electricity (kWh)
1 (poorest)	72.64
2	127.06
3	174.76
4	247.11
5 (richest)	500.44
Total	224.39

Source World Bank calculation based on extrapolated HBS 2005. Note: *HSB* household budget survey; *kWh* kilowatt hour

Table 8.12 Impact on well-being of fuel subsidies reform in August 2014, in percent

Quintile	Kerosene	LPG	Gasoline	Diesel	Total
1 (poorest)	−1.0	0.0	0.0	0.0	−1.1
2	−0.7	0.0	−0.1	0.0	−0.8
3	−0.5	0.0	−0.2	0.0	−0.7
4	−0.4	0.0	−0.2	0.0	−0.6
5 (richest)	−0.2	0.0	−0.3	0.0	−0.5
Total	−0.4	0.0	−0.2	0.0	−0.6

Source World Bank calculation based on extrapolated HBS 2005. Note: *HSB* household budget survey

Table 8.13 Impact on well-being of full elimination of fuel subsidies, in percent

Quintile	LPG	Gasoline	Diesel	Total
1 (poorest)	−0.73	−0.04	0.00	−0.77
2	−0.69	−0.14	0.00	−0.83
3	−0.62	−0.16	0.00	−0.79
4	−0.56	−0.23	0.00	−0.80
5 (richest)	−0.34	−0.38	−0.01	−0.72
Total	−0.50	−0.26	0.00	−0.77

Source World Bank calculation based on extrapolated HBS 2005.
Note: *HSB* household budget survey

References

Breisinger, C., W. Engelke, and O. Ecker. 2011. *Petroleum subsidies in Yemen leveraging reform for development.* Policy Research Working Paper 5577. Washington, DC, World Bank.

Commander, S. 2012. *A guide to the political economy of reforming energy subsidies.* Bonn, Germany: IZA (Institute for the Study of Labor) Policy Paper 52.

GIZ (Deutsche Gesellschaft für Internationale Zusammenarbeit, Federal Ministry for Economic Cooperation and Development). 2012–13. *International Fuel Prices 2012/2013.* Eighth edition.

IMF (International Monetary Fund). 2010. Republic of Yemen: request for a three-year arrangement under the extended credit facility—Staff report. Press Release on the Executive Board Discussion; and Statement by the Executive Director for Yemen. IMF Country Report 10/300. Washington, DC: International Monetary Fund.

IMF (International Monetary Fund). 2013. *Case studies on energy subsidy reform: lessons and implications.* Washington, DC: International Monetary Fund.

IMF (International Monetary Fund). 2014. Republic of Yemen staff report for the 2014 article IV consultation and request for a three-year arrangement under the extended credit facility. IMF Country Report 14/276. Washington, DC: International Monetary Fund.

Komives, K., V. Foster, J. Halpern, and Q. Wodon. 2005. *Water, electricity, and the poor: Who benefits from utility subsidies? Directions in development series.* Washington, DC: World Bank.

Salisbury, P. 2011. Yemen's economy: Oil, imports and elites. Middle East and North Africa Programme Paper 2011/02. London: Chatham House.

Vagliasindi, M. 2014. *Implementing Energy subsidy reforms: Evidence from developing countries. Directions in development series.* Washington, DC: World Bank.

World Bank. 2005. Household energy supply and use in Yemen. Energy Sector Management Assistance Program Working Paper ESM 315/05. Washington, DC: World Bank. http://documents.worldbank.org/curated/en/2005/12/6743106/household-energy-supply-use-yemen-vol-1-2.

World Bank. 2012. Republic of Yemen joint social and economic assessment. Report 69388-YE. Washington, DC: World Bank.

World Bank, UN (United Nations), EU (European Union), and IDB (Islamic Development Bank). 2012. *Joint social and economic assessment for the Republic of Yemen.* Washington, DC: World Bank.

Author Biography

Aziz Atamanov is an economist at the World Bank working on poverty and inequality issues in the Middle East and North Africa Region. His areas of interest include poverty and inequality analysis, international migration, and social protection. Aziz is also engaged in regional work on microdata management, harmonization, and visualization. He holds a Ph.D. degree in development economics from Maastricht University.

Chapter 9
Djibouti: Subsidies, Tax Exemptions and Welfare

Stefanie Brodmann and Harold Coulombe

Introduction

Djibouti is one of the smallest countries in Africa. It covers an area of 23,200 km^2 and is home to a population of fewer than 900,000. The country is almost a city-state with 80% of the population living in the capital, Djibouti City. The rural population mainly consists of poor pastoral and nomadic peoples who sparsely occupy the hinterland, an extension of the deserts of Ethiopia and Somalia. As in other small states, the size of Djibouti's economy limits its ability to diversify production and increases its reliance on foreign markets, making it more vulnerable to external market downturns and hampering access to external capital. With less than 1000 km^2 of arable land (4% of the country's total land area) and an average annual rainfall of 130 mm, Djibouti depends completely on imports to meet its food needs.

Although Djibouti's economic outlook is generally favorable, significant risks to growth remain. Economic growth, which averaged 4.5% per year during 2009–12, was projected to reach 5% in 2013 (World Bank 2014). Growth is driven by strong foreign direct investment (FDI) inflows and public investment. Transport and logistics, such as transit trade with Ethiopia and transshipment activities, are the backbone of Djibouti's economy, with port activities contributing almost 20% to its gross domestic product (GDP). However, Djibouti is left vulnerable to major risks to growth and macroeconomic stability including fuel and food price shocks and natural disasters such as droughts and floods. Poverty has been exacerbated by drought conditions since 2007—the worst in 60 years. The drought is estimated to have affected at least half the rural population, with annual economic losses of 3.9% of GDP over the period 2008–11 and a substantial flow of refugees from neighboring countries that also suffer from drought. With its strategic location in the

S. Brodmann (✉) · H. Coulombe
World Bank, Washindton, DC, USA

P. Verme and A. Araar (eds.), *The Quest for Subsidy Reforms in the Middle East and North Africa Region*, Natural Resource Management and Policy 42,
DOI 10.1007/978-3-319-52926-4_9

Horn of Africa and at the southern end of the Red Sea, Djibouti is affected by adverse economic or security developments in neighboring countries. Domestic social and political instability also present potential risks to growth.

Djibouti's external position has deteriorated as a result of a significant increase in the level of imports. The current account deficit is estimated to have widened to about 13.1% of GDP in 2013 from 5.1% in 2010. Imports grew by 18% per year on average, in nominal terms, during 2011–13, as compared to 13% for exports. This deficit has been financed in part by significant FDI inflows, which were expected to rise from 2.4% of GDP in 2010 to 18.6% in 2013. Djibouti requires significant reserves for imports of food, fuel, and manufactured goods. The real effective exchange rate fell by about 4% in 2011–12, as declining food and fuel prices led to lower inflation (World Bank 2014).

Universal tax exemptions were introduced in response to the food crisis and to shield the population from price shocks on essential food products. Djibouti depends massively on imports to meet its food needs, and a large fraction of the population faces food insecurity. Practically all food items are imported, and increases in international food prices directly affects Djibouti's poor people, who spend up to three-quarters of their income on food. Due to severe and prolonged droughts, at least 20% of the capital's population and three-quarters of rural households are vulnerable to moderate to severe food insecurity, according the Emergency Food Security Assessment carried out by the World Food Programme in 2013. In response to the stark food price increases, the government has exempted five essential food items from domestic consumption tax since 2008. According to estimates of the International Monetary Fund (IMF), Djibouti forgoes 0.5% of GDP (2009) on rice, edible oil, sugar, flour, and powdered milk.

Similarly, discretionary price adjustments on certain energy products, such as gasoline (super) kerosene, and diesel, have been in operation since 2009. The government's Department of Customs and Excise, after consultation with oil companies, operates a monthly adjustment of prices at the pump to minimize the negative impact of fluctuating international prices of super, kerosene, and diesel. According to estimates of the IMF, Djibouti forgoes an estimated 2% of GDP (2011) on certain energy products (De Broek et al. 2012). The findings in this chapter are part of a broader dialogue on energy tax reform and the effort to strengthen social safety nets in Djibouti. As part of a possible reform of energy taxes, the government of Djibouti has sought the support of the World Bank to better understand how such a policy reform can be pro-poor.[1]

Untargeted tax exemptions reach a wider part of the population than targeted programs, but have high benefit leakage and are regressive compared to some targeted

[1]The study was designed and implemented by a multisectoral committee composed of various stakeholder institutions, including the Ministry of Economy and Finance, the Ministry of Budget, the secretary of state responsible for National Solidarity (SESN), the Department of Statistics and Demographic Studies (DISED), the Ministry of Energy, and the Ministry of Transport, with whom the teams of the World Bank and the International Monetary Fund collaborated throughout the process of preparation of the study.

transfers that appear generally more progressive. Tax exemptions on basic food items reach the majority of the poor and nonpoor, with close to 95% of the population benefiting. In contrast, targeted programs, such as food rations and cash transfers, generally benefit the rural population and the poor. More than half of the transfers for food rations are received by the poor (bottom quintile), and almost 80% of beneficiaries are in the bottom two quintiles and live in rural areas (84.2% of benefits received). In contrast, the population living in urban areas receive the majority of tax exemptions on food and fuel products, 85 and 97%, respectively. The majority of these beneficiaries are from the richest two quintiles, 56 and 87%, respectively, making these programs regressive. Only 15% of the tax exemption benefits on food and less than 3% on fuel go to beneficiaries living in rural areas, and only 10% and less than 1%, respectively, are received by those in the poorest quintile.

The government of Djibouti is currently considering abandoning the use of the discretionary tax, which can be either positive or negative, on retail prices of fuel. As of December 2013, such a reform would result in a small drop in gasoline and kerosene prices, but an increase of around 13% for diesel. Therefore, it is likely that a jump in fuel costs brought about by the abolition of the discretionary tax could lead to higher ticket prices for public transport. Combining the possible increase in diesel prices (12.5%), relative to the level in December 2013, with a fuel cost share of 30% suggests that an increase in the cost of passenger fares of 4% would be justified to allow bus companies to pass on the effects of the higher fuel prices to passengers. In fact, car ownership and utilization of public transport is a strong indication of welfare. One-fourth of the richest quintile owns a car, and car ownership is basically negligible in the other quintiles. In addition, only 10% of the poor use public transport (buses, taxis, and school buses) compared with almost 60% in the richest two quintiles.

The next section provides a short summary of the evolution of subsidies, followed by an overview of the distribution of various fuel and food products by welfare quintiles. The following section presents simulations that eliminate the discretionary tax elements on fuel (super and diesel) and food products and shows the potential impact of this removal on household welfare and government budget. The final sections discuss reform options, show the result of different simulations on the welfare effects of various reform options on poverty head count and poverty gap, and offer conclusions.

Evolution of Subsidies

Djibouti relies entirely on imports for its supply of petroleum products. All imports come through Djibouti port. Of these imports a substantial portion is re-exported, with large volumes in transit to Ethiopia. A large fraction of the net imports are destined for foreign armies with bases in Djibouti, for international airlines, and for maritime transport. Although there are no official figures for imports and consumption of petroleum products, a recent study for the government of Djibouti

Table 9.1 Imports and domestic consumption of petroleum products by Djibouti in 2012 (million liters)

Total imports	530
Re-export	283
Consumption by foreign military, airlines, and shipping	163
Domestic consumption:	84
Diesel (gasoil)	61
Gasoline (super)	6
Kerosene *(pétrole lampant)*	11
Fuel oil	6

Source Cap Gemini Consulting, April 2014

surveyed all parties involved in the import and sale of petroleum products and produced reconciliation for 2012. The resulting data are shown in Table 9.1 and indicate that diesel dominates domestic consumption.

The same study also presented a forecast of domestic consumption until 2017. Diesel is expected to reach 91 million liters; kerosene, 17 million liters; gasoline, 9 million liters; and fuel oil, 8 million liters. These figures indicate that the change in taxation of diesel will be particularly important in terms of government revenue. The domestic consumption of petroleum products is divided between households and businesses that pay all taxes and duties and a number of parties, such as certain businesses, embassies, and the Republican Guard, that receive some tax exemptions.

Fuel prices, especially of gasoline, are higher in Djibouti than in neighboring countries. Transportation fuel prices in Djibouti can be compared to those from other non-oil-producing countries in the region in 2012. With the exception of Eritrea, prices in Djibouti, especially for gasoline, were higher than neighboring countries (Table 9.2). The higher prices are due to the small size of the domestic market, resulting in loss of economies of scale. Diesel prices are nearer to those of neighboring countries, in part due to discretionary tax offsets that have been used for diesel.

The retail prices of petroleum products in Djibouti are regulated by the Ministry of Budget according to a formula that includes predetermined and discretionary elements (costs and taxes). In 2009 the government signed a memorandum of understanding with the oil companies that allows for a monthly review of the complete price and cost structure. Costs include an import component and various domestic items. The allowable amounts for domestic costs are changed occasionally, and tax rates are fixed except for a discretionary component *(ajustement en faveur de l'Etat)* that is used to smooth out fluctuations in retail prices that would

Table 9.2 Prices of transportation fuels in 2012 (US$/liter)

Country	Gasoline (super)	Diesel (gasoil)
Djibouti	1.8	1.2
Eritrea	2.5	1.7
Ethiopia	1.1	0.9
Kenya	1.4	1.3
Lebanon	1.1	0.9
Tanzania	1.3	1.3

Source GIZ (2012–13)

otherwise be caused by fluctuations in the import cost. This component can be either positive (extra tax) or negative (tax offset).

The exact determination of the smoothed retail price is not made according to a formula; rather, it depends on judgments made by the government. In principle, such an approach to smoothing out import cost fluctuations could result in no additional long-run net benefit or cost to the government. At times, however, the discretionary component has been negative (because of the low final retail price set by the government) and produces tax revenues persistently below the amount that would have resulted from the application of the nondiscretionary tax structure. The government is now considering abandoning the discretionary tax component so that retail prices would be predictably linked to the allowable costs and the import cost of the products. This change would mean that the full tax revenue implied by the formula would be collected from retail sales.

At present, kerosene is provided through two routes, yielding the same retail price due to a discretionary tax element. In addition to the established marketing of kerosene, the government has made an arrangement with the SDVK (*La Société de Distribution et de Vente de Kérosène*) to sell and distribute kerosene nationwide (although at present it serves only Djibouti City and suburbs). The government allows the SDVK to include a fee in the price charged to build its network and exempts the price from the domestic consumption tax (TIC) and the value-added tax (VAT). The price does include a discretionary tax element so that the retail price of this kerosene supply is the same as the general retail price of kerosene.

Determination of the Retail Price

The various components of the pricing formula are set by the government in agreement with the oil companies. Table 9.3 illustrates the structure of the gasoline retail price (De Broek et al. 2012). The price for delivery at Djibouti port is set as follows.

- Free on board (FOB) prices in international markets are collected monthly, as averages of daily FOB prices for the preceding month quoted in *Platt's Oilgram Price Report*. An exporter's margin, cost of shipping and insurance, and port fees are added. The commercial margin is updated every six months based on invoice information about actual FOB prices paid by oil companies in the preceding six months.
- Duties and taxes include TIC and VAT at rates set by legislation—currently 26 and 7%, respectively. Excise duties are set by legislation, and royalties are determined annually in the budget.
- The transport, operational, and storage costs and the commercial margins of distributors and service station operators are set by the government. These charges can be changed after discussion with the relevant parties.

Table 9.3 Price build-up for retail gasoline, in DF

Category	DF
PF (FOB price)	137.57
MF (maritime freight)	3.24
EM (exporters margin)	4.36
PF + MF + EM = PC (CIF price)	145.18
SE (extra storage cost)	2.60
FP (port fees)	0.68
PC + SE + FP = PP (price at port)	148.46
TC (domestic consumption tax) = 0.26 * PP	38.60
TE (excise duty)	49.50
TR (royalty)	32.13
TD (discretionary tax adjustment)	5.84
DD (various distribution costs)	11.65
PP + TC + TE + TR + TD + DD = PV (price subject to VAT)	286.18
TV (VAT) = 0.07* PV	20.03
CT (terminal transport cost)	1.76
PV + TV + CT = PS (price received at service station)	307.98
RM (retail margin)	7.02
PS + RM = PR (retail price)	315.00

Source Ministry of Budget. *Note* The price buildup for retail gasoline is illustrated with the case of gasoline (super) for December 2013 (December 11, 2013–January 10, 2014) in Djibouti francs (DF) per liter

- A discretionary tax component is used to smooth out retail prices in the face of volatile FOB costs and to reduce inflationary pressure on low-income households in times of rising international prices. This component varies each month and is calculated so as to produce a desired retail price linked to the other costs by the formula.

The regulated prices for petroleum products sold to special groups also allow for various exemptions on taxes, and these exemptions are expected to continue so that tax revenue from these groups is lower than that from the purely retail market. Such groups include the French military (50% exemption on domestic consumption tax and 50% exemption on excise duties); exempt businesses (zero domestic consumption tax and zero excise tax); embassies and domestic security forces (zero domestic consumption tax, zero VAT, zero excise tax, and zero royalty). The effect of these exemptions is to forgo tax revenue that would otherwise have accrued to the budget had the products been sold at the same price as to the general public.

The government has entered into an arrangement with the SDVK to sell and distribute kerosene to make it more widely available. A service fee was included in the price markup on top of other port and distribution charges. To encourage the company to set up the network required to expand the market for kerosene, the government exempted this kerosene from the TIC, excise duty, and VAT. A royalty

Table 9.4 Retail prices and discretionary taxes for petroleum products in 2013 (DF/liter)

Month	Gasoline				Kerosene (SDVK)				Diesel			
	FOB price	Retail price	Discretionary tax	Other taxes	FOB price	Retail price	Discretionary tax	Other taxes	FOB price	Retail price	Discretionary tax	Other taxes
January	139.27	310.00	−11.47	141.70	137.66	195.00	8.68	7.00	135.08	210.00	−28.47	75.40
February	139.27	310.00	−11.47	141.70	142.02	195.00	4.29	7.00	139.79	210.00	−34.44	76.65
March	139.27	310.00	−11.47	141.70	148.65	200.00	2.61	7.00	146.46	215.00	−38.23	78.69
April	142.58	310.00	−5.90	140.59	136.31	190.00	5.04	7.00	135.44	210.00	−28.92	75.51
May	142.58	310.00	−5.31	141.26	128.29	190.00	13.12	7.00	127.98	210.00	−19.46	73.57
June	137.57	310.00	1.17	139.94	127.88	190.00	13.53	7.00	128.47	210.00	−20.08	73.70
July	137.57	310.00	1.17	139.94	129.52	190.00	11.88	7.00	131.44	212.00	−21.98	74.60
August	137.57	315.00	5.85	140.26	134.89	195.00	11.47	7.00	136.16	215.00	−25.16	76.02
September	137.57	315.00	5.84	140.26	138.39	195.00	7.95	7.00	136.73	215.00	−25.88	76.16
October	n.a.	n.a.	n.a.	n.a.	n.a.	n.a.	n.a.	n.a.	n.a.	n.a.	n.a.	n.a.
November	137.57	315.00	5.84	140.26	136.50	195.00	9.85	7.00	136.42	215.00	−25.49	76.08
December	137.57	315.00	5.84	140.26	136.25	195.00	10.01	7.00	136.09	215.00	−25.07	76.00

Source Ministry of Budget 2013. *Note DF* Djibouti franc; *FOB* free on board; *SDVK* La Société de Distribution et de Vente de Kérosène was charged, and the discretionary tax was set so as to bring the retail price to the same level as the charge for the traditional method of selling kerosene.

Table 9.4 shows the retail prices and discretionary tax elements for 2013. The data for gasoline prices illustrate how the retail price was smoothed by varying the discretionary tax through the year. In January 2013 the adjustment was negative, indicating that the government was holding down retail prices by forgoing a certain amount of tax revenue. By the end of the year, the retail price had risen slightly, but the discretionary tax had become positive, indicating that the government was now collecting some extra tax revenue. For diesel, the government was forgoing a certain amount of tax revenue throughout the year to hold retail prices down. It is important to note that the government during this period was still a net recipient of tax revenue from diesel as "other taxes" were much larger that the negative discretionary tax. For kerosene, the government collected some tax revenue through royalty as well as a small amount from the (positive) discretionary tax. The net effect of this sales arrangement for kerosene was that the total tax revenue per liter was much lower than for gasoline and for diesel.

The calculation of the discretionary element is similar for the exempt organizations, but it has to be interpreted differently. The price calculation for the Republican Guard is an illustration. In December 2013 the price at the port (PP) for gasoline was Djibouti francs (DF) 148.46; domestic tax, excise tax, royalty, and VAT were all zero; distribution costs (DD) were DF 11.65; terminal transport cost was DF 1.76; and the retail margin was DF 7.02. The sum of these costs was DF 168.89, and this was the charge to the Republican Guard. Relative to the retail price of DF 315, the charge to the Republican Guard was a tax exemption of DF 146.10, which can be seen as a transfer from one segment of the government to another.

Distribution of Subsidies

Data for this chapter are from the third round of the *Enquête Djiboutienne auprès des ménages* (EDAM 3), a representative household survey that includes detailed information on household expenditures and receipt of certain cash and in-kind benefits. To ensure consistency across chapters, the analysis uses 2014 prices, with inflation rates of 2.5 and 2.9% for 2013 and 2014, respectively. The EDAM 3 survey was conducted in 2012 and has a nationally representative sample of the sedentary population composed of 5880 households with 31,686 individuals. The EDAM 3 questionnaire covers many aspects: demography, education, employment, mortality, governance, housing, access to basic social services, durable goods ownership, and finally, expenditures and revenues. Of particular importance is information on household expenditure on tax-exempt food (flour, rice, oil, sugar, and milk); certain fuel items (kerosene, butane, and fuel expenditure on transport); and electricity, as well as information on cash and in-kind benefits. The EDAM 3 dataset has been used to compute total expenditure aggregates of households, which the Department of Statistics and Demographic Studies (DISED) has used to produce their recent poverty profile, yielding 40.8% of poverty and 23% of extreme poverty.[2]

As is common for household surveys, the EDAM 3 data are representative only of the sedentary population. The EDAM 3 sample leaves out the nomad and homeless populations (*population flottante*) and individuals living in collective households (hotels, prison, military camps, and orphanages). According to the most recent census conducted in 2009, Djibouti's total population was 818,159 individuals, of which 161,132 were nomads and 149,022 either lived in collective households or were homeless. Having household surveys solely covering the sedentary population is standard practice because surveying nomad and homeless populations creates important conceptual and logistic issues.

Five quintiles based on per capita expenditure have been constructed based on the per capita expenditure welfare index. The first quintile includes the poorest 20% of the sedentary Djibouti population; the second quintile includes the next 20%, and so on up to the top quintile with the richest 20% of the population. For the purpose of this study, the destitution[3] line is defined as the upper limit of the first quintile. Therefore, the destitution head count rate is de facto set to 20%.

Energy Products

The following analysis includes all the tax-exempt fuel products available in the household survey. The survey does not differentiate between diesel and super (lumped together as *carburant* in the EDAM 3 questionnaire), but data from the *Enquête de Budget et Consommation* (EBC) survey (an urban-only survey done in 2013) show that around two-thirds of spending by households on *carburant* is on diesel. Furthermore, the survey shows that almost all direct spending on *carburant* is by the richest quintile. The simulations of subsidy reforms, discussed n the next section, assume that the price of fuel purchases will increase from DF 215 to DF 242 per liter.

Car ownership and utilization of public transport is a strong indication of welfare. Car ownership is not widespread in Djibouti—only 6% of households own a car and 1% own a motorcycle. One-fourth of the richest quintile owns a car, and car

[2]The EDAM 3 sample slightly underestimates the size of households, and the level of average per capita total household expenditure is therefore slightly overvalued in this survey. Because this study focuses primarily on expenditure quintiles, the effect of this general overvaluation is marginal. Furthermore, and in contrast to the recently updated national poverty profile that combines data from EDAM 3 and the Budget and Consumption Survey (EBC), this study uses data from EDAM 3 and its expenditure aggregate only. The aggregate used in this study, however, is highly correlated with that used for the poverty profile produced by the DISED. We do not see any conflict between the analysis in this study and the figures recently approved by the government.

[3]In this chapter we try to avoid the terms *poverty line* and *poverty head count* in order to differentiate our analysis from the poverty profile produced by the DISED.

Table 9.5 Percentage of households owning a car or motorbike or using buses, by quintile and area

	Car	Motorbike	Public transport	School transport
Quintile				
1 (poorest)	0.0	0.1	12.4	6.9
2	0.4	0.5	37.4	21.9
3	1.7	0.6	53.2	37.2
4	3.0	1.3	62.0	47.0
5 (richest)	25.3	3.3	58.0	41.9
Area				
Urban	7.1	1.3	51.4	36.7
Rural	0.7	0.2	9.7	1.2
Total	6.1	1.2	44.6	31.0

Source World Bank calculation based on the EDAM 3. Note: *EDAM* Enquête Djiboutienne auprès des ménages. *Note EDAM* Enquête Djiboutienne auprès des ménages

ownership is basically negligible in the other quintiles (Table 9.5). Most cars are owned by urbanites, and therefore *carburant* is essentially consumed by urban households and the richest quintile (Table 9.6). Utilization of public transport (buses, taxis, and school buses) is also highest among the richer quintiles. Only 12% of the poor (quintile 1) use public transport compared with 60% in the richest two quintiles. More than half of the population in urban areas makes use of public transport, but less than 10% in rural areas. Utilization of school transportation is also highly skewed toward richer and urban households.

Djibouti households spend about DF 7.96 million on subsidized fuel products (that is, fuel at the pump, public transport, and school transport), about 6.75% of their total annual expenditure (Table 9.7). On an average, households spend DF 25,400 on fuel at the pump, DF 27,400 on public transport, and DF 30,600 on school transport (Table 9.6). Tax exemptions on fuel products do not benefit the poorest as they consume little fuel and hardly use public transportation. As shown in Table 9.5, possession of cars and motorbikes is essentially limited to the richest quintile, which consumes DF 96,847 per household on fuel at the pump, about 4%

Table 9.6 Expenditures per household (in 2014 DF), by quintile

Quintile	Fuel	Public transport	School transport	Total
1 (poorest)	0	2142	2381	4523
2	499	13,196	13,192	26,887
3	617	25,352	31,755	57,724
4	4093	38,002	46,889	88,985
5 (richest)	96,874	49,837	50,932	197,643
Total	25,422	27,381	30,622	83,425

Source World Bank calculation based on the EDAM 3 (2014 prices). *Note EDAM* Enquête Djiboutienne auprès des ménages

Table 9.7 Expenditure on subsidized products over total expenditures (in %), by quintile

Quintile	Fuel	Public transport	School transport	Total
1 (poorest)	0.00	0.79	0.88	1.67
2	0.07	1.89	1.89	3.86
3	0.06	2.57	3.22	5.85
4	0.31	2.87	3.54	6.72
5 (richest)	3.93	2.02	2.07	8.02
Total	2.06	2.22	2.48	6.75

Source World Bank calculation based on the EDAM 3 (2014 prices). *Note EDAM* Enquête Djiboutienne auprès des ménages

of the total annual household expenditure. Spending on public and school transport is also considerably lower in the poorest quintile (DF 2142 and DF 2381 per household, respectively) than in the richest quintile (DF 49,837 per household). Already the second quintile spends considerably more on public transport than the very poor (Table 9.6). For the poor, expenses on fuel and public and school transport amount to less than 2% each of the overall household expenses (DF 4522), whereas the richest quintile spends about 8% of total household expenditure (DF 197,643) on these fuel products.

Food Products

Poor households spend relatively more on tax-exempt food products than richer households. Household expenses on tax-exempt food products amount on average to DF 153,629 per household, which is equivalent to 12.4% of total household spending. Table 9.8 shows household expenses on tax-exempt food products, and Table 9.9 shows the proportion of annual household spending. Of these basic food items, sugar is the most consumed item in terms of expenditure (DF 37,622). Although rice consumption is higher, only a tiny fraction of rice is actually tax exempt and therefore has been excluded from our analysis. Tax-exempt products are relatively more important for the poor, as the expenditure share of these products is

Table 9.8 Expenditures per Household (in DF), by quintile

Quintile	Powdered milk	Flour	Cooking oil	Sugar	Total
1 (poorest)	4250	17,455	8262	22,193	52,161
2	17,189	27,000	17,573	36,717	98,480
3	26,579	25,541	20,486	40,253	112,858
4	35,266	28,348	23,782	41,760	129,156
5 (richest)	55,248	31,814	33,213	45,082	165,357
Total	29,529	26,350	21,450	37,622	114,951

Source World Bank calculation based on the EDAM 3 (2014 prices). *Note DF* Djibouti franc; *EDAM* Enquête Djiboutienne auprès des ménages

Table 9.9 Expenditure on subsidized products over total expenditures (in %), by quintile

Quintile	Powdered milk	Flour	Cooking oil	Sugar	Total
1 (poorest)	1.57	6.46	3.06	8.22	19.31
2	2.47	3.88	2.52	5.27	14.14
3	2.69	2.59	2.08	4.08	11.43
4	2.66	2.14	1.80	3.15	9.75
5 (richest)	2.24	1.29	1.35	1.83	6.71
Total	2.39	2.13	1.74	3.04	9.30

Source World Bank calculation based on the EDAM 3. *Note EDAM* Enquête Djiboutienne auprès des ménages

much higher for the very poor than for the very rich. In the poorest households, 19% of the total expenses correspond to tax-exempt food products, while these products account for less than 7% of the richest households' total expenses.

Simulation of Subsidies Reforms

This section presents two simulation scenarios. The first focuses on fuel products and estimates the effects of removing the discretionary tax on retail prices on super and diesel. The survey database used does not differentiate between expenditure on super and diesel, but because it can be shown that by far the largest part of spending on fuel is on diesel, we would assume that all such fuel spending is on diesel. Kerosene would be excluded from such a reform. The second simulation focuses on four basic food items and estimates the effects of introducing a consumer tax. The latter reform is currently not under consideration by the government, and the simulations are for illustrative purposes only.

Impact of Removing the Discretionary Tax on Fuel Products

The proposal to remove the use of discretionary tax on certain fuel products is currently under consideration by the government. Other tax rates could be varied by legislation, as at present, but would normally be stable for lengthy periods. Allowable costs along the supply chain could also be varied if justified by the circumstances of the entities involved. To simulate the effect of removing the discretionary tax element on prices, it is assumed that all other tax rates and costs remain at the levels of December 2013.

For gasoline and diesel, the removal of the discretionary tax component has two effects on the retail price that would have to be charged. First, when the discretionary tax is positive, its removal would contribute to lowering of the retail price by this amount. Second, because the VAT at 7% is charged on the discretionary tax

Table 9.10 Retail petroleum product prices with and without the discretionary tax (December 2013), in DF/liter

Gasoline			Diesel		
Before	After	% Change	Before	After	% Change
315.00	308.73	−2.0	215.00	241.82	+12.5

Source World Bank data and calculations. *Note DF* Djibouti franc

element, the result would be a further lowering of the retail price. Similarly, when the discretionary tax is negative, its removal would raise retail prices by 1.07 times the amount of the discretionary tax. Table 9.10 illustrates the effects on retail prices if the tax had been removed in December 2013.

The removal of discretionary tax would have resulted in a small drop in gasoline price, but an increase of around 13% for diesel. The comparison between the before and after prices in December 2013 is possible because the government's action with respect to the determination of the retail price (and the associated discretionary tax) is a known fact. Simulating the effect of removing the discretionary tax under different circumstances is possible, but it is not possible to give a "before" calculation because it is not known what the government would have decided to do with retail prices had it kept the discretionary tax.

To illustrate the range of retail prices that might be experienced if the discretionary tax were abandoned, simulations of the impacts of a 20% increase and a 20% decrease in the FOB prices (relative to the levels of December 2013) are constructed and the results are shown in Table 9.11. It is assumed that all other costs, taxes, and duties remain unchanged, and in all cases there is no discretionary tax element. The results of the calculations show gasoline price varying by between plus or minus 12%, and diesel prices by plus or minus 15%. The larger fixed elements for gasoline (excise duty and royalty) mean that the percentage swing in the FOB price (which is similar for all three products) is damped down more than is the case for diesel.

The substantial fall in crude oil prices is relevant to the calculations shown. In December 2013 Brent crude sold for about $110 a barrel and remained around that level until July 2014. Since then it has steadily declined until falling to around $50 a barrel in September 2015. Considerable uncertainty remains about the price of crude oil.

The simulations of the effect of removing the discretionary tax focused on December 2013 actual FOB prices and included a sensitivity analysis of a 20% drop of those prices (Table 9.11). This drop would have corresponded to a Brent crude

Table 9.11 Results of simulation: range of retail prices (DF/liter)

	Gasoline	Diesel
December 2013 FOB	308.7	241.8
December 2013 FOB plus 20%	345.8	278.5
December 2013 FOB minus 20%	271.6	205.1

Source World Bank data and calculations. *Note DF* Djibouti franc; *FOB* free on board price of about $90 a barrel. The actual fall has been almost twice that allowed in the sensitivity analysis. Simple extrapolation indicates that, in the absence of discretionary taxes, a 40% fall in FOB prices would result in gasoline prices of 235 DF/liter and diesel prices of 169 DF/liter.

Diesel Prices and Transport Costs

The analysis of the impact of removing the discretionary tax element on households proceeds through the use of an expenditure survey, coupled with the calculated changes in petroleum product prices. The shares of total household expenditure allocated to each of the two petroleum products is directly available from the household expenditure survey and can be combined with predicted price changes to estimate the expenditure change required to purchase the same amounts of each product.

In addition to the direct effects on household budgets, there are indirect effects caused by the impact of rising petroleum product prices on other goods and therefore on the household budget. Without a detailed input-output table it is not possible to quantify all such links, but the most important link for petroleum products in Djibouti is transport costs. Because the costs of travel by bus or taxi can be a substantial component of household expenditure, we must consider the link between product prices and transport costs.

As diesel is used as fuel for commercial transportation vehicles, the key question is the nature of the link between the gas oil price and the price of transportation services. Bus fares are regulated and have changed very little in the last decade. It is likely that a jump in fuel costs brought about by the abolition of the discretionary tax, which was holding down costs by about 12% in December 2013, could provide an opportunity for the bus sector to ask for higher ticket prices to cover increased costs. Many factors might enter such a negotiation, including previous loss of profitability caused by the government holding prices steady for a long period. A full justification of an allowable fare increase would require detailed analysis of the economics of the bus and taxi sectors. In the absence of such a detailed study, a first approximation can be obtained by combining the fuel share in total costs with the percentage increase in fuel costs.

Evidence from other countries on the share of fuel costs in the total costs of operating a bus fleet can serve as a marker for any assumption that is made for Djibouti. ESMAP (2011) refers to a study in India where the share of fuel cost in Andhra Pradesh amounted to 31% of total costs. A World Bank study analyzed factors affecting bus performance in middle- to low-income countries and provided values indicative of the range of cost breakdown as shown in Table 9.12. The following remarks from the study are relevant to Djibouti: "In the case of informal small-scale operation using rehabilitated or locally fabricated buses, financed by overseas remittances, depreciation and interest costs are much less (only about 10% of total costs), while driver and other staff costs can be relatively more (20–30%)

Table 9.12 Shares of operating cost of a bus fleet in developing countries

Cost item	Proportion of operating cost (%)
Variable costs	
Fuel	20–30
Lubricating oil	1–5
Tires	5–10
Spares	5–10
Fixed costs	
Driver and other platform staff	10–15
Other labor	About 5
Depreciation and interest	20–30
Overheads and other costs	5–15

Source IBRD (2015)

due to the higher number of people employed per unit of capacity (often including the owner)" (ESMAP 2011, 10).

Fuel costs can range between about 50 and 75% of variable costs depending on circumstances. A survey carried out by the secretary of state responsible for National Solidarity (SESN) and the Department of Statistics and Demographic Studies (DISED) in Djibouti City in 2014 indicated that averaged over all forms of passenger road transport, fuel accounted for 80% of variable costs and that there was little variation in this ratio among the different forms of passenger transport. The closeness of these figures suggests that it is reasonable to assume that fuel costs in Djibouti are about 30% of total operating costs (the high end of the range given in Table 9.12, corresponding to the 75% share of variable costs).

Combining the information on the possible increase in diesel prices (12.5%) relative to their level in December 2013 with a fuel cost share of 30% suggests that an increase of 4% in passenger fares would be justified to allow bus companies to overcome the effects of higher fuel prices. If the government decided to permit a larger price rise, perhaps to allow for catching up with previous cost increases, there is more likelihood of public opposition to the change.

Impact of Fuel Subsidy Reform on Household Welfare, Government Budget, Poverty, and Inequality

Abandoning the discretionary tax on super and diesel retail prices would imply a loss of DF 510.8 million (or 0.2% of GDP)4 for the population. Table 9.13 shows the impact of the reform on the welfare of the population for each quintile; Table 9.14 shows the impact of the reform on the per capita welfare of each quintile; and Table 9.15 shows the impact as the proportion of total household expenditure.

Table 9.13 Total impact on the population's well-being (in DF millions), by quintile

Quintile	Fuel	Public transport	School transport	Total
1 (poorest)	0.0	−1.5	−1.7	−3.1
2	−1.0	−8.1	−8.1	−17.3
3	−1.3	−16.3	−20.4	−38.0
4	−9.7	−26.8	−33.0	−69.5
5 (richest)	−292.7	−44.6	−45.6	−382.8
Total	−304.8	−97.3	−108.8	−510.8

Source World Bank calculation based on the EDAM 3 (2014 prices). *Note EDAM* Enquête Djiboutienne auprès des ménages

Table 9.14 Impact on the per capita well-being (in DF), by quintile

	Fuel	Public transport	School transport	Total
1 (poorest)	0	−14	−15	−29
2	−10	−76	−76	−161
3	−12	−152	−190	−354
4	−90	−249	−307	−646
5 (richest)	−2734	−417	−426	−3576
Total	−568	−181	−203	−951

Source World Bank calculation based on the EDAM 3 (2014 prices). *Note EDAM* Enquête Djiboutienne auprès des ménages

Table 9.15 Impact on well-being (in %), by quintile

Quintile	Fuel	Public transport	School transport	Total
1 (poorest)	0.00	−0.03	−0.03	−0.06
2	−0.01	−0.07	−0.07	−0.15
3	−0.01	−0.10	−0.12	−0.22
4	−0.04	−0.11	−0.13	−0.28
5 richest)	−0.49	−0.08	−0.08	−0.65
Total	−0.26	−0.08	−0.09	−0.43

Source World Bank calculation based on the EDAM 3 (2014 prices). *Note EDAM* Enquête Djiboutienne auprès des ménages

For fuel bought directly at pump, the impact of the reform on poor households is negligible, but it increases with welfare and represents the highest loss among rich households (2734 DF per capita), equivalent to 0.5% of total household spending. The poorest two quintiles spend considerably less on public and school transport than the richer quintiles, partly because the poor live in areas with no such transport available, such as the rural areas. The same conclusion, however, holds when restricting the analysis only to urban areas. The impact of the reform on the poorest 40% is less than DF 80 per capita on either public or school transport, compared to more than DF 800 (for both public and school transport combined) among the

Table 9.16 Impact of the reform on the government revenue (in DF millions), by quintile

Quintile	Fuel	Public transport	School transport	Total
1 (poorest)	0.0	1.2	1.3	2.5
2	0.8	6.5	6.5	13.8
3	1.1	13.0	16.3	30.4
4	7.8	21.4	26.4	55.6
5 (richest)	234.1	35.7	36.5	306.3
Total	243.8	77.8	87.0	408.6

Source World Bank calculation based on the EDAM 3 (2014 prices). *Note EDAM* Enquête Djiboutienne auprès des ménages

richest quintile. In terms of household spending, this would amount to a loss of 0.06% of welfare for the poorest quintile and 0.16% for the richest quintile. The middle class would experience the largest reduction in well-being—about 0.22%.

The impact of the reform would result in a gain for the government budget, with the highest gain coming from fuel bought directly at the pump. Table 9.16 shows the impact of the reform on the government budget from the different subsidized products. The impact of the reform would result in a total gain of DF 408.6 million (or 0.16% of GDP). Sixty percent of that gain would come from fuel sold at the pump (96% of the 60% will originate from the richest households), and the remaining 40% will come from public and school transport. It should be noted that because we assume a price elasticity of minus 0.2, the amount gained by the government is less than the loss incurred by the different households.

Because the poor spend most of their income on food-related products, the elimination of tax exemptions on fuel products would reduce inequality but with no apparent impact on poverty. The elimination of tax exemptions on fuel would not affect the poorest because the consumption of this product is negligible among the poor. On the other hand, the consumption of this product is one of the highest among the subsidized products in rich households, and an elimination of tax exemption would result in a reduction in inequality by 0.12 percentage points.

Our results show that an elimination of tax exemption on fuel at the pump offers potential for higher government revenues without impacting poverty. An increase of prices on public transport would increase poverty, but at a lower rate than increases on school transport (see Table 9.23).

Impact of Introducing Consumer Tax on Basic Food Items

The government is not considering levying a consumer tax on basic food items, and the next simulations are merely for illustrative purposes. As mentioned, among the basic food items that are tax-exempt, only a certain quality or type is exempt (for example, broken rice). For rice, only 6% of the imported rice is exempt, but about

Table 9.17 Total impact on the population's well-being (in DF, millions), by quintile

Quintile	Powdered milk	Flour	Cooking oil	Sugar	Total
1 (poorest)	−3.1	−24.8	−7.3	−18.4	−53.6
2	−11.2	−34.0	−13.8	−27.0	−86.0
3	−18.1	−33.4	−16.7	−30.8	−99.0
4	−26.3	−40.8	−21.3	−35.1	−123.5
5 (richest)	−52.4	−58.1	−37.8	−48.2	−196.6
Total	−111.2	−191.0	−96.8	−159.6	−558.7

Source World Bank calculation based on the EDAM 3 (2014 prices). *Note EDAM* Enquête Djiboutienne auprès des ménages

88% of flour, about 60% of sugar and edible oil, and about 50% of powdered milk products are exempt. The implicit subsidy represents 7% of the unsubsidized price. Given the minimal proportion of rice being tax-exempt, we exclude it from our analysis.

Introducing consumer taxes would imply a loss of DF 558.7 million (or 0.22v of GDP) for the population. The per capita values indicate that the loss would be considerably higher for the richest in absolute terms (Table 9.17). Overall, the impact of the reform on the poorest quintile would imply a decrease in well-being by DF 500 or 1.06% of household spending. For the richest quintile, the loss would be equivalent to DF 1,836 or 0.33% of household spending. This comparison shows that the poor spend more in relative terms on tax-exempt food products. Therefore, introducing consumer taxes would affect poverty (Tables 9.18, 9.19 and 9.20).

Table 9.18 Impact on the per capita well-being (in DF), by quintile

Quintile	Powdered milk	Flour	Cooking oil	Sugar	Total
1 (Poorest)	−29	−231	−68	−172	−499
2	−104	−316	−128	−251	−800
3	−169	−312	−156	−288	−924
4	−245	−379	−198	−326	−1148
5 (richest)	−490	−543	−353	−450	−1836
Total	−207	−356	−180	−297	−1041

Source World Bank calculation based on the EDAM 3 (2014 prices). *Note EDAM* Enquête Djiboutienne auprès des ménages

Table 9.19 Impact on well-being (in %), by quintile

Quintile	Powdered milk	Flour	Cooking oil	Sugar	Total
1 (poorest)	−0.06	−0.49	−0.14	−0.37	−1.06
2	−0.10	−0.29	−0.12	−0.23	−0.75
3	−0.11	−0.20	−0.10	−0.18	−0.58
4	−0.11	−0.16	−0.08	−0.14	−0.49
5 (richest)	−0.09	−0.10	−0.06	−0.08	−0.33
Total	−0.09	−0.16	−0.08	−0.14	−0.47

Source World Bank calculation based on the EDAM 3. *Note EDAM* Enquête Djiboutienne auprès des ménages

Table 9.20 Impact of reform on government revenue (in DF millions), by quintile

Quintile	Powdered milk	Flour	Cooking oil	Sugar	Total
1 (poorest)	2.5	19.8	5.8	14.7	42.9
2	9.0	27.2	11.0	21.6	68.8
3	14.5	26.7	13.4	24.7	79.2
4	21.1	32.6	17.0	28.1	98.8
5 (richest)	42.0	46.5	30.2	38.6	157.2
Total	89.0	152.8	77.5	127.7	447.0

Source World Bank calculation based on the EDAM 3 (2014 prices). *Note EDAM* Enquête Djiboutienne auprès des ménages

The Political Economy of Reforms

Following the previous section where we looked at the impacts of the proposed reforms, here we examine the safety nets in place in Djibouti and attempt to estimate the effect of compensating schemes to offset perverse effects on poverty.

Fuel Subsidies

The government is currently considering abandoning the use of the discretionary tax element on certain fuel products (super and diesel) for private consumers, but the privileges for other exempt groups such as the military and embassies would remain. At the time of analysis (based on prices of December 2013), such a reform would have resulted in a small reduction in super prices and an increase of around 13% for diesel. The substantial fall of crude oil prices is relevant to the calculations shown. In December 2013, Brent crude sold for about US$110 a barrel, and it remained around that level until July 2014. Since then it has steadily declined until falling to around US$50 a barrel in January 2015.

Before the drop in oil prices, the government had not taken any firm decision, in part due to fears that higher fuel prices would increase inflation. In addition, there are concerns over the impact on the poor, the middle class, and certain sectors, such as transport, fisheries, and bakeries. The impact of fuel subsidy reforms on the transport sector is of particular concern to the government. Ticket prices for public transport are set by the state and have been more or less stable since 2006. The bus and taxi fleet is outdated, and current discussions center on decreasing the cost of transport by updating the fleet. The government is considering financing new vehicles, which the bus and taxi operators would pay back over time, thereby reducing the consumption of fuel.

If the government wanted to abandon the discretionary tax, this would be the time for action. With falling oil prices, an elimination of the discretionary tax elements would not necessarily lead to higher prices for consumers. In fact, given the low prices seen in early 2015, removal of discretionary tax on diesel would be small in comparison to the fall in underlying costs—so that the effect of its removal will be negligible and the effect on bus prices will be easily absorbed. If bus operators do not lower their prices at all, their margins will increase.

With the elimination of discretionary tax on fuel products, however, the government would relinquish a tool to smooth fuel prices in times of price fluctuations. With falling oil prices, government tax revenues will decrease accordingly. The removal of discretionary tax at this point would lower the tax revenue further. It is likely that the government has adjusted the magnitude of the discretionary tax since January 2014, which would warrant further analysis. Furthermore, an analysis of the optimal tax structure would be warranted. The following analysis based on December 2013 prices confirms that a negative tax on fuel products effectively subsidizes the better-off. Any reform of the current energy tax system should be pro-poor,and social safety nets would be the channel to reinvest savings in pro-poor policies.

Social Safety Nets

In this subsection we examine first the efficiency of the current safety nets in Djibouti and then look at the impacts of reforming the safety net already in place, including eliminating the tax exemption on a few key items. And finally we estimate the effects on poverty of different compensating schemes following the proposed reforms.

Role of Social Safety Nets

Currently, untargeted tax exemptions (implicit subsidies) reach a wider part of the population than targeted programs. Table 9.21 shows the percentage of the population (by welfare quintile) receiving seven types of transfers: pensions (private or public), compensation for health care expenditure, food rations, cash transfers from the government or nongovernmental organizations (NGOs), publicly provided food

Table 9.21 Coverage of transfer programs (in %), by quintile

Quintile	Pensions	Compensation for health care expenditure	Food rations	Transfers from government or NGOs	Food subsidies	Fuel subsidies	Remittances
1 (poorest)	5.3	1.3	27.0	5.8	77.3	17.1	29.7
2	8.6	3.5	8.6	1.3	98.1	48.2	23.6
3	10.5	4.2	2.5	1.5	99.7	66.9	20.2
4	8.5	5.5	1.3	0.9	99.3	76.2	18.3
5 (richest)	9.6	6.9	1.1	0.8	99.2	82.5	13.5
Total	8.5	4.3	8.1	2.1	94.7	58.2	21.0

Source World Bank calculation based on the EDAM 3. *Note EDAM* Enquête Djiboutienne auprès des ménages. *NGO* nongovernmental organization subsidies, publicly provided fuel subsidies, and private transfers received from family and friends. Tax exemptions on basic food items reach the majority of the poor (77.3% in the poorest quintile) and almost the totality of individuals in the other four quintiles. Tax exemptions on certain fuel products, on the other hand, benefit only 17% of the poorest quintile but more than 82% of the richest. About a quarter of the population in the poorest quintile benefits from food rations, making it a program with relatively effective targeting. Compensation for health expenditure disproportionately benefits the richer quintiles. Very few households (less than 10%) benefit from pensions. Finally, 21% of Djibouti households receive private transfers (international or national), and these transfers benefit the poorest households in a larger proportion.[4]

The intended beneficiaries of social safety net programs should be the poor. Therefore, the performance of such programs can be assessed by estimating program leakage. One way to measure such leakage is by determining the share of total transfers received by nonpoor beneficiaries. In a well-targeted progressive program, the poor receive the highest share of transfers; this share declines as welfare increases. Table 9.22 shows the distribution of benefits by area and welfare quintile. In Djibouti, food rations and cash transfers generally fit this description as the poor receive most of the transfers, in fact, more than half of the transfers for food rations. In contrast, tax exemptions on food and fuel items predominantly benefit the urban population and nonpoor, making these programs regressive. The majority of food and fuel subsidy resources (85 and 97%, respectively) are received by those living in urban areas and by those from the richest two quintiles (57 and 89%, respectively). Only 15% of food subsidy benefits and less than 3% of fuel subsidy benefits go to beneficiaries living in rural areas, and only 10% and less than 1%, respectively, are received by those in the poorest quintile. Pensions and compensation for health care expenditure transfers are received mainly by nonpoor beneficiaries and the population living in urban areas.

The generosity of social safety net programs in Djibouti is generally very low, which limits the impact on poverty. Only two programs (pensions and private transfers from family and friends, which strictly speaking are not social assistance programs), of the seven types of programs available seem to have an impact on the consumption levels of the population in general. On the contrary, by focusing on the poorest quintile, food rations also have a significant effect even if private transfers are by far the most efficient vehicle. The impact of cash transfers from the government or NGOs and tax exemptions on food on the welfare of the poorest quintile is extremely modest, and that of tax exemptions on fuel items is negligible.

Impact of Reforming Tax Exemptions and Safety Nets on Poverty

Discretionary energy taxes have benefited the better-off in times of higher fuel prices (the analysis in this study is based on December 2013 prices). An

[4] GDP for 2013 is estimated at US$1.456 billion.

Table 9.22 Distribution of benefits (targeting accuracy), by quintile and area

Type of benefit	Area of residence		Quintiles of per capita consumption				
	Urban	Rural	1 (poorest)	2	3	4	5 (richest)
Pensions	85.6	14.4	4.5	10.9	17.5	19.3	47.9
Compensation for health care expenditure	88.0	12.0	3.5	11.1	17.2	23.4	44.9
Food rations	15.8	84.2	56.2	21.2	10.7	4.3	7.5
Transfers from government or NGOs	44.7	55.3	45.1	16.9	13.6	11.7	12.7
Food subsidies	84.9	15.1	9.5	15.4	17.8	22.0	35.3
Fuel subsidies	97.2	2.8	0.6	3.4	7.5	13.5	75.0
Remittances	75.6	24.4	20.8	15.4	20.7	15.0	28.1

Source World Bank calculation based on the EDAM 3. *Note* Benefits incidence is the transfer amount received by the group as a percentage of total transfers received by the population. Specifically, benefits incidence is (sum of all transfers received by all individuals in the group)/(sum of all transfers received by all individuals in the population). Aggregated transfer amounts are estimated using household size-weighted expansion factors. *EDAM* Enquête Djiboutienne auprès des ménages; *NGO* nongovernmental organization

elimination of tax exemptions on fuel products would reduce inequality but would not have any apparent impact on poverty. Savings from a possible tax reform and other funding resources could be rechanneled toward the poor and vulnerable. But the key component of any poverty alleviation program is effective targeting of the poor. The government of Djibouti with the support of the World Bank is currently developing a social registry to increase equity in the distribution of resources and to promote greater social inclusion for the most vulnerable groups. Over the course of the technical assistance provided to the government of Djibouti, a number of policy recommendations have emerged, and some have already been taken into consideration in the design of a stronger social protection system. These recommendations are derived from a poverty and social impact analysis and include:

- Savings on energy tax reforms and other funding resources, including those spread over a number of very small safety net programs, should be channeled to a cash-transfer program targeting the poorest;
- A proxy means test (PMT) should be used to determine the households' poverty score, and all safety net programs should target the poorest (as defined by the PMT) rather than targeting rural households based on geography[5];

[5]This functionality will be part of the forthcoming social registry that will be used to identify, classify, and target households that would be considered poor or vulnerable, to improve the delivery of assistance to them.

Table 9.23 Reform, destitution head count, and gini index

	Destitution level	Change in destitution	Gini index	Variation in Gini
Prereform	20.00	–	45.13	–
Powdered milk	20.00	0.00	45.13	0.00
Flour	20.05	0.05	45.18	0.05
Cooking oil	20.01	0.00	45.15	0.01
Sugar	20.01	0.01	45.17	0.04
Fuel	20.00	0.00	45.01	−0.12
Public transport	20.00	0.00	45.13	0.00
School transport	20.00	0.00	45.14	0.00
Post reform	20.17	0.17	45.13	−0.02

Source World Bank calculation based on the EDAM 3. *Note EDAM* Enquête Djiboutienne auprès des ménages

- Similarly, current and future safety net programs should first target poor households based on the relative poverty score, and then use other (categorical) factors to determine program eligibility.

As the poor spend most of their income on food-related products, the elimination of tax exemptions on such products would have the highest impact on poverty and inequality, while the elimination of tax exemptions on fuel products would reduce inequality but with no apparent impact on poverty. However, these effects would be minimal, almost negligible. Table 9.23 shows the impact of the reform on destitution and inequality. (Recall that the destitution line is defined as the upper limit of Quintile 1.) Globally, a reform of taxes on fuel and food products alone would not have a significant impact on destitution and no impact on inequality. In particular, the destitution rate would increase by 0.17 percentage points from 20.00 to 20.17%. The elimination of tax exemptions on flour would increase destitution by 0.05 percentage points (from 20 00 to 20.05%), and inequality by 0.05 percentage points (from 45.13 to 45.18%). The effect of the elimination of the discretionary tax adjustment on fuel would not affect the poorest as it would result in a reduction of inequality by 0.12 Percentage points. The consumption of fuel is negligible among the poor, but it is one of the highest consumed products among the subsidized products in rich households.

Likely Impact of Compensation Policies Through Social Safety Nets Programs

Reform options based on a number of transfer schemes and budget envelopes were discussed with the government. The different transfer schemes proposed are defined in Table 9.24 and could be implemented at an individual or household level. In the

Table 9.24 Definition of the different transfer schemes

Transfer no.	Selection criteria	Beneficiary	Amount transferred per unit (in DF)
1	Rural + urban outside Djibouti City	Individual	6935
2		Individual (in Eq.Ad.)	9268
3		Household	35,826
4	Rural only	Individual	11,560
5		Individual (in Eq.Ad.)	15,717
6		Household	54,940
7	Rural + urban in quintile 1	Individual	7675
8		Individual (in Eq.Ad.)	10,259
9		Household	42,550
10	First quintile with unique transfer	Individual	9306
11		Individual (in Eq.Ad.)	12,418
12		Household	58,748
13	Quintile 1 with 2 steps	Individual	Percentile 0–10: 13,960 Percentile 10–20: 4673
14		Individual (in Eq.Ad.)	Percentile 0–10: 18,811 Percentile 10–20: 6176
15		Household	Percentile 0–10: 90,133 Percentile 10–20: 28,863
16	Quintile 1 with 4 steps	Individual	Percentile 0–5: 15,245 Percentile 5–10: 12,670 Percentile 10–15: 7066 percentile 15–20: 2288
17		Individual (in Eq.Ad.)	Percentile 0–5: 20,629 Percentile 5–10: 17,001 Percentile 10–15: 9313 percentile 15–20: 3031
18		Household	Percentile 0–5: 110,709 Percentile 5–10: 73,607 Percentile 10–15: 42,777 Percentile 15–20: 14,417

Source World Bank calculation based on the EDAM 3 (2012 prices). *Note DF* Djibouti franc; *EDAM* Enquête Djiboutienne auprès des ménages; *Eq.Ad. equivalence adult scale*

latter case, the amount transferred is the same for any household meeting the selection criteria irrespective of the household size. On the other hand, the "individual" schemes depend on household size. For example, a nine-member household would receive three times the amount received by a three-member household.

Table 9.25 Effect on Destitution Gap of the Different Transfer Schemes

Transfer no.	Selection criteria	Beneficiary	DF 1 billion	DF 2 billion	DF 3 billion
1	Rural + urban outside Djibouti City	Individual	5.5	4.3	3.3
2		Individual (in Eq.Ad.)	5.6	4.4	3.4
3		Household	5.7	4.6	3.8
4	Rural only	Individual	5.0	3.4	2.2
5		Individual (in Eq.Ad.)	5.0	3.5	2.3
6		Household	5.3	4.0	3.1
7	Rural + urban in first quintile	Individual	5.0	3.4	2.2
8		Individual (in Eq.Ad.)	5.0	3.5	2.3
9		Household	5.1	3.8	2.7
10	Quintile 1 with unique transfer	Individual	4.6	2.9	1.6
11		Individual (in Eq.Ad.)	4.7	3.0	1.7
12		Household	4.6	2.9	1.8
13	Quintile 1 with 2 steps	Individual	4.4	2.1	0.6
14		Individual (in Eq.Ad.)	4.5	2.2	0.8
15		Household	4.3	2.3	1.1
16	Quintile 1 with 4 steps	Individual	4.4	1.9	0.3
17		Individual (in Eq.Ad.)	4.4	2.0	0.4
18		Household	4.2	2.0	0.8
Without transfer			6.9	6.9	6.9

Source World Bank calculation based on the EDAM 3. *Note DF* Djibouti franc; *EDAM* Enquête Djiboutienne auprès des ménages

An intermediate measure is based on a calorie-requirement–based equivalence adult scale (Eq.Ad.).

The largest decline in destitution (poverty) head count is achieved when targeting Quintile 1. The destitution head count (P0) is defined as this quintile. Overall, with a total budget of DF 1 billion, the effect on the destitution head count is limited if we concentrate mainly on rural households without taking into account urban households from Quintile 1. The largest decline in the destitution head count with a budget of DF 1 billion targets that quintile and transfers a uniform amount.

With a larger budget of DF 3 billion, it would be possible to almost halve the destitution head count using any of the schemes that target Quintile 1. By using such a destitution head count as a measure of efficiency, however, it is not clear whether an individual scheme or a household-based scheme is more efficient at reducing destitution. The main problem in using a destitution head count to assess the different schemes is that no weight is given when an extremely poor household receives an important transfer while remaining below the poverty line. Actually, we can imagine an extreme case where all the poorest households would be better off but still poor if the amount transferred makes them go over the poverty line. Therefore, we should focus on the destitution gap as a measure of destitution.

To reduce the destitution gap, targeting Quintile 1 is more efficient than any of the schemes focusing on rural households. The poverty gap index (PGI or P1) estimates the depth of destitution by considering how far, on average, the poor are from that destitution line. It is defined as the average destitution gap in the population as a proportion of the destitution line. In a graph presenting the cumulative welfare function, this is the area below the destitution line and on the left-hand side of the function. Before any transfer, the destitution gap index associated with the destitution line is measured as 6.9% (last line in Table 9.25). On average, the poor individual has expenditures (as measured by the PMT) 6.9% below the destitution line (DF 77,926 per capita in 2012 prices). The preferred transfer scheme to reduce the destitution gap would be to target Quintile 1 with a four-step transfer amount depending on destitution. Schemes 16 or 17 would be by far the best—focusing on Quintile 1 but with the amount transferred being dependent on destitution (as defined by the PMT). In this case, the poorest 5% would receive more than the penultimate 5%, and so on (see Table 9.24).

Conclusion

The government of Djibouti is currently considering abandoning the use of the discretionary tax element on certain fuel products (super and diesel) for private consumers. This chapter shows that the effects of removing tax exemptions on food and fuel globally would have a marginal effect on poverty, but would keep inequality unchanged. Among the poorer quintiles, the loss in welfare as a result of the reform would be the highest on food-related items; among the richer quintiles it would be the highest on fuel products. Figure 9.1 shows the impact of the reform on the welfare of the population as a proportion of the total spending by quintile and for each subsidized product group. In terms of food-related products, the reform would result in a significant loss of welfare among the poorest quintile (1.12% of total spending) but this loss decreases as welfare increases. The reform would result in a minimal loss among the richest quintile for fuel products, and this loss decreases as welfare decreases and becomes negligible for the poorest quintile.

The impact of the reform on government budget would result in a gain, the highest coming from fuel. The impact of the reform on government budget would result in a total gain of DF 856 million (or 0.33% of GDP): 28% of that gain would come from fuel (96% of the gain from fuel will originate from the richest

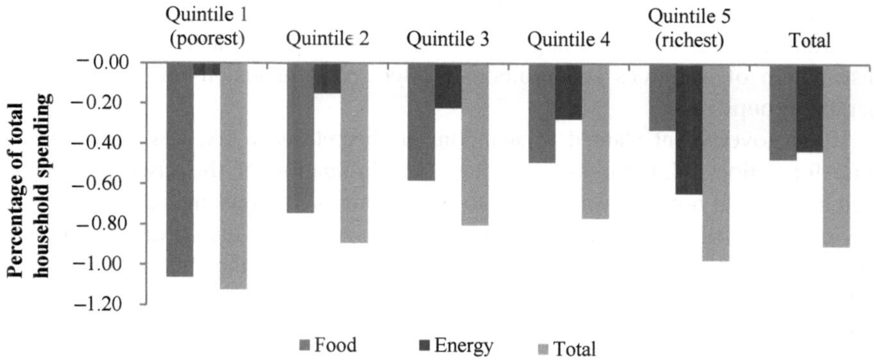

Fig. 9.1 Impact on Well-being, by quintile. *Source* World Bank calculation based on the EDAM 3. *Note EDAM* Enquête Djiboutienne auprès des ménages

households), 18% from flour, and 15% from sugar. The highest gain in the government budget will come from the richest households (54%). This gain decreases as welfare decreases to reach the lowest share among poor households (5%). This result is consistent with the finding that the highest loss of welfare in the population would come from fuel, and particularly among the rich.

Figure 9.2 shows the impact on government revenues as the price of each subsidized product increases. The most important revenue gain to the government would come from increasing the price of fuel, while the least would come from increasing the price of cooking oil

To reduce poverty, savings from a possible tax reform on fuel products and other funding resources could be rechanneled toward the poor and vulnerable. To reduce poverty, however, effective targeting of the poor is important. A key element to strengthening social safety nets in Djibouti is the creation of a social registry of poor and vulnerable households, which will be the single platform used by all social assistance programs. Such a measure would result in significant cost savings and

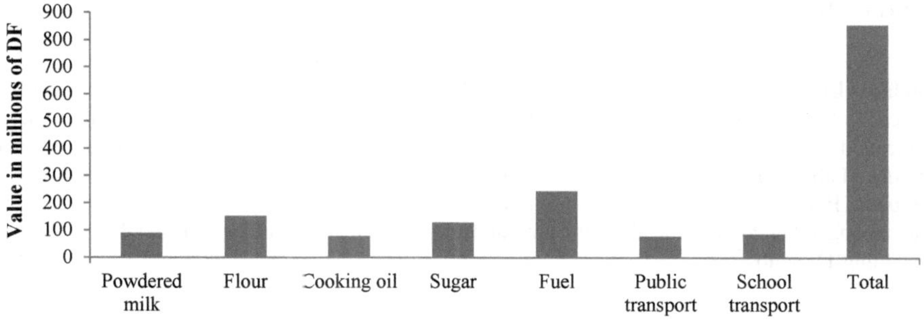

Fig. 9.2 Impact of the Reform on the Government Revenue (DF), by product. *Source* World Bank calculation based on the EDAM 3 (2014 prices). *Note DF* Djibouti franc; *EDAM* Enquête Djiboutienne auprès des ménages

substantial improvements in targeting the poorest households. In addition, the government is considering a targeted cash-transfer system to increase equity in the distribution of resources and promote greater social inclusion for the most vulnerable groups.

If the government wanted to abandon the discretionary tax, this would be the time for action. With falling oil prices, an elimination of the discretionary tax elements would not necessarily lead to higher prices for consumers. In fact, given the low prices seen in early 2015, removal of discretionary tax on diesel would be small in comparison to the fall in underlying costs—so that the effect of its removal will be negligible and the effect on transport prices, a key concern to the government, will be easily absorbed.

Acknowledgements We thank Robert Bacon, Ines Rodriguez Caillava, and Angela Elzir for their contributions to this chapter.

References

Cap Gemini Consulting. April 2014.

De Broek, M., A. Kangur, and R. Kpodar. 2012. *Djibouti: Fuel Price Subsidy Reform*. IMF, May 2012.

ESMAP (Energy Sector Management Assistance Program). 2011. Transit bus operational and maintenance practices to maximize fuel economy. Report 63116–GLB.

GIZ (Deutsche Gesellschaft für Internationale Zusammenarbeit, Federal Ministry for Economic Cooperation and Development). 2012–13. *International Fuel Prices 2012/2013*. Eighth edition. https://www.energypedia.info/index.php/International_Fuel_Prices.

IBRD (International Bank for Reconstruction and Development). 2015. Poverty and social impact analysis: Strengthening safety nets in Djibouti. Report AUS7544, World Bank, Washington, DC. www.worldbank.org/transport/roads/rdt_docsannex1.pdf.

World Bank. 2014. *Djibouti country partnership strategy 2014–17*. Washington, DC: World Bank.

Author Biographies

Stefanie Brodmann is a senior economist at the World Bank's Social Protection and Labor Global Practice. She has worked on issues related to labor markets, entrepreneurship, safety nets, education-to-work transition, and labor migration. She holds a doctorate from the Universitat Pompeu Fabra in Barcelona, was a visiting Ph.D. student at Harvard University, and a postdoctoral fellow at Princeton University prior to joining the World Bank in 2009. Her current work focuses on, among other topics, social safety nets and targeting in the Middle East and North Africa, including Djibouti.

Harold Coulombe has been an international freelance consultant for over twenty years, mainly on World Bank projects, but also with other UN organisations (UNDP, UNFPA, UNICEF, and DESA). His most recent mandates have been focused on different applications of the census-based poverty map methodology in collaboration with the World Bank's Research Department and Education Network. He is also collaborating on a series of studies on different poverty and social protection issues. Prior to his current status, he spent five years as a researcher at the University of Warwick where he also obtained his Ph.D. in economics.

Chapter 10
Consumer Subsidies in the Islamic Republic of Iran: Simulations of Further Reforms

Mohammad H. Mostafavi-Dehzooei and Djavad Salehi-Isfahani

Introduction

The Islamic Republic of Iran is a major producer of oil and gas, and therefore it is not surprising that the country subsidizes energy heavily. In 1995 energy subsidies were estimated at $5 billion or 6% of gross domestic product (GDP) (Salehi-Isfahani 1996), and with rising world prices in the following decades, the subsidies rose several times over to reach more than 15% of GDP (Jensen and Tarr 2003; Salehi-Isfahani 2014). During the oil boom of the 2000s, when the world price of energy trebled, the country's domestic price failed to keep pace, and subsidies ballooned. Despite several small adjustments in the domestic price of oil and gas since 1995, energy prices in the Islamic Republic of Iran diverged from their opportunity cost.

In January 2010 a bold law was enacted that required the government to raise energy prices to a level equal to 90% of the free on board (FOB) price of energy in the Persian Gulf. The law also stipulated that the revenues from the price increases should be divided into three parts: 50% to compensate households, 20% to compensate firms, and the remaining 30% to be added to government revenues. In December 2010 prices of energy products were increased, by factors ranging from 2 (for bread) to 9 (for diesel), and monthly cash transfers of 455,000 rials (Rls), or about $90 (U.S. dollars) in purchasing power parity (PPP) per capita started reaching about 95% of the population.

Although the reform was successful in raising energy and bread prices several times over and the cash transfer scheme allowed the price shock to go forward without any protest, four years later much of the program's initial gains have been lost to inflation, and opposition to further sharp price adjustments is strong. In the meantime, the collapse of the price of oil in the world markets has narrowed the gap

M.H. Mostafavi-Dehzooei (✉) · D. Salehi-Isfahani
Virginia Tech, Blacksburg, USA

P. Verme and A. Araar (eds.), *The Quest for Subsidy Reforms in the Middle East and North Africa Region*, Natural Resource Management and Policy 42,
DOI 10.1007/978-3-319-52926-4_10

between prices in the Islamic Republic of Iran and the outside world, diminishing the urgency of further subsidy reform. President Hassan Rouhani, who took office in August 2013, introduced the second phase of price increases, raising the average price of energy and bread by about 30%. His administration appears determined to follow up with gradual increases in energy prices. This chapter examines the consequences of further price reforms for consumer welfare and the government budget. It presents simulation results that compare the effects of gradual price reform, which is the likely course of action, with a one-time increase that removes all the subsidies, similar to the 2010 reform.

Although energy subsidies are lower than they were in 2010, the logic of removing them is stronger, especially for the government. Lower world oil prices, which have ostensibly reduced the need to raise domestic prices, have at the same time made it more urgent for the government to seek more revenue from its domestic sale of energy, which is more than three times what it exports.

Besides budgetary concerns, energy subsidies raise equity issues because they distribute the national hydrocarbon wealth unequally. This chapter shows that subsidies for energy products accrue mainly to upper-income groups, who use more energy than the poor. Efficiency is another concern. Decades of cheap energy distorted Iranian production to be more dependent on energy and less efficient in its use. As shown in Fig. 10.1, before 1987 the Islamic Republic of Iran consumed less energy for each dollar of production compared to the world and Organisation for Co-operation and Development (OECD) countries. Since then the country has increased its use of energy per dollar of GDP, while the rest of the world has decreased it. In 2009 the Islamic Republic of Iran consumed 50% more energy per unit of GDP than the rest of the world. Moreover, subsidized energy is detrimental to the environment. The country produces more than its share of greenhouse gases,

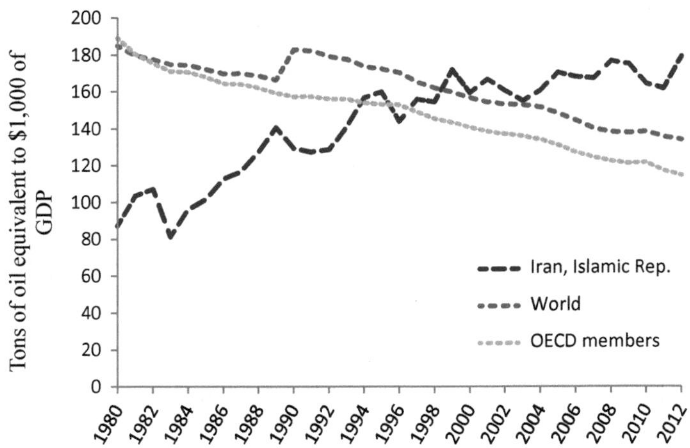

Fig. 10.1 Energy consumption in the Islamic Republic of Iran, the world, and OECD countries. *Source* WDI various years, World Bank calculations. *Note GDP* gross domestic product; *OECD* Organisation for Economic Co-operation and Development

and pollutants have made the air in its major urban centers unbearable. As with snow days in the United States, Tehran's schoolchildren get days off from school because of pollution, which has become a part of normal life. Finally, low energy prices have also encouraged the use of capital-intensive technologies, which limit demand for labor at a time when youth are entering the labor force in record numbers.

There is a small literature on the Islamic Republic of Iran's subsidy reform. Several papers describe the reform (Guillaume et al. (2011), Salehi-Isfahani et al. (2013), Salehi-Isfahani (2014)). Salehi-Isfahani and Dehzooei (2015) evaluate the impact of the cash transfer on household labor supply. Gahvari and Karimi (2013) use an Almost Ideal Demand System (AIDS) model to study the reform and find that cash transfers improve welfare, at least for poor deciles. Gahvari and Taheripour (2011) use prereform data and the Quadratic Almost Ideal Demand System (QAIDS) to predict the impacts of a price reform in the country. In their general equilibrium framework, they find that eliminating subsidies for utilities results in substantial welfare losses. Jensen and Tarr (2003) use a computable general equilibrium (CGE) model to simulate the effect of reform of subsidies and find that "even nontargeted direct income payments to all households (not just the poor) would enormously and progressively increase the incomes of the poor."

The plan of this chapter is as follows. The next section offers a more detailed account of the evolution of subsidies and is followed by a section that explains our sources of data. The next sections derive the distribution of subsidies as they existed in 2013, present the simulations results, and discuss the political economy of subsidy reform.

Evolution of Subsidies

The Islamic Republic of Iran has subsidized a variety of goods besides energy—bread and medicine, in particular—but energy subsidies have been by far the largest part and the part that has increased the fastest in recent decades. One reason for this increase was the rise of global oil prices. From 1999 to 2008 the price of oil increased tenfold, raising the opportunity cost of oil used domestically and the amount of subsidies to oil-based products. Energy subsidies have also increased because domestic consumption of oil and gas has grown from about 1 million barrels per day (mbd) in the 1970s to about 4 mbd oil and gas in 2013.

In oil exporting countries, subsidies tend to rise and fall with the global price of energy. Governments let energy prices stagnate during the periods of rising global oil prices because they are flush with revenue and see no need to charge domestic consumers the world price. Distortions increase further because the expenditure of rising oil revenues leads to inflation, led by the price of nontradable goods and services, which reduces the price of energy products relative to other goods. At the end of an oil boom, as in 2014–15, revenues from exports decline, and governments become more interested in eliminating subsidies.

The Iranian government delivers more than 4 million oil equivalent barrels of energy (gasoline, natural gas, and electricity) each day to consumers inside the country. In 2013, before the collapse of oil prices, the total value of this energy reached $100 billion per year. With the domestic price of energy roughly about one-third of the world market, some $66 billion of this can be counted as subsidy. In 2014, as a result of the collapse of oil prices, the amount of the implicit subsidy declined substantially. Given the uncertainty about the future price of oil, it is difficult to define a zero-subsidy price for future years.

A major part of subsidies in the Islamic Republic of Iran are implicit and due to the gap between the domestic and world price of energy, but a good part, especially the subsidies for food and medicine, are explicit and are financed from the general budget and therefore compete with other expenditures more directly. The rationale for both types of subsidies is social protection. Protecting the poor was a widely stated slogan of the 1979 revolution. Although subsidies existed for many of these commodities before the revolution, they took a more essential role as the ethos of the populist state.

There were several attempts at energy price reform in the 1990s, but none succeeded in closing the gap between prices in the Islamic Republic of Iran and the world markets to any significant degree. During the administration of President Mohammad Khatami (1997–2005), the conservative political opposition dominated the parliament and stymied any major reduction in subsidies. Going further, in 2004 the conservative-dominated parliament passed a law preventing the government from raising energy prices.

Figure 10.2 shows the history of energy prices since 1994 in Iranian rials (Rls) and in U.S. dollars ($).[1] The impact of fixing the price of energy products is visible in this graph after 2004 when global crude prices doubled.

Khatami's populist successor, Mahmoud Ahmadinejad, had the support of the parliament for energy price reform, but little was done on this during most of his first term (2005–09). In 2008 the government and the parliament started discussions for a major price reform, which eventually became the Targeted Subsidy Reform Act in January 2010, six months after Ahmadinejad's controversial election to his second term, 2009–13. Subsidy reform was the centerpiece of his economic program, but its implementation was delayed until December 2010, when prices for bread and energy products were raised in one go by factors varying from 2 to 9 times.

The decision whether to increase prices in one step or gradually was a difficult one. Gradual increases are preferred if they can be maintained over several years as prices catch up with their intended targets. In the Islamic Republic of Iran the experience with gradual increases had not been encouraging. Getting both the government and the parliament to commit to future increases proved unsuccessful because of the country's fluid politics. Small increases in one year were rarely followed by further increases as

[1]In this chapter we use the market exchange rate for energy prices because we are interested in measuring their opportunity cost in the world market. Elsewhere, when reporting on household expenditures, we use the PPP rates for private consumption taken from *World Development Indicators* on January 26, 2015.

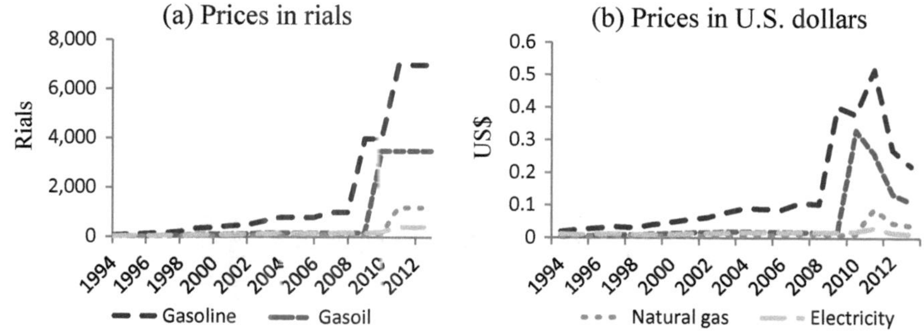

Fig. 10.2 Energy prices in the Islamic Republic of Iran, 1994–2012. *Source* Ministry of Energy (2013). *Note* During much of this period the Islamic Republic of Iran had multiple exchange rates. We use the rial-dollar exchange rate that is reported by the Central Bank of Iran for the parallel or free market. For energy prices with two rates, rationed and free, we use the latter

the powerful lobbies for low energy prices (such as the petrochemical and auto industries) often mustered enough support in the following year to block further increases. This experience, plus the government's interest in generating enough revenue for redistribution, provided the rationale for shock therapy.

The reform included a massive cash transfer program, which was launched simultaneously with the price hikes. The cash transfer program was efficiently executed, depositing Rls 445,000 per person per month in individual bank accounts. Initially, this amount was 28% of the median household income, and 50% of the income of a minimum-wage worker with a family of four (Salehi-Isfahani et al. 2013). According to the government, during the first four months of the program, about 62 million people (about 82% of the total population) started to receive cash transfers. This number increased quickly to cover about 95% of the population. Survey data indicate that coverage in rural areas where banks are less accessible was lower than in urban areas (Salehi-Isfahani et al. 2013).

Data

The data used in this chapter are derived from the Household Expenditures and Income Survey (HEIS) collected annually by the Statistical Center of Iran (SCI). The survey is nationally representative and two-stage stratified, at the urban and rural level and by province The survey is weighted, and the sampling weights are provided by the SCI. This survey includes information on expenditures and incomes of urban and rural Iranian households. We use the most recent sample collected in Iranian year 1392, which corresponds to March 20, 2013, to March 19, 2014, and we refer to it as 2013–14 hereafter.

Table 10.1 presents the descriptive statistics for the 2013–14 sample. The survey frequencies have been inflated using sampling weights to reflect population level

Table 10.1 Population and household expenditures, 2013–14

Expenditure decile	Population ($\times 10^6$)	Number of households ($\times 10^6$)	Household size	Total expenditures ($\times 10^{12}$ rials)	Expenditures per capita ($\times 10^6$ rials)	Expenditures per household ($\times 10^6$ rials)
1 (poorest)	8.1	1.8	4.5	116.4	14.5	65.4
2	8.0	1.9	4.2	174.9	21.7	92.1
3	8.0	2.0	4.0	217.9	27.1	109.3
4	8.1	2.1	3.8	260.4	32.3	123.9
5	8.0	2.2	3.7	304.2	37.9	140.4
6	8.1	2.3	3.6	358.6	44.5	158.3
7	8.0	2.3	3.4	426.1	53.0	182.2
8	8.0	2.4	3.3	516.0	64.1	213.1
9	8.1	2.6	3.1	671.2	83.4	256.2
10 (richest)	8.1	3.0	2.7	1242.8	154.4	409.8
Total	80.5	22.6	3.6	4288.5	53.3	189.6

Source World Bank calculation using SUBSIM and HEIS (2013)

Note We use the sampling weights provided for the HEIS by the Statistical Center of Iran to inflate sample values to population level. These weights overestimate Iran's population by about 3 million. *HEIS* Household Expenditure and Income Survey; *SUBSIM* SUBsidy SIMulation values. The population of 80 million is divided into ten equal size deciles (with varying number of households). Per capita expenditures is Rls 53 million per year (about \$1664 and \$6200 in PPP).

Prices of subsidized items were set through both government control and subsidy. For bread, for example, the government bought domestically produced wheat at Rls 10,150 per kilogram in 2013–14, which was close to international market price. Wheat was then sold at the subsidized price of around Rls 460 to flour producers, who sold it at Rls 5900 (\$0.20) per kilogram to bakers. The government thus controled the price of bread sold at bakeries. In 2014 each kilogram of bread was sold at Rls 10,274 on average. In rural areas, where most households bake their own bread, the government sells flour up to a quota at the subsidized price. Liquefied petroleum gas (LPG) is also sold at a subsidized price mostly in regions without piped natural gas. Alongside bread, LPG and kerosene have linear pricing, but other subsidized items are subject to nonlinear pricing with quotas that vary according to season and a region's climate (natural gas and electricity) and type of vehicle (gasoline and diesel). LPG sold at Rls 1800 (\$0.06) per kilogram at the time, and kerosene at Rls 3500 (\$0.11) per liter. Prices of subsidized goods are given in Table 10.2.

Gasoline had a two-tier price to begin with: Rls 1000 per liter for rationed and Rls 4000 for free market gasoline from 2010, and these prices rose to 4000 and 7000, respectively, in 2013.

To control the quota, all vehicles had an electronic card that kept track of their monthly consumption. The quota differed by type of vehicle. Motorcycles had 25 L per month of the subsidized gasoline in 2013–14. Cars, other than taxis and government vehicles, had 60 L. In our data, we have the information only on how much gasoline each household bought altogether, but a household may have a car, a motorcycle, or both. In our calculations we assume that all consumed gasoline is used in cars.

Natural gas and electricity prices have more tiers, and they also depend on the season and regional climate. The effective national average price of natural gas was Rls 742 per cubic meter (m^3) (Ministry of Energy 2013). Prices started at Rls 700 per m^3 (about \$0.01), increasing to Rls 3500 (about \$0.12) for large users. Similarly, the average price of electricity for households was Rls 337 per kilowatt hour (kWh), with tariffs increasing from Rls 300 to Rls 2150 per kWh. The rising tariff for natural gas is shown in Fig. 10.3.

Distribution of Subsidies

This section describes the distribution of subsidies for bread and energy products in 2013–14. Calculating the exact level of the subsidy is not a trivial task. Many subsidies, such as gasoline sold to households, are direct, while others, such as gasoline used in transportation, are indirect. Here, we are concerned with direct subsidies only. The calculation of direct subsidies is also complicated by two facts.

Table 10.2 Price of subsidized items and free market

	Gasoline		Diesel (L)	Kerosene (L)	Natural gas (m^3)	LPG (m^3)	Electricity (kWh)	Bread (kg)	Flour (kg)
Price in 2013	Up to 60 L	More than 60 L							
Iran, Islamic Rep.	4000	7000	3500	1000	742[a]	1800	337.5[b]	10,274	5900
Free market	23,811[b]	23,811[b]	22,986[b]	22,639[b]	13,317[c]	10,800[c]	4800[d]	21,800[e]	14,700[e]

Source Ministry of Energy (2013), except for explicit data in the note

Note

[a]Effective national average price, Ministry of Energy (2013)

[b]Based on FOB Persian Gulf price, Platts.com

[c]Average Europe price, FERC and www.cngeurope.com, 2013

[d]Price in Turkey, Turkish Statistical Institute (2013)

[e]Based on international wheat price and authors' calculations

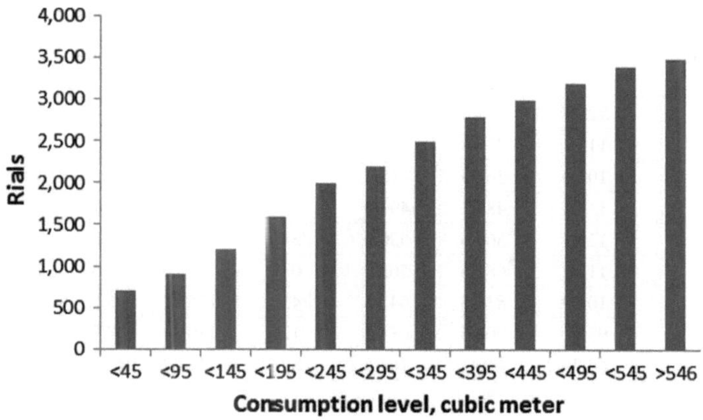

Fig. 10.3 Natural gas price schedule in 2014, in rials per cubic meter. *Source* National Iranian Gas Company, 2013

First, most of the subsidies are implicit, so they do not appear in the budget. World market prices serve to estimate the value of implicit subsidies. Second, except for bread, kerosene, diesel, and LPG, other subsidies are nonlinear. Gasoline is sold at two prices—a rationed and a free price—and tariffs for natural gas and electricity are differentiated by volume. In addition, prices for electricity and natural gas vary according to the season and a region's climate.

At the start of the reforms in 2010, gasoline had a two-tier price: Rls 1000 per liter for rationed and Rls 4000 for free market gasoline. In December these prices were increased to 4000 and 7000, respectively. The new free market price was about $0.70 per liter, which was close to its border price, but by 2014, following the 200% depreciation of the rial, it had fallen to about $0.25 per liter, well below the border price. The price of diesel, which had the highest subsidy, was initially set to increase 22 times, but was reduced to 9 times following protests by truck drivers. In 2013–14, the price of diesel was raised again, to Rls 3500 ($0.11) per liter, which was about one-sixth of its border price. Table 10.2 presents the prices of the main energy products and bread in 2013–14 and their respective free market levels.

The prices we use in the calculation of subsidies in this section, as well as in simulations in the next section, are more detailed than appear in Table 10.2; in particular, they take into account the nonlinear price structure of energy products in the Islamic Republic of Iran. For example, the effective national average price of natural gas was Rls 742 per m^3 (Ministry of Energy 2013). In reality, prices started at Rls 700 per m^3 (about $0.01) and increased to Rls 3500 (about $0.12) for big users. Similarly, the average price of electricity for households was Rls 337 per kWh, and tariffs increased from 300 per kWh to 2150 for the high-end users.

Bread prices are set through government control and subsidy. The government buys domestically produced wheat at Rls 10,150 per kilogram, which is close to international market price. Wheat is then sold at the subsidized price of around Rls

Table 10.3 Expenditures per capita on subsidized products, in thousand rials

Expenditure decile	Kerosene	Gasoline	Electricity	Diesel[a]	Bread[b]	Natural gas[c]	LPG	Total
1 (poorest)	72.6	166.0	291.9	0.8	1100.8	213.0	121.3	1966.1
2	112.2	275.8	382.6	3.2	1182.9	326.1	101.4	2384.0
3	103.0	365.3	416.6	0.0	1187.5	422.6	92.5	2587.3
4	119.5	481.2	490.0	4.5	1252.0	509.7	87.5	2944.2
5	125.3	569.6	530.6	3.0	1251.9	566.0	76.0	3121.9
6	114.7	681.5	563.8	0.4	1331.0	661.5	70.8	3423.2
7	104.9	836.6	643.5	4.8	1259.7	776.6	65.4	3691.2
8	98.1	902.6	681.2	12.2	1309.4	807.0	54.7	3865.1
9	67.7	1199.5	762.6	3.6	1321.3	942.8	42.1	4339.2
10 (richest)	100.5	1843.0	1147.8	12.2	1364.3	1196.2	45.9	5709.3
Total	101.8	732.2	591.1	4.5	1256.1	642.2	75.7	3403.3
Ratio of richest to poorest decile	1.38	11.10	3.93	15.37	1.24	5.62	0.38	2.90

Source World Bank calculation using HEIS (2013)
Note
[a]Household consumption of diesel fuel is small compared to its use in transportation, which is included in the indirect effects
[b]Bread includes flour
[c]Natural gas data included compressed natural gas (CNG) used in cars
HEIS Household Expenditure and Income Survey

460 to flour producers. In 2013–14 flour sold at Rls 5900 ($0.20), per kilogram to bakers. Each kilogram of bread was then sold at Rls 10,274.

Using these data from the survey with SUBSIM (SUBsidy SIMulation) enables us to estimate the distribution of subsidies among households. Table 10.3 shows the distribution of per capita expenditures on subsidized goods by deciles of per capita expenditures. Except for bread and kerosene, per capita expenditures on subsidized goods increase sharply with the decile of expenditures. The ratio of expenditures on bread between the richest and poorest deciles is 1.24, compared to 11.1 for gasoline and 3.7 for natural gas (household consumption of diesel is very small, so this ratio is not very informative). The SUBSIM estimates show that the total value of the subsidy paid directly to households (implicit plus explicit subsidies) amounted to Rls 540 trillion per year, or about $18 billion at the market exchange rate (Rls 30,000 = $1.00). This amount is considerably below the $66 billion mentioned at the beginning of this chapter. That calculation was based on the gap between the total value of energy products consumed in the Islamic Republic of Iran evaluated at world and domestic prices. For detailed information on the value of subsidies paid to each item see Table 10.16 in the appendix.

Viewed from the perspective of incidence, the value of subsidies for the poor and the rich is quite different. Defining incidence as the proportion of subsidies in household expenditures, we can see from Table 10.4 that subsidized products matter much more for the poor than for the rich. The poorest decile spent 13.6% of

Table 10.4 Expenditure on subsidized products over total expenditures, in percent

Expenditure decile	Kerosene	Gasoline	Electricity	Diesel	Bread	Natural gas	LPG	Total
1 (poorest)	0.5	1.1	2.0	0.0	7.6	1.5	0.8	13.6
2	0.5	1.3	1.8	0.0	5.4	1.5	0.5	11.0
3	0.4	1.3	1.5	0.0	4.4	1.6	0.3	9.6
4	0.4	1.5	1.5	0.0	3.9	1.6	0.3	9.1
5	0.3	1.5	1.4	0.0	3.3	1.5	0.2	8.2
6	0.3	1.5	1.3	0.0	3.0	1.5	0.2	7.7
7	0.2	1.6	1.2	0.0	2.4	1.5	0.1	7.0
8	0.2	1.4	1.1	0.0	2.0	1.3	0.1	6.0
9	0.1	1.4	0.9	0.0	1.6	1.1	0.1	5.2
10 (richest)	0.1	1.2	0.7	0.0	0.9	0.8	0.0	3.7
Total	0.2	1.4	1.1	0.0	2.4	1.2	0.1	6.4

Source World Bank calculation using SUBSIM and HEIS (2013)
Note HEIS Household Expenditure and Income Survey

its expenditures on subsidized goods compared to 3.7% for the richest decile. The poor's dependence on subsidies was greatest for bread, natural gas, and electricity. Households in the poorest decile spent 7.6% of their budget on bread compared to less than 1% for those in the richest decile. The gasoline subsidy, which is unequally distributed between the poor and the rich, accounted for similar proportions of the budgets of different deciles. As a result, the poor would sooner agree to a price reform for gasoline, which would not affect them much, than bread, which makes up a larger proportion of their budget. With compensation, they would stand to actually gain from a gasoline price reform.

Figure 10.4 combines the information in Tables 10.3 and 10.4 to depict the main dilemma of subsidy reform. The shaded areas are expenditures per person per year, measured in Rls 1000, on various energy products and bread (left y-axis). Assuming that the subsidies that directly accrue to households (as distinct from the

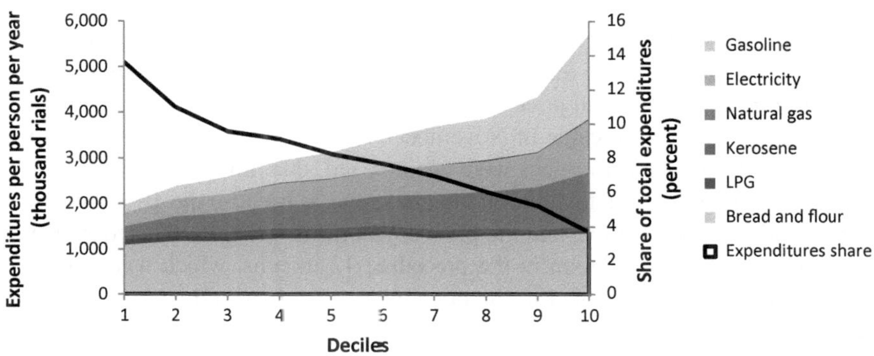

Fig. 10.4 Expenditures per person per year on subsidized goods and their share in total expenditures in 2013–14, by decile (1000 rials). *Source* Data from Tables 10.3 and 10.4

indirect benefits from lower transportation costs, for example) are proportional to expenditures on these items (which is the case with linear prices), this graph also depicts the distribution of the subsidies. The richest decile spent on average more than Rls 5 million per person (about $584 PPP) per year on these subsidized products, compared to Rls 2 million for the poorest decile (about $234 PPP). In a sense, the gasoline subsidy is the most regressive because the richest decile receives about 15 times as much of it as the poorest decile. By contrast, the bread subsidy is almost uniformly distributed.

The right y-axis captures the main political economy dilemma in subsidy reform. The solid line shows the share of expenditures on subsidized products in total expenditures for each decile of per capita expenditures. As a proportion of total expenditures, the poorest decile spends nearly four times as much on subsidized goods—13.6% compared to 3.7%—and therefore stands to lose more if energy prices are increased without compensation. This chart shows that we should expect the direct welfare effects of price reforms to be greater for the poor than the rich. The indirect effects, through higher prices in other goods and services that use energy, are more equally distributed and rise with income. Still, the overall negative effect on the poor is sufficient to justify some form of social protection, either direct compensation or reliance on the existing social protection mechanisms.

Simulations of Subsidy Reform

This section presents the simulation results of two hypothetical price reforms. Scenario 1, labeled "gradualist," increases the prices of subsidized goods by 10% across the board. Scenario 2, "full adjustment," assumes a much larger adjustment, taking all prices to close to their FOB or European levels (for electricity and natural gas) in 2014. Scenario 1 is interesting because it is the choice likely to be implemented. Scenario 2 is not on the agenda at present, but it is useful to consider because it was adopted in 2010 and serves as a comparison for the gradualist scenario.

Since taking office, the Rouhani government has opted for small price adjustments. Following the country's bad experience with full adjustment in 2010, there is a no public support for a large price increase. The sharp decline in the global price of oil in 2014 has also reduced the need or urgency for raising domestic prices of energy. In spring 2014 all prices for subsidized goods were raised by about 30% (the bread price increase came in November), except gasoline, which went up by about 50%. In spring 2015 prices were again raised, this time by about 15%. Both of these increases are less than our gradualist scenario because the 10% increase in our scenario is in real terms, and the price adjustments under Rouhani were hardly enough to correct for inflation in the preceding 12 months, which were 34.5% in 2013–14 and 15.5% in 2014–15. The price increases that would have matched this scenario would have been 44.5% in 2014 and 25.5% in 2015.

Scenario 2 assumes that global oil prices recover to their average for 2014; that is, it aims for full elimination of subsidies. For bread a 60% increase brings its price close to the zero-subsidy level. Bread prices are set by a combination of government control and subsidy. Flour is sold at subsidized prices to bakers, whose prices are monitored. A substantial part of the wheat consumed in the country is imported, which can be considered as opportunity cost. In 2013 the support price set by the government for domestically produced wheat was Rls 10,150 ($0.30) per kilogram, which is close to the world market, so it can be used as the target price. Currently, however, the government sells flour to bakers at Rls 8490 per kilogram, which would not reach the zero-subsidy level with a 10% increase.

Determining the energy prices that would fully eliminate the energy subsidies is difficult. Given the volatility in the global price of oil, it is hard to pinpoint the medium-term opportunity cost of Iranian oil and gas. At $50 a barrel, for example, the FOB price of gasoline in the Islamic Republic of Iran is about the free-market price of gasoline. Scenario 2 assumes that the world oil price returns to the average for 2014, $96.30.

The list of target prices used in both scenarios is presented in Table 10.5. For traded commodities, we set the target price at opportunity costs as implied by the average crude price in 2014. For gasoline, diesel, and kerosene, whose global prices declined by nearly 50% during 2014, we take the average FOB Persian Gulf level—Rls 21,950 ($0.69) per liter for gasoline, Rls 21,189 ($0.66) for diesel, and Rls 20,869 ($0.65) for kerosene. These average prices would equal opportunity cost if world oil prices were to return to the level prevailing around September 2014.

The price of natural gas varied much less than crude oil during 2014, but has its own complexity because there is no regional market as transparent as the one for gasoline. We set the target price for natural gas at Rls 11,358 per m^3 (about $0.35), which is less than the export price of Iranian gas to Turkey (about $0.50), but closer to the export prices charged by Azerbaijan for exports to Turkey. The prices combine compressed natural gas (CNG), used in transportation, with the natural gas supplied to consumers.

There is no regional market of any kind for electricity that would guide the setting of the subsidy-free price. The Islamic Republic of Iran does export some electricity to Iraq, but there is no information on pricing for these exports, and in any case may involve a subsidy of its own due to political considerations. We therefore picked the target price of Rls 2720 ($0.09) per kWh, which is close to the rate in Turkey but below the average in most middle-income developing countries (EIA 2015). This price is close to the prevailing price in Turkey, India, and Brazil.

We use a demand price elasticity of −0.2 to calculate the postreform consumed quantities of subsidized goods and changes in government subsidy payments.

Scenario 1: Direct Effects

This section reports the results of the gradualist scenario, increasing prices by 10%. We evaluate the impact of this reform on individual welfare and government revenues, starting with the direct effects of price increases on energy and bread. Direct

Table 10.5 Price of subsidized items, in rials

	Gasoline		Diesel (L)	Kerosene (L)	Natural gas (m^3)	LPG (m^3)	Electricity (kWh)	Bread (kg)	Flour (kg)
Price	Up to 60 L	More than 60 L							
2013	4000	7000	3500	1000	742.2[a]	1800	337.5[a]	10,274	5900
Scenario 1 (10% increase)	4400	7700	3850	1100	816.42	1980	371.25	11,301	6490
Scenario 2 (opportunity cost price)	24,000[b]	24,000[b]	23,000[b]	22,600[b]	11,358[c]	10,800[c]	2,720[d]	20,548[e]	13,900[e]

Source Ministry of Energy (2013), except for explicit data in the note

Note

[a]Effective national average price, Ministry of Energy (20130

[b]Based on FOB Persian Gulf price, Platts.com

[c]Average Europe price, FERC and www.cngeurope.com (2014)

[d]Price in Turkey, Turkish Statistical Institute, 2014

[e]Based on international wheat price and authors' calculations

Table 10.6 Direct effects of the gradualist scenario on per capita well-being (thousand rials)

Expenditure decile	Kerosene	Gasoline	Electricity	Diesel	Bread	Natural gas	LPG	Total
1 (poorest)	−7.3	−16.6	−29.2	−0.1	−110.0	−21.3	−12.1	−196.6
2	−11.2	−27.6	−38.3	−0.3	−118.2	−32.6	−10.1	−238.4
3	−10.3	−36.5	−41.7	0.0	−118.7	−42.3	−9.2	−258.7
4	−11.9	−48.1	−49.0	−0.4	−125.2	−51.0	−8.7	−294.4
5	−12.5	−57.0	−53.1	−0.3	−125.1	−56.6	−7.6	−312.1
6	−11.5	−68.2	−56.4	0.0	−133.0	−66.1	−7.1	−342.3
7	−10.5	−83.7	−64.3	−0.5	−125.9	−77.7	−6.5	−369.1
8	−9.8	−90.3	−68.1	−1.2	−130.9	−80.7	−5.5	−386.5
9	−6.8	−120.0	−76.3	−0.4	−132.1	−94.3	−4.2	−433.9
10 (richest)	−10.1	−184.3	−114.8	−1.2	−136.4	−119.6	−4.6	−570.9
Total	−10.2	−73.2	−59.1	−0.4	−125.6	−64.2	−7.6	−340.3

effects measure the losses in welfare as reductions in real expenditures for households in different deciles of per capita expenditures. The model takes into account consumer responses to the price increases for these products, but ignores indirect or secondary effects caused by increases in prices of other goods and services. These secondary effects are considered in the next section, indirect effects.

We present our estimates of the direct effects on well-being in Table 10.6 and as proportion of per capita household expenditures in Table 10.7. The data show that the largest effect in level and share is due to the increase in the price of bread, an average loss of welfare of Rls 125,600 per person per year and 0.24% of expenditures. The second largest average loss is for gasoline at Rls 73,200. The reason bread has a relatively large impact is that the average Iranian spends 67% more on

Table 10.7 Direct effects of gradualist scenario on well-being, in percentage of household expenditures

Expenditure decile	Kerosene	Gasoline	Electricity	Diesel	Bread	Natural gas	LPG	Total
1 (poorest)	−0.05	−0.11	−0.20	−0.00	−0.76	−0.15	−0.08	−1.36
2	−0.05	−0.13	−0.18	−0.00	−0.54	−0.15	−0.05	−1.10
3	−0.04	−0.13	−0.15	−0.00	−0.44	−0.16	−0.03	−0.96
4	−0.04	−0.15	−0.15	−0.00	−0.39	−0.16	−0.03	−0.91
5	−0.03	−0.15	−0.14	−0.00	−0.33	−0.15	−0.02	−0.82
6	−0.03	−0.15	−0.13	−0.00	−0.30	−0.15	−0.02	−0.77
7	−0.02	−0.16	−0.12	−0.00	−0.24	−0.15	−0.01	−0.70
8	−0.02	−0.14	−0.11	−0.00	−0.20	−0.13	−0.01	−0.60
9	−0.01	−0.14	−0.09	−0.00	−0.16	−0.11	−0.01	−0.52
10 (richest)	−0.01	−0.12	−0.07	−0.00	−0.09	−0.08	−0.00	−0.37
Total	−0.02	−0.14	−0.11	−0.00	−0.24	−0.12	−0.01	−0.64

bread than gasoline. Expenditures on bread amount to more than one-third of the total expenditures on subsidized goods.

The losses due to the increase in the bread price are more uniformly distributed across deciles of per capita expenditures than other commodities, increasing by 24% from the poorest to the richest decile. In the case of gasoline this increase is more than 10 times. The total loss on all items is on average Rls 340,300 per person per year (PPP $39.75), which is less than 1% of expenditures. The ratio of the overall loss in the richest to poorest decile is 2.9.

The loss of welfare is better stated as proportion of household expenditures (Table 10.7). Contrary to the picture obtained from levels in Table 10.6, the distributional impact of gasoline seems the least unequal and for bread the most unequal. Losses due to price increases for bread, natural gas, and gasoline figure prominently in the poorest decile's budgets, but all are less than 1%. The overall impact is small because the share of these products in average per capita expenditures is 6.4%, so a 10% increase in their price does not have a large impact on the average consumer's budget. Changes in quantities reported in annex Table 10.17 are also modest, showing average reductions of 7 kWh per person in electricity and 5 m^3 of natural gas. Given the elasticity assumptions of −0.2, a 10% price increase reduces the quantity consumed by 2%.

The sensitivity of the change in government revenue to the size of the price increase of individual subsidized goods is shown in Fig. 10.5. Government revenue is most sensitive to the size of increase in the prices of bread, natural gas, and gasoline. For example, a 100% increase in the price of bread increases government revenues by Rls 100 trillion (PPP $11.7 billion, or 5% of total government revenues), compared to Rls 80 trillion for natural gas and Rls 75 trillion for gasoline. In the present scenario, the total amount of subsidies paid out declines from Rls 484 trillion (PPP $56.5 billion) to Rls 447 trillion ($52.2 billion), a savings of Rls 37 trillion ($4 billion) for the government (see Table 10.18 in appendix).

We now turn to the impact of the gradualist reform scenario on poverty and inequality. We measure the poverty rate using the poverty lines of Rls 18 million per person per year in urban areas and Rls 12 million in rural areas. Implementing

Fig. 10.5 Price changes and the impact on government revenue. *Source* World Bank calculation using SUBSIM and HEIS (2013). *Note HEIS* Household Expenditure and Income Survey

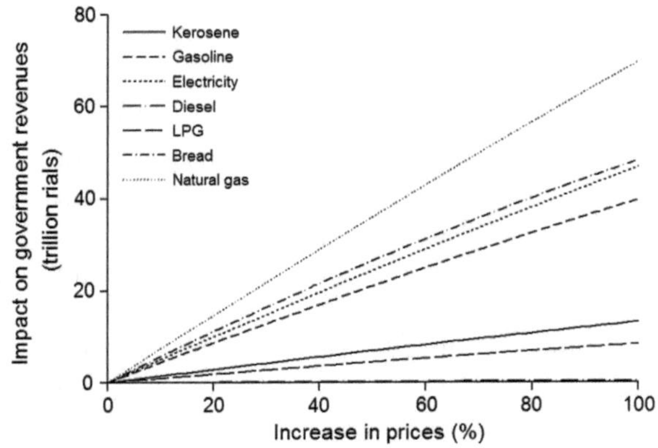

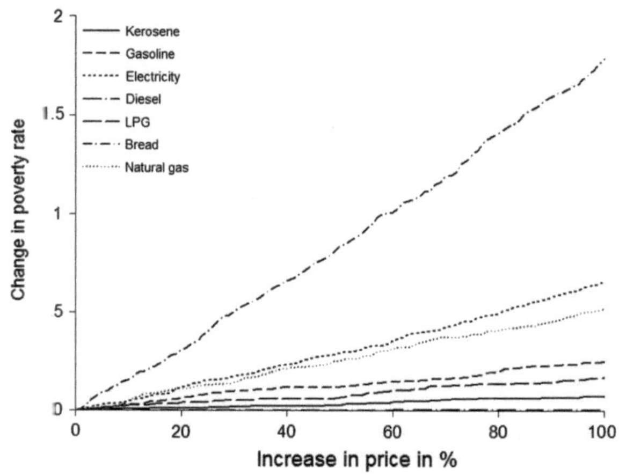

Fig. 10.6 Percentage change in the poverty rate by the size of price increases. *Source* Authors' calculation using SUBSIM and HEIS 2013. *Note HEIS* Household Expenditure and Income Survey

the gradualist price reforms increases the poverty rate from 4.95 to 5.30% and the poverty gap from 0.98 to 1.04%. Inequality, as measured by the Gini index, increases slightly from 37.36 to 37 49. These small changes are not surprising given the small price adjustment envisioned in the gradualist scenario.

How sensitive are these changes in poverty to the size of the price increase? Figure 10.6 shows the sensitivity of the poverty rate to the size of price increases by commodity. Again, from the point of view of increase in poverty, bread is the most important commodity; a 60% increase in its price increases the head-count ratio by 1 percentage point. Energy products have much smaller impacts.

If the government wishes to keep the poverty rate from increasing, it must offer compensation. Figure 10.7 estimates the effect of universal and uniform transfers on the poverty rate. To prevent the poverty rate from increasing as a result of the direct effects of the 10% price adjustment, the government needs to pay each person Rls 204,703 per year (about $23.40), which is less than 4% of the current level of transfer). Doubling this amount reduces the poverty rate by 0.35 percentage points.

Scenario 1: Indirect Effects

The indirect effects are the secondary effects on the consumer budget that result from the increase in prices of energy-using sectors. SUBSIM uses an input/output table to take these secondary effects into account. The quality of the indirect estimates depends crucially on having an up-to-date I/O table. The latest I/O table for the Islamic Republic of Iran is from 2001, when energy prices were very low. SUBSIM uses the rial values of intersector flows as input. We update the rial values

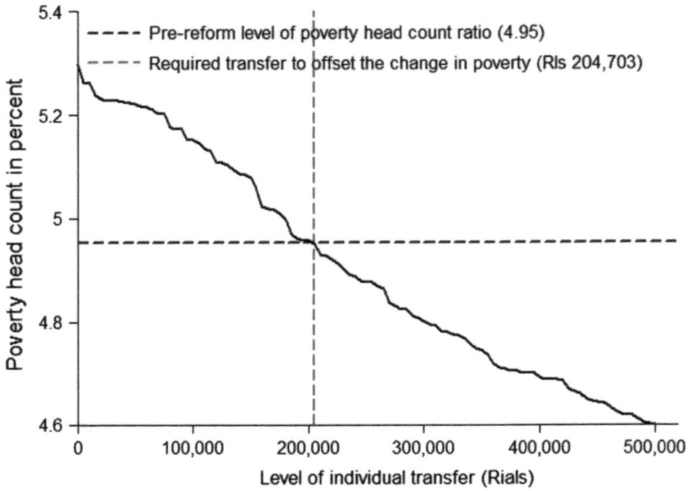

Fig. 10.7 Impact of the level of transfer to compensate indirect effects on poverty in the gradualist scenario. *Source* World Bank calculation using SUBSIM and HEIS (2013). *Note* Direct effects of the reform on well-being are considered only. *HEIS* Household Expenditure and Income Survey

of the I/O table to 2013 using the consumer price index (CPI). This calculation underestimates the dependence of other sectors on energy products because energy prices rose by a larger factor than the CPI during 2001–13. The CPI rose by a factor of 7, and energy prices rose by factors ranging from 10 to 20.

The country's I/O table does not show individual prices for subsidized products; instead, it combines diesel, gasoline, and kerosene into one group. We include electricity and natural gas as separate items. As with direct effects, we raise the price of the group and individual items by 10% in real terms.

In Table 10.8 we add the indirect and direct effects to get a more comprehensive picture of the impact on well-being of the gradualist scenario. These results update the direct estimates of impact shown in Tables 10.6 and 10.7 (column 1 reproduces the totals column in Table 10.6, and column 4 reproduces the totals column in Table 10.7). Looking at per capita losses, we note that except for the tenth decile, indirect effects are smaller than the direct effects, but they are less equally distributed. The ratio of the loss suffered by the richest to the poorest decile is 2.9 compared to 5.2. Losses as proportion of household expenditures, shown on the right side, indicate that direct effects, measured relative to household expenditures, are smaller than direct effects and their distribution is more equal. Including the indirect effects does not change our assessment of the impact of the price increase on poverty and inequality by much (Table 10.9).

As before, we calculate the required transfer to prevent an increase in poverty. To compensate for the indirect effect so that poverty rate remains at 4.95%, the government needs to pay Rls 131,824 per person per year (Fig. 10.8), compared to Rls 204,703 for the direct effects (Fig. 10.7).

Table 10.8 Direct and indirect effect of the gradualist scenario on household welfare

	Per capita, in rials			Percent of total expenditures		
Expenditure decile	Direct effects	Indirect effects	Total	Direct effects	Indirect effects	Total
1 (poorest)	−196.6	−121.3	−317.9	−1.36	−0.77	−2.13
2	−238.4	−169.9	−408.4	−1.10	−0.71	−1.81
3	−258.7	−180.3	−439.0	−0.96	−0.6	−1.56
4	−294.4	−207.5	−501.9	−0.91	−0.58	−1.49
5	−312.1	−234.6	−546.7	−0.82	−0.56	−1.38
6	−342.3	−251.0	−593.3	−0.77	−0.5	−1.27
7	−369.1	−341.8	−710.9	−0.70	−0.58	−1.28
8	−386.5	−333.2	−719.7	−0.60	−0.46	−1.06
9	−433.9	−386.3	−820.2	−0.52	−0.41	−0.93
10 (richest)	−570.9	−631.9	−1202.8	−0.37	−0.37	−0.74
Total	−340.3	−292.6	−632.9	−0.64	−0.48	−1.12

Source World Bank calculation using SUBSIM and HEIS (2013)

Table 10.9 Direct and indirect impacts of gradualist subsidy reform on poverty and inequality

	Prereform	Postreform
Change in per capita expenditures (thousand rials)		−632.91
Poverty head count (%)	4.95	5.48
Poverty gap (%)	0.98	1.072
Gini (%)	37.36	37.55

Source World Bank calculation using SUBSIM and HEIS (2013)

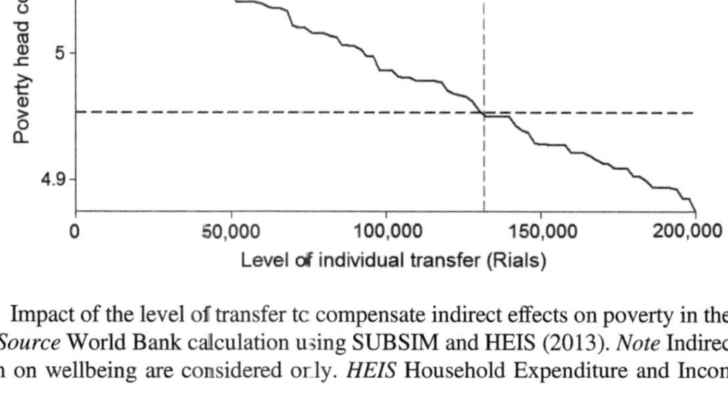

Fig. 10.8 Impact of the level of transfer to compensate indirect effects on poverty in the gradualist scenario. *Source* World Bank calculation using SUBSIM and HEIS (2013). *Note* Indirect effects of the reform on wellbeing are considered only. *HEIS* Household Expenditure and Income Survey

Scenario 2: Direct Effects

In the full adjustment scenario we increase prices according to the values in Table 10.5 by factors ranging from 2 for bread to 20 for kerosene. We use the Cobb-Douglas routine of SUBSIM because the marginal approach is much less accurate for large price changes. We present the results for this scenario first for the direct effects followed by the indirect effects.

As expected, the impact on household welfare in this scenario is much larger than the gradualist scenario. Looking at the impact as a percentage of per capita expenditures (Tables 10.10 and 10.11), we note that the average impact is 11.46% compared to 0.64% in the gradualist scenario, higher by a factor of 17 (compared to a higher average price increase of 7 times). The loss for the poorest decile increased from 1.36% in the gradualist scenario to 24.06% in full adjustment. The richest decile's loss increased from to 0.37 to 6.61%, which is similar to the change in impact for the poor.

In contrast to the gradualist scenario, we see a significant quantity adjustment in this case (Table 10.12). Average electricity consumption declines by 105.78 kWh (a decline of 30% in consumption), and natural gas by 161.77, which is a decline of less than one-forth. The natural gas consumption by the poorest decile is estimated to decline by about 78%, which is unrealistic, and the result of assuming a fixed elasticity for all levels of consumption and income. In this scenario bread continues to have the largest impact on the welfare of the poor, followed by natural gas and LPG.

Naturally, the impact of full adjustment on poverty and inequality are larger (Table 10.13). The poverty rate increases to 11.59%, more than doubling, and the poverty gap more than triples, 0.98% compared to 3.91%. The Gini index increases from 37.36 to 40.70. The Gini index changes because the reform impact is different for each decile. The poor are affected more by the program relative to their total expenditures compared to the rich (see Table 10.11). Note that this impact is before any cash transfer is paid to individuals. The cash transfer necessary to keep the poverty rate from increasing is estimated at Rls 4.4 million per person per year, 20 times higher than in the gradualist scenario (Fig. 10.9). However, as Table 10.13 shows, the savings of the government outweigh this amount of transfer by Rls 139 trillion (PPP $16 billion), which is a substantial amount (about 9% of total government revenues).

Scenario 2: Indirect Effects

To implement the price changes according to this scenario we need to find the average price increase for energy products that appear in one group in the I/O table. We use a weighted average of increases for prices of gasoline, diesel, and kerosene, which comes to 600%. For individual commodities, we assume a 200% increase for natural gas, 100% for bread, and 700% for electricity.

Table 10.10 Direct effects of the full-adjustment scenario on per capita well-being, (thousand rials)

Expenditure decile	Kerosene	Gasoline	Electricity	Diesel	Bread and flour	Natural gas	LPC	Total
1 (poorest)	−432.1	−390.8	−210.2	−4.0	−1169.7	−664.0	−606.5	−3477.5
2	−668.3	−640.8	−260.8	−16.4	−1236.3	−1005.3	−507.0	−4334.9
3	−613.7	−840.2	−282.4	−0.2	−1227.2	−1255.2	462.4	−4681.3
4	−711.5	−1094.5	−316.6	−22.7	−1286.8	−1481.4	−437.4	−5351.1
5	−746.4	−1292.6	−337.1	−15.0	−1283.6	−1607.8	−380.2	−5662.7
6	−683.0	−1542.0	−353.5	−2.2	−1355.2	−1850.8	−353.8	−6140.6
7	−624.6	−1885.7	−387.0	−24.2	−1283.0	−2114.1	−326.8	−6645.5
8	−584.6	−2030.8	−404.1	−61.7	−1327.3	−2191.2	−273.5	−6873.2
9	−403.3	−2679.6	−451.0	−18.4	−1335.9	−2574.4	−210.3	−7672.9
10 (richest)	−598.7	−4075.1	−596.4	−61.5	−1375.7	−3274.2	−229.7	−10,211.2
Total	−606.6	−1647.3	−359.9	−22.6	−1288.1	−1801.9	−378.7	−6105.3

Source World Bank calculation using SUBSIM and HEIS (2013)

Table 10.11 Direct effects of full adjustment scenario on well-being, in percentage of household expenditures

Expenditure decile	Kerosene	Gasoline	Electricity	Diesel	Bread and flour	Natural gas	LPG	Total
1 (poorest)	−2.99	−2.70	−1.45	−0.03	−8.09	−4.59	−4.20	−24.06
2	−3.07	−2.95	−1.20	−0.08	−5.68	−4.62	−2.33	−19.93
3	−2.27	−3.10	−1.04	−0.00	−4.53	−4.63	−1.71	−17.28
4	−2.20	−3.39	−0.98	−0.07	−3.98	−4.59	−1.35	−16.56
5	−1.97	−3.41	−0.89	−0.04	−3.39	−4.25	−1.00	−14.96
6	−1.53	−3.46	−0.79	−0.00	−3.04	−4.16	−0.79	−13.79
7	−1.18	−3.56	−0.73	−0.05	−2.42	−3.99	−0.62	−12.55
8	−0.91	−3.17	−0.63	−0.10	−2.07	−3.42	−0.43	−10.72
9	−0.48	−3.21	−0.54	−0.02	−1.60	−3.09	−0.25	−9.21
10 (richest)	−0.39	−2.64	−0.39	−0.04	−0.89	−2.12	−0.15	−6.61
Total	−1.14	−3.09	−0.68	−0.04	−2.42	−3.38	−0.71	−11.46

Source World Bank calculation using SUBSIM and HEIS (2013)

Table 10.12 Impact on the per capita consumed quantities in the full adjustment scenario, direct effects

Expenditure decile	Kerosene (L)	Gasoline (L)	Electricity (kWh)	Diesel (L)	Bread and flour (kg)	Natural gas (m^3)	LPG (m^3)
1 (poorest)	−24.20	−12.65	−66.91	−0.23	−26.56	−61.85	−67.39
2	−37.40	−20.43	−81.01	−0.93	−27.00	−94.15	−56.33
3	−34.35	−26.46	−87.46	−0.01	−26.07	−116.68	−51.37
4	−39.82	−34.00	−95.88	−1.29	−26.96	−135.76	−48.61
5	−41.77	−40.05	−101.22	−0.85	−26.73	−146.86	−42.24
6	−38.22	−47.59	−105.48	−0.12	−27.72	−166.70	−39.31
7	−34.96	−57.92	−113.00	−1.37	−26.26	−187.02	−36.31
8	−32.72	−62.23	−117.07	−3.49	−26.82	−195.06	−30.39
9	−22.57	−81.37	−130.44	−1.04	−26.81	−228.62	−23.37
10 (richest)	−33.51	−122.11	−159.34	−3.48	−27.40	−284.93	−25.52
Total	−33.95	−50.48	−105.78	−1.28	−26.83	−161.77	−42.08

Source World Bank calculation using SUBSIM and HEIS (2013)

The results are presented in Table 10.14. In contrast to the gradualist scenario, for richer deciles the indirect effects are larger than direct effects, though on average the effects of the two types are similar in size. The additional transfer required to maintain the poverty rate at prereform level of 4.95% is Rls 3.2 million per person per year (Fig. 10.10). Thus, the total required compensation for both the direct and indirect effects is Rls 7.5 million (PPP $876), which is about 40% larger than the current level of compensation. However, if we compare the same amount paid in 2011, the first year of the 2010 reform, with the estimated compensation here, we

Table 10.13 Direct impacts of full-adjustment subsidy reform on poverty, inequality, and government budget

	Prereform	Postreform
Change in per capita expenditures (Rls thousand)		−6105.34
Poverty head count (%)	4.95	11.59
Poverty gap (%)	0.98	3.91
Inequality (%)	37.36	40.70
Subsidies (Rls trillion)	491.41	0
Transfers (Rls trillion)[a]	0	352.06
Change in total budget (Rls trillion)		−139.35

Source World Bank calculation using SUBSIM and HEIS (2013)
Note HEIS Household Expenditure and Income Survey
[a]The transfer refers to the required amount to offset the change in headcount poverty

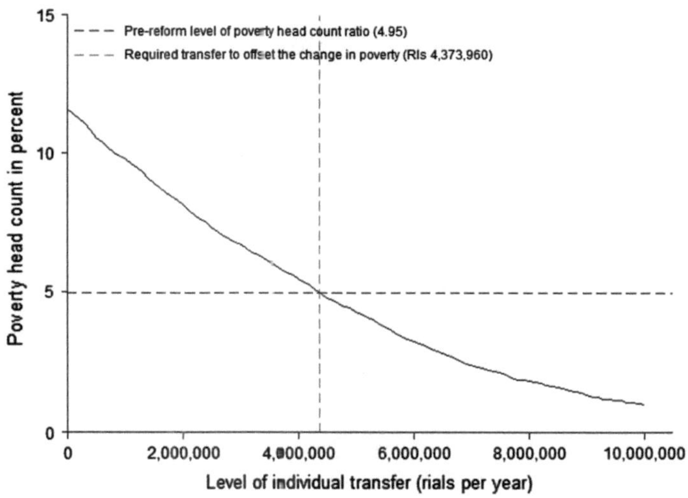

Fig. 10.9 Impact of the level of transfer to compensate for the direct effects on poverty in the full adjustment scenario. *Source* World Bank calculation using SUBSIM and HEIS (2013). *Note* Direct effects of the reform on well-being are considered only. *HEIS* Household Expenditure and Income Survey

learn that the Ahmadinejad compensation plan exceeded what was necessary to keep poverty constant, by some 70%.[2]

The overall impact on poverty and inequality is reported in Table 10.15. As a result of full adjustment, assuming no compensation, the head count ratio jumps fourfold, increasing from 4.95 to 20.12%, and the poverty gap increases sevenfold, from 0.98 to 7.31%. The Gini index increases by 5.05 points, which is large and

[2]The value of the Rls 445,000 per person, per month paid out in 2011 is about Rls 756,000, which is 70 percent higher.

Table 10.14 Direct and indirect effects of price increases on well-being in the full adjustment scenario

	Per capita, thousand rials			Percent of total expenditures		
Expenditure decile	Direct effects	Indirect effects	Total	Direct effects	Indirect effects	Total
1 (poorest)	−3477.5	−2631.0	−6108.5	−24.1	−18.2	−42.3
2	−4334.9	−3702.1	−8037.0	−19.9	−17.0	−37.0
3	−4681.3	−4372.0	−9053.3	−17.3	−16.1	−33.4
4	−5351.1	−4868.6	−10,219.7	−16.6	−15.1	−31.6
5	−5662.7	−5626.8	−11,289.5	−15.0	−14.9	−29.8
6	−6140.6	−6284.0	−12,424.6	−13.8	−14.1	−27.9
7	−6645.5	−7182.9	−13,828.4	−12.6	−13.6	−26.1
8	−6873.2	−8411.0	−15,284.2	−10.7	−13.1	−23.8
9	−7672.9	−10,318.9	−17,991.8	−9.2	−12.4	−21.6
10 (richest)	−10,211.2	−16,333.4	−26,544.6	−6.6	−10.6	−17.2
Total	−6105.3	−6973.4	−13,078.7	−11.5	−13.1	−24.6

Source World Bank calculation using SUBSIM and HEIS (2013)

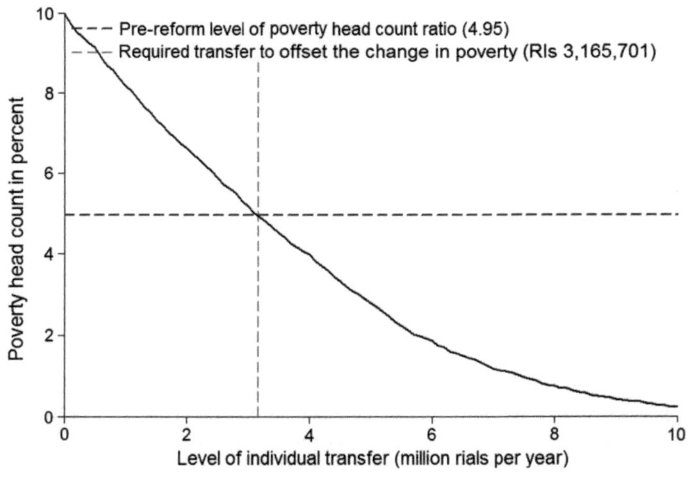

Fig. 10.10 Impact of the level of transfer to compensate indirect effects on poverty in the full adjustment scenario. *Source* World Bank calculation using SUBSIM and HEIS (2013). *Note* Indirect effects of the reform on wellbeing are considered only. *HEIS* Household Expenditure and Income Survey. The value of 1.00e+ is 10,000,000

shows that price increases for all the items considered here have a greater effect on the poor than on the rich. Removing subsidies has a large adverse impact on inequality because, as shown in Table 10.4, the poor spend a larger proportion of their income on subsidized goods. The share of the expenditures on all subsidized goods to total expenditures is 13.6% for the poorest decile and 3.7% for the richest

Table 10.15 Total impact of price increases on expenditures, poverty and inequality in the full adjustment scenario

	Prereform	Postreform
Change in per capita expenditure (Rls thousand)		−13,078.73
Poverty head count (%)	4.95	20.12
Poverty gap (%)	0.98	7.31
Gini (%)	37.36	42.41

Source World Bank calculation using SUBSIM and HEIS (2013)
Note HEIS Household Expenditure and Income Survey

decile. The highest disparity is for bread which, in 2013 accounted for 7.6% of the poorest decile expenditures compared to 0.9% for the richest decile. The next least equally distributed expenditure shares are for electricity, and here the share for the poorest decile is three time higher than for the richest decile. Naturally, any increase in price that is not moderated by a significant decrease in consumption will have a much larger impact on the poor than on the rich, thus increasing the inequality.

It appears that the indirect effects are as important in increasing inequality as the direct effects. The change in the Gini coefficient as a result of the direct effects of removing the subsidies (in scenario 2) is from 37.36 to 40.70, which a about half of the change in Gini with the indirect effects added. This result suggests that half of the adverse impact of the removal of subsidies on inequality comes from the indirect effects.

The Political Economy of Reforms

The most important political economy aspect of subsidy reform in the Islamic Republic of Iran is that much of the subsidies are government forgone earnings rather than cash expenditures. The government delivers daily about 4 million equivalent barrels of oil and gas, about three times as much as it currently exports, to domestic consumers, enterprises, and power companies at very low prices.

When oil prices are high the government is flush with revenues and does not feel the need to raise domestic prices of energy in tandem with global prices. When the world price of oil is down, government revenues and household incomes are also down, and that is the worst possible time to raise domestic energy prices. Given such price fluctuations, divergence between local and world prices of energy seems a natural part of the country's political economy.

Another political economy reason that energy subsidies are endemic in the Islamic Republic of Iran (and in other oil-rich countries) is that although energy subsidies are unevenly distributed, with most of it going to higher-income brackets, removing them hurts the poor more than rich. As shown in Fig. 10.4, as a share of household expenditures subsidies are larger for the poor than the rich. Moreover, the credibility of Iranian governments to remove energy subsidies and promise to spend the proceeds more equitably and efficiently is low, which explains why the large price reforms of 2010 had to include a generous cash transfer program.

The unhappy history of energy price reform since 2010 also complicates the political economy of further energy price reform. Since 2010, for reasons unrelated to subsidy reform—sanctions and mismanagement of the economy—Iranians have experienced four years of stagnation and inflation, making them apprehensive of any new government-initiated price reform. A good part of the inflation in the four years following the reform had little to do with energy and bread price increases, but the Iranian media and public opinion believe otherwise. One contributor to inflation was that cash transfers were too generous and as a result the program was not fully funded. The government filled that gap with borrowing from the Central Bank, which fueled inflation. Another contributor to inflation was the low-cost housing Maskan Mehr program. According to the government, 40% of the monetary base was created to cover the deficit in this program. In addition to social spending, the country suffered sizable supply shock during 2011–13, as international sanctions tightened and disrupted its oil sale and general trade. As Fig. 10.11 shows, monthly rates of inflation decreased a few months after the reform but jumped back up with sanctions and devaluation. The much smaller price hikes in 2014, which were not followed up by other shocks, raised the rate of inflation for a few months before declining.

An important solution to the political economy of reform has been the cash transfer scheme that started in December 2010. Unfortunately, it has come under criticism so that it may not be part of any future reform. There have been claims of negative effects of cash transfers on the incentives of the poor to work. Although

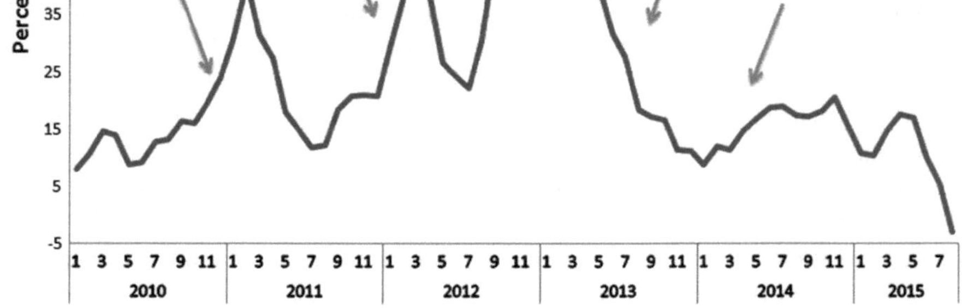

Fig. 10.11 Rates of inflation and macroeconomic shocks from January 2010 to September 2014, 3-month moving averages with annualized rates. *Sources* Central Bank of Iran, various years, and World Bank calculations

the evidence does not support such claims, anecdotes of poor agricultural workers abandoning their farms continue to appear in the Iranian media (Salehi-Isfahani and Mostafavi-Dehzooei 2016). The cash transfer program has also been criticized for its unsound targeting because even the richest Iranians receive cash transfers every month. Several attempts have been made to limit cash transfers to poor families only. The 2014–15 budget law required the government to find a way to exclude the richest families from the transfer scheme, but so far the government has avoided the issue because it lacks the necessary mechanism to identify high-income families.

Despite setbacks in public support for the continuation of subsidy reform, the government has strong motivation to raise energy prices and replace lost revenues from oil exports with revenues from the domestic sale of energy. The proposed budget for fiscal 2015/16 projects revenues from oil exports to fall by 24% in real terms, forcing the government to cut real current expenditures by 3.3%. The increased motivation for raising energy prices is, however, tempered by at least two factors. First, the government itself is very apprehensive of rekindling high inflation. Second, its willingness to raise the price of domestic energy is closely related to the outcome of the current nuclear negotiations, which affect the level of oil exports, and the need for more revenues from other sources. Following the July 14, 2015, nuclear accord between Iran and the six world powers, international sanctions against Iran are expected to be gradually lifted, allowing Iran to export more oil. But this may not be enough to close the budget gap if oil prices continue to remain in the low $50 range per barrel. There is considerable uncertainty regarding the future of oil prices, which suggests that budgetary pressures to raise domestic energy prices could continue for the next several years. Furthermore, the pro-market Rouhani government has already demonstrated its willingness to raise energy prices to market levels, so we should expect further adjustments in energy prices in the near future.

Conclusions

Despite the significant reform of subsidies in 2010, the Islamic Republic of Iran still subsidizes energy. The public debate over energy subsidies is lively and largely negative, often emphasizing how reform leads to inflation and stagnation. Given the large role that this public debate plays in the internal politics of the country, especially in the parliamentary elections of March 2016, knowledge of how energy price reform affects household welfare is key to the future of energy price reform in Iran. In this chapter we evaluate the impacts on household welfare, poverty, and inequality, for two reform scenarios, gradualist and full adjustment. There are important lessons to be learned from each exercise.

A simple analysis of household budgets using the country's 2013 household survey shows that although the benefits of the subsidies generally accrue to richer families, they make up a larger proportion of the income of the poor. This result implies that reform without compensation hurts the poor more than the rich and is likely to face serious opposition. Households in the poorest decile on average spend 13.6% of their expenditures on subsidized items, compared to 3.7% for the richest decile.

We then incorporate the same survey data into the SUBSIM model to simulate the direct and indirect effect of energy price increases on household welfare. Several interesting policy implications emerge. First, we find that a gradualist approach to energy price reform, even without compensation, does not increase poverty or inequality significantly. The baseline poverty rate of about 5% (using a $5 PPP per day poverty line) increases by less than one percentage point as a result of a 10% increase in bread and energy prices. The Gini index increases by about 0.2 Gini points. The price increase simulated in this scenario is larger than what the Rouhani government has managed to push through since March 2014. These price increases have barely adjusted energy prices in real terms. So, our simulations indicate that even without compensation, a larger increase that reduces the subsidies in real terms will not cause a significant increase in poverty or inequality.

To keep poverty from increasing, we estimate that about half the savings from price reforms is needed as transfers back to all households. The rest would be added to government revenues, raising them by 0.86%. An additional benefit of this scheme is a reduction in inequality of 0.1 Gini points compared to the no-reform case. The necessary amount paid per person is about Rls 28,000 per month, which is quite modest compared to the Rls 445,000 per person per month distributed now. According to this scenario, price increases of 10% in real terms (above the rate of inflation) could include modest compensation that insulates the poor and makes further price increases politically easier to implement.

We also simulated the results of a larger one-time adjustment in bread and energy prices that would completely eliminate subsidies. This scenario, which is similar to the price hikes of 2010, serves as a comparison for the gradual case. Without compensation, price reforms have a large effect on the poverty rate, which rises fourfold from 4.95 to 20.12%. This is important to know in view of the widespread criticism of the 2010 cash transfer program. Without it, from a social and political point of view, the price reform would not have been possible. To keep poverty from increasing under this scenario, the necessary monthly transfer is Rls 629,000, which is 29% less than the current value of the cash transfers paid in December 2010 (about Rls 875,000). Critics of the implementation of the 2010 cash transfer program have pointed out that the amount paid at the time was too generous and was more than the program's earnings. The financing of the deficit contributed to inflation and thereby undermined the energy price reform (Salehi-Isfahani et al. 2013). Under this scenario, the government actually ends up with more revenues, about 5.9% more, and inequality drops by 1.2% Gini points compared to the no-reform case.

Finally, our simulations provide evidence of the relative sizes of the direct and indirect effects. The indirect impact on welfare, through energy used in the production of other goods and services, appears quite significant, about 13.1% of total expenditures compared to 11.5% for the direct effect. For the poor the direct impact is higher, whereas for higher expenditure groups it is the indirect effect that dominates.

Annex

See Tables 10.16, 10.17 and 10.18.

Table 10.16 Total and per capita benefits from subsidies (2014)

Expenditure decile	Kerosene	Gasoline	Electricity	Diesel	Bread	Natural gas	LPG	Total
		Total (billion rials)						
1 (poorest)	3826	3526	1692	36	9417	6546	4883	29,837
2	5907	5779	2098	145	9944	9880	4078	37,615
3	5428	7584	2272	2	9876	12,324	3721	40,959
4	6304	9901	2553	202	10,374	14,575	3527	47,074
5	6591	11,654	2708	133	10,313	15,743	3054	49,922
6	6048	13,943	2848	19	10,919	18,182	2850	54,441
7	5524	17,030	3114	215	10,323	20,734	2629	59,177
8	5170	18,343	3252	547	10,680	21,468	2201	61,375
9	3569	24,224	3631	163	10,756	25,271	1693	69,049
10 (richest)	5297	36,847	4802	546	11,075	32,249	1849	92,352
Total	53,665	148,831	28,970	2007	103,678	176,972	30,486	541,802
		Per capita (thousand rials)						
1 (poorest)	475	438	210	4	1170	813	607	3706
2	734	719	261	18	1236	1228	507	4677
3	675	942	282	0	1227	1531	462	5090
4	782	1228	317	25	1287	1808	437	5839
5	820	1451	337	17	1284	1959	380	6213
6	751	1731	353	2	1355	2257	354	6757
7	687	2117	387	27	1283	2577	327	7355
8	642	2280	404	68	1327	2668	273	7627
9	443	3008	451	20	1336	3139	210	8575
10 (richest)	658	4577	596	68	1376	4006	230	11,471
Total	667	1849	360	25	1288	2199	379	6731

Source Authors' calculation using SUBSIM, HEIS (2013), and the Statistical Center of Iran
Note HEIS Household Expenditure and Income Survey, free market prices are assumed according to Table 10.2

Table 10.17 The impact on per capita consumed quantities, direct effects, gradualist scenario

Expenditure decile	Kerosene (L)	Gasoline (L)	Electricity (kWh)	Diesel (L)	Bread (kg)	Natural gas (m^3)	LPG (m^3)
1 (poorest)	−0.48	−0.51	−3.69	−0.00	−2.42	−1.56	−1.35
2	−0.75	−0.84	−4.73	−0.02	−2.52	−2.40	−1.13
3	−0.69	−1.10	−5.14	−0.00	−2.47	−3.07	−1.03
4	−0.80	−1.44	−5.93	−0.03	−2.58	−3.66	−0.97
5	−0.84	−1.70	−6.38	−0.02	−2.56	−4.04	−0.84
6	−0.76	−2.03	−6.74	−0.00	−2.69	−4.68	−0.79
7	−0.70	−2.48	−7.58	−0.03	−2.55	−5.42	−0.73
8	−0.65	−2.67	−7.98	−0.07	−2.62	−5.66	−0.61
9	−0.45	−3.53	−8.92	−0.02	−2.63	−6.59	−0.47
10 (richest)	−0.67	−5.39	−12.83	−0.07	−2.70	−8.23	−0.51
Total	−0.68	−2.17	−6.99	−0.03	−2.57	−4.53	−0.84

Table 10.18 Impact of the reform on the government subsidy payments, gradualist scenario (billion rials)

Expenditure decile	Kerosene	Gasoline	Electricity	Diesel	Bread	Natural gas	LPG	Total
1 (poorest)	−127	−194	−264	−1	−1057	−275	−193	−2111
2	−196	−320	−343	−5	−1131	−419	−161	−2576
3	−180	−423	−374	−0	−1134	−535	−147	−2794
4	−209	−557	−438	−7	−1196	−642	−140	−3189
5	−219	−656	−472	−5	−1192	−704	−121	−3368
6	−201	−787	−502	−1	−1269	−821	−113	−3692
7	−183	−963	−570	−8	−1199	−953	−104	−3980
8	−171	−1039	−602	−20	−1246	−989	−87	−4154
9	−118	−1378	−674	−6	−1257	−1159	−67	−4660
10 (richest)	−176	−2110	−1002	−20	−1297	−1471	−73	−6149
Total	−1780	−8427	−5242	−72	−11,977	−7966	−1207	−36,671

References

CNG Europe. 2014. Map of CNG Stations and Prices by Country in Europe. http://www.cngeurope.com.

EIA (Energy Information Administration). 2015. Electricity Prices for Households for Selected Countries. http://www.eia.gov/countries/prices/electricity_households.cfm.

FERC (Federal Energy Regulatory Commission). 2014. Market Oversight. http://www.ferc.gov/oversight.

Gahvari, Firouz, and Farzad Taheripour. 2011. Fiscal Reforms in General Equilibrium: Theory and an Application to the Subsidy Debate in Iran. *The B.E. Journal of Economic Analysis & Policy* 11 (1): 1–54.

Gahvari, Firouz, and Seyed Mohammad Karimi. 2013. Export Constraint and Domestic Fiscal Reform: Lessons from 2010 Subsidy Reform in Iran. *Working Paper*, Department of Economics, University of Illinois, Urbana-Champaign, IL.

Guillaume, Dominique, Roman Zytek, and Mohammad Reza Farzin. 2011. Iran–The Chronicles of the Subsidy Reform. *IMF Working Paper 11/167*, 1–28. International Monetary Fund, Washington, DC.

HEIS (Household Expenditures and Income Survey). 2013. Statistical Center of Iran, Tehran.

Jensen, Jesper, and David Tarr. 2003. Trade, Exchange Rate, and Energy Pricing Reform in Iran: Potentially Large Efficiency Effects and Gains to the Poor. *Review of Development Economics* 4: 543–562.

Ministry of Energy. 2013. Energy Balance Sheet. Tehran, Iran.

Platts.com. 2014. Asia Pacific/Persian Gulf Marketscan. McGraw Hill Financial.

Salehi-Isfahani, Djavad. 1996. *Government Subsidies and Demand for Petroleum Products in Iran*. Oxford, U.K.: Oxford Institute for Energy Studies.

Salehi-Isfahani, Djavad. 2014. Iran's Subsidy Reform; From Promise to Disappointment. *Policy Perspective* 13: 1–11. Economic Research Forum, Cairo, Egypt.

Salehi-Isfahani, Djavad, and Mohammad Mostafavi-Dehzooei. 2016. The Impact of Unconditional Cash Transfers on Labor Supply: Evidence from Iran's Energy Subsidy Reform Program. *ERF Working paper*, Economic Research Forum, Cairo, Egypt.

Salehi-Isfahani, Djavad, Bryce Wilson Stucki, and Joshua Deutschmann. 2013. The Reform of Energy Subsidies in Iran: The Role of Cash Transfers. *Emerging Markets Finance and Trade.*

Author Biographies

Mohammad H. Mostafavi-Dehzooei received his PhD in Economics from Virginia Tech in 2016. He holds a Masters degree in Economics (2011) and a Bachelors degree in Electrical Engineering (2008) from Sharif University of Technology. He was a consultant to the World Bank (2015 and 2016). Mohammad's research has been in development economics, labor economics, economic policy, and the economics of the Middle East.

Djavad Salehi-Isfahani received his PhD in economics from Harvard University in 1977. He is currently professor of economics at Virginia Tech and a nonresident senior fellow at the Brookings Institution. He taught at the University of Pennsylvania (1977–84) and was visiting faculty at the University of Oxford (1991–92), the Brookings Institution (2007–08), and the John F. Kennedy School of Government at Harvard (2009–10, and fall 2013). He has served on the Board of Trustees of the Economic Research Forum in Cairo and the Middle East Economic Association and as the associate editor of the *Middle East Development Journal.* His research has been in energy economics, demographic economics, and the economics of the Middle East. He has coauthored two books, *Models of the Oil Market* and *After the Spring: Economic Transitions in the Arab World*, and edited two volumes, *Labor and Human Capital in the Middle East* and *The Production and Diffusion of Public Choice*. His articles have appeared in *The Economic Journal, Journal of Development Economics, Health Economics, Economic Development and Cultural Change, Journal of Economic Inequality, International Journal of Middle East Studies, Middle East Development Journal*, and *Iranian Studies*, among others.

Appendix

SUBSIM
A User Guide

Abdelkrim Araar and Paolo Verme

SUBSIM is a product of the World Bank. The authors are grateful to the many people who have tested SUBSIM in various countries or provided comments over the past three years. We wish to thank in particular Aziz Atanamov, Shanta Devarajan, Gabriela Inchauste, Michael Lokshin, Jon Jellema, Umar Serajuddin and Quentin Wodon. We are also grateful to the World Bank PSIA Trust Fund and the MENA Chief Economist Office for funding during the preparation of the model and country studies.

Introduction

SUBSIM is an automated subsidies simulation model designed to carry out distributional analyses of subsidies and simulations of subsidies reforms. The model estimates the impact of subsidies reforms on household welfare, poverty, inequality, and the government budget. It can also estimate these impacts in the presence of compensatory cash transfers. SUBSIM currently comes in two flavors:

1. **SUBSIM Direct.** This version uses only one household budget survey to estimate direct effects of subsidies reforms on household welfare and on the government budget. This version presents results by subsidized products and by quintiles of household expenditure or other group variables indicated by users.
2. **SUBSIM Indirect.** This version combines data from input-output (I/O) tables and household budget surveys to estimate direct and indirect effects of subsidies reforms. This version presents results by sets of consumption items that match economic sectors and by quintiles of household expenditure or other group variables indicated by users.

P. Verme and A. Araar (eds.), *The Quest for Subsidy Reforms in the Middle East and North Africa Region*, Natural Resource Management and Policy 42,
DOI 10.1007/978-3-319-52926-4

SUBSIM is a product of the World Bank and has been designed to assist policy makers who need to make rapid decisions on subsidies reforms. For more information about the SUBSIM project, please visit: www.subsim.org.

Installation

To install SUBSIM simply execute the following command in STATA:

```
set more off
net from http://www.subsim.org/Installer
net install subsim_part1, force
net install subsim_part2, force
cap addSMenu profile.do subsim_menu
```

Note: The last Stata command line tries to add the file profile.do automatically or add the command _subsim_menu in the file profile.do if the latter exists already. If this last command does not function, you have to copy the profile.do file in:

a. *Windows OS system:* copy the file in **c:/ado/personal/**
b. *Macintosh system:* copy the file in one of the Stata system directories. To find these directories, type the command sysdir.

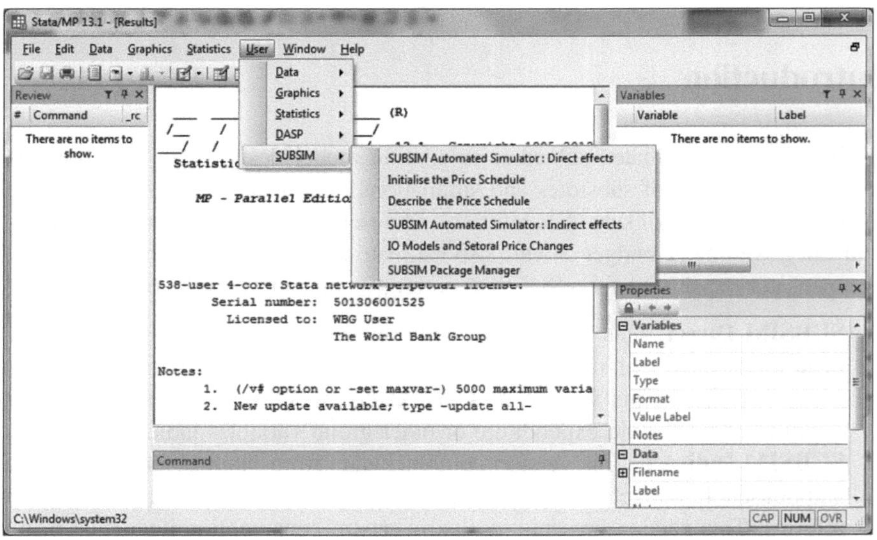

The SUBSIM Automated Simulator: Direct effects is the automated model to run the SUBSIM Direct version. This is complemented by two other tools. The first tool (Initialize the price schedule) is designed for goods priced according to tariffs'

blocks (nonlinear pricing) such as electricity and water where different tariffs correspond to different quantities consumed. This tool is also useful if subsidized goods have a quota system whereby consumers receive the subsidized price only on a limited amount of goods consumed. Note that this tool is also available within the automated simulator and is not normally used independently. The second tool (Describe the price schedule) is designed to graph and compare nonlinear pricing structures. This tool can be useful if users want to compare different tariffs structures for items such as electricity.

The SUBSIM Automated Simulator: Indirect effects is the automated model to run the SUBSIM version for direct and indirect effects combining household budget survey and input-output data. This is complemented by one other tool designed to manage and use input-output tables only (I/O Models and Sectoral Price Changes). For example, if users do not have a household budget survey and wish to make simulations of price changes only, they can use this tool working with input-output tables only.

Note: By *direct* effects, we mean the impact of a price change on household well-being via the consumption of subsidized products. By *indirect* effects, we mean the impact of a price change on household well-being via the consumption of products that are affected indirectly by the change in price of subsidized products. For example, a change in the price of gasoline has direct effects on households who consume gasoline and indirect effects on households that consume products that use gasoline as a production input, such as transportation services. Partial equilibrium models generally provide results for direct effects only. This is the case of SUBSIM Direct for example. General equilibrium models generally provide results for both direct and indirect effects. However, they require lengthy preparation, numerous data sets, several behavioral assumptions, and the convergence of multiple equations toward a general equilibrium. The I/O model can be viewed as a simple general model that can capture the bulk of the welfare effects in the absence of detailed specific behavioral responses for all agents and markets. CGE (computable general equilibrium) and I/O models are expected to reach similar results with moderate exogenous price shocks. SUBSIM Indirect was designed to estimate direct and indirect effects

SUBSIM also provides the SUBSIM package manager to check for updates, read the reference material, or visit the SUBSIM website as shown below.

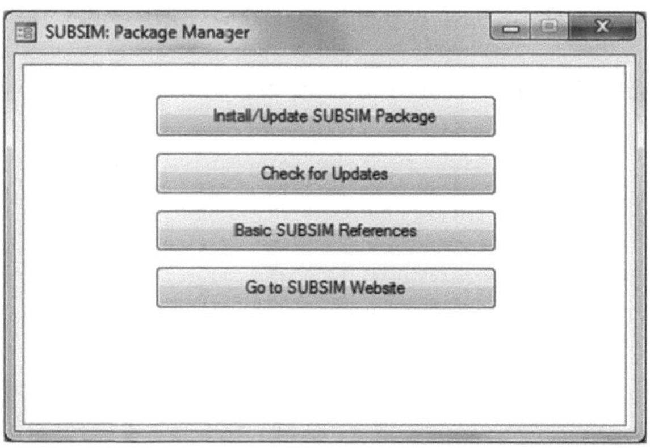

SUBSIM Direct and Indirect versions have similar interfaces organized into four tabs:

- Main
- Items
- Tables options
- Graph options

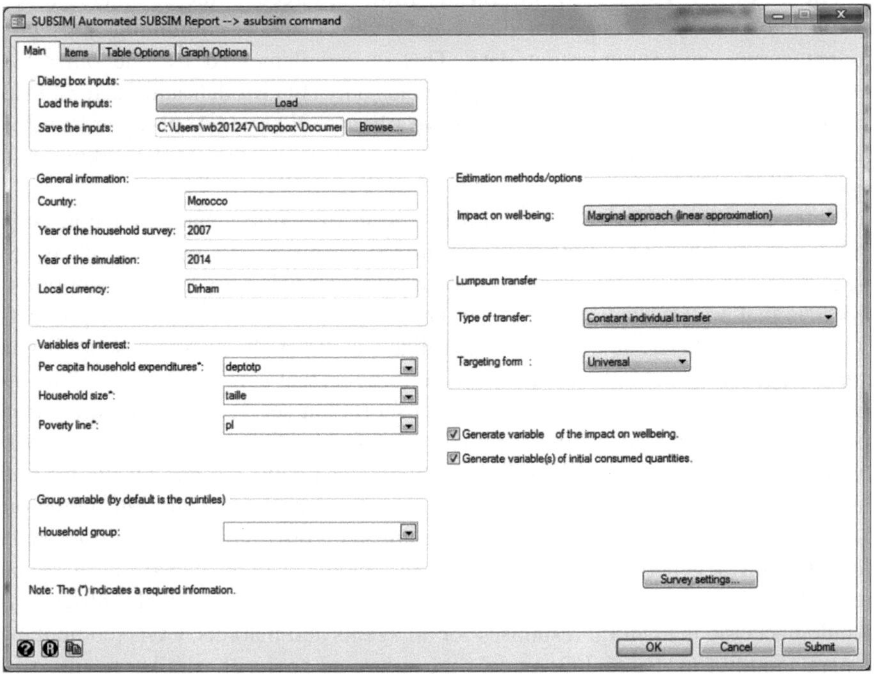

The tabs “Main” and “Items” are designed for data *inputs* and are different between SUBSIM Direct and SUBSIM Indirect. The tabs “Tables options” and “Graphs options” are designed to control *outputs* options and are identical between the two versions. These last two tabs are described under the SUBSIM Direct version only.

Note: Inputs that are compulsory for the simulations are indicated with an asterisk (*).

SUBSIM Direct Effects

Tab "Main"

The tab "Main" contains six boxes for data input:

Dialog Box Input. This box is used to load and save input data. The box enables the user to load information already saved into the SUBSIM window or to save the information inserted in the dialogue box in a file to be stored for future simulations. This information is stored in text files with the extension "*.prj". You can test this feature by uploading the file "example_1.prj" provided with the toolkit. Note that you can load the file from one directory ("Load the Inputs") and save it in a different directory with a different name ("Save the Inputs").

General Information. The box General Information enables the user to insert some helpful information, such as the name of the country or the local currency. This information will be saved in the file of results. Remember that the basic background information about the simulation is displayed and saved in the Excel file of results.

Variables of Interest. The box Variables of Interest enables the user to insert key variables such as the per capita expenditures or income, the household size, and the poverty line.

Note: The key income or expenditure variable should be prepared in advance in per capita terms.

Group Variable. The box Group Variable enables the user to insert a population group variable. This variable captures a sociodemographic group, such as gender or urban-rural. By default, results are shown by quintile. When you select a different group variable, the results will be displayed using this variable. Note that only one variable can be chosen for each simulation. If results are needed by more than one variable the user will have to re-run SUBSIM each time.

Estimations Methods/Options. The box Estimation Method/Options enables the user to select different modeling estimation options. This concerns the selection of the approach to be adopted to assess the impact on well-being. In addition to the popular marginal approach which uses a Laspeyres variation formula, SUBSIM offers a second option which models the consumer behavior with a Cobb-Douglas function. In this case, the impact on wellbeing is measured with the equivalent variation formula. For more information, see Annex with formulae.

- The marginal approach (Linear approximation)
- The behavioral approach (Cobb-Douglas Utility Function)

Lump-sum Transfer. The box "Lump-sum Transfer" enables the user to indicate information on cash transfers. In some cases, the government may want to compensate the population affected by subsidies reforms with cash transfers. This box allow users to choose whether this transfer should be allocated to individuals or households (**Type of transfer:** Individual or household) or whether the transfer should be universal or targeted to particular population groups (**Targeting form:** Universal or population group). There is no need to indicate the amount of transfers. Results are reported in graphs, and the user can select a range of values of transfers (the min and the max, see graphs options) and see results for all values included in the range specified.

The tab "Main" also offers the options of leaving behind the welfare variables of the impact on well-being and the quantities variables before and after simulations for each product. These quantities are estimated by SUBSIM using information on expenditure and unit prices. If these boxes are ticked, users will find these variables in the data set after SUBSIM has finished running.

Note: If users want to target a specific population group, the corresponding indicator should be prepared in advance if not already part of the variables set. For example, poor = 1 and non-poor = 0, if the poor only should be targeted. If the group variable is not specified, SUBSIM will produce the graphs on transfers with universal transfers.

Note: Survey settings. Remember to set the survey settings before you launch SUBSIM including sampling weights and sampling design information. This can be done with the command "svyset" in Stata or you can use the button "Survey Settings…" located in the bottom right-hand corner of the SUBSIM "Main" tab. For more information on survey settings, see the Stata manual.

Tab "Items"

The tab "Items" is conceived to insert information about the goods concerned in the simulation, including initial prices, final prices, and unit subsidies.

Initialize Information: The information on products can be initialized manually by inserting the information for each item (option "parameters values") or by selecting variables already created and available in the data set (option: "variables"). The "example.dta" contains these special variables. Users would normally input data manually using the parameters values option unless one needs to analyze more than 10 items, which is the limit in the dialogue box. Doing so is usually not recommended because listing more than 10 items makes graphs messy. If you have more than 10 items, divide them in separate simulations, for example, food subsidies and energy subsidies.

Number of Items. This is to select the number of items to consider. The maximum number allowed is 10.

Option "Parameter Values": With this option the user can input the information for each item manually including name, quantity, per capita expenditure variables, type of price schedule, initial price, unit subsidy, final price, and elasticity.

Short names: This is the name of the variable as it should appear in the output files. This is imputed manually.

Q. Unit: Used to insert the unit quantity (kg, liters, etc.). This information will be displayed in the results tables.

Varnames: These variables are selected from the data set and indicate the variables that contain information on expenditure per capita of the item considered.

Price schedules. Users have an option to choose linear and nonlinear prices. The schedule refers to whether the price is equal for all quantities consumed by households or changes according to quantities. This is the case, for example, of electricity or a product with a quota system where households are entitled to subsidized prices only up to a certain quantity (quota).

Initial Prices. This is the pre-reform price, usually the subsidized price as found at the time of simulations.

Subsidy: This is the unit subsidy. This information is usually provided by ministries or specialized government agencies. Unit prices can also be estimated manually if the total amount of subsidies on a product is known together with information on the quantity of subsidized product consumed. Note that SUBSIM can also be used to simulate price increases or decreases in the absence of subsidies. In this case, unit subsidies are set to zero.

Final prices: This is the simulated price. If one wants to remove subsidies completely, this price will be simply the sum of the initial price and the unit subsidy. If one wants to estimate other price increases or reduction in subsidies, this final price will be lower.

Elasticity. This is the own-price (quantity/price) elasticity. The user can insert any value, and this is used to estimate changes in quantities consumed and other impacts. See section SUBSIM Basic Formulas for a discussion on how to specify the value of elasticity.

As an example, assume that the actual initial price is 0.1 monetary unit and the unit subsidy is 0.3. In the absence of subsidies, the price of flour would be 0.4. We can simulate any increase in price, such as an increase in prices of 0.1, which leads to a final price of 0.2. In this case, our inputs will be 0.1 for the initial price, 0.3 for the unit subsidy and 0.2 for the final price. For rice, we can input, as an example, 0.14 for the initial price, 0.4 for the unit subsidy and 0.24 for the final price (Fig. A.1).

If you are using the **nonlinear option**, you will have to initialize initial and final prices. If you click on "initialize," another window will open for this purpose. It will allow you to specify prices by tariffs block and also change the number of blocks if you wish to simulate a reform that implies changing the tariffs structure, not just the prices. Clicking on "Initialize" will open a window as shown in Fig. A.2.

Tariff Structure. Electricity or water tariffs are generally organized in quantities blocks, where a different tariff corresponds to each block of quantities. These prices can be "marginal," meaning that they apply only to the block where the consumer is located, or "flat," meaning that they apply to all quantities consumed up to the block where the consumer is located. The first type of tarification is called *increasing*

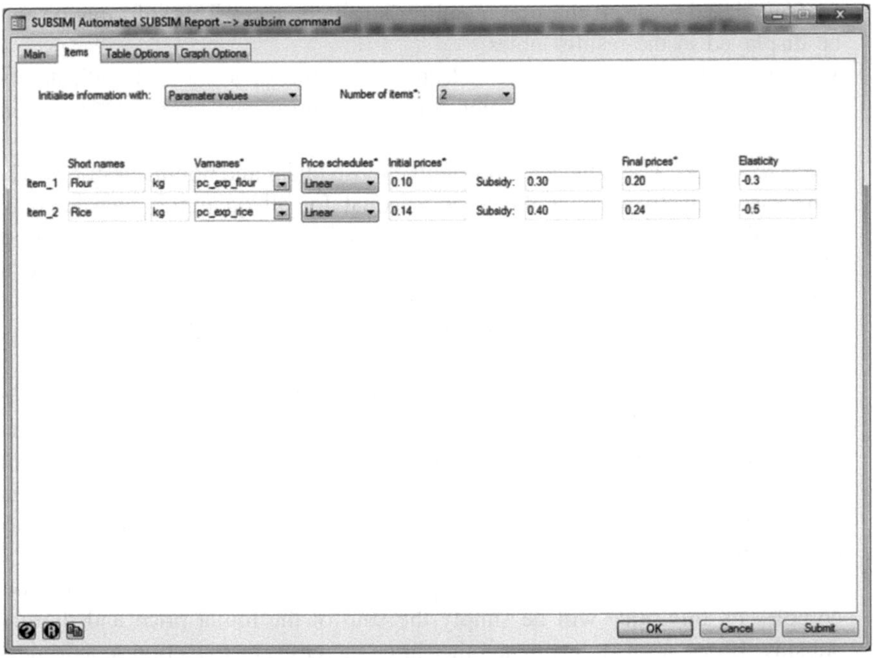

Fig. A.1 Tab *Items* of SUBSIM dialog box

block tariffs (IBT), and the second type is called *volume differentiated tariffs* (VDT). The nonlinear option in SUBSIM can simulate both types (IBT or VDT) and can also simulate combinations of both.

Blocks Defined By. Tariffs blocks can be defined by household consumption or by individual consumption. Make sure that you choose the right option. Also check whether your data in the household budget survey report expenditure by month, quarter, year, or other periods. Tariffs blocks are defined in quantities such as kilowatt hours, and these quantities refer to specific period such as a month or a quarter.

Number of Brackets. You can set up to 10 tariffs blocks.

Subscription Fee. Sometimes, tariffs for electricity or water include an initial fixed cost for the meter or the service. This tariff can also be modeled by including the amount in the "Subscription fee" box.

Option "Variables". This applies to the main "Items" tab and to the "Initialize" button. With this option, the user can select the data on products by selecting variables directly from a pre-prepared data set. This option is suitable when the user has a large number of items so that it may be easier to prepare first a spreadsheet with all the key information including names of items, prices, units, and elasticities. SUBSIM allows the user to upload this information and use it for the analysis. Note that the spreadsheet has to contain all the information needed for the analysis in the

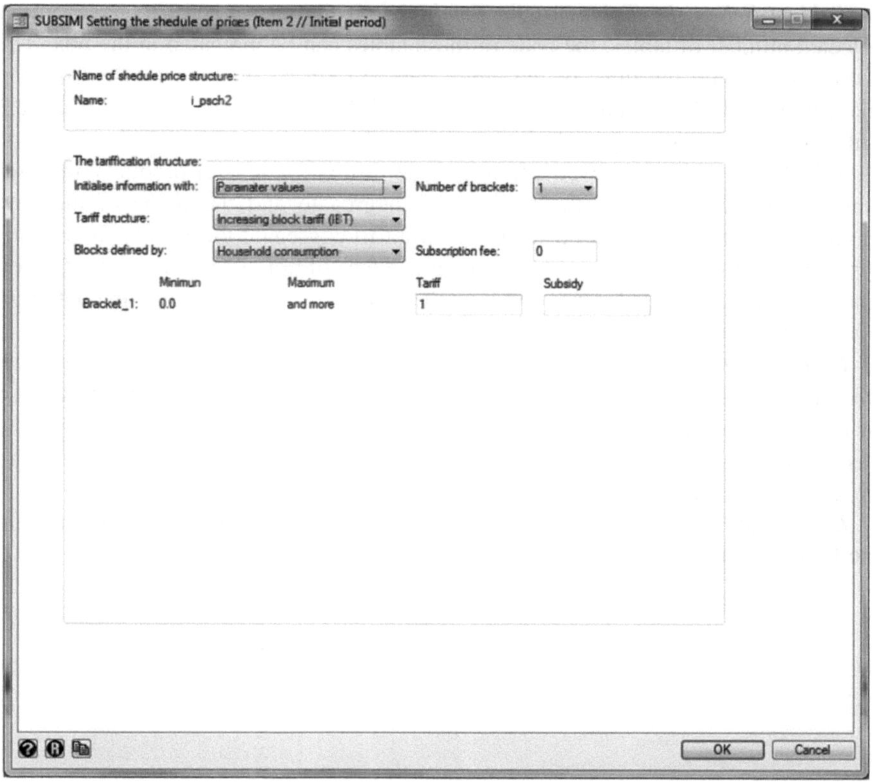

Fig. A.2 Price schedule dialog box to set initial prices

form of variables. This option will be treated more in detail in Example 3. We usually do not recommend using this option because it is time-consuming to prepare the data and using more than 10 products clogs the output graphs and tables. If you have more than 10 products simply run SUBSIM for different groups of products such as food or energy products.

Tab "Tables Options"

This tab allows the user to select the tables' options (Fig. A.3). The default option when you do not select the tables and override options is the production of all tables.

Tables: Select the Tables to Be Produced. If the user wishes to have only a selected number of tables, the code of these tables can be indicated in the box. The list of codes with the titles of the tables can be seen by clicking on the question mark button [?]. For example, you can type "*11 23*" to produce Tables 1.1 and 2.3 only (no commas, one space between numbers).

Join Items. If the user wants to aggregate results for several products, the user can indicate the codes of the products to aggregate and the name of the new aggregated item. For example, you may want to aggregate the results for various types of sugar (items 4, 5, and 6) and various types of flour (items 7 and 8). Or you may want to add results for rice and flour. This may be done by adding the option: 4 5 6 : "Sugar" | 7 8 : "Flour."

Produce an Excel File of Results. This box allows the user to define the Excel file where all tables should be stored. The user can select an existing file to override or create a new file. The user can either specify the name of the file or not. In the case of an existing file, the user should make sure that this file is closed when the program is launched, otherwise an error message will appear.

Language: Users can choose the language for all results. English and French are the two languages currently available.

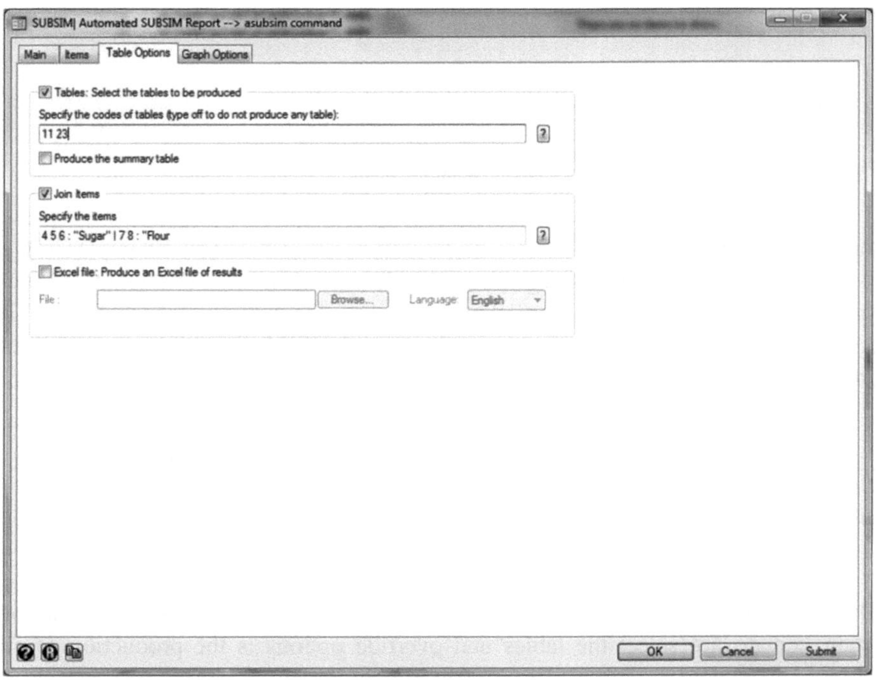

Fig. A.3 Tab *Table Options* of SUBSIM dialog box

Tab
"Graph Options"

Graphs: Select the Graphs to Be Produced. This option allows the user to save only selected graphs by indicating the code of each graph. The list of codes with the titles of the graphs can be seen by clicking on the question mark button?. For example, if the user wishes to produce only Graphs 1, 2, and 4, the user will simply type "1 2 4" (no commas, one space between numbers).

Join Items: If the user wants to aggregate results for several products, the user can indicate the codes of the products to aggregate and the name of the new aggregated item. For example, you may want to aggregate the results for various types of sugar (items 4, 5 and 6) and various types of flour (items 7 and 8). This may be done by adding the option: 4 5 6 : "Sugar" | 7 8 : "Flour."

Select the Folder of Graphs Results. This option allows the user to select the directory where the saved graphs should be stored. Note that all graph files are saved in three formats: .gph. .pdf, and .wmf. SUBSIM will save a folder with the name "Graphs" in the directory selected.

Graph Options. For each graph, the user can select options regarding the y-axis scale (min and max) and other two-way graphs options as indicated in the Stata graph help files. For example, users may want to limit the range of the graphs to a specific interval such as between 10 and 80. This can be done by indicating minimum and maximum values. Or users may want to omit titles of the graphs and add these titles separately in the report. This can be done by adding the stata option "title ("")" (Fig. A.4). Note that these options need to be specified separately for each of the 10 graphs produced by SUBSIM.

Examples

For the examples, you will need to download first the data set and the examples files from the following website:

http://www.subsim.org/examples/example_dir.rar

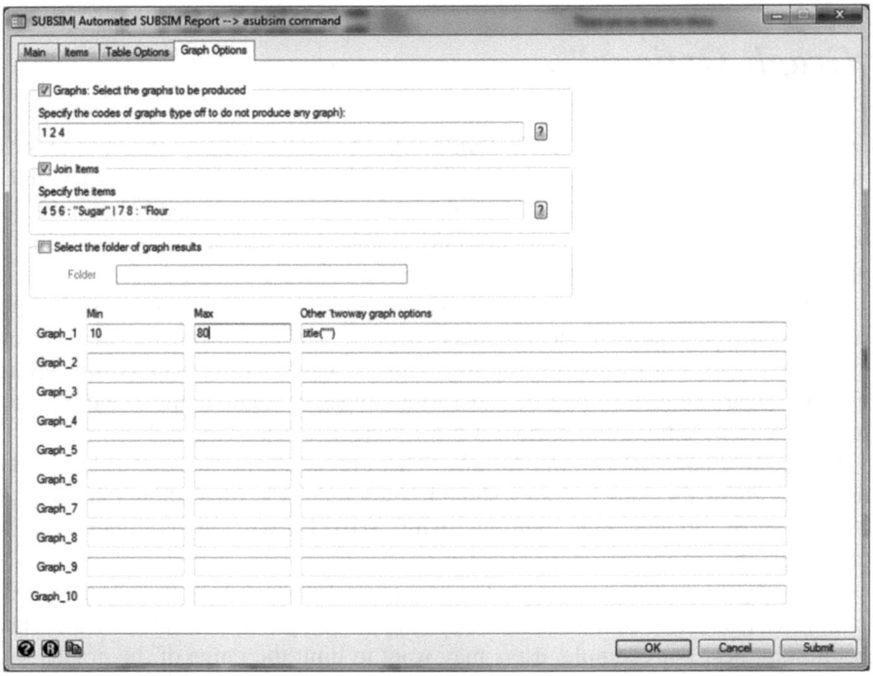

Fig. A.4 Tab *Graph Options* of SUBSIM dialog box

Example 1 Linear Subsidies

The following examples are based on the data set "example.dta" provided with the toolkit. To be sure that SUBSIM has been correctly installed, the user should run the example with the data provided before testing SUBSIM with other data.

As a first step, load the *example.dta* data into STATA. Then open SUBSIM Direct and load the pre-prepared example data in *.prj* format using the load option in the tab "Main" (Fig. A.5). Then indicate in the "Save the inputs" box the full directory where you want to store the *.prj* file.

In this example, our country of interest subsidizes two goods, flour and rice. We wish to simulate the impact of a subsidy reform (price increase) on well-being and government revenue. In the example in Fig. A.6, the initial prices for flour and rice are 0.10 and 0.14 respectively, the unit subsidies are 0.30 and 0.40, and the final prices to simulate are 0.20 and 0.24. Note that this is not a complete removal of subsidies because the final price is not equal to the initial price plus the subsidy.

Next, make sure that the directories for the input data, tables, and graphs to save are the correct one that you want to use (see instructions for tabs). Then simply run SUBSIM clicking on "OK" or "Submit" and let the model complete its work.

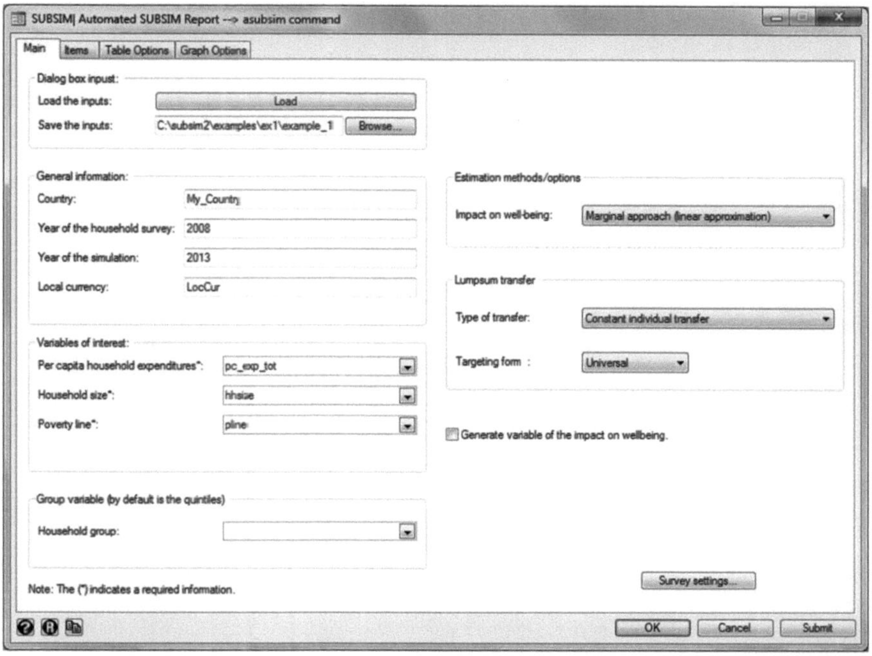

Fig. A.5 Tab *Main* of SUBSIM dialog box

When SUBSIM finishes, the Excel file of results with all tables will open automatically. If you wish to look at the graphs, open the Graphs folder under the graph directory you have indicated. The only difference between the "OK" and "Submit" execution buttons is that "Submit" will keep the SUBSIM window open while "OK" will not.

Note: Make sure that you specify directories correctly. SUBSIM does not accept spaces in directories or certain symbols, such as an exclamation point. This may stop SUBSIM from executing the full routine.

Example 2
Nonlinear Subsidies

By nonlinear subsidies we mean to describe subsidies that change according to different levels of quantities consumed by households. The case of nonlinear subsidies is typically of two forms: the quota system and the blocks system.

The **quota** system refers to subsidies administered via allotments. For example, households may be entitled to a subsidized price for bread up to a certain quantity purchased, say 10 kg per month. Beyond that quantity, consumers buy bread on the

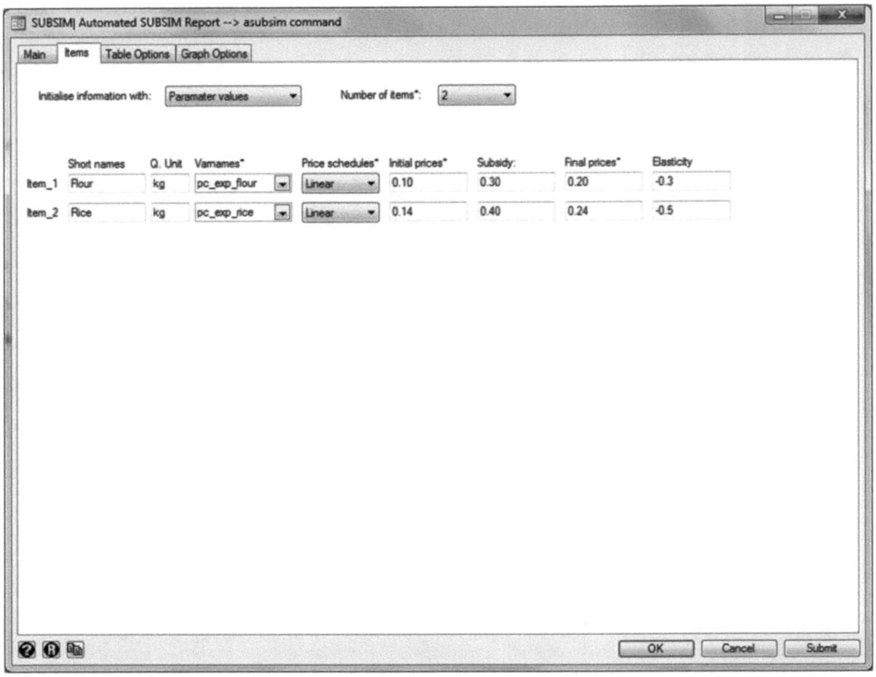

Fig. A.6 Tab *Items* and insertion of information with editable fields

free market at unsubsidized prices. This system usually makes use of quantity cards or vouchers that households can use to purchase certain quantities at subsidized prices.

The **blocks** system is one in which different prices apply to different bundles of quantities consumed. This system is typically used for electricity or water subsidies where the electricity or water prices are set by the regulator at different prices for each quantity block. For example, a price is set for consumption of 0–150 kWh per month, and a higher price for the consumption of 151–300 kWh per month, and so on. In this case, the number of blocks can be small or large depending on the choice of the regulator.

From an economic and modeling perspective, the quota and blocks systems are equivalent. In fact, the quota system can be considered as a block system with a two-block structure. Therefore, in what follows, we will limit our discussion to the quota system, but the same explanations apply to the blocks system.

Suppose now that subsidies are administered through a quota system where all individuals are entitled to fixed quantities at subsidized prices. For example, imagine that the annual per capita quota for flour is 36 kilograms. Assume also that the nonsubsidized market price is equal to 0.4. This implies that the price of flour is nonlinear; it changes with different quantities consumed (Table A.1). Consumers

Table A.1 Nonlinear schedule price for flour

Block	By	Subsidy	Price
0–36 kg	individual	0.3	0.1
36 kg and more	–	0.0	0.4

pay a subsidized price up to 36 kilograms per person and the unsubsidized price for any additional quantity purchased.

This nonlinear schedule price must be first declared in SUBSIM. To this end, the user has to perform the following steps (Fig. A.7):

Example 3
Simulation with Large Number of Items

If the subsidy reform concerns more than 10 items, the user can insert information on items using variables by selecting the "Variables" option from the "Items" tab. Note that the spreadsheet has to contain all the information needed for the analysis in the form of variables as shown in Fig. A.8.

Once the data are uploaded into STATA, the user can draw from the spreadsheet by using the items dialogue box as shown in Fig. A.9. (For this example, load the example_3.prj.) When the information is uploaded through variables, it is possible to ask SUBSIM to perform the computation for up to three scenarios. For example, in scenario 1 the reduction in subsidies is 30%, and in scenario 2 it is 100%. In this case, the Excel output file will contain estimations for both scenarios.

When you have tested the three examples, you are ready to use SUBSIM Direct with your own data. Don't forget to prepare your data file in advance following the indications provided.

SUBSIM Indirect Effects

The main objective of SUBSIM Indirect is to estimate the direct and indirect effects of a price change on household well-being combining a Household Budget Survey (HBS) and Input-Output (I/O) tables for a particular country. Note that SUBSIM Indirect focuses only on the goods that are concerned by the exogenous price shocks. Thus, this version is more appropriate to assess the indirect effect rather than the full direct effect of the subsidy reform. Direct effects are better estimated with SUBSIM Direct.

A. Indicate that the price schedule is nonlinear for the item: flour.	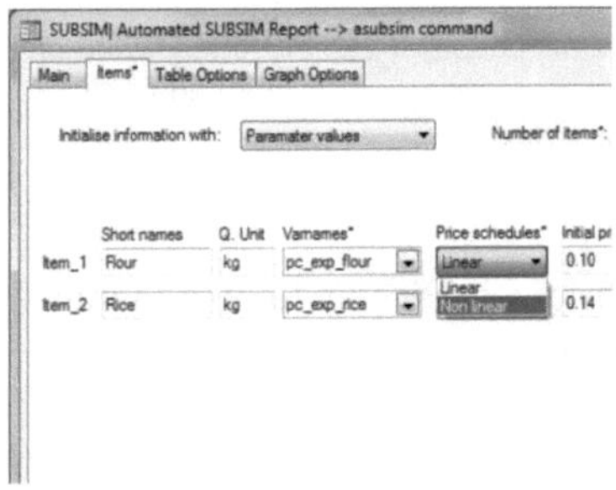
B. Click on the button "Initialise."	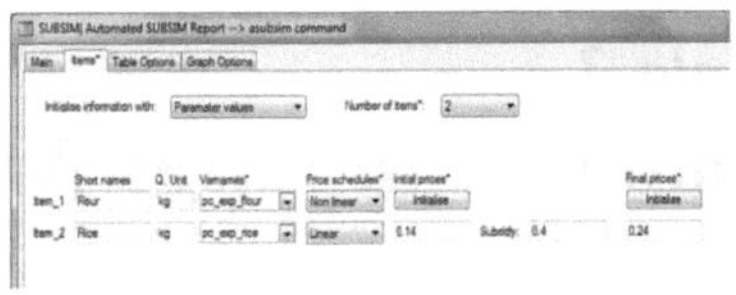
C. Initialize the opening prices for each block.	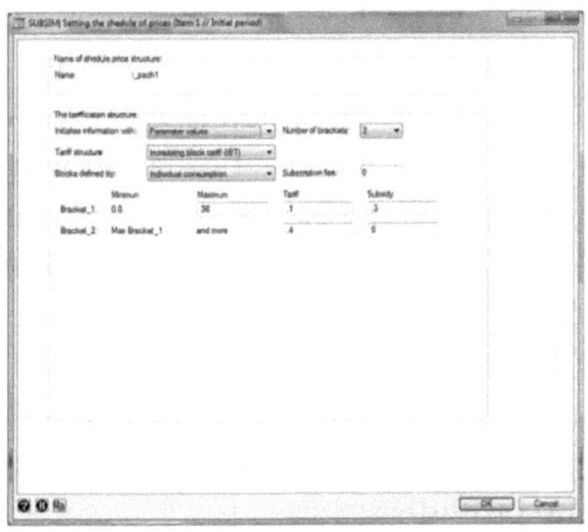
D. Initialize the final prices for each block. Note that we do not need to indicate the unit subsidy for the final period because SUBSIM estimates it starting from the initial subsidy and the change in prices: $(ds = -dp)$.	

Fig. A.7 Steps to initialize prices in SUBSIM

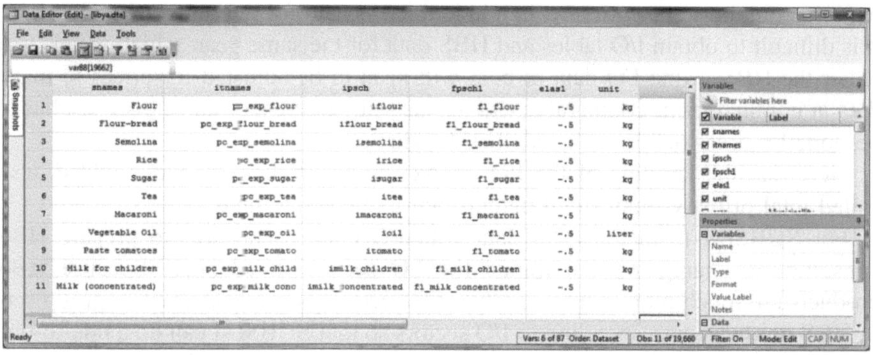

Fig. A.8 Use of Stata variables to declare information on items

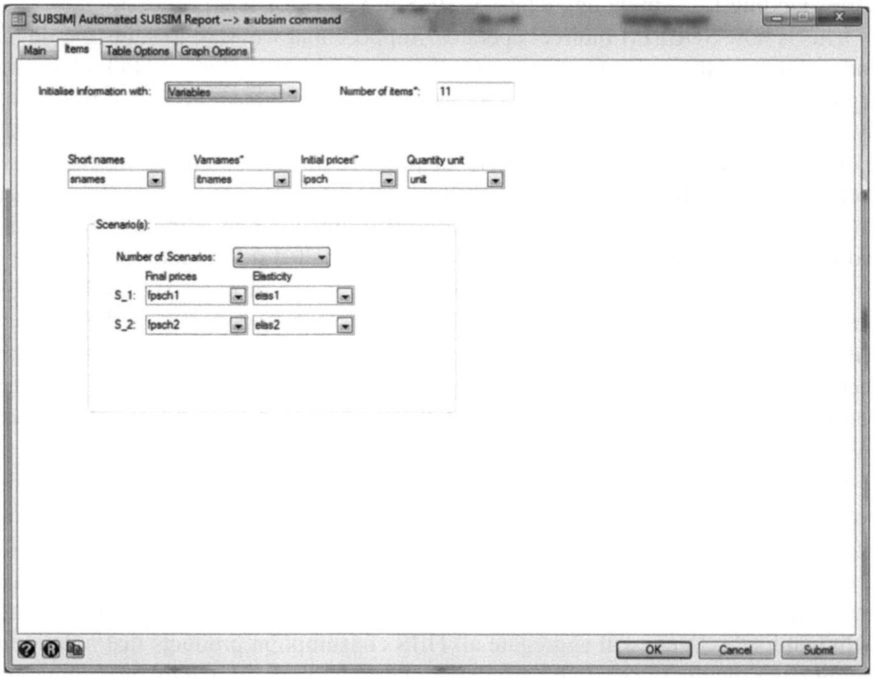

Fig. A.9 Tab *Items* and insertion of information with Stata variables for the case of two simulated scenarios

Data and Methodology

SUBSIM Indirect requires at least one Household Budget Survey (HBS) and an Input-Output (I/O) matrix (file). The I/O matrix required is the output matrix expressed in local currency. It is important that the I/O data and the HBS data are expressed in the same currency, in nominal terms, and for the same year. However, it is difficult to obtain I/O tables and HBS data for the same year, which means that either the HBS or the I/O data or both will need to be adjusted for prices to make data in nominal terms comparable and for the same reference year. This work has to be done by users before using SUBSIM Indirect.

Note that the last line of the I/O matrix should be the total value added, also called total primary input (total output-total intermediate inputs).

For SUBSIM to match HBS data with I/O data, users have to prepare HBS consumption aggregates that mimic the I/O sectors in advance. Because HBS products are much more numerous than I/O sectors, one would want to group sets of HBS products corresponding to I/O sectors so that SUBSIM can do a one-to-one matching between HBS aggregates of products and I/O sectors. In some cases, one HBS product may span across several I/O sectors. SUBSIM can also handle that situation. The user will simply indicate in the dialogue box multiple I/O sectors corresponding to a single aggregate of HBS products (or one product).

This is how SUBSIM Indirect operates. Suppose that we want to study the direct and indirect welfare effects of a price increase of gasoline. Because I/O tables are organized by sector, and it is very rare for researchers to have access to I/O tables by individual product, the study of indirect effects can be done only by sector and group of products and not by individual product. In our example, we have one sector called "petroleum products," which includes gasoline as well as other products. We can shock this sector with a price increase and study the direct and indirect effects on final consumers. If users have detailed information on the sector structure and want to study the effect of a price change of only one product, it is possible to make the price shock proportionate to the importance of the product within the sector. For example, if gasoline accounts for only 20% of the petroleum sector and we wish to increase only the price of gasoline by 10%, we can shock the petroleum sector by 2% (10% of 20%). This is a user's choice and does not make any difference to how SUBSIM operates.

Continuing with the same example, suppose now that we shock the whole petroleum sector with a price increase. Users will have prepared in advance aggregates of consumption products that roughly correspond to I/O sectors. In Fig. A.10, we have n consumption items present in the HBS represented by the list on the first column and 12 sectors in the I/O matrix represented by the list on the right hand side. Users will aggregate all HBS consumption products that belong to the I/O petroleum sector (e.g., gas, gasoline, and kerosene) into one item and prepare similar aggregates for the other sectors. SUBSIM will first load the HBS and I/O data and then match I/O economic sectors with HBS consumption products following the indications provided in the dialogue box.

Note: Some products, such as food in Fig. A.10, may belong to more than one I/O sectors, and in other cases, such as gas, gasoline and kerosene, several products belong to one sector. To accommodate simulations for both cases, it is important that users construct in advance HBS aggregates for those products that belong to only one sector. For example, the variable "gas, gasoline, and kerosene" is constructed by users in advance to allow SUBSIM to match products with sectors.

The price change of the HBS items is estimated in two steps. In the first step, the price change of the I/O sectors is estimated based on the selected I/O model. In the second step, by using the sectoral price changes, the price change of HBS items are estimated based on the matching information indicated by the user and the importance of each sector. For example, assume that the price change in sector 8 is dp_S8 = 0.1 and the one in sector ten is dp_S10 = 0.2. Further, assume that the value of total product of the sector eight is S8 = 100 and that of sector ten is S10 = 400. Then a weighted price change of food is equal to: (100/500) * 0.1 + (400/500) * 0.2 = 0.18.

SUBSIM Indirect has the same tabs as SUBSIM Direct. The Tables and Graphs tabs are identical but the "Main" and "Items" tabs are different and described below.

Tab "Main"

The "Main" tab window has one choice box in addition to what is available in SUBSIM Direct. This is the box "**I/O price change model.**" Here users can chose between different types of simulation models:

- **M1: Cost-push prices.** The main assumption here is that producers "push" the increase in prices onto consumers via the increase in prices of market products.

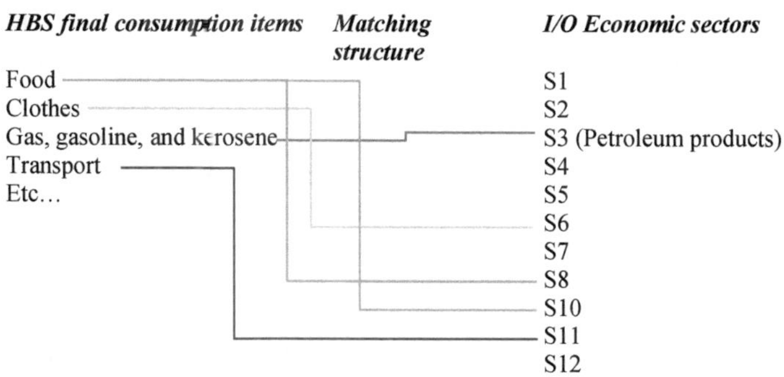

Fig. A.10 Map of matching between grouped consumption items of household surveys and I/O economic sectors

SUBSIM Indirect offers two sets of options (exogenous/endogenous model and short-term/long-term).

Endogenous and exogenous models refer to the sector that is shocked. With the endogenous option, we enable for the price adjustment of the shocked sector after the shock period. With the exogenous option, we assume that the price of the shocked sector does not change after the introduction of the price shock. The selection of the appropriate model will depend on the country context. For example, if the country is a net importer of the shocked good, and we assume that its economy cannot influence the world price, it may be appropriate to select the exogenous model.

Short-term or long-term options refer to the time horizon of the price effects measured in terms of successive rounds of price adjustments. The short-term option considers only the first round effects. The long-term option considers infinite rounds.

- **M2: Marginal profit-push prices.** The main assumption here is that markets are competitive and reach full price adjustments and producers maintain their marginal profits in the long term. For the formulas corresponding to this choice see Appendix B.

Tab "Items"

The new 'Items" tab window has two panels: Items info and Price shock and I/O matrix info. Remember that items indicated with an asterisk (*) are mandatory.

Items Info. This panel is designed to input data from the HBS file. Here you have two options. If you have up to 10 items, you can input the information related to these items directly from the window (option "Parameters value"). If you have more than 10 items, you need to prepare these items in advance in the HBS file (option "Variables"). In this case, the HBS file has to be prepared and loaded in advance and must contain the variables that indicate the item names, the corresponding variables names, and elasticity if required by the user. Look in the example provided to see how the key variables are constructed.

Short names. This is the space to indicate the names of items as displayed in results.

Varnames. The user should also indicate the variable that contains the items already matched with the I/O economic sectors. This variable will contain the group of HBS products that roughly correspond to I/O sectors.

Elasticity. This is the own-price elasticity to use for the simulations. See section "Elasticity" for more information on how to set elasticities.

Matching I/O sectors. This is where the I/O sectors matching the HBS variable indicated in "Varnames" are indicated. Because HBS products are more numerous than I/O sectors, one would want to group sets of HBS products under individual

I/O sectors so that SUBSIM can do a one-to-one matching between HBS aggregates of products and I/O sectors. However, in some cases, one group of HBS product may span across several I/O sectors. SUBSIM can also handle this. The user will simply indicate multiple I/O sectors corresponding to a single aggregate of HBS products in the box "Matching I/O sectors." Otherwise, this box will contain only one matching sector. Matching sectors are indicated with numbers as found in the I/O data file.

Note: The file directory of the input file should not contain any space and the last line of the I/O matrix data file must contain the added values as shown in Fig. A.11 for a hypothetical I/O matrix with four sectors.

Figure A.11 shows an I/O matrix with four sectors. The last line contains the added values. For example, the first sector uses its product as an input with a cost of 1 unit; it uses the good of sector 2 with cost of 2; and so forth. The total cost of intermediate goods is 9. The added value (labor and capital rents) is 4. The value of the total product of the first sector is 13.

As already indicated, the Tabs "Tables options" and "Graphs options" are described under the SUBSIM Direct version. These tabs are the same for both SUBSIM versions.

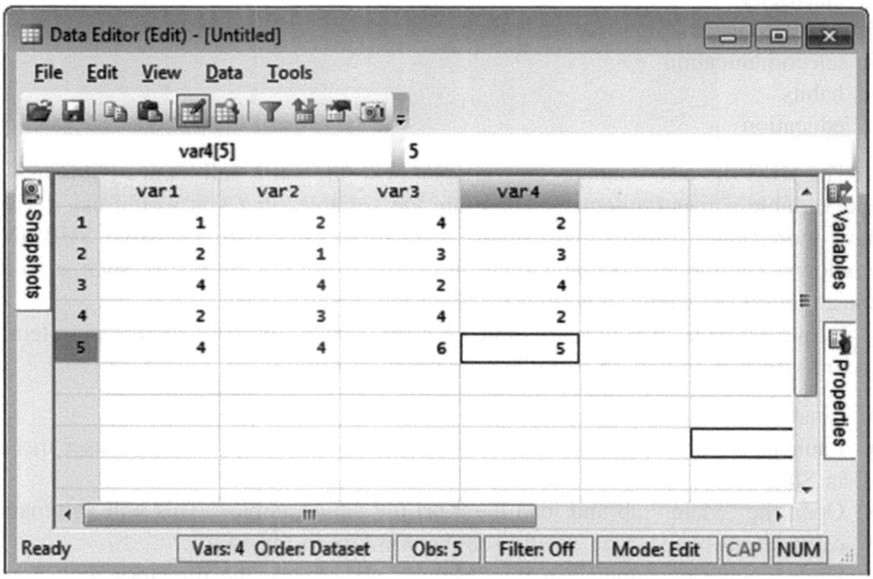

Fig. A.11 Illustrative example with a fictive input output matrix

Example

As an example, load the zipped file below from the Internet and unzip the file in your working directory:

http://www.subsim.org/examples/example_ind.rar

The zipped file contains data files (.dta) and preloaded input file (.pri). The three data files include a HBS file ("example_ind_eff.dta"), an I/O data file ("iomv.dta") and a file containing the sectors legends of the I/O file ("sec_info"). The pri files contain information on examples that can be directly loaded into windows.

Note: The .pri file extension is used in place of the .prj file extension so as to distinguish between SUBSIM Direct and SUBSIM Indirect input files.

As you can see, the I/O file ("iomv.dta") contains 50 lines and 49 columns (49 sectors plus one line for the value added). The HBS file ("example_ind_eff.dta") contains the per capita consumption of nine main items:

1. food
2. clothes
3. **energy (dir_eff)**
4. transport
5. electricity
6. travel_tourism
7. telecomunication
8. habits
9. education

The HBS file also contains the variables with the items full names ("itnames") and variable names ("nitems"). These are the variables that you would use if you have more than 10 items and cannot create these same variables from SUBSIM windows. The file also contains other information used by SUBSIM, such as total consumption per capita, household size, or the poverty line.

In our example, we want to simulate a price shock of 10% for the petroleum sector, which is in line 15. Here are the steps to follow:

- Load the HBS pre-prepared data
- Launch "SUBSIM Automated Simulator: Indirect Effects" from the user menu in Stata
- Open the "Main" tab and load the *.pri file "myexample." This will automatically fill all boxes. You should see the window in Fig. A.12:
- Under "Save the inputs" in the "Main" Tab, replace the directory with your directory to make sure that you save the inputs file "myexample" in your working directory, otherwise SUBSIM will produce an error.
- Make your choices in the tab "Main" and box "I/O price change model" regarding the options as described in the previous section.

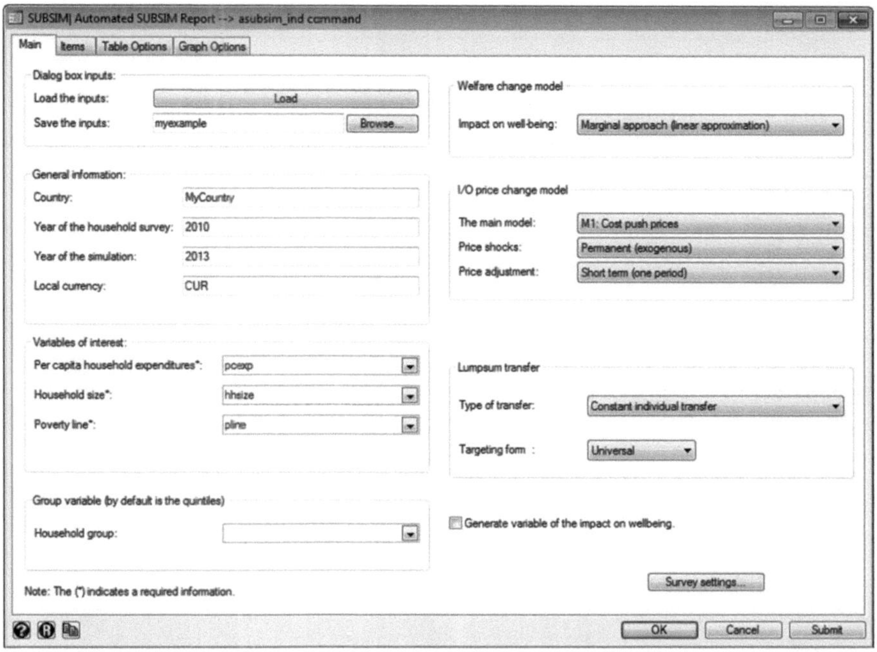

Fig. A.12 Dialog box of SUBSIM indirect effect

- Make sure that the Stata working directory is that where the file iomv.dta is located.
- Open the "Items" Tab and check the information loaded. You should see the window in Fig. A.13.

If the user wishes to focus only on the pure indirect effect, the item *Energy* should be removed from the list of items, as Fig. A.14 shows. Remember, however, to keep the price shock information (see also the example: *myexample_ind.pri*).

As you can see, we are ready to increase the price of sector in line 15 of the I/O file by 10%. Doing so will affect the HBS items directly via the increase in price of the consumption products that are included in the petroleum sector and indirectly by increasing the price of nonsubsidized products that are affected by the price change in the petroleum sector. Note that the user can select between two options to insert the information about the aggregated HBS items as already explained (options "Parameters values" for up to ten items and "Variables" for more than 10 items). In this example, we assume that only one economic sector is affected by the exogenous price shock. However, SUBSIM 3.0 enables users to introduce up to six shocks as shown in Fig. A.15.

You are now ready to run SUBSIM (click on "ok" or "submit"). Output tables are organized by group of products corresponding to I/O sectors (in columns) and provide totals as sums of all effects (direct and indirect). In this way, you will be

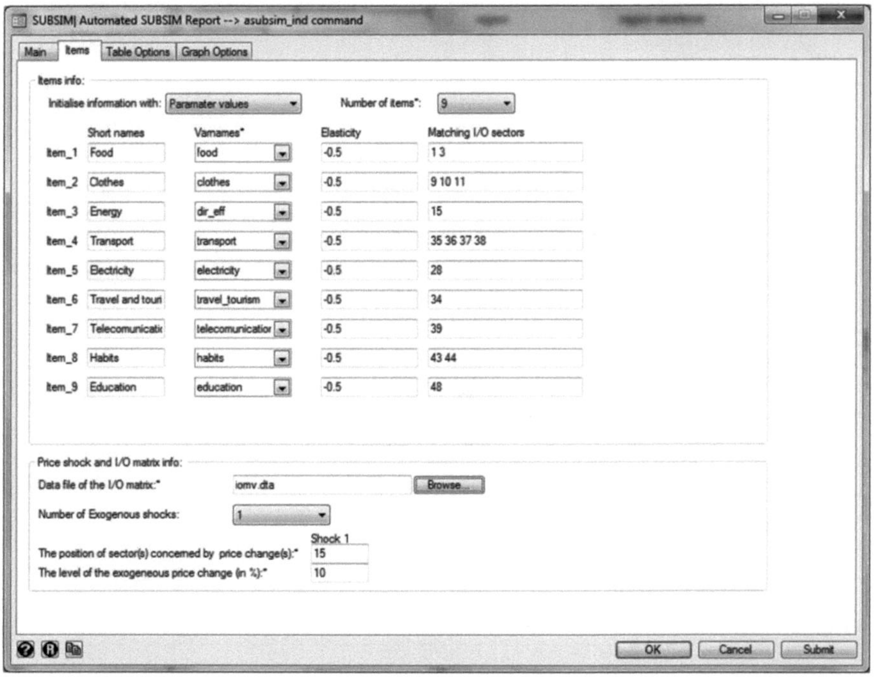

Fig. A.13 Tab *Items* and insertion of information on items and on corresponding matching I/O sectors

able to distinguish between direct effects and indirect effects and also have the total effect, which can be compared with the output of a general equilibrium model.

Note: To avoid typical mistakes, make sure that the HBS data have been loaded in advance; the specified directory for the I/O data is correct and without spaces; and the specified directory under "Save the inputs" in the "Main" tab is your directory and not the one preloaded.

When you run SUBSIM the program follows the following sequence of actions:

1. Matches products with sectors using information provided in the tab "Items";
2. Picks the simulation algorithm selected with choices in the tab "Main";
3. Produces the matrix of coefficients "A" (see section SUBSIM Basic Formulas)
4. Introduces shocks to the system following the choice made in the tab "Items";
5. Calculates the impact on all sectors;
6. Derives the impact on group of products as selected in the tab "Items";
7. Produces tables of results in one Excel file as indicated in the tab "Tables";
8. Produces a folder with figures as indicated in the tab "Figures."

To give a flavor of the impact of different choices on results, Table A.2 provides results for all options under the cost-push framework and using data in example 1. As expected, long-term effects and endogenous shocks produce larger impacts than

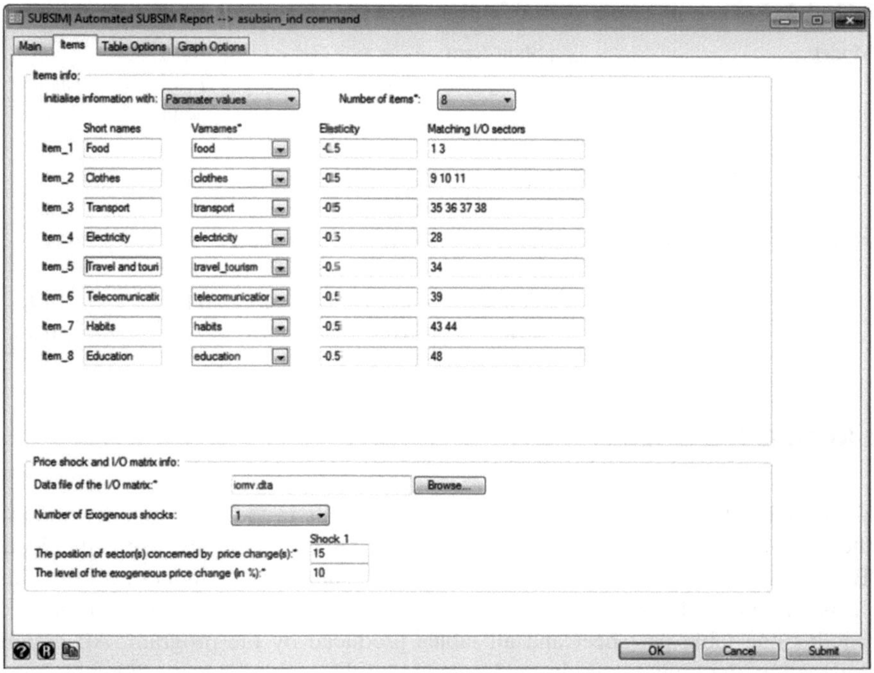

Fig. A.14 Tab *Items* and selection of indirect effect items

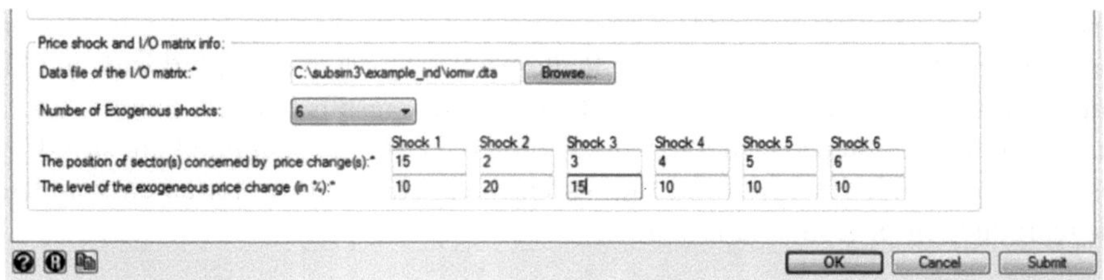

Fig. A.15 Tab items and simulation of several price's exogenous shocks

short-term effects and exogenous shocks. This result is clearly visible if we look at impacts on welfare per capita. As one should expect, however, the differences in impact on poverty is much smaller, and the differences in impact on inequality are nonexistent. Therefore, in applied works, reporting results obtained with different methods may be worthwhile only if differences are large.

Once you have run the example successfully, inspect the results and try to repeat simulations with your own data and parameters.

Table A.2 Example of alternative modeling choices

Model		Short term			Long term	
		Prereform	*Postreform*	*Change*	*Postreform*	*Change*
Exogenous	Welfare (per capita)	3022	3002	**−19.8**	2999	**−23.6**
	Poverty (%)	11.4	11.6	**0.2**	11.6	**0.2**
	Inequality (%)	39.6	39.6	**0.0**	39.6	**0.0**
Endogenous	Welfare (per capita)	3022	2994	**−28.0**	2984	**−38.5**
	Poverty (%)	11.4	11.6	**0.2**	11.8	**0.4**
	Inequality (%)	39.6	39.6	**0.0**	39.6	**0.0**

Launch SUBSIM

When SUBSIM is launched, it will display all results in the Stata output window. The user can stop the command at any stage of execution by using the Stata "Break" button. If the user has selected to save the table results in an Excel file, this file is automatically opened once the computation ends. The Excel file produced contains one table per sheet and all tables produced by the program. All graphs produced by the program are instead saved in a folder with the name "Graphs," and in three formats (pdf, gph, and wmf).

The complete set of tables and graphs can then be used to prepare a report on the distribution of subsidies, on the impact of subsidies reforms on household welfare and government revenues, and on the impact of compensatory cash transfers on poverty and the government budget. If the user is familiar with SUBSIM and all input information is available, SUBSIM will produce results in a few minutes and a full report can be prepared in a few days. Moreover, all the data input are saved by users in a file with the .prj or .pri files extensions, which allows for an easy update or reproduction of results at any time.

Comparing SUBSIM Direct and SUBSIM Indirect Effects

SUBSIM Direct and SUBSIM Indirect can be used independently depending on data availability and simulation needs. In some cases, users may want to use both versions and compare results. This section explains how to compare and interpret results for direct and indirect effects when both models are used. Recall that SUBSIM Direct produces only direct first-round effects and SUBSIM Indirect produces direct and indirect effects combined for first and higher rounds.

As a first rule, SUBSIM Direct will always be more accurate than SUBSIM Indirect to estimate direct effects because results are displayed by individual product and the price shocks can be applied to individual products rather than economic sectors. SUBSIM Direct uses the best available HBS information, and results in SUBSIM Direct should be used as the reference results for direct effects in empirical analyses.

It is also possible to separate direct and indirect effects using SUBSIM Indirect by opting for the cost-push model with the exogenous option. The exogenous option is enough to ensure that the introduced price shock in sector X does not affect the same sector in subsequent rounds. For single-products simulations and with the cost-push exogenous option, results of SUBSIM Indirect under the shocked sector are the same as SUBSIM Direct results under the shocked product (see example).

Note that comparing SUBSIM Direct and SUBSIM Indirect is possible if one shocks one product at a time. More complex simulations with multiple price shocks will make comparisons between the two SUBSIM versions more complex because of cross-products and cross-sectors effects. Therefore, a good strategy is to analyze one product at a time and see how important direct effects relate to indirect effects. This strategy is also useful because different products typically have different shares of direct and indirect effects. For example, diesel, which is largely used for commercial transport but not by households, has large indirect effects but moderate direct effects. Vice versa, LPG, which is largely consumed by households but not much used as a production input, will have large direct effects but small indirect effects. An analysis that combines simultaneous shocks on diesel and LPG will miss on these important differences.

As an example, we compare simulations for a price increase in diesel with SUBSIM Direct with a corresponding price increase in the diesel sector (petroleum) with SUBSIM Indirect. The case study is Morocco and the increase in price of diesel is 11.35%. This is the price increase used in SUBSIM Direct. For SUBSIM Indirect we need to multiply this price increase for the share of diesel in the petroleum sector. The result: the price shock to apply in SUBSIM Indirect is [11.35 * (57.23/100)] = 6.5%.

It is important to note here that the share of diesel in the sector is not derived from I/O data but from HBS data. In this particular case, we have only two products that correspond to the oil-refining sector in I/O tables, and these two products are grouped under the HBS sector "Petroleum." Diesel represents 57.23% of the petroleum sector according to HBS data and this is the share (weight) to use for the simulations in SUBSIM Indirect. The baseline data for the simulation are provided below.

Table A.3 SUBSIM indirect: welfare impact of alternative simulation options (millions DH)

Option	Food	Housing	Electricity	Water	Petroleum	Total
Exogenous/short term	−695.4	−1076.9	−145.8	−7.2	−421.0	−2346.2
Exogenous/long term	−904.6	−1157.9	−155.6	−9.6	−421.0	−2648.6
Endogenous/short term	−1128.7	−1277.8	−262.3	−9.4	−463.1	−3141.3
Endogenous/long term	−2071.1	−1794.0	−356.2	−21.9	−542.9	−4786.1

Baseline Data

Unit	L
Subsidized unit price	9.69
Unsubsidized unit price	10.79
Price increase (%)	11.35
Share in HBS sector	57.23
I/O sector shock	6.50
HBS sector	Petroleum
Corresponding I/O sector	D23-oil refining

A price increase of 11.35% with SUBSIM Direct has a welfare impact of 421 million. We can compare this estimate with those provided by a shock of 6.5% of the petroleum sector with SUBSIM Indirect under various modeling options. Table A.3 shows results using the four options provided under the cost-push model. It is evident that the option "Exogenous" in SUBSIM Indirect produces the same results as SUBSIM Direct in correspondence of the Petroleum sector and this is the case whether we use the short-term or long-term option. Therefore, with the option "exogenous," SUBSIM Indirect provides the same results as SUBSIM Direct in correspondence of the shocked sector, which allows the researcher to separate direct and indirect effects.

SUBSIM Basic Formulas

This Appendix provides a brief introduction to the basic formulas used by SUBSIM. The first version of SUBSIM (SUBSIM 1.0) was accompanied by a full paper (Araar and Verme 2012), which includes a general section on subsidies simulations, a section on the economic theory behind SUBSIM, and the SUBSIM 1.0 users' guide. Here, we below integrate and update the theoretical part of the paper for SUBSIM 2.0.

Changes in Welfare

Let e = monetary expenditure; p = price and q = quantities with the superscripts' representing the postreform values, the subscript 1 representing the subsidized product and the subscript 2 representing the bundle of all other consumed products. It is well known that the total expenditures (e) can be used as a money metric measurement of well-being. The change in welfare, due to an increase in price, depends on the change in consumed quantities. Mainly, we have:

$$e = p_1 q_1 + p_2 q_2$$
$$e' = p_1' q_1' + p_2 q_2'$$

When prices are normalized at consumer equilibrium, the last consumed units of each of the two goods will generate the same level of utility. With the assumption of marginal or moderate change in prices, the consumer can select any combination of quantities (q_1', q_2'), but the decrease in well-being is practically the same. Based on this assumption, an easy way to assess the change in well-being is the case where the change in quantities concerns only the first good.

$$\Delta w = \Delta q_1 = -q_1 \, dp_1$$

Because prices are normalized, we can also write:

$$\Delta w = -e_1 \, dp_1$$

where *dp* represents the relative price change $(\Delta p_1 / p_1)$. This is the most popular method to estimate changes in welfare subject to changes in prices, and it is the same approach proposed by Coady et al. (2006) among others.

Note that this formula applies with any behavioral response on the part of households, including changes in quantities consumed of the subsidized products or substitution of the subsidized product with consumption of other products. This means that the use of elasticities in SUBSIM does not affect the estimation of the impact of subsidies reforms on household welfare. Households can reorganize consumption as they wish, but the impact on total household welfare will not change.

In the case of multiple pricing of the product considered (for example, electricity with different tariffs for different quantities consumed) the formula for the changes in household welfare is as follows:

$$\Delta w_h = -\sum_{b=1}^{B} e_{1,h,b} dp_{1,b}$$

where *b* represents the blocks and *h* households. The sum across households represents the total change in welfare.

Note that all of the reported formulas are for the IBT price structure. However, these formulas can be easily generalized for the VDT structure or for the mixed IBT/VDT structure. For example, with the VDT structure, the formula of the impact on household well-being can be written as follows:

$$\Delta w_h = -\sum_{b=1}^{B} e_{1,h,b} dp_{1,b,z|q_h}$$

where $dp_{1,b,z|q_h}$ refers to the change in price of good 1 for the consumed quantities within the block b, and this is based on the block z, which depends on the total consumed quantity of the household (q_h).

Example 1

Block	Initial price (IBT)	Final price (VDT)
000–100	0.10	0.10
100–300	0.20	0.30
>300	0.30	0.40

Note If the total consumed quantity is 250, then $dp_{1,1,2} = 0.2$ and $dp_{1,2,2} = 0.10$
If the total consumed quantity is 350, then $dp_{1,1,3} = 0.3$ and $dp_{1,2,3} = 0.20$

Example 2

Block	Initial price	Structure	Final price	Structure
000–100	0.10	IBT	0.10	IBT
100–300	0.20	IBT	0.20	IBT
300–400	0.30	IBT	0.30	VDT
>400	0.40	IBT	0.40	VDT

Note
If the total consumed quantity is below 300, then $dp_{1,1,1} = 0$ and $dp_{1,1,2} = 0$
If the total consumed quantity is 350, then $dp_{1,1,3} = 0.2$ and $dp_{1,2,3} = 0.10$
If the total consumed quantity is 450, then $dp_{1,1,4} = 0.3$, $dp_{1,2,4} = 0.2$ and $dp_{1,3,4} = 0.1$

SUBSIM also allows researchers to model household behavior using a Cobb-Douglas function. In the case of multiple pricing of the product considered the formula is as follows:

$$\Delta w_h = e_{1,h}\left(\frac{1}{\prod_{m=1}^{M} \varphi_{m,h}^{\alpha_{m,h}}} - 1\right)$$

where $\varphi_{m,h}$ is the average weighted postreform price (the postreform price in the linear case) of household h for the good m and $\alpha_{m,h}$ is the expenditure share of household h for the good m.

The marginal approach is the most common method and it is usually accurate for small or moderate price increases. For very large price increases, the marginal approach tends to overestimate the welfare impact and it is recommended to use the Cobb-Douglas approach.

Changes in Quantities

Estimates of changes in quantities in the consumption of the subsidized product are useful to have an idea on the impact of the subsidy reforms on quantities consumed and, by consequence, on production of subsidized goods. They are also essential to estimate the impact of reforms on government revenues given that the government reduces expenditure on subsidies when households reduce consumption of subsidized products. Estimates on changes in quantities, in turn, require knowledge of the demand function and the price-quantity elasticity of the subsidized product.

SUBSIM assumes a linear demand function and allows for imputing elasticities. The basic formula for the estimation of changes in quantities of the subsidized product is

$$\Delta q_1 = q_1 dp_1 \varepsilon_1$$

where the own-price elasticity ε_1 is typically negative and between 0 and −1. Note that we are assuming that all households behave equally so that the total impact on quantities is just the sum of the changes in quantities consumed across all households.

Elasticity

The formula for the estimation of changes in quantities consumed uses the own-price uncompensated elasticity. One of the main difficulties in subsidies simulations is to specify the value of this elasticity correctly. There are at least three major difficulties.

The first difficulty is attempting to estimate elasticities when products are subsidized. When prices are subsidized, and especially when only one price is applied nationally and on all quantities, it is not possible to estimate the own-price elasticity with cross-section household data (there is no price variation). Sometimes, the subsidized price changes over time, and one may have available several household consumption surveys that cover the period when price changes occurred. However, this occurrence is rare, and it is difficult to isolate the impact of the price change in the subsidized product from other effects on expenditure over time. Therefore, subsidies analysts can rarely estimate elasticities for the country of interest.

The second difficulty relates to the use of known elasticities from the literature and other countries. Sometimes, it is possible to derive elasticity parameters from the specific literature on products. For example, the own-price elasticity for gasoline is quite well known and has been estimated widely worldwide, and the user could simply use estimations made for similar countries to the country of interest. However, known elasticities are typically estimated at free market prices, and they are point elasticities that apply to prices that are not subsidized. The point elasticities at subsidized prices may be very different and cannot be assumed to be the same. Therefore, it is difficult for subsidies analysts to simply "borrow" elasticities from elsewhere.

The third difficulty is that the formula presented in the previous section is designed for small changes in prices (marginal changes) and does not function well for large price changes. When the product between changes in prices and elasticity ($dp_1\varepsilon_1$) is greater than 1, the postreform quantity can become negative using this formula. Unlike other simulations of price changes, changes in subsidized prices can be very large, especially when governments want to remove subsidies altogether. In these cases, it is not unusual to have price increases of several times over so that dp_1 can be very large. Therefore, subsidies analysts cannot simply use standard parameters for elasticities like −0.3 or −0.5 but have to consider more specifically the relation between subsidized and unsubsidized prices before specifying elasticities.

To overcome these problems, SUBSIM has three main solutions. The first solution is that, by design, SUBSIM does not allow quantities to become negative ($-Q_0$) because the postreform quantity has a lower bound of zero. However, one should be aware that when results on quantities in the Excel output file show zero values, it is most likely that the specified elasticities are too large. Subsidized products are usually essential consumption items, and it is unlikely that households stop consuming these products altogether if the price increases. It is more likely that our specification of elasticity is incorrect.

The second solution is to use the value of elasticity at unsubsidized prices from another country and derive from this elasticity the correct elasticity to use for the subsidized price. When the subsidized price is several times lower than the unsubsidized price, this means that the subsidized price is extremely low. But if this price is extremely low and quantity is initially high, we should expect the own-price elasticity to be very low. If prices increase a little around the subsidized price, consumers will tend to reduce quantities by small amounts. On the contrary, if the subsidized price is close to the unsubsidized price then it is more likely that increases in prices will lead to large decreases in quantities and that the elasticity will be large. Therefore, either the elasticity ε_1 is large or the relative change in price dp_1 is large, but they should not be both large at the same time. As a rule of thumb, if the new price is three times the current price and the known elasticity at unsubsidized prices is (say) −0.3, then the elasticity to use in the formula may be around a third of that value, say 0.1.

With the assumption of a straight linear demand function, it is also possible to calculate precisely the initial elasticity (the elasticity at the subsidized price) using the final elasticity (the elasticity at the unsubsidized price). The formula is as follows:

$$\varepsilon_1 = \frac{\left(\frac{1}{\left(1 - \frac{\varepsilon_1'(p_1' - p_1)}{p_1'}\right)} - 1\right)}{(p_1' - p_1)} p_1$$

The third (and perhaps the most sensible) solution is to run SUBSIM with different assumptions about the elasticity and compare results. In this case, it is useful to use zero as a lower bound and the expected value of elasticity at the unsubsidized price as an upper value. This is what we would recommend especially when price increases are large.

Changes in Government Revenues

Having discussed elasticities and changes in quantities, we can now estimate changes in government revenues. We may face two situations, one where we know the unit subsidy and one where we do not know the unit subsidy in advance. If we know the unit subsidy, the formula is as follows:

$$\Delta r = \sum_{h=1}^{H} \epsilon_{k,h} dp_k (1 - \varepsilon_k (s_k - dp_k))$$

where s_k is the unit subsidy for product k.

In the case of large price changes and in order to constrain the maximum decrease in quantity to that of the initial quantity, the formula becomes:

$$\Delta r = \sum_{h=1}^{H} e_{k,h} dp_k + \max(\varepsilon_k e_{k,h} dp_k; \; -e_{k,h})(dp_k - s_k)$$

If we do not know the unit subsidy in advance, we can then approximate the change in government revenues with the change in producers' profits as follows:

$$\Delta r = \sum_{h=1}^{H} -e_{k\,h} dp_k (1 + \varepsilon_k (1 + dp_k))$$

SUBSIM will use one or the other formula depending on whether users specify unit subsidies or not in the tab "Items."

Formulas for Input-Output Simulations

SUBSIM Indirect provides various options for the simulation of indirect effects with input-output tables. The two sets of choices for the **cost-push model** will select one of four options for the estimation of direct and indirect effects. The formulas of the four options are listed in Table A.4.

Where I is the identity matrix and the matrix $\overline{A}$ is similar to A by replacing the elements of the ith line and the ith column of the shocked sector by zeroes. For example, with a three sectors' matrix and a price shock to the second sector

$$A = \begin{bmatrix} 0.2 & 0.2 & 0.3 \\ 0.0 & 0.3 & 0.4 \\ 0.5 & 0.2 & 0.1 \end{bmatrix} \quad \text{and} \quad \overline{A} = \begin{bmatrix} 0.2 & 0.0 & 0.3 \\ 0.0 & 0.0 & 0.0 \\ 0.5 & 0.0 & 0.1 \end{bmatrix}.$$

If we have an increase of 10% in price of sector 2, then:

$$S = \begin{bmatrix} 0.0 \\ 0.1 \\ 0.0 \end{bmatrix} \quad \text{and} \quad U = \begin{bmatrix} 1 & 0 & 0 \\ 0 & 0 & 0 \\ 0 & 0 & 1 \end{bmatrix}$$

where S is the vector of initial price shocks and U is the identity matrix with zero in correspondence of the shocked sector. Assume now that dP_t denotes the vector of price changes after t lapses of time (years or months). Just after the introduction of the price shock, the initial reaction will generate a change in price that is equal to:

$$dP_0 = (S'A'U) + S = \begin{bmatrix} 0.00 \\ 0.10 \\ 0.04 \end{bmatrix}$$

The four cost-push options provide welfare impacts that are ranked in the following order: (1) < (2) and (3) < (4) and (1) < (3) and (2) < (4) so that option 1 is the lower bound and option 4 is the upper bound (see also example in text). Note that the International Monetary Fund (IMF) adopts the cost-push model and the option of choice for this institution is option (4). A good choice is also to model upper and lower bounds and report both bounds in empirical analyses.

Table A.4 Summary of formulas for alternative modeling options

	Short term ($t = 1$)	Long term ($t = \infty$)
Exogenous model	(1) $dP_{t=1} = dP_0 + \left(dP_0'\overline{A}\right)'$	(2) $dP = \left(I - \overline{A}'\right)^{-1} dP_0$
Endogenous model	(3) $dP_{t=1} = dP_0 + \left(dP_0'A\right)'$	(4) $dP = (I - A')^{-1} dP_0$

The formula applied for the **marginal profit-push model** is the following:

$$P_1 = (I - A * T)^{-1} V$$

where T is the diagonal matrix of price changes and V is the vector of added values. Example:

$$T = \begin{bmatrix} 1 & 0 & 0 \\ 0 & 1.1 & 0 \\ 0 & 0 & 1 \end{bmatrix}$$

References

Araar A, Verme P. Reforming subsidies: a toolkit for policy simulations. World Bank Policy Research Working Paper 6148. Washington, DC: World Bank; 2012.

Coady D, El-Said M, Gillingham R, Kpodar K, Medas P, Newhouse D. The magnitude and distribution of fuel subsidies: evidence from Bolivia, Ghana, Jordan, Mali, and Sri Lanka. International Monetary Fund Working Paper WP/06/247; 2006.

MIX
Papier aus verantwortungsvollen Quellen
Paper from responsible sources
FSC® C105338

If you have any concerns about our products,
you can contact us on
ProductSafety@springernature.com

In case Publisher is established outside the EU,
the EU authorized representative is:
Springer Nature Customer Service Center GmbH
Europaplatz 3, 69115 Heidelberg, Germany

Printed by Libri Plureos GmbH
in Hamburg, Germany